THE SASH MY FATHER WORE

The Sash My Father Wore

An Autobiography

Robert Greacen

MAINSTREAM
PUBLISHING

EDINBURGH AND LONDON

For my friend Alex Comfort whose poetry — as well as his achievements in other fields — I have admired for over half a century

First published in Great Britain in 1997 by
MAINSTREAM PUBLISHING COMPANY (EDINBURGH) LTD
7 Albany Street
Edinburgh EH1 3UG

ISBN 1 85158 923 6

A catalogue record for this book is available from the British Library

The first part of this book was previously published as *Even Without Irene* (1969)

Typeset in Perpetua
Printed and bound in Great Britain by Butler and Tanner Ltd, Frome

My son used to say: 'Whatever oppresses
a man must be wrought out in another
medium' and when he himself suffered
any ill, he made a poem out of it.

– J.W. Goethe's mother

Acknowledgements

The extract on page 180 from *Huxley in Hollywood* by David King Dunaway published by Bloomsbury Publishing in 1985, £18.95, is reproduced with their kind permission.

The front cover photograph, *The Twelfth of July in Portadown* (1928), by Sir John Lavery (1856–1941) and © Mrs Jacqueline Donnelly is reproduced with the kind permission of the Trustees of the Ulster Museum, Belfast.

Contents

ONE

The Londonderry Air

Mother's name was Elizabeth and, like the mother of John the Baptist, she was over 40 when her first and only child, myself, was born. The date was 24 October 1920. Many years later, when I started to work for the United Nations Association in London, I was told that 24 October was the most important date in their year – United Nations Day. My life has been associated with 'foreigners'. I spent much of it teaching English as a foreign language.

The name of the city I was born in is disputed. At the time of my birth it was called Londonderry. Now the majority of its people simply call it Derry. If people in Ireland ask me where I was born I can, if wishing to be politic, say 'The Maiden City' or use the more recent coinage, 'Stroke City'.

I was delivered by a Dr McCurdy. Of that gentleman I know nothing else, but, to me at least, his name is blessed except in fits of depression. It seems I was not expected to live, but I have always delighted in confounding the expectations of others. Father came from further south in Ulster, Co. Monaghan. My natal year saw the start of partition when the island of Ireland was divided into Northern Ireland and what, for some years, was called the Irish Free State.

As every Irish schoolboy knows, or used to know, Derry/Londonderry is often referred to as the 'Maiden City' because of the fight for survival of the Protestant inhabitants during James II's siege in 1689. G.M. Trevelyan, the great historian, wrote: 'The burghers of Londonderry endured the famous siege, facing starvation in the spirit that the citizens of Haarlem and Leyden had shown in like case against the Spaniard.'

The city – whatever name you care to give it – was and is a place

9

steeped in tradition and continuity. Even today, one finds there readily enough a reminder of the brutal facts of history – the walls that have been celebrated in ballads, the River Foyle that leads to the ancient city on the hill and the two cathedrals, as well as the British Army presence.

History – or what passes for history – for the Irish has a reality that can be frightening and which can perpetuate ancient feuds. As a boy, from my aunts and mother I heard many a story of the suffering endured by the defiant Protestant citizenry, and in language no less eloquent than that of Trevelyan. I heard of the so-called traitor Lundy who had the same significance for us as Quisling for Norwegians during the Second World War. These tales of heroism and stoic endurance were, it was true, told me in Belfast to which my family had moved. Derry indeed was in decline. The Protestants were moving east as the city became more and more populated by Catholics. But even in true-blue, loyalist Belfast, the hearts of my mother and her sisters were still in the Maiden City of their youth when their lives had centred round the Presbyterian Church in Carlisle Road.

Derry for them – they said 'Derry' in conversation but used 'Londonderry' officially – meant Protestant Derry. History meant Protestant history. Suffering and heroism meant that undergone by Protestants. There was never a whisper of the sixth-century Derry that had become a great centre of missionary zeal, long before we Scots-Irish had settled there – along with some English – sword in one hand and Bible in the other.

Nobody told me of Colmcille who founded a monastery on the hill overlooking the wide tidal river. Nobody spoke of how, in 563, now named St Columba, he created a great Christian settlement in Iona, so spreading the Gospel through pagan Scotland and northern England. Nor did I know of how Irish monks brought Christianity to western Europe after the fall of Rome and of how the saint wrote of his beloved place:

> Were all the tributes of Scotia mine,
> From the midland to its borders,
> I would give all for one little cell
> In my beautiful Derry.

No, not a syllable of all that history was uttered, for the very good reason that my mother and aunts knew nothing of it. Theirs, I repeat, was the Protestant version of history – the near-disaster of the 105-day siege in 1689 before the boom was broken and ships sailed up the Foyle with food for the gallant Protestants. And of course they were gallant and determined, but no more exclusively in the right than their opponents. The past in Ireland, especially in the north, hangs round people's necks like a gigantic albatross.

None of us could foretell that history had not finished with the Protestant city which was so rapidly turning into an Irish Catholic city. Nobody guessed that one day this place would erupt violently, that television would bring names like Creggan and Bogside into English living-rooms. It could not be foreseen that on 30 January 1972, British paratroopers would shoot dead 13 Catholics and that this 'Bloody Sunday' would lead to the burning down of the British Embassy in Dublin. History, God knows, has scourged Ireland for centuries. The pity of it is that it has struck so frequently at elegant, beautiful Derry.

As a boy, I often had to listen to the praise of things past and people long dead. What, I used to wonder, had it to do with me? I was interested in sex and Hollywood movies, not in all these old wives' tales of conflict. My aunts and mother might have been talking of the early Christians being thrown to the lions for all I cared. Their anecdotes of their own early lives I found just as boring. Now they, too, have passed into history and it is too late for me to take notes.

What can I remember of those first five or so years of my life in Derry? I can see myself at the age of three or four, in the early 1920s, standing in Bennett Street, where Dr McCurdy had delivered me, looking through my legs at a fascinatingly topsy-turvy world. Another image of myself is of stroking a grey horse that pulled a bread cart, and marvelling at the size and beauty of the animal, and wanting yet fearing to touch its smartly groomed tail.

I recall too, being taught to say 'Logan's Loaf' and rendering it as 'Ogan's Oaf' to an amused feminine audience. 'L' and 'r' were as difficult for me to master as they proved for Japanese students I was to teach several decades later. I used to proclaim my name, with some pride, as 'Lobelt'. I was taught a few simple Bible stories and I think the hope existed that this only child might one day feel 'the call' to the Presbyterian ministry. These stories I was encouraged to repeat in my

11

lisping accents and I soon realised that a storyteller can capture and hold an audience.

I was particularly addicted to the story of Moses, with variations on the theme. The Old Testament for us was as real, perhaps even more so, than the New. Jews were respected as the people of the Book, not thought of with contempt or hatred. So it proved that bulrushes, wilderness, rock, children of Israel, were colourful props for an exhibitionistic little boy. I liked to emphasise the length and tedium of Moses' journey using repetition: '. . . and he go-ed and he go-ed'. This, I sensed, would bring the house down.

How many years I spent in Derry I cannot accurately remember, but an old directory lists my grandmother's name until 1925, so I think it must have been five. I have not forgotten, however, the sensation of being, as I believed, deserted by my parents and left in the care of my maternal granny and her two daughters. I cried bitterly for my mother. When I asked for her, granny said: 'She's gone away for a wee while.'

'Where? Where?'

'To a big, big city called Belfast.'

'What for?'

'To earn pennies for her Robbie.'

This news was not comforting. It alarmed me, saddened me. I felt betrayed. It was as if the sky had fallen on my head. It could not be. She could not have left me. Nothing would console me, not even the grey horse to which I once delighted to feed lumps of sugar. Nor the recital of that story about some old Jew called Moses. No, I did not want granny or my two aunts – kind and loving though they were.

Aunt Annie begged me to look at the man in the moon. Man in the moon, indeed! Had I but known the words, what obscenities I would have uttered! But small children know only the language of yells and sobs. They know betrayal, too. The parting, as it happened, was not final by any means, yet the relationship with mother never fully recovered. She lived to be nearly 90 and we were on loving terms – and yet . . .

Time and again, I have made an effort to re-establish the early sense of harmony, oneness, completeness. Time and again, I have endeavoured to re-enter the lost paradise. Is it like catching a soap bubble and holding it in one's hand? The Belfast novelist Forrest Reid, the first writer I ever met, put forward in his autobiography, *Apostate*, the suggestion that a certain kind of creative artist finds his motivation in discontent, so that, as Reid puts it, 'his art is a kind of crying for Elysium'. He may well have revealed the reason why, as a grown man, I have felt the necessity to write poems. Poetry is the antidote for hurt and frustration.

But I often think back to those Derry days. Aunt Annie, kind soul then and in later years, apart from attempting to make me believe in the reality of the man in the moon — a ploy I stubbornly resisted — used to take me out for what she called 'air'. She could ameliorate yet not dissolve the bitterness in my infant heart. The giants of the adult world, I felt, were not to be trusted. Kindness might mask betrayal.

Throughout my life, when I hear the bitter-sweet strains of the 'Londonderry Air' — as haunting a melody as has ever come out of Ireland, north or south — I think of my native city and of being taken out for 'air'. I recall with affection, not unmixed perhaps with some shame, of this good aunt of mine and her long perambulations with a fractious, self-willed, dreamy little boy along Shipquay Street and the Waterside. And I have sometimes wondered how my life would have turned out had I spent my boyhood on the banks of the River Foyle in Colmcille's 'beautiful Derry'.

TWO

Where the Wild Thyme Grows

A golden-curled girl of 11 took me by the hand to St Simon's School in Belfast's Donegall Road and so introduced me to 'education'. After a short sojourn in paradise – being coddled by the golden-haired girl and moulding plasticine – I was, for some reason, abruptly despatched to a school at the top of Broadway ruled by a Mr McDougall. Here, there were tough boys around and no golden-haired girls. I feared the worst but do not remember being bullied. I remember singing for the first time 'Rock of Ages' and having no idea what it was about, being in particular puzzled by the phrase 'cleft for me'. I only knew that the hymn had something to do with Christianity.

Mr Taylor, a pleasant young man, was my teacher. Aunt Tillie – now I was living with my two aunts who ran a shop at the corner of Broadway and the Donegall Road – used to wake me in the morning and hurry me out of bed with the words:

> Ding-a-ling-a-ling, the old school bell,
> Mr Taylor's up to say that all is well.

Or else she would greet me with the verse:

> Get up lazy Robert, get up lazy Rob,
> The sun through your window is shining.
> If you only but knew, it is saying to you
> Time's precious, don't waste it in dreaming!

I remember watching older and daring boys walk across a parapet over the Blackstaff river which flowed along a few doors from the corner house. Another memory is of using a net and putting tiny fish into a glass jam jar, and then of falling into the river and being hauled out again.

My grandmother, whose maiden name had been Smyth and who had been brought up in County Tyrone, was a tight-laced, black-clad, at times stern, at times kindly, old body who lived contentedly and God-fearingly with her two daughters, my aunts. She and they prayed for guidance, for they had no men to look after them and my father only posed problems for them. They all believed in honesty, hard work, thrift. Holidays were unknown, not even a half-day at the nearby seaside town of Bangor. Yet cheerfulness prevailed.

Then mother and father appeared once more and claimed their boy. I cried and asked to stay with granny and the two aunts, but I had to go. That meant a move to the country when I was somewhere between eight and nine, in the last years of the 1920s. This mysterious and forbidding place, 'the country', proved to be a farm about three or four miles from the town of Castleblayney in County Monaghan. We went across the border into what was then called the Free State. Even so, we were still in the historic province of Ulster where Protestant influence, though declining, was still fairly strong.

A few miles outside Castleblayney, on the way to Ballybay, my Aunt Liz-Ann, a widow, ran a hill farm with the help of her brother George, who owned a nearby farm. An adjoining farm had been taken by my father who, tired of fortune-hunting in the big city, had decided to try his hand at the rural pursuits of his ancestors. He never really liked farming, however, and I often heard him speak contemptuously of the back-breaking effort that, in the end, brought little reward other than rheumatism and bankruptcy. Still, he had ventured forth, probably on the advice of his brothers and sister, and with the insurance money he had received when his Belfast shop had burned down. Back to the plough and the cart and the dung heap, if not to the plough and the stars, in the county of little fields and lakes whose stony soil would be the inspiration of the poet Patrick Kavanagh.

Father was a restless man. He wanted quick results. His reach tended to exceed his grasp. When disappointed, he turned to the whiskey bottle rather than to the Bible for comfort. This dismayed both his own family and mother's, except that his own kin found excuses for him:

'Harry suffers from his nerves . . . that's what it is. He needs a tonic.' Mother's family made more abrasive comments, for granny had been against him from the beginning and advised mother not to marry him. I think he was over-sensitive and under-confident. He kept hoping that his day would come but it never did. He gradually slid down the social and economic scale.

I cannot remember as much as I would like about these far-off days in the late 1920s when father ploughed and hoed and swore and kept pigs. I was sent to a shack-like country school where I was the only Protestant and excused prayers on that account – much to my satisfaction. On one occasion, I fell on top of a pile of sharp stones and cut my knee so that there is still a scar on it. I always had shoes to wear, but I envied those hardy lads who walked through field and bog and over uneven road surfaces in their bare feet. They were tough and, like all boys, I admired toughness. I never found any hostility because of my minority religion. I sensed a difference from the others without quite knowing why it existed.

We had a cat called Polly and Aunt Liz-Ann had a collie named Victor. I loved both cat and dog. One window of our house was edged with bits of coloured glass and this seemed to me extremely grand. Father beat me once, hitting me round the head, for bad handwriting, having tried to 'teach' me in his own amateur fashion. I fell to the floor sobbing and I think it was then that the bitterness I felt for him began. For years we were to clash. Father represented authority simply because he was older. I started to resent authority, but had the sense to conceal my hostility. The injustice of the world began to impinge.

It may possibly be too fanciful to suppose that Father's sneer at my inability to 'write' set up a process of over-compensation that made me determine, a few years later, to become a professional writer, come what may. Certainly, at that period the relationship with Father had not deteriorated to the extent where I consciously wished to kill him and have Mother all to myself. Under the surface of polite obedience of course that is precisely what I *did* want. He sensed it, I suppose, and only used my inability to 'write' as a rationalisation of his jealousy. Often he would tell me that my teachers had complained to him of my 'stupidity' and lack of concentration. If so, they gave me no sign of their displeasure.

The lilac at Aunt Liz-Ann's enchanted me as did the army of spring daffodils in Uncle George's semi-wild garden. My aunt was kind and chatty, Uncle George was kind and silent, but loved playing practical jokes. Asked by my aunt if he intended tackling a particular job the next day, he would be silent for a long time. Then he would answer in a monosyllable – ay or no. At times I could not help wishing that Uncle George had been my father. Children know what adults to like, just as they know which animals to trust. I trusted Uncle George's collie, Victor, and I hoped he trusted me, though sometimes I teased him. I longed to trust my father, but somehow sixth-sensed it would be a mistake.

After nearly a year in the country, Mother and I went to visit her relatives in Belfast. That was a pleasant expedition to a formerly well-known feminine world, a world of security and affection that I had lost. Not a detail of that visit stands out, for happiness leaves no trace on the map of memory.

But the time came to return to Castleblayney. There we hired a car for the journey home. The familiar lanes came in sight, fresh and clean-smelling after the chimney smoke of the city. When our house came into view, Mother burst into tears, then sobs. She took me in her arms. 'Robbie,' she began. 'Robbie . . .' I looked out of the car, focused my short-sighted brown eyes on a blackened skeleton. Our home had been burned down! I felt numb, tearless with apprehension and excitement.

Some of the furniture had been saved and taken up the hill to Aunt Liz-Ann's, where we all stayed while Father debated the next move. I wondered if he had started the fire himself. In imagination, I could see his lean figure sprinkling petrol from a can. Then I could see him strike the match that started the great blaze. Polly had disappeared, burned to death perhaps. I cried for the cat I loved, not for our homelessness.

Weeks passed and one day Father received what was described as a 'big cheque'. The bigger the sum of money, the bigger the cheque, I supposed. Memory may be playing a trick on me, but I recall the actual sum as being £600. I heard a neighbour remark, 'Harry's on the pig's back now'. Flushed with triumph, Father appeared in a roseate hue as an organiser of victory. To me, he seemed a prince of fire-raisers but, of course, I may be quite wrong. I wanted to ask him if he had started the fire, but was afraid to mention the subject. The witnesses all died many years ago and the secret – assuming there was a secret – is buried with them.

We were soon to hear about the next venture, a new business in Belfast. Back again to the city of red trams and slogan-daubed walls and shipyard gantries and the sad hooting of ships' sirens. Father explained that farming was dirty, back-breaking work, fit only for the unambitious. Now he had the greatest idea of modern times, one whose imaginative sweep would dwarf the notions of Ford or Nuffield.

I was entranced with the spectacle of the tycoon-to-be and looked forward to being a rich man's son. Father decided to take over a newsagent's shop, a business that apparently could be run profitably by a child. Newspapers, tobacco, cigarettes, snuff, bundles of sticks, firelighters, simple toys, sweets and assorted 'fancy goods' – these were always in demand by the workers in east Belfast. So off we went, our small family of three, to Belfast, city of mercantile dreams. Father had the addresses of several shops with 'a good passing trade' on main roads. These he visited and assessed. He chatted with proprietors, asked awkward questions, scrutinised accounts, considering both tactics and strategy.

All the chatter and to-and-froing excited me, for I knew that the trade winds were blowing hard, now that the hedgerows and potato drills and carts had been left behind. It was hurrah for each till whose every ring would be the music of thanksgiving, a salute to Protestant enterprise. Farewell to the little school where I was an honoured heretic, and goodbye to the sickly warm stench of Castleblayney market days full of pigs' squeals and horny-handed cattle-dealers' be-Jasuses – and a sad goodbye to Victor, wisest of collies.

After much enquiry and reflection – and perhaps even prayer by Mother – Father settled for a newspaper shop on the Newtownards Road, called the Kenilworth. The good passing trade was an attraction for him, just as the association with Sir Walter Scott was an attraction for me. He opened an account with the Northern Bank at the top of the road, near the Holywood Arches. We would end up with a store like Robb's or even Woolworth's in the High Street near the Albert Clock, but naturally one had to start somewhere.

I was enrolled at the new elementary school in Templemore Avenue, the biggest building but for the City Hall I had yet seen. It smelled of fresh paint, wood shavings and disinfectant. Unfortunately for me, it was solidly Protestant – so there would be no way of escape from morning assembly. I consoled myself with the fact that Protestants prayed less than Catholics. O bustling, rainy city with swings and slides in the children's playground at Scotch Row (locked up, of course, on Sundays when all good children were at home studying the Bible or at Sunday School).

But have I, by any chance, suggested that delighted were hard to come by? Time took care of that. I discovered the solidarity and the intrigues of the back streets, the politics of children's leisure time. By politics I mean the little groupings and alliances, the fallings-out and the fights, all based on personal attractions and clashes. Mother gave strict instructions that I could not absent myself without permission given or refused at our business headquarters, the Kenilworth, where we lived over the shop. I often had to ask the question: 'Have you the right time, mister?'

Crowds of boys appeared on all sides – new potential friends, new potential enemies. Helpful, cheerful, tidy little boys roamed the streets, as did others who were double-faced, malicious, dirty. Yet they were all of the Protestant tribe. It was considered wrong, even dangerous, to tangle with the Catholic nationalist tribe. We thought of 'us' and 'them' – we were the good guys, they were the bad guys. Every boy jack of these new boys I began to meet was crammed with city lore. How did you straighten out the metal top of a lemonade bottle? Simple – just place it on a tram-line and wait for the tram to pass. How did you see part of a football match? Wait outside until half-time and then walk in. What did the sign 'FP' mean? Father's prick, of course.

Now my own father could hardly be called a bookman, although he did express admiration for Samuel Lover's novel, *Handy Andy*. But, to give him his due, he assiduously combed through the racing pages of the newspapers like a true student of form. From gambling, as from his business venture, he had high hopes of making a fortune. This hope was dashed in the end for, in his own words, his horses 'never ran fast enough'. The handful of books in our home were all musty Victorian or Edwardian novels that had survived two fires and a number of removals. I remember there was a book entitled *A House Divided*, a good forecast of what our home would be in the years to come.

Mother liked a 'nice story', but never seemed to have time to settle with a book or magazine. She could never understand why I shied away from writing 'nice stories', nor could she understand why editors would pay to have novels reviewed. This amazed her as much as D.H. Lawrence amazed his father when he showed him a cheque that was an advance on an early novel. The father is supposed to have exclaimed: 'Eh, Bert, and to think tha's never done a day's work in thy life!' Father's advice was to write something that would 'take' and that could be done by making people laugh.

He used to nip out to McMahon's pub or the Green Bar for a 'wee drink' more frequently than befitted a respectable merchant hoping to rake in the shekels in an acquisitive society, and in which the ugly spectre of unemployment was never absent. We lived, after all, in the hungry 1930s and the north of Ireland was a depressed area. Our prosperity as shopkeepers depended fairly directly on conditions at 'the Island', where the ships were built. A cold fear gripped us when we heard that a large number of men had been paid off or that Belfast had lost an order to the Clyde. Didn't everyone know that our ships were the best in the world! We didn't care to dwell on the fate of the 'unsinkable' *Titanic*.

As Father became more experienced, he talked less about shops being gold mines. Snags were discovered. Times were hard, money was tight, newsboys unreliable, assistants dishonest and customers owing bills could do a midnight flit to somewhere in the Shankill. There we were, then, surrounded by newspapers, weekly magazines, big jars of brightly coloured 'boilings' (sweets guaranteed to rot the teeth), packets and packets of cigarettes (guaranteed to make boys into men), mellow-smelling bars of plug tobacco bought by mature citizens and canisters of snuff for the elderly ladies. I was allowed to serve in the shop and I loved it. There seemed an insatiable appetite for our wares – an appetite so tremendous that if the shop were unattended for a few minutes it could mean a theft!

We were proud of the gentle craft of newsagency. Not every Tom, Dick and Harry could set up as a supplier of the *Belfast Telegraph*, the *Northern Whig* and *News Letter* to customers eager for the latest developments in football, horse racing and local politics. I often pored over these pages myself and read of 'Slip-it-to Joe' Bambrick's latest triumph at Windsor Park. I read too of the burning of some building in Berlin called the Reichstag and what a man called Herr Hitler had just said or done. He always seemed in bad temper, whoever he was.

Mother said she could not understand why the Germans had fought a war against us. They were Protestants, weren't they? I learned what I could about local politicians – Lord Craigavon, J.M. Andrews, Sir Wilson Hungerford, Tommy Henderson, the Labour leader Harry Midgley. I absorbed information about foreigners too. There was a Herr von Papen who always seemed to be travelling throughout Europe. I often wondered what he was up to. Then there was the man who ruled Italy, Signor Benito Mussolini, but all I knew about Italians was that they made good ice-cream. Perhaps Signor Mussolini's father had been one of their notable ice-cream merchants. Not least I liked to read about the kings of sport, men like Don Bradman and Kaye Don.

Occasionally, I was sent down – great privilege that it was – to collect our copies of the sixth edition at the *Belfast Telegraph* offices or, as we preferred to call it, Baird's. A sharp-eyed newsboy might catch a glimpse of the legendary figure of Sir Robert Baird. At 'the hole' could be seen a cross-section of Belfast youth who had entered the world of commerce at an early age. These lads seethed with energy. They had ready fists in case of dispute and some were well equipped with an extensive vocabulary of obscene language. Those not so tough would hurl milder threats at their rivals.

It was after a visit to 'the hole' that I conceived the idea that when I grew up I would not merely sell newspapers, like Father, but would – heaven help me! – actually write in them. I had seen films of American newspapermen in shirt-sleeves and wearing eyeshades – such a career seemed romantic, though how one went about translating romance into reality I had no idea whatever. I was silly enough to mention my dream to Father. His comment was like a blow on the head: 'These journalist fellows drink like fish and they usually die in the workhouse.' No matter, I thought, that's what I'll be one day – a journalist. Didn't the novelist Dickens start out as a journalist? If he could do it, why couldn't I? He too had had some trouble with his feckless father.

In truth, father's opposition stimulated me as I had come to suspect that his attitude towards me was based less on an objective study of the situation than sheer jealousy. As a child I did not quite see it in that light – I would never have used 'jealousy' in my own mind. But I felt there was something odd about his readiness to throw cold water on my dreams.

Since I have grown up — and especially since his death in 1950 — I have frequently relived the various crises in which he and I confronted each other, and which have had so strong an influence on my subsequent emotional life. The father-son relationship, always difficult — sometimes to the point of impossibility — was rather bitter in our case; and it seems likely that Father had been driven to repeating with me the pattern he had established with his own father. Another revealing aspect of Father's behaviour was his refusal to attend his mother's funeral. Did he feel that he had been unjustly deprived of love? That the other sons had been preferred at his expense? It seems a likely explanation for his having taken to drink as a solution for his problems.

As the years passed, I grew more and more like the other 'wee fellows'. I steered a course between being an ill-mannered roughneck on the one hand and a 'cissy' on the other. I had no great taste for the rough-housing that was practised, but I would not stand for being bullied. I made it a rule to let the other fellow strike the first blow. Then I would hit him back — harder, if I possibly could. It was a philosophy widely understood in east Belfast. Perhaps it is a philosophy that is understood everywhere.

From time to time, I would walk as far as the Queen's Bridge or the Albert Memorial with its enormous clock. On the bridge, I would look eagerly at the ships that voyaged to fabulous places like Liverpool and Glasgow. Among the people I knew, few ventured far except those driven out by poverty and the hope of employment elsewhere. Tourism lay in the distant future.

A one-legged man used to sit on the bridge. It seemed wrong to me as a child that a man should expose his injuries for gain, that he had no one to look after him. Had God punished him for some terrible sin? Had he been the victim of a stroke of ill luck? Was he just lazy? I did not know the answer. Some boys said that begging was a trade like any other. Beggars did well out of it. I did not know. Life around me had its visible quota of poverty and suffering. Times were hard, as I was constantly reminded. All around I could see ragged, smelly children, some of them suffering from rickets or TB. I could also see shawled, anaemic women, brutal men, cripples and deaf-mutes and the blind, tramps and derelicts. What was the meaning of it all? Perhaps one day I would find out.

It was a world of characters too. Old soldiers, now stiff and peevish, would speak of trench warfare in the 'Big War' and boast of how many Huns they had killed. Or they might go further back in history and talk of their service in South Africa or the Punjab. Then there was the less martial, but certainly not less dignified, personage called Joe, who was in command of the trap which delivered copies of the *Belfast Telegraph*. Vans were in fairly general use even then, but they could not compete in smartness with a trap drawn by a well-groomed horse.

On Sundays, I was packed off to Sunday school and church – as much to get me out of the way as to have me save my immortal soul. Not that being 'saved' had a high place in Presbyterianism. What seemed to matter more was to live an upright life. Moral and religious instruction was pleasant, since there was no fearsome exam to be passed at the end of it. The exam, so to speak, was life itself. Eventually one had to face the Supreme Headmaster and account for what one had done and not done on this earth. Sunday was a shut day for the pubs, so Father never drank on the Sabbath – as we sometimes called Sunday – for no strong drink was kept in the house. I think this was not so much a matter of principle but rather because Mother had threatened to pour down the sink any alcohol she came across.

Sunday work was deprecated and I used to be reminded that homework done on a Sunday would not prosper, though it seemed to me not a matter of much concern to my schoolmasters. I detected an element of hypocrisy here, as in so many other matters. Good Presbyterians did only necessary work on a Sunday, but how exactly did one define the adjective 'necessary'? Sunday was the day I most enjoyed our mid-day meal, 'dinner' as we called it, which usually consisted of roast beef or boiled beef with the inevitable potatoes and cabbage, followed by jelly and strong tea. On Saturday evening, I delighted in cutting up the large square of thick jelly, pouring boiling water over it and floating slices of banana on top. The Sunday meal could be relished, for not only would Father be sober but we could eat unhurriedly. There would be no rushing out to the shop when the bell rang to serve customers, as often happened during the week, and coming back to find on one's plate a tepid, greasy mess.

On Saturdays, I went to the butcher's and picked up a nice joint or piece of boiling beef. I was quite a judge of prices and was encouraged by my thrifty mother to find bargains. Value for money was what I aimed at. While not being poor, like people in the drab side-streets, we still had to count every penny. Nothing that could be used was thrown away. There was much worry about money and this seemed to me to contradict our belief that God would provide. Still, bills had to be paid and Mother believed in prompt payment. Father helped himself too readily to the takings, squandering money on drink and betting. We never had the feeling of financial security. My parents' house had in it little affection and laughter, and too much anger and bitterness.

'If a man hasn't made his fortune by the time he's forty,' said Father, 'then he never will.' He himself had failed to make the fortune he talked about or, if he had, he had lost it. As I lay in my attic bed and twilight deepened into darkness, and the shrill noise of lads and girls still at play lessened, I pondered this question of a fortune in the candlelight. How much was a fortune? £100? £1,000? £10,000? Rich men, it was well known, wore plus-fours, played golf, drank champagne for breakfast and lived in enormous houses. And yet, oddly enough, the Bible did not seem to favour rich men. They had to die just like tramps and the one-legged beggar who sat on the Queen's Bridge. Rumour had it that the rich were unhappy. What a puzzling world we lived in! I wished to chat with a wise man who would straighten out my contradictory notions.

At school, I began to hear whispers, and more than whispers, of the strange thing called 'sex'. Some of the bolder and more precocious boys, especially those who had sisters and brothers older than themselves, began to speak of secret practices and delights. Willie Taggart had tales to tell of what he had actually seen in dark entries or deserted quarries. His stories were corroborated by other boys, some of whom I had actually seen exposing their genitals to tittering girls. The general belief was that sex was both disgusting and delightful. If it was disgusting, why did people indulge in it? I was genuinely puzzled, but the matter remained mysterious. Not one of the adults I knew could be questioned on such a topic.

Willie Taggart had an Answer Book in which could be found the solutions to arithmetical problems. I got into the habit of going to his house after school and copying down the answers. Then I knew how many sums I had got right before spotty Mr Ferguson examined my work. (I always aimed at getting three or at most four right out of five. Five out of five would look suspicious.) In the security of his home, where I never met either of his parents, Willie played the genial host and undertook further lessons in my sexual education. Sometimes I emerged rather shamefaced. I at last stopped quarrelling with his facts, for he showed me diagrams in a well-thumbed book to back up his assertions. But I refused to believe that the sort of people we knew did the things Willie said they did. Willie Taggart affronted me by saying that even clergymen did these things.

'Why do they preach against sex, then?' I asked him.

'That is simple,' Willie replied. 'They're all hypocrites. That's what me da says.'

When I went home and thought over what Willie had told me, I found my belief in the purity of clergymen somewhat weakened. Teachers, too, I wondered, and doctors and perhaps my own parents? It did not bear thinking about. Then I reflected that Willie had known how to get hold of an Answer Book. He had actually ventured into some posh bookshop – I had never set foot in such a place – and bought it with his pocket money. Had I entered a bookshop, I imagined I would be confronted by a grim, bald gent (a BA no doubt) who would have asked gruffly: 'And why might you want an Answer Book, young man?'

Why, he might even have called a policeman and then I would have been in real trouble. Such a picture of events would not have occurred to the matter-of-fact Willie. Willie knew how things were done in the world. He knew that, if you had the money in your hand, you could buy almost anything. He was a realist, I a romantic.

Though sex seemed disgusting, I used to daydream of marrying a beautiful girl when I grew up, someone who looked like a princess. She would have long blonde hair and speak like one of those ladies I heard on the wireless, and I would be heroic and famous, perhaps having rescued her from drowning. Some of the local girls were pretty, though they were far from being princesses, as I discovered in the case of Mary Anderson. When Mary came into the shop I always gave her a few extra sweets. Evidently she told her friends, for they began to think I had cheated them. My interest in Mary ended abruptly when I heard her make a coarse remark. Girls then were not exclusively made of sugar and spice, but had other aspects too. Willie Taggart could have informed me about girls.

One day I woke up with a really nasty cold. The day after that I was even worse. I was in great discomfort, for my nose and throat were sore and inflamed. I could not eat. At the hospital in Templemore Avenue, they discovered, by means of a swab, that I had diphtheria. Next came the ambulance and a drive through the streets out to Purdysburn Fever Hospital where I found myself in a ward full of subdued children and cheerful nurses. I remember having injections in the thigh and wondering whether I would live. Would my sins be forgiven?

Soon the cloud lifted. I grew stronger and was transferred to a convalescent ward where I luxuriated in the company of a swarm of noisy extroverts. Father came laden with bananas and sympathy and wearing his nattiest blue serge suit. I felt proud of him. Why could he not always be like that? I enjoyed my status as the Boy Who Had Nearly Died. When I went home, the house smelled fresh. It had been fumigated and then repainted.

Soon after my return, Mother opened a letter with a Free State stamp on the envelope. It was from Aunt Liz-Ann down in County Monaghan. She would be delighted to have me there, the country air and fresh eggs and cream and butter and home-cured bacon would soon have me as right as rain. I could stay at least a month. A month in the country! No school, fields to roam at will, droll Uncle George with his tall stories, the collie dog to play with, the wild cats to chase . . . a dream world was opening up for me.

Mother hesitated. She was afraid I might not be able to get there by myself and there was nobody to accompany me. But I set her mind at rest. Yes, of course I could travel to Castleblayney on my own . . . I was a big boy now, nearly 12 . . . yes, of course I would get into the right train when I changed at Dundalk. I could read! I could ask! Uncle George would be at Castleblayney Station with his mare, Bessie, to meet me. Nothing has ever been so delightful both in anticipation and in the event.

On the day of my leaving for the Great Northern Station, I was atingle with excitement. My shiny brown suitcase had been crammed with socks and shirts, and patched old trousers for country wear, and I was shod in a pair of gleaming black boots that would soon be muddied in the country fields and lanes. I went up to the butcher's for a pound of pork sausages, for Mother intended to send me off with a full stomach. I ran into Willie who was mitching that day. I told him where I was going. He was incredulous.

'But that's in the Free State,' he exclaimed. 'You'll be murdered there.'

'No, I won't,' I said. 'I lived there for a while once and went to a village school where I was the only Protestant.'

'Didn't the Fenians beat you up?'

'No, they didn't. I got friendly with a Catholic boy called Seán. I'll be seeing him soon.'

Willie was astonished.

He changed the subject. He sniggered and whispered confidentially: 'Now when you're in the country, take a keek at them bulls an' cows. I saw what they were up to once.'

Willie was a practical lad, a wise urchin of the back streets, cunning and canny yet loyal to his friends. There was so much he knew that I didn't. But I had the feeling that perhaps I knew a thing or two undreamed of in Willie Taggart's philosophy.

Willie would not understand that, in the shadowy fields where dusk would find me, there were banks 'on which the wild thyme blows/Where oxlips and the nodding violet grows'. That was what I had read and remembered from some book at school. It sounded lovely, though I knew poetry had no practical value, except perhaps in exams. I did not know what 'thyme' was and was not sure of the pronunciation. The country sights were before me as I stood clutching my brown-paper parcel of pork sausages, and the scent of the country was already in my nostrils. In a few hours' time, the hills and lakes of County Monaghan would be as real as Fraser Street, where I said goodbye to Willie Taggart.

THREE

The Sash My Father Wore

I shuttled between two houses: the house-cum-shop my aunts Tillie and Annie ran in Broadway, and the Kenilworth, my parents' house-cum-shop in the Newtownards Road. From west Belfast to east Belfast, only a few miles apart – but, for a child, the North and South Poles. Sometimes, I would stay for long, idyllic periods – months in duration – with my aunts, weekending reluctantly with my parents, in tears when at last I boarded the red tram taking me to the Junction, where I got on another red tram which would cross the Queen's Bridge into territory for which I had no liking.

There was a time when I must have spent up to three years with my parents, only occasionally visiting Broadway and going on the annual jaunt to County Monaghan, where I often stayed as long as six weeks with father's sister. This was the Belfast period when I was a pupil at the huge, glassy, shining school in Templemore Avenue. I endured, rather than enjoyed, that school though it had its satisfactions – such as my friendship with Willie Taggart, Dickie Best and Fat Mayne. I had my second fight on the way home from school (the first fight, a less serious affair, was at a Cub meeting when the other lad had made my nose bleed). Fortunately, I put up a reasonable show, so that I did not shame my friends. Cowardice might even have left me friendless. It was the willingness to fight that counted, not the winning.

I loathed my parents' house as much as I loved my aunts'. In one there was dissension and quarrelling, in the other cheerfulness and good humour. My aunts believed in God and prayer, and they made a success of their business. Mother did not seem to have much imagination, but had the virtues of hard work and patience with which to withstand the moods and inadequacies of Father. His dreams of business success had crumbled. During the boom of the First World War, he had done well, exporting eggs and butter to hungry England. Those were the days when England's difficulty had been Ireland's opportunity. What did the slaughter in France matter, so long as hard-faced men could make money? Not, indeed, that Father was hard-faced. He was simply weak.

I often wondered what he had looked like as a young man. It seemed to me that, with his dark, glossy hair and faintly Spanish appearance, he must have been attractive. Mother no doubt had believed what he told her about his future prospects, though her mother and sisters had disapproved of him. She was big-boned and fair, and I resembled her.

Mother was meek and conformist, which I was not. Boys at the elementary school had told me that fighting back accomplishes more than giving in to the other fellow. Yet Christ, I had been told, said one should not hit back. Willie Taggart's philosophy was one of cheerful aggression and of taking small, calculated risks. All this confused me. Yet it seemed pretty clear that people, especially adults, did not practise what they preached. Catholics and republicans were our enemies, weren't they? Jesus said we should love our enemies and there was general agreement we should follow the Master. Did we love our enemies? We did not.

'Ven' was the name which my mother and her two sisters used when they met in a coven and talked about my father. They could safely use it when the old boy was within hearing distance. He never cottoned on, and thought perhaps they were gossiping about someone they had known in the old days in Derry. Ven was an abbreviation for Venezuela, and they sometimes giggled as they spoke the longer form. This nickname seemed to cause them infinite amusement. It helped them to overcome their contempt for somebody they considered a drunken failure. I never did find out why they had chosen this particular nickname. Perhaps he had once read out a news item or something of the kind from the 'Tally' – as everyone called the evening paper, the *Belfast Telegraph* – that had to do with the South American republic. Children sometimes ask a lot of questions. But about some matters they wisely kept quiet, believing that acceptance is best. They know that grown-ups will not answer certain questions truthfully. I never heard the old man refer to Venezuela or South America, for his terms of reference were strictly local. He had never been further away from base than London and I remember him telling me about a big railway station there called Houston or so I imagined him to say. Perhaps he unconsciously had picked up a cockney porter's rendering of Euston.

I tried to please him but found I could not, so in the end I gave up trying. As I grew older, we had more and more disputes. He had a violent, uncontrollable temper. He often frightened me and I feared for my life as for my mother's. In a drunken rage, he would throw his dinner into the fire and, on one occasion, I remember he pulled an electric light fitting out of the wall in the kitchen so that the wires dangled obscenely. Violence seemed something that men indulged in – or some men at least, for I had never seen my uncles behave in such a way.

But it would be wrong to suppose that Father and I were always at enmity. Sometimes, when he was in a good mood, I would sit on his knee and comb the dark hair that was beginning to silver at the sides. Or we would go out together on placid, golden-tinted summer evenings, sauntering up the drab Short Strand and onwards to the leafy oasis of Ormeau Park, where decades earlier the young Forrest Reid used to listen to the strains of a German band. Mother talked about these German bands that had been a feature of Ulster life before the First World War. The only foreigners in Belfast in my time were a handful of Italians, who ran ice-cream shops and sold fish and chips. Nobody I knew would have touched pasta.

I had a football which I obtained by saving up a set of football cards (each card represented a team and could be found in copies of boys' papers such as *The Wizard* and *The Rover*). As a newsagent's son, I was in a favoured position so, in the end, I completed the set. I posted it off to the publishers in London and got my football. Dad and I would find a secluded place in the Ormeau Park where we could kick it around for fun, free from the deadly competitiveness of boys for whom football was a religion. He would advise me on such excursions to work hard at school so that I would be a credit to the family. Yet he had some reservations about 'the family'. I sensed a bitterness in him for – referring to the family, his brothers and sister – he would say: 'Get yourself a good job and then you can snap your fingers at the whole lot of them.'

Perhaps he had been dependent on their help and resented being patronised. I was too young to understand and, in later years, have regretted that I never came to understand his viewpoint and the cause of his being the black sheep.

We would begin our journey home, ball safely tucked under oxter. The way back would then turn into a roll-call of pubs – Kelly's, Murphy's, the Marble Bar, the City Lights, the Britannia. I would wait outside each one and listen to the sea-noise of babble within. I would walk up and down, bounce the ball on the pavement, and wince as groups of rough lads went past spitting out side-of-the-mouth jeers at the too-respectable-looking boy with a football – 'Did ya knuck it from the Athletic Stores, you?' Out father would come at last, flecks of sawdust on his laced-up boots and we would soldier on through the now lighted streets.

After every stop for refreshment, he would be that bit less sure-footed. Near the end of the journey, his earlier good humour would have disappeared. He would grasp me by the arm and mutter incoherently that Mother's family had robbed him and that he would have a writ served on them and get every penny piece back. My cheeks damp with tears and my heart bursting with shame, the pair of us would shuffle back to the Kenilworth to hear Mother's lamentations: 'I might have known it.' It did not always end so badly, and my hopes of a pleasant outcome were not always frustrated. Yet I tend to recall the occasions when a drunken father would unlace his boots and kick them off in the kitchen before crawling upstairs to bed. I learnt the hard way about the abuse of alcohol.

Father had few friends for he preferred to drink alone, and to go from pub to pub rather than have a local. But for a time he had indeed one friend, a merry-eyed, cuddly little man called Alfie Duggan. Alfie bubbled over with cheer and chatter. His words frothed out of him and he laughed, so Mother said, 'fit to beat the band'. Alfie was employed as a canvasser for the *Daily Herald*, a newspaper that offered free gifts in return for taking the paper for a specified period. These gifts were sets of Dickens or encyclopaedias that most working-class people would open a few times and then set aside for ever, but which their wives would dust with that Protestant zeal for cleanliness which, I learned at Sunday school, is next to godliness. With his sense of fun, Alfie proved a success as a canvasser. Many would do anything if they were 'codded' into it, including buying newspapers they did not want so as to get free gifts they did not want.

The bond between Father and Alfie was membership of the same Orange lodge, Loyal Orange Lodge No. 525, a number that pleased me because it read the same from right to left as from left to right. Father's joyless, anxious temperament was drawn to Alfie's fizzy extroversion. Mother approved of Father's membership of the Order. Was it not right and proper that a man should uphold his religious principles in the face of Catholic wiliness and Fenian treachery? Just look at the face of that half-Spaniard de Valera and note the trickiness written all over it! You couldn't trust one of them.

Yet Mother had to admit that some Catholics were good people and some Protestants bad people. I found all this talk puzzling. I liked black-and-white situations. Then there was the fact that being an Orangeman in east Belfast was good for business. Even Catholics – and some were customers whom we served with courtesy and efficiency – respected a man who stood firm on fundamental issues. There was no clash between devotion to the Crown and the half-crown. God, it was widely understood, favoured those who helped themselves. He favoured Presbyterians in particular. Another puzzle for me lay in a phrase in one of our prayers: 'the holy Catholic Church'. I assumed the printer was either no theologian or else a Catholic who cunningly inserted it as propaganda for Rome.

It was odd that our great folk hero was a Dutchman, William III – no Presbyterian, surely? Then there were the more recent, local heroes like the histrionic southerner Lord Carson, or Sir Edward Carson as older people called him, and the granite-faced Sir James Craig, who had been elevated to Lord Craigavon. Mother had her doubts about Craigavon, since she believed he had made money out of whiskey. Of all our folk festivals, the crowning one took place on 12 July and it, as every schoolboy knew, celebrated the Battle of the Boyne in 1690 when William of Orange defeated the forces of Catholic James II.

We had all heard of the historic toast that runs: 'To the glorious, pious and immortal memory of King William III, who saved us from rogues and roguery, slaves and slavery, knaves and knavery, Popes and Popery, from brass money and wooden shoes . . .' Another great festival was the 12 August celebration in Derry, or Londonderry, when the Apprentice Boys, an organisation separate from but parallel to the Orange Order, took to the streets and vowed never to be subject to rule from Dublin or Rome. Mother and my aunts, with their Derry background, believed the Apprentice Boys to be the truest defenders of our faith and way of life.

I did not learn the Protestant version of history from books, but by word of mouth passed on from generation to generation. The 'quality', who had education and leisure, knew the details and the dates, but ordinary folk like ourselves carried the facts – or alleged facts – of history in our very bones and in our hearts. We were the people who had never surrendered and would never surrender. As each Twelfth of July came round, Protestant fervour would rise again and be reaffirmed.

In Sandy Row and the Shankill and the Newtownards Road, street would vie with street in putting up decorative arches tricked out with the symbols we knew and loved: the open Bible, William crossing the Boyne on his white horse, a black servant kneeling at the feet of his sovereign lady, Queen Victoria. Even the name Victoria – Victory – had a triumphalist tone. Crude but emotive paintings of scenes from history would appear on gables in working-class streets. So would slogans such as 'No Surrender', 'Remember 1690' and 'Ulster is not for sale'.

Coming up to the Twelfth, father and Alfie used to show some signs of excitement: Lodge No. 525 must be one of the smartest in the five-mile walk to Finaghy – 'the walk' was the term used, presumably to show it was civilian in nature – where speeches would be made and all the old slogans repeated. Finaghy was known as 'the field' and sympathisers who were not themselves Orangemen would also go there. Orangemen tended to wear an unofficial uniform, a blue serge suit and a bowler hat. These Sunday suits needed to be pressed and ironed and made ready for the great day. Alfie would call at the shop and chaff us all, including the customers, and tell a joke or two before he and father sallied out to McMahon's Select Bar for a half-un of Bushmills ('a wee Bush') whiskey and a pint of Guinness or a black-and-tan.

'Me and Harry's goin' for a wee drop o' holy water,' he would say apologetically to mother, knowing that she disapproved.

One story Alfie told with glee was about a visiting Englishman – and strangely enough the abstraction 'England' was loved but the English were treated with some reserve – who watched a Twelfth of July procession with its banners tossing in the wind and its brawny men flagellating Lambeg drums until the drummers' wrists ran with blood, and its flute and pipe bands accompanying the marchers, and its ranks of besashed, determined Ulstermen who had summoned up all their martial qualities for the occasion. Well, this Englishman watched the tribal display and was impressed by its ferocious dedication, but being an Englishman, and by definition ignorant of even the basic facts of Irish – or indeed *any* – history, could make nothing whatever of it.He turned to a bystander and said in his BBC-ish voice: 'Could you please tell me what these good people are celebrating?' The bystander, scandalised by both the display of ignorance and the English upper-class accent, retorted more in sorrow than in anger: 'Away home, maun, an' read yer Bible.'

On the eve of the Twelfth, bonfires were lit and for weeks beforehand children went around shops and houses scrounging wooden boxes and anything that burned readily. These bonfires – pronounced 'bone-fires' – were held in districts where arches and red, white and blue bunting had already been put up. Some said the biggest bonfire of all was in Sandy Row. Others swore by the Shankill and some voices – of which mine was one – were raised on behalf of the Newtownards Road, a district where, in late June and early July, men would be busy painting their houses, frequently – so it was said – with paint purloined from Harland & Wolff's shipyard.

Catholics were reputed to stay behind locked doors on the evening of 11 July, except for those among them spoiling for a fight with the Billy Boys. In my time, such fights might result in some injury but not in death, as had happened in the past and was to happen in the future. I was a devotee of bonfires, not so much for their political or religious significance as for their friendly pagan warmth. The crackle and the flames inflamed excitement, and gave some of us Prods a deep sense of belonging. God's Chosen People – not the Jews, but ourselves – would leap and skip and caper round the blaze and, when the great fire had been reduced to a few smoking embers, we would creep sadly away to snatch a few hours' sleep before the start of the truly serious business of the following day.

It was on a drizzling Twelfth of July in the early 1930s that I stood on the Newtownards Road and watched the Ballymacarret and East Belfast Orange contingents marching – walking? – towards the central meeting point from which the assembled lodges of the Belfast area would move towards Finaghy. There they would picnic, drink beer (except for the minority of rabid teetotallers), eat ice-cream and listen to the thunder of the orators. I watched eagerly for a glimpse of Father and Alfie, those pillars of Ulster-is-Right-and-Ulster-will-Fight philosophy. My guarder-of-Derry's-walls father walked in the over-sober, rather stiff way affected by heavy drinkers who, for once, must rely on their own will and nerve. He wore the regulation blue suit with a snowy white handkerchief peeping out of the breast pocket, and a bowler hat he had borrowed from Mr Hanna, the proprietor of the nearby hardware shop. Alfie half-danced along at father's side, grinning and waving to acquaintances in the crowd who would wave back. He looked too jovial a man to be a descendant of the stern Scottish settlers of the 16th century. I began to suspect that wee Alfie had a drop of foreign blood in him.

The crowd roared in delight as the flute band played the stirring song that has carried many a Protestant into battle, not least some of the soldiers of the Ulster Division who died on the Somme – 'The Sash My Father Wore'. Bystanders waved Union Jacks with abandon and joined in the words of the old Orange classic:

> It's old but it is beautiful,
> Its colours they are fine,
> It was worn at Derry, Aughrim,
> Enniskillen and the Boyne.
> My father wore it when a youth
> In bygone days of yore,
> So on the Twelfth I proudly wear
> The sash my father wore.

My mind turned to the sash my father was wearing. It was kept in a metal box in the coal-hole and the mothballs had preserved it from all harm. Once a year, the old, frayed sash was taken out with due reverence. One day, I thought, I will be wearing it.

The procession moved on. I had watched father and Alfie and their fellow lodge members go by with pride, but also with a sense of bitter disappointment. As well as the two stalwart Orangemen supporting each banner, there were also a couple of lads who held the strings that kept the banner in position, especially on a windy day. I had wanted to hold a string and begged Father to ask the Master of his Lodge if I might have that honour. Father said yes, he would, but he reckoned without Aunt Tillie.

'It looks as if I'm going to hold a string on the Twelfth,' I told her artlessly.

'You'll do no such thing,' Aunt Tillie replied.

'But Father says I can – I mean, if the Master of the Lodge agrees,' I insisted.

'I don't care what your father says or what the Master of the Lodge says or what Lord Craigavon himself says, you will not go traipsing through the streets of Belfast on the Twelfth or you'll know the reason why.'

Now when Aunt Tillie made up her mind, she really meant what she said. I could defy father or disobey mother, but I could not oppose Aunt Tillie on an important issue. I knew that of them all she loved me most. I would have to obey.

'But why shouldn't I?' I demanded, for I never gave in without a fight. 'Willie Taggart's doing it and so is Tommy Patterson. Why not me?'

'Because,' she said, 'you are not Willie Taggart or Tommy Patterson. They will leave school at fourteen and go to work in the shipyard or as a message boy for a grocer. I want to see you become somebody, a Presbyterian minister or a doctor. I'm as loyal as the next, but you can put the notion of walking through the streets right out of your head.'

It was noteworthy that, except for the teetotallers among the Orangemen, the homeward procession was more joyous and relaxed than the journey out to the field. The movements of the banner-bearers were more balletic, less stiff. Their joints had been oiled by John Barleycorn. Father and Alfie were not counted among the teetotallers, so they came back clutching each other for support.

'Hi, you two, are youse married?' cried a wit among the onlookers.

Alfred lunged out ineffectively and cried, 'Get out of the road, ye Fenian bugger!'

And so another Twelfth of July ended with more whimper than bang. But there would be another and another and another, as long as the Protestant enclave existed in Ireland's north. Once again the patriarchs of the Order would sit like graven images in horse-drawn landaus and the men in blue serge and bowlers would step out briskly to the music, sometimes merry, sometimes provocative. Occasionally, there would be an eruption of violence when fists and stones would fly. Worse still, there might be a crackle of gunfire. Or the sky at evening would redden from a blaze that signalled the burning of a Catholic house in a Protestant area or a Protestant house in a Catholic area. Our side was naturally always in the right. We never started trouble. 'They' did.

The watered-silk sash father had worn so proudly was wrapped up in tissue paper, along with the mothballs, and placed reverently in the tin box. Sometimes it was taken out and shown to a tipsy companion as proof of father's commitment to King Billy's cause. But, as the years passed and the creditors pressed for payment, Father lost interest. He stopped going to lodge meetings and even lost touch with Loyal Orange Lodge No. 525. The business gradually declined. Competition was strong. Mother could not cope with all the work on her own. Father drank more and more heavily, and took less and less responsibility.

In the end, the Kenilworth was sold up and my parents went their separate ways. And the sash? What happened to it? It would be pleasing to think that Father took it with him in the tin box to his lodgings, but I have no reason to think that he did. Was it left behind in the coal-hole? Did he pawn it for the price of a few whiskeys? Now that Father is dead, I shall never know. Yet I sometimes wonder where it got to – and, when I do, I see Father and little Alfie stepping out to the brave music. The sacred Orange words come into mind:

> My father wore it when a youth
> In bygone days of yore,
> So on the Twelfth I proudly wear
> The sash my father wore.

FOUR

The Streets of Freedom

'Now I don't want you to play with these rough wee fellows,' said Mother. She went on: 'The chemist across the road, Mr Quirke, has three of the nicest boys you would find anywhere. Why don't you play with them?'

In the Kenilworth, we sold the local and English newspapers, bar tobacco, cigarettes, snuff, lemonade and a strange drink called Sarsaparilla, chocolate, boiled sweets, firelighters, bundles of sticks and balls of string, to mention a few items at random. I helped myself to sweets and lemonade fairly generously, though within limits set by Mother who warned me 'not to eat the profits'.

We belonged to the class of small but respectable shopkeepers whose function had not been usurped by the large combines, although that process had already started. People of our sort hated, really *hated*, the Co-operative Society, and had a distaste for the chain shops that could under-cut us. We believed in a sort of one-man-one-shop economy. Nor did we subscribe to the philosophy that all men were equal. We felt superior to manual and skilled workers – after all, we were small-scale capitalists.

Yet being your own master, though it sounded marvellous, meant that you were everybody's servant. It meant being pleasant to people you might detest. It meant longer hours of work than if you were an employee protected by a trade union. Even so, we took a great pride in deluding ourselves that we could do as we pleased.

Mother had had a hard life, having been one of a family of four children when her mother was left a widow with next to no financial resources. How my grandmother managed to bring up her children I never discovered. Mother, like her two sisters, wanted life to be easier and more secure for me. How better, then, than to have me cultivate the children of a professional man – 'Mr Quirke is almost a doctor, you know' – and keep clear of the riff-raff who lived in tiny kitchen houses and shamelessly hung out their washing?

On mother's prompting, I approached the eldest of the Quirke children, a boy named John, who was approximately my own age. This John turned out to be thin and chalky-faced, as if he lived his life in a basement where they grew mushrooms. He was too polite and, worst of all, he lisped. I knew that, despite his father being 'almost a doctor' and John's having won Sunday school prizes, he would never be a friend of mine.

I yearned for the streets of freedom in which the scruffy children played late and early in their torn jerseys. They shinned up walls, they got their knees cut, they tormented cats, they teased shop assistants, they used bad language, they formed themselves into gangs that fought other gangs, they went off with jam jars and nets to catch spricks, and some rose to heights I did not aspire to, like breaking windows and shoplifting. These were my heroes and I wanted to be accepted by them. Live dangerously – well, in moderation, for I had a sneaking feeling I was too conformist by half.

Now, Willie Jeffers was a hero. He knew how to get into the cinema and football grounds without payment. He rode free inside tramcars or clung outside, to the annoyance of conductors who tried to beat him off, but feared he might be killed when the tram was in motion. Willie knew where to find conkers and luscious blackberries. He terrorised rivals, but led a band of disreputable friends. If he were to be sent to a reformatory, he said he knew how to escape, not that he was ever put the test. Willie had a strong contempt for girls and the games they played, their skipping and 'shop' and mother-and-child.

Streetwise lads like Willie were football mad; not that any of them owned a leather ball. At a pinch, a tin can would serve and goal-posts could be outlined with a piece of chalk some enterprising boy had filched from his classroom. If anyone actually wanted to play proper football, then he and his pals would leave the streets and find a piece of waste ground where they could play, undisturbed by silly girls and envious boys not asked to join in.

Next to football came go-car racing. These vehicles were made out of old soap boxes fitted out with small wheels, and a piece of string for steering. A boy pushed until the contrivance went at such speed that he could no longer keep up with it. There used to be races round the streets — and heaven help the pedestrian who got in the way of a competitor. Respect for person or property was not part of the creed of these youthful aces, who dreamed of one day taking part in the Ulster Tourist Trophy race that brought great racing motorists to our province.

Bicycle racing was another pastime and outlet for the competitive instinct. The only prize for winners was the knowledge that he was a champ. Everybody seemed to be graded according to ability. It was just like school, only that the values were different.

Billy Wilson was a champ at marbles, Jimmy Hanna was the acknowledged wizard in soapbox racing, Alec Dunn was an artist with anything round and bounceable. There existed a hierarchy of ability and achievement. A useful pair of fists got a boy quick acceptance into whatever group he fancied, for fights were a common occurrence.

These fights did not last long and seldom left an aftertaste of bitterness. Fair play predominated. There was often a kind of affectionate fighting between us, the teasing playfulness of energetic young animals. Sometimes we heard tell of real, big-scale battles and for us, in our polarised society of rampant sectarianism, these meant clashes between rival gangs of Protestants and Catholics. Encounters took place in which the principal weapons were stones, and real injuries could be inflicted, but I was fortunate never to witness any such battle. Exaggeration was not unknown and sometimes, after a squabble, a boy would limp away, tenderly caressing some part of his body as if he were an old sweat back from the trenches. But boys are shrewd and we always knew if someone had suffered a real injury. Then we gave quick aid to friend or enemy.

Playing 'May Queens' was popular with girls, who dressed up their queen in clothes resembling wedding dresses. They would dance her along the streets with a shrill vocal accompaniment. Groups of children and teenagers in high-heeled shoes and old lace curtains would escort their queen and one girl would collect money in an old tin can. If they met a rival queen with her attendants, the air would be filled with angry cries. Part of the May Queen song went something like this:

Our Queen up the river
with your yah-yah-yah
Your Queen down the river
with your yah-yah-yah
Our Queen up the river
And we'll keep her there for ever
with your yah-yah-yah.

At Hallowe'en, we used to wear false faces and try to frighten old ladies. Our toy guns would emit loud bangs and we would let off rockets and Catherine-wheels, and hold sparklers in our hands. If we had collected enough empty boxes from shops, we would then start a bonfire. Toffee apples on sticks would make their appearance in shops and I think these usually sold for a halfpenny each.

Some amusements were more passive. Film-going meant attendance at the special children's matinee held on Saturday afternoons at the Pop – the Popular Cinema being its grand title – where admission was one penny or, as we said, 'a wing'. Did I say passive entertainment? Hardly so, for the child audience loudly cheered its heroes and equally loudly hissed its villains. We stood up and shouted our approval or disapproval. Cowboys and rustlers appeared more real to us than our next-door neighbours.

Football matches we looked on as religious rites, but few lads could afford the entrance money to watch the gladiatorial contests between teams such as Linfield and Glentoran. My own loyalty was divided between those two teams, since my aunts lived in the Linfield supporters' area and my parents in a solid Glentoran district. One learnt that it was possible to get in free at half-time when, if the match had been half-hearted, some men would come out muttering darkly about the decline in football standards and obviously heading for the nearest pub to drown their disappointment in a half-un of Bushmills.

One of the great local footballers was Joe Bambrick and a favourite catchphrase of boys playing in the streets would be 'Slip it to Joe'. The giants of the football field such as Bambrick and Elisha Scott were revered by us all. It came as no surprise to me that, many years later, Belfast should produce a footballer of world stature in George Best.

The days I am talking about were spent at the elementary school in Templemore Avenue, a school that seemed to me an immense building with a fantastic acreage of glass. Social contacts came mainly through school and church, the church in question being Westbourne. But I had another way of making acquaintance with those around me. Whenever I could evade mother's vigilant eye, I would make a sortie at evening into the streets – Austin Street, Kenilworth Street, Fraser Street, Wolff Street, Harcourt Street. These for me were the streets of freedom. In them I could be myself, far removed from the do-gooding adults who ran activities such as the Cubs.

My parents employed a couple of part-time lads to deliver newspapers. I helped sometimes and did a little round every Sunday morning before going off to Sunday school. At Christmas, I used to get presents from some of our customers who appreciated my skill in pushing *The People* or the *Sunday Express* so expertly through their letter-boxes.

One boy we employed was called James Haig Mackie, the 'Haig' having been given him at baptism in honour of the First World War general. 'Haig,' said Mother, 'is as honest as the day, not like some of them who would steal the eyes out of your head.' Yes, Haig was upright, hard-working, well-mannered and destined for higher things than the delivery of newspapers. The odour of tobacco had not polluted Haig's lips. Nor had he ever tasted strong drink, or ever entered a betting shop. I had entered a betting shop when Father sent me to put on bets for him – I have the impression that such places were, strictly speaking, illegal, but the police simply turned a blind eye. Haig's secret was that he was, as the Belfast phrase put it, 'good living'. He had been saved.

Haig attended the Elim Tabernacle Church, whose great figure in distant England was called Principal George Jeffreys. On one of Principal Jeffreys' visits to Belfast, that city of a thousand sects, Haig got me to attend a meeting for healing and salvation. As the proceedings went on, I contrasted the emotional atmosphere with that of the Presbyterian church. I was half-attracted and half-sickened by it. Some people went up to the front to be saved. I wavered but, in the end, I decided to stay in my place. So I missed my opportunity which no doubt would have opened up a new way of life for me. Back I went to my double life – pretending to be conformist yet, all the while, seething with revolt and, at every opportunity, seeking out the boys Mother had warned me against. Haig became a pastor of the Elim Tabernacle. I preferred, for the time being at least, to roam around the streets of freedom.

FIVE

Once Upon a Christmas

Ilooked out through the kitchen window at the drizzle. Would it snow? It always snowed at Christmas in times past, I thought, for snow, deep and crisp and even, appeared in most of the Christmas card scenes. 'It's been a tiring day,' said Mother, 'not that there's much money to show for it.' I was used to hearing it said that times were bad, money was tight and so on. But my mind was on a higher thing than paying the bills. Snow.

I thought of the gentle way snowflakes would fall on the hills ringing the city, on Divis and Cave Hill. Snow in all its virgin purity I would imagine floating down to whiten the rooftops. Not least I could see snow gradually cap the dome of the City Hall and cling to the statues of those Victorian worthies that stood in their frock coats around the huge edifice. Like them, time itself would stand still in an Arctic world.

'Is it going to snow?' I asked.

'It isn't cold enough, thank goodness,' Mother answered. 'Och, it makes such a mess when people tramp through it.'

Mother moved over to the fire and warmed her hands over it. They were red and blotched because she suffered badly from chilblains.

'He's away to the usual place,' she said. I knew this meant McMahon's pub. I had often peeped in through the frosted glass windows at the dim interior where working men in cloth caps drank their pints of Guinness and the occasional half-un of malt, and talked, sometimes with passion, of horses and football. I should say *gambling* on horse racing, for the average Belfast worker had nothing to do with the horses which were rapidly disappearing from the streets.

Hands warmed, she went back to the shop, for the furious jangling of the bell announced a new customer. I took some greasy dishes into the scullery and placed them in the discoloured sink. Then I lifted a food-stained newspaper off the table and replaced it with a clean inside sheet of the *Belfast Telegraph*. We saved tablecloths, pure linen ones, for rare occasions like Christmas Day dinner or when visitors turned up. Then I went out to the shop where Mother was cutting bar tobacco.

'Can I help?'

'Yes,' Mother answered, 'you could weigh out half-an-ounce of snuff for Mrs Gill.'

I did the job with exaggerated precision, standing well away from the dull brown powder so as not to get any in my nostrils and start sneezing. I imagined I was a famous scientist, someone like that Lavoisier I'd heard about at school, conducting an experiment.

It was past ten in the evening when Father returned. The pubs closed at ten. The shop had just been closed, and Mother and I were sitting by the fire drinking tea. Father brought a man with him called Mr Ansell who also frequented McMahon's. Mr Ansell had a great roll of fat at the back of his neck, his belly bulged out like a Lambeg drum and he wore wide, dark-grey trousers. Mr Ansell contrasted with lean, dark Father in his shiny, navy blue serge.

'So you're back,' Mother said. 'You might have come earlier and given me a hand.'

'Oh, but I had a wee bit of business to see to. I knew what I was doing, don't you fret, woman. Many's the bit of business is done over a wee drink.'

Father winked at Mr Ansell, who winked in return. They silently congratulated themselves on being members of a man's world.

Mother shook her head unbelieving. 'Good evening to you,' she said unenthusiastically to Mr Ansell.

'Good evening ma'am,' said Mr Ansell, with slight flattery in his voice. 'I hope I am not intruding.'

Within minutes, Father had ordered me cheerily to get out the dartboard. I was delighted. Mr Ansell's jaws trembled like jellies as he stood a trifle unsteadily and aimed at the board. I noticed how bloodshot Father's eyes were and how his voice came more country-slow and slurred than when he was sober. It reminded me of those voices just across the border — still Ulster in quality, but with the merest hint of southern intonation. Mother disappeared to get tea for the two men, and the clink of cups and saucers added a treble to the bass of the men's half-drunken cries. Soon dart-playing was over and they were sucking tea noisily out of saucers under Mother's disapproving eye. I remember that she used to say: 'Even if you live in a pig-sty, you don't have to behave like a pig.'

'A sup of tea,' said Father, 'is hard to beat.'

'Ay, it is that,' agreed Mr Ansell.

'Especially when a body's tired after a hard day's work,' said Mother quietly, but the irony was lost on the tea-drinkers, who had started to cope awkwardly with wedges of plum cake.

When there was nothing more to eat or drink, Father called for a song. He got up from his swivel-chair and placed a gaunt wooden chair in the centre of the kitchen.

'Now, wee Robbie,' he announced, 'will entertain our gallant fighting man, Corporal Ansell, who by rights ought to be a sergeant-major. But sure there's no justice in this life.'

Mr Ansell grinned toothily. Eager to demonstrate my lung-power and win an audience, I stood to attention on the chair and launched into 'Danny Boy', a song I attacked with more gusto than finesse. 'It would make you cry,' said Father, meaning, I hope, that the song was moving, not that my performance was pitiable. 'There's nothing like the old Irish songs,' he added. 'Now gives us "The Minstrel Boy".'

I sang as if the minstrel boy's wild harp had been slung behind me and Mr Ansell made noises of approval. I ended up by reciting Kipling's 'If', a poem whose moral uplift made it a popular piece in the puritan North.

'I'll make a preacher of that boy,' Father declared. 'I can see him in the pulpit wearing a black gown and warning them against the Devil and all his works. All he needs is a bit of Latin and Greek.'

'There's nothin' like the church,' chimed in the old soldier. Mother had retreated upstairs from what she regarded as an entertainment for drunk men.

Mr Ansell began to be nostalgic.

'When I was with "the Skins" in the Punjab,' he began, 'once the Colonel, he says to me – oh a fine gentleman from Limavady he was – well, as I was saying, the Colonel he says, "Corporal Ansell" . . .'

By this time I was feeling drowsy, for it was past my normal bedtime, and the Colonel's words were lost forever. I bade the two men goodnight and climbed the stairs, candlestick in hand.

I slept at the top of the tall brick house and into my little room came the whine and grind of tramcars to-and-froing on the Newtownards Road. I heard, too, the diminishing shouts in the side-streets of the workers' children. I watched the play of shadows on the wall while my mind turned to coming excitements. My friend Johnny Carson had asked me to a party where there was sure to be fizzy drinks and spongy cakes. Perhaps Johnny and I would go to the Picturedrome on Boxing Day to see Jeanette MacDonald and Nelson Eddy in *Rose Marie*. But, above all, I thought of powdery snowflakes and frozen ponds and the slides we would make in the narrow streets off the road. These for me were, after all, the streets of freedom. Snow would make them even more exciting.

I woke with a start to see Mother standing beside my bed, crying softly into her dress.

'Get up, Robbie, and put on you,' she whispered. 'It's your granny. She's . . .'

Father, Mother and I hurried out into the night drizzle, down Middlepath Street and over the Queen's Bridge, where only a few muffled phantoms slithered homewards and a bull-like lorry butted against the unfriendly night. Out of half-closed eyes, I saw the indistinct outline of the cross-channel vessels and then the hands of the Albert Clock.

Father ran over to the taxi rank and, in a moment, we were being driven smoothly up Great Victoria Street and towards Shaftesbury Square. The taxi was roomy and smelled of rich leather. The rain spat lazily against the windows. The taxi driver was saying something about the Christmas displays in the shops, but his words petered out for lack of response.

The house of death was crowded with neighbours huddled together in the gaslit kitchen. Some of them drank tea out of enamel mugs and spoke in conspiratorial tones. The air was thick and tense. A bearded old fellow smoked a pipe, emitting fumes at random and mouthing something about God and mercy. My aunts appeared, spare Aunt Annie and plump Aunt Tillie, both red-eyed. A clock ticked with busy insolence. My parents and I tiptoed upstairs. We passed the sitting-room where I had practised scales and where hung the painting of the old farmhouse in County Tyrone where granny had been a girl. We passed the print of the Stag-at-bay on the landing and went into the room of the dead woman.

Aunt Annie opened the door and then burst into tears. 'Here she is,' she whimpered, 'the best mother anyone ever had.' I looked at the stiff figure that had already been washed and laid out. The dead woman's hands rested on a Bible, those hands that had both punished me with a tawse for naughtiness and rewarded me with silver coins for virtue. I felt myself gasping for breath, unable to transform my feelings into words. It was as if the angel of death were still loitering in the room. I wondered how I ought to behave. Such a situation was outside my experience.

Back in the kitchen, the smell of death was still in my nostrils. I glanced at the assembled faces that looked as if they had been sprayed yellow by the gaslight. I noticed the food stains on the old man's beard. Then the old man sat up with a start, for there was a loud rapping at the door. Aunt Tillie rushed to it. I heard a voice and caught some of the words: '. . . told me the sad news . . . come to offer . . .'

A man came in. 'This is Mr Clarke,' said Aunt Tillie. 'I'm sure some of you know him.'

There was a ragged chorus of helloing and come-in-out-of-the-wet-mister. I had seen the stranger once or twice before. I took in the grey cloth cap, the long trailing muffler and the wrinkled, paint-splashed macintosh. I had heard this man described as 'Bolshy', whatever that was.

'That's a cruel night, friends, so it is,' said Mr Clarke, wiping his forehead with a big handkerchief.

'It is now, to be sure,' agreed father, making way for the newcomer.

'I wouldn't put a dog out in it.'

'Would you like a cup of tea?' asked Aunt Tillie.

'I wouldn't say no to a wee drop,' said Mr Clarke.

The bearded man stirred and heaved himself erect in his chair.

'She's up in heaven now,' he said, lifting his eyes piously and fixing them on the ceiling like a street evangelist trying to attract a crowd.

'What's that you said?' asked Mr Clarke sharply.

'I said she's up in heaven now, good Christian that she was,' replied the bearded man.

'A good woman, yes I agree with that,' answered Mr Clarke, 'but that stuff about heaven and harps is a fairy tale for wee childer.'

There was a stunned silence and then a roar from the bearded one.

'How dare you deny your Maker?' he screamed. 'How dare you!

You Russian atheist! God might strike you dead this minute for your blasphemy.'

Everyone was now in a timeless vacuum. Silence reigned. The tick of the clock came loud and clear.

'Then let Him strike me dead,' said Mr Clarke, calmly. 'I'll give Him exactly 60 seconds to do it.'

The old man's beard trembled with passion as if every white hair in it had been individually insulted.

'No wonder they call you Bolshy, you Russian pig,' shouted the old man.

The word 'pig' had barely been pronounced when Mr Clarke's fist struck the nose of the bearded Christian. 'Pig yourself!' retorted Mr Clarke. 'Now men, steady on,' cried Father, somewhat indecisively.

But my two aunts had by now leapt to their feet almost simultaneously. Aunt Annie clutched the old man and Aunt Tillie held Mr Clarke's arms in a vice-like grip.

'Now that's as much from either of you as I want to listen to,' said Aunt Tillie firmly. 'My poor mother is lying dead upstairs and all you two can do is to start fighting. Two grown-up men, you should be ashamed of yourselves.'

The two offenders muttered apologies and seated themselves at some distance from each other. The 60 seconds Mr Clarke had given his Creator to strike him dead were long up. I was surprised that Mr Clarke was still breathing, but God I knew was merciful to miserable sinners. 'It's time you were in bed, Robbie,' said mother. 'Come along now, you've had more excitement this night than is good for you.'

I lay awake a long time in a strange bed after mother had kissed me goodnight. It would soon be Christmas. Would there be snow? I prayed to God for snow. Then the image of my dead granny came into my mind and I felt guilty for having thought first of snow. Suppose there was no heaven as Mr Clarke had maintained? But I knew that Mr Clarke was wrong. Granny must be in heaven.

As I drifted into sleep, I saw the flakes falling and settling on the beard of the old man, so that the food stains were cancelled out and the beard was immaculately white. The beard gradually turned into a tombstone. A dark bird flew to the tombstone and perched on it. Then it started to peck at the stone. It did this until Granny's name and her dates of birth and death appeared. Suddenly there was a flash of lightning that lit up the graveyard and then a thunderclap. The tombstone dissolved. Next I saw the old man with the beard flying heavenwards. Dangling from the end of a rope was the limp body of Mr Clarke wrapped in his wrinkled macintosh, the muffler flying in the wind. Out of his mouth there issued thick black coils of smoke.

In the days that followed, carollers appeared in the streets, shop windows were decorated with bits of cotton-wool to simulate snow and people hurried along with bulging baskets and parcels wrapped in coloured paper. But I kept remembering that Granny was dead and that we had driven into the heart of Tyrone to bury her at Leckpatrick. Mr Clarke had not been among the mourners. Had God struck him dead after all? I did not care.

When I woke on the morning of Christmas Day, I jumped out of bed and ran eagerly to the window. There was no snow on the ground, so my prayers had gone unanswered. But at least the ground and windows were frosted. Even in my room the air had a nip in it, a fresh edge that was exhilarating. I looked everywhere for a present but could not find one.

Father and I hurried off to church after breakfast, but I had no ears for the hymns and psalms and the long-winded sermon. The absence of a present, or any mention of one to come, kept nagging. Outside church the air sparkled in the winter sunshine. I asked Father to let me go for a wee run and he dismissed me with the warning not to be late for dinner. 'We've got a big fat goose from Monaghan,' he said. I knew it had been sent to us by his sister Liz-Ann.

I headed towards the Holywood Arches, running and jumping with relief that the church service was over. I had gone only a few hundred yards when I bumped into Fat Wilson and Willie Anderson. Fat was resplendent in new kid gloves and swinging his arms as if to demonstrate his superiority. Willie, a pale, stunted boy – did he smoke butt ends of cigarettes picked up in the gutter? – hopped along beside Fat like a sparrow trying to keep on friendly terms with a pigeon.

'Hi there, you! Does yer ma know you're out the day?' was Fat's cheeky greeting. Willie chuckled obsequiously at the sally.

Unable to think of a suitable riposte, I said lamely, 'We've got a goose, a big one.'

'Did you ever hear the like of that, Willie?' demanded Fat, removing his left glove with calculated elegance. 'Sure everybody except the riff-raff has a turkey at Christmas. We've got a turkey and two chickens and lots of sausages and mince pies and *everything*.'

'My old man bought a turkey in the market,' said Willie, probably lying.

'Them's nice gloves,' I said to Fat in an attempt at appeasement.

'"Nice", says he,' retorted Fat. 'You mean them's the best bloody gloves money could buy in this city or even in London.' But worse was to come.

'What have you got for Christmas?' he asked. Malice shone out of his piggy eyes. 'I've got . . . I've got . . .' I stammered, 'a pair of roller skates.'

'Liar! Liar! Liar!' answered Fat, who had shrewdly noted my hesitation. Then he rubbed salt into the wound. 'I can't see that hopeless old da of yours buying you anything. Doesn't he spend all his money on drink in McMahon's?'

I blushed.

'Well,' I said loyally, 'he spends his own money. He doesn't borrow from anybody.'

Fat snorted contemptuously. He knew he had won. Now he ignored me.

'Come on, Willie,' he said. 'Come on back with me for a couple of hot mince pies.'

Upset, I was left standing on the pavement. It was as if the crisp air had gone soggy and clammy and the bright sky had suddenly darkened. I thought for a moment it was going to rain and even stretched out my hand to feel the first raindrops, before I realised that I had fallen into a dream state.

I was late for dinner.

'What have you been up to?' Mother asked crossly. The goose was already being carved, but the normal high spirits of a family gathered round the table on Christmas Day were singularly absent. Granny's recent death weighed on us all.

I listened moodily to the conversation and only vaguely heard the words of my parents as they spoke of Christmases long before I was born. I day-dreamed of how I might borrow a pair of skates so that I could rush past nasty old Fat and shove him into the gutter and then push the contemptible Willie on top of him. Revenge was sweet.

'What's wrong with you today?' asked Father, with a little bit more concern in his voice than usual. 'Don't you like the goose? It seems tender enough to me.'

'The goose is fine,' I said with a marked lack of enthusiasm.

'Are you grieving for your granny?' asked Mother.

'Only a wee bit,' I said truthfully. 'You see . . . you see . . . I met Fat Wilson up the road and he was boasting and showing off as usual. He said some horrible things to me, and Willie Anderson was backing him up.'

'Don't let it worry you,' said Mother.

'Well,' said Father, after swallowing a dollop of stuffing, 'if he goes on like that you'll have to use your fists on him one of these fine days.'

'Now don't encourage the child to fight,' said Mother.

Father put his hand in his pocket and drew out a fistful of coins. He selected one. 'We hadn't time to buy you anything for Christmas, what with all the upset over Granny. Take this and buy yourself something.' I took the shilling he offered and put it – with a polite word of thanks – into my hip pocket. I was not pleased with the gift.

I asked permission to go out for a walk. Having crossed the city, I went over to the south side. I made my way up University Road, passed the Museum and Art Gallery on the Stranmillis Road and headed in the direction of the Lagan towpath. I had thought of calling at Johnny Carson's house. Johnny always stood by me and might even have helped in planning revenge on Fat. But I felt I could not unburden myself, not even to Johnny. I knew that Fat would spread the news of his encounter with me and tell others that I was a liar. *One day . . .* I thought . . . *one day* . . . and I clenched my fists.

I felt an anger, a turbulence within me that was at odds with the season of peace and goodwill. Coming to a bridge, I leaned over the parapet and looked dully at the moving water. Almost before I knew what I was doing, I pulled the shilling out of my pocket and threw it into the river. I shivered at the recklessness of what I had done and a tear trickled down my cheek. I started the trek home. As I neared the straggle of houses at the city's edge, the lights were going up one by one. I started to whistle, whether to cheer myself up or because the tension had gone, I did not rightly know.

SIX

Waiting for Lefty

In September 1933, at the age of 13, I left the school in Templemore Avenue and made my début in the Lower Fourth at the Methodist College in Belfast. I was overawed by the sense of purpose, organisation and the sheer size of everything. Obviously one had gone there to *work*, not to enjoy a rest-cure. The first few days were tough and bewildering. Yet it was clear that discipline would not be imposed by the slaughterhouse methods of the primary school where caning was an everyday occurrence. No, there was not a cane in sight at Methody and not one of the masters looked like a butcher. Nonetheless, these gowned and learned figures had an indefinable air of authority. They were *masters* in the real sense of the word, and would stand no nonsense. Or would they? I decided to play it safe.

At Templemore Avenue, my teachers had all been Ulstermen, mostly local men at that. We spoke the same dialect more or less, and shared practically all the same assumptions; and our prejudices largely coincided. Here at Methody a high proportion of the staff were Englishmen, Scots and Welshmen. The headmaster, an awe-inspiring, Jehovah-like person, was a Scot named Henderson. The next in command, Mr John Falconer (also a Scot), pulsated with energy. It was Mr Falconer who was in charge of the Lower Fourth, the newcomers – apart from a handful of boys who had been at the Methody prep school, Downey House – so to some extent we judged all the masters by Mr Falconer. Within minutes the brighter among the new recruits knew somehow that he was called 'The Hawk' and had a reputation for severity tempered with justice. It was whispered that he was all right if you obeyed him. If you failed him, you were for it; and if you 'cheeked' him, heaven help you! The Hawk certainly put the fear of God into me, if not into one or two rougher, more insolent lads. Commands issued in that resonant Scots voice were given to be obeyed – or else!

The Hawk and I were to come into conflict on very few occasions. Yet collide we did – and I always got the worst of it. I could not complain that he had been the least bit unfair, even in his punishment. If a boy were not guilty, he need have no fear in stating his case to 'Johnny' Falconer. He lashed me with his tongue on at least two occasions when I had been guilty of an offence – once when I had cut my name on a desk, and once when I had been discovered talking to another boy at prayers in morning assembly. I heard of only one boy who had actually dared to be insolent to The Hawk, a vicious boy whom I had reason to dislike and who was later expelled for, I believe, breaking a window deliberately. I may say that Mr Falconer, in my later years at Methody, more or less indicated his friendly interest in my literary ambitions. As editor of the school magazine, *MCB*, he was to publish my early efforts in verse and prose. Mr Falconer became headmaster after my time, but even in that exalted position I doubt whether he appeared more impressive to my successors in the Lower Fourth than he did to my contemporaries.

It was a strange sensation to be associating with potential young gentlemen. That is not to say they were above larking about or throwing their weight around. On a few occasions there were real stand-up fights, but these were rare. More often there were scuffles in the locker room or threats exchanged in a half-humorous, half-angry tone. The manliness of these boys did not consist in simple punching and kicking, but took on subtler guises. A tiny few were determined to make their mark both academically and on the sports field. Some were scholars pure and simple. Others looked forward mainly to the shove and thrust of rugger. Most were undistinguished on the playing field or in the classroom; but, of course, certain boys had individual interests they pursued with intensity. The really stupid were as rare as the really brilliant, though one wondered about a handful of lads how they had managed to get let in at all. Had a guardian angel stood at their right hand and guided the pen with which they wrote their English essays and coped with their mathematical problems?

For myself, I went to Methody full of resolve for hard work and giving as little trouble as possible to those whom God had ordained as my superiors. As the years passed, alas! and as conditions at home became more and more strained, I took to inward (rather than outward) rebellion. *Non serviam* became my motto. I later did less and less work, except at those subjects, like English and history, in which I could do fairly well, anyhow, with a minimum of effort. I had rebelled against sport after the first two or three years so that, by the time I had reached the upper forms, I had gracelessly bowed myself out of that arena. (One of my problems on the sports field was my indifferent eyesight. Should I take my glasses off and see badly, or keep them on and risk having them broken? Another problem was that I longed to be more than just another mediocre player. Yet I knew I was no giant, no Colquohoun or Grimshaw.) At science and mathematics, I was indifferent, so the only thing for me was to be 'literary'. What else could I do well? By the age of 16 I was beginning to send out an occasional article and poem here and there, for I felt I could find myself only in verbal self-expression. And so it has proved. That process of 'finding myself' has continued to this day – and it is a process that will end only with death.

At 13, then, I first entered the dewy world of infinite possibility. Eagerly I joined in work and play and friendship. It was all so simple. Life was there for the grasping. Go on, grasp it, Robert! Doubt and rebellion came with adolescence. But as I write, well advanced in years, I think my sympathies have returned to my 13-year-old, enthusiastic self. The world is indeed there for the taking, if only we have the courage not to be dismayed by apparent, yet often unreal, difficulties. In his *Margin Released*, J.B. Priestley remarks on the importance of character for anyone who wants to become and stay a writer. In youth one tends to overrate talent and underrate those qualities of grit and determination and courage in the face of odds that we sum up in the word 'character'. Of one thing I am certain – and that is the futility of taking the advice of others in important matters. Similarly, I believe the advice of others can be immensely useful in coping with minor affairs. These truths, however, were only to come with the years; and they had to be bitterly paid for.

Neither truly introverted nor extroverted, I found little difficulty in making friends. Among boys there tends to be quick shifts in friendship, for they enjoy playing at what one might call social politics. Alliances form, dissolve and new patterns come into being. The close friend of a

13-year-old may be forgotten in three years' time. We are, of course, inevitably drawn to those with whom we share interests yet who are unlike us in temperament. Optimist and pessimist consort together. During my first few weeks at Methody, I made a number of new friends, but only one of them was to last a lifetime. That was Leslie Baxter, a tall, unusually helpful, well-mannered and serious boy with a strong vocation for teaching. I do not think that Leslie and I have been at all alike temperamentally; nor have our interests and ideas coincided. One of our bonds has been our common interest in the arts. When Leslie left school he went to the College of Art in Belfast – an institution which was then, it always seemed to me, to be unfittingly housed in the 'Tech' building – and there qualified as an art teacher, making a subsequent career for himself in that field. Unlike me, he has not been tempted to stray from his native place, apart from making summer excursions to continental art galleries and churches. What a pub crawl is to other men, a church (or cathedral) crawl is to a person like Leslie Baxter!

It would be invidious to pick out the names of boys with whom friendship suddenly ripened and then, more often than not, ceased equally suddenly, and for no very obvious reason. That is the way of young animals not yet set in their ways. A boy with whom friendship extended beyond school was Ernest Baird, who shared my enthusiasm for books. Often at his home we discussed our reading into the small hours – I remember how amused we once were when we came across a remark of Arnold Bennett's (was it about a novel by the Scottish writer, Lewis Grassic Gibbon?) to the effect: 'It cannot not be a classic.' We found Bennett's *Literary Taste* a useful signpost to further reading.

Oddly enough I was to meet some Methody boys in later life and I am glad to say the old school has produced a number of writers of more than local fame, and whom I counted among my friends. Of these I mention John Hewitt, poet, art critic and man of letters, and another poet, Richard Kell. It is a pity that Hewitt, Kell and I were not contemporaries.

I can remember getting into one serious 'scrape' at Methody, but have only the vaguest memory of the details. Even at the time, I found myself implicated in happenings I did not fully understand. It was a case of the 'innocent bystander' being hit by a bullet. Some sort of rough-housing was apparently going on in the vicinity of the locker room and lavatory. Within minutes The Hawk had swooped. 'See he-rrr-e me boy . . .' he began. A group of boys, of whom I was one, was swiftly rounded up, caught in the act. Neither then or now do I know what the act happened to be! Protestations of innocence with regard to whatever mischief had been afoot were to no avail. The only other boy I remember being implicated was Ernest Paul, whom I knew well then and afterwards. We were all suspended for an indefinite period. What would happen? Would we all be expelled? It was all the more ghastly for me since I had little idea of what it was about. If I had been clearly guilty, I could have owned up. As it was, my general feeling of guilt had been aroused and I was a bit like one of those Russians during the Stalinist era who were prepared, after brainwashing, to write full confessions about crimes they had not committed. Of one thing I was sure – I ought not to have been out of my classroom at the time I was caught. A minor offence had rapidly become a major one. As usual I set off for school each morning – not having breathed a word of the suspension to any outsider – but, being barred from classes, simply mooched around the grounds with some of my fellow culprits or wandered listlessly and aimlessly through the city streets. Expulsion from Methody was not to be taken lightly. The others involved in the offence would not talk about it, so the mystery thickened. One day I was told by an assistant master that, if I wrote an apology, it had a chance of acceptance; he gave me a general outline of what I might say. It was all up to the headmaster . . . there was no guarantee that the apology would be accepted.

I began a letter, hinting at guilt but not quite admitting it and beginning 'Dear Headmaster'. A day passed and I prayed as I had never prayed before. But the prayer was answered. I was pardoned, and only a few of the real culprits punished. Nobody was expelled. A chastened Robert went back to classes. The whole experience made me doubt the validity of the concept of justice, yet I clung as best I could to the idea that in the end the innocent would come out with no mark against their names. It had been horrible, however, to have been in a position where one had appeared to be guilty of some unknown offence. I decided one not only had to be innocent, but to be clearly seen to be innocent. No doubt the headmaster, Mr Henderson, realised that the boys caught by The Hawk were not truly wicked or insolent. I certainly had no criminal record. Back at classes I realised that I had a certain glamour, especially for the average boy who probably supposed I had done something really naughty and had survived it. I had come through the fire unscathed after all. I settled down as quickly as I could to humdrum anonymity – even though I did nurse a certain sullen and hidden discontent – all heroism spent. Just as earlier I had played the role of The Boy Who Had Nearly Died, now I played that of The Boy Who Had Nearly Been Expelled. At least it lifted one out of the common run, though I knew it would never do to get a reputation for being a bad 'un.

Examinations could be a nightmare. After the expulsion threat, for a time I was unusually quiet and industrious, but soon I was in a rebellious mood again. As notions of revolt grew in me, industry decreased, and I followed my own devices more and more. The result was that I came to fear exams – end of term exams, Junior and then Senior – for which I knew myself, in some subjects, to be ill-equipped. This was all the more devastating since my masters kept telling me I could do really well if I tried. But why should I? Unusually energetic in some ways I gradually drifted into being an idler academically, with the result that in most exams I just managed to scrape through, except in the one or two subjects I found easy. The only piece of homework I started to take seriously was the weekly essay, which increasingly became a labour of delight. I took pleasure in being deliberately exhibitionist and outrageous in my essays, setting off squibs for all I was worth – squibs that frequently expressed left-wing, free-love, and violently anti-bourgeois opinions that no doubt seldom found their way into the essays of Belfast grammar school boys.

My masters, however, were exceptionally tolerant, I must say. They probably realised that I was having a more than normally disturbed adolescence. Having discovered D.H. Lawrence's *Sons and Lovers*, I became a devoted Lawrentian; and my admiration for Lawrence the writer, if not the thinker, has never really cooled. James Joyce was soon added to the figures in my private gallery of the truly great of the 20th century. Is it surprising, in view of what I have already written about my adolescence, that my admiration was given so unstintingly to two lifelong rebels, who, like me, had early decided they would not serve that in which they had ceased to believe? I remember one of my masters being shocked when he read in the school magazine an article that expressed my interest in D.H. Lawrence. Perhaps, for him, Lawrence just seemed the abominable author of the then whispered-about *Lady Chatterley's Lover*. Yet Mr Falconer, more tolerant than the more 'advanced' boys would have supposed, was willing to print my views – in a slightly toned-down form – in, of all journals, *MCB*. Perhaps I was not so unlucky in my school after all.

Among the masters who impressed me, there was one I came to admire, almost love, when I reached the higher forms. That was Ronnie Marshall, a Cambridge aesthete – or so he seemed to me – who taught English and history. Ronnie had a sophistication I had never come across before and it appealed to me forcibly. Immaculate in his appearance, arresting in expression (enhanced with a slight lisp) of at times somewhat unconventional views, Ronnie treated us not as pimply schoolboys but as intellectual equals. That, I think, is what endeared him to me. One did not have the impression of an adult 'talking down', as with some of the other masters. He seemed to be saying, as it were: 'Well, you are all old enough now to form your own opinions. Go ahead and do so. I'm here to give you the background of fact on which to base them.' Not least impressive was that Ronnie was an Italophile, who spoke Italian fluently and had made a special study of Italian history. Perhaps my liking for pasta comes from his influence.

Rebellion did not just take a negative form and was not just a matter of being against all forms of authority. I had chanced to come into contact with a group of young Queen's graduates who told me of the exciting new developments in Russia, or, as they preferred to say, the Soviet Union, a country that was proud to call itself 'One Sixth of the Earth'. They assured me that reports about concentration camps not so very different from the Nazi model, and the extermination of the Kulaks and minority peoples were lies – plain capitalist lies – and that our newspapers had to build up the Red Bogey. What else, they insisted, *would* our newspapers say? I began to read the *Daily Worker* and the yellow-orange-covered Left Book Club books they lent me; I tried manfully to read Marx's *Capital* but shamefacedly gave up. I found the *Communist Manifesto* easy going and thrilled to the sentiment: 'There is a spectre haunting Europe . . . the spectre of Communism.' 'Workers of the world unite, you have nothing to lose but your chains' began to seem more and more true.

If we do not stop the Nazis in Germany and the Italian Fascists, said my new friends, humanity is lost. The clouds darkened in Spain and the Spanish Civil War was upon us. That Franco was supported by the Roman Catholic Church did not seem a good omen to Protestant

Ulstermen. 'No Pasarán' became a slogan as real to me as the 'Remember 1690' scrawled or painted on gables. Mass action! On Guard for Spain! A Popular Front Now! Chamberlain Must Go! Workers of Hand and Brain Unite!

All is not yet lost, urged my new mentors, whom I met with pleasurable eagerness. We have friends in high places, they said. Don't worry, we can eventually capture the citadels of power in the Labour Movement. I became more and more interested in these new and stimulating ideas. Who gave a damn for Senior Certificate when there was a world to be lost and a world to be won? Instead of doing my homework in those last anxious years of the '30s, I would sneak of an evening to some out-of-the-way hall and listen to a Marxist analyse the current situation. Or I would go to watch a Soviet film made by Pudovkin or Eisenstein, or see some play such as Clifford Odets' *Waiting for Lefty*. Or in the vastness of my little bedroom-cum-study I would read the stirring political poems of Auden and Spender and C. Day-Lewis. I could indeed hear the 'opening of a new theme'. Bliss was it in that Red Dawn to be alive, but to be young was a veritable Soviet heaven.!

Within a year or two, I was to be sadly disillusioned by it all. The dream crumbled before the iron realities like the Soviet-German pact and the disclosures of savage Stalinist repression of the kind that came to be openly admitted by Soviet leaders. The god had failed. For the time being there was blinding new light in eastern Europe, and it was spreading a crimson glow over the sleeping west. Awake! Awake! Even in faction-ridden, obscurantist Belfast, if one peered closely into the heavens, it was possible to discern the proud Red Star. It could shine for us, too, and the Lagan could flow crimson.

All this time, during this new surge of hope – days and nights of it – I was going to Methody as usual and being as discreet as possible about my views to my elders and betters, some of whom would have been angry, while others would have merely laughed. At Methody, however, I found a few boys who were willing to sympathise and read the subversive literature I smuggled in. This was read with as much zest as other lads showed in poring over pornography. Soon I would be a man, I thought, and able to play my part on the stage of the big world. Even schooldays must come to an end. Then I would set the Lagan on fire. O dreams, O destinations!

SEVEN

Heroes This Way

Johnston was a big fellow with slouching movements and slow speech. He was determined to be a boss. A good sportsman, he captained the junior rugby team and would one day, everyone believed, be captain of the 1st XV, which in itself conferred heroic status. His academic performance was mediocre. Nobody liked him particularly, but it would be untrue to say that he was hated. Though feared, he harmed nobody so long as he was not crossed. Cross him and, once his slow mind had decided what was to be done, he would surely do it in his own apparently lazy yet determined way.

It must have been in my second year at Methody that I became aware of Johnston. Nobody called him by his Christian name, Julian, perhaps because it was the only Julian one had heard of. He was Johnston and nothing else. That was the name he scrawled on his exercise books. If he came into the locker room for his books, he elbowed everyone else aside, definitely but not viciously. If you had already opened your locker drawer and were sorting out books or gear, you automatically made way and let Johnston go ahead. It was an unwritten rule.

Johnston said no word of thanks, but took it as a *droit du seigneur*. He had a natural ascendancy over other boys, even over clever, quick-witted boys. 'When I'm captain of the 1st XV . . .' he would drawl. Johnston had an uncanny feeling of rightness even when he was dead wrong. He once disputed the spelling of a word with the English master, who proved Johnston was wrong by pointing out to him the word in a dictionary. Johnston would not admit his mistake. 'I know it as a fact,' he announced, and some of his toadies agreed that the dictionary must be wrong. Perhaps they were hoping for a place in the 1st XV one day.

I remember that, in the locker room, a boy called McAllister said to Johnston, 'I was here first and I'm in a hurry.' Johnston stopped and looked hard at him.

'What did you say?' Johnston did not always quite get it first time.

'I said I was here before you and that I'm in a hurry.'

'So you're in a hurry,' said Johnston, emphasising every word. 'Are those your books?'

'Yes,' said McAllister.

'Give them to me.'

McAllister meekly handed a pile of books to Johnston. Johnston held them above his head like a rugby ball and then flung them with all his might into the far corner of the locker room. Now McAllister, who was no coward – I had seen him fight valiantly – said nothing but walked away defeated. He never challenged Johnston again.

Another place dominated by Johnston was the bicycle shed. Five or ten minutes before morning assembly, the shed would be a seething mass of boys dismounting and storing away their bicycles. One morning, Johnston arrived just as another boy was putting his bike into position in the spot Johnston generally chose.

'That's *my* place,' said Johnston.

'Then why didn't you get here before me?'

'That's *my* place,' repeated Johnston.

The boy walked off before Johnston could think of what to do next.

I knew slightly the pale, dark-haired boy who had dared to displease Johnston. He was a newcomer to the school, one Clive Dunton, a boy from Lancashire whose father was a Salvation Army major. Dunton was a bit of a dandy with oiled hair and beautifully creased pants. Johnston was not in the habit of bothering to address nonentities like myself, but he was obviously crestfallen. He turned to me and said, 'I won't take cheek from anybody and least of all from that oily English bugger.' I nodded, for I had no wish to be involved. I had enough problems to occupy my attention.

At break I looked around for Johnston, for I expected he would be on the prowl for Dunton with a view to physical rather than verbal aggression. Not so, for Johnston lay sprawled on the steps of the canteen, surrounded by several admiring younger boys and deep in conversation with his crony, Dick Watters. Watters was a sly fellow. He flattered Johnston and carried out little jobs that Johnston wanted done, but were too important or lazy to do for himself.

When I went, after school, to pick up my bike, Johnston and Watters were hanging around. They watched several boys push off home. Watters came over to me.

'Would you like to see a little bit of fun?' he asked.

'Fun? What sort of fun?' I asked.

'Just a wee bit of fun,' said Watters with a grin.

I should have jumped on my bike that minute and made off. I watched with Watters while Johnston put his hand in his pocket and pulled out a razor blade. He flashed the blade in the sunshine with a Byronic gesture before walking over to the bike that had been stowed away in the wrong place, *his* place. Slash! Slash! Slash! He ripped both tyres with a few beautifully co-ordinated movements. I could not help admiring his dexterity, though the deed appalled me.

Watters laughed and clapped his hands. 'What happened just now?' he demanded.

'Johnston slashed the tyres of Dunton's bike.' It was obvious, surely.

'What big eyes you have, granny,' said Watters sharply. He reached towards me and pulled my glasses off.

'How handsome you are, granny,' said Johnston. 'Ask him the question again.'

'What happened just now?' Watters asked. 'Think before you reply.'

A minute passed before I could bring myself to give the answer required.

'Nothing,' I said.

'You're not as stupid as I thought,' said Watters. 'Give him back his glasses,' said Johnston.

Watters pushed the glasses roughly into my hands.

'Bugger off,' said Johnston.

Next morning the headmaster, after prayers, said he had a special announcement to make. He spoke of 'unparalleled hooliganism . . . great discourtesy to a new boy and a stranger to our city . . . duty to the school . . . the community'. We filed out. The words buzzed in my head. Johnston was getting away with too much. Big-headed bully. Bullies should not get away with it. The headmaster was right, though I generally thought him a pompous ass. I would tell. Yes, I would tell.

The bell released me into the clamour of tuckshop and playground.

I walked along the corridor, head down. *Must tell.* Suddenly, Johnston and Watters appeared.

'Going for a walk?' Watters enquired.

'Heroes this way,' said Johnston, seizing my arms and dragging me into an empty classroom.

'Why don't you own up?' I said weakly. 'You heard what the headmaster said at assembly.'

'He only heard one side of the story,' said Watters, as if he were Johnston's lawyer. 'He only heard what the Salvationist swine had to tell him. Bloody foreigner. I'll bet he didn't say a word about being offensive to Johnston.'

Johnston looked at me.

'You hear what Watters says,' he said.

Johnston put his hand in his pocket and pulled out a tin box that had once held tobacco flakes. He opened it slowly and took out a razor blade.

'This is sharp,' he said. 'A beautiful edge. Best quality Sheffield steel.'

Watters grinned in his nasty way. 'High time you started shaving,' he said.

'Ask him some questions, Watters,' said Johnston.

'Did you see anything interesting yesterday?' asked Watters. 'At the cycle shed, say?'

There was a long pause while Johnston stroked the razor blade.

'I don't think so.'

Johnston and Watters laughed. They walked off together and left me standing there nervously. I can still hear their laughter as they ran down the corridor and out into the playground.

EIGHT

Butterfly

Butterfly may seem a strange name for a hefty schoolboy with black hairs on his wrists, a larger-than-average head and blue eyes that gazed into infinite space. James Walter Brown was his real name but we always called him Butterfly because he had written in a composition: 'A bat is a sort of big blind butterfly.' Even if Butterfly had given a definition of 'bat' equal to that in the *Concise Oxford Dictionary*, we would have sniggered anyway and said he had copied it from a book. We never allowed Butterfly to win, as, by consensus of schoolboy opinion, Butterfly was only one remove from being an idiot.

Big and shambling, neither at home in classroom nor playing field – and not even when larking around the locker room where our small dramas were enacted – Butterfly was an odd boy out. Those of us who were none too sure of our own place in the hierarchy knew one fact for sure: Butterfly was at the bottom of the form and he was going to stay there. One might not be awfully bright, but one was brighter than that big slob.

Funny when you thought about it, because Stewart was really dense, but if you hinted at his denseness, you would most likely get a vicious blow in the groin. Dixon kicked a ball like a girl and actually enjoyed the academic grind, but you dared not offend him or he would not lend a hand with Latin homework. I could cobble sentences together and so make a little knowledge go a long way, and as a result was in demand as a writer of letters to the headmaster that were supposed to come from parents. Truancies could be explained away as illnesses or family commitments. Many a boy owed me a debt of gratitude for having explained how he had to attend his grandfather's funeral in a remote village.

I was not a bully, yet I must confess that I occasionally bullied Butterfly in a mild sort of way. Sometimes, when the mood was on me, I defended him. I quite liked Butterfly, in spite of his daft ways, but I had not the guts to stand up for him unequivocally. Life with Father was difficult and schoolmasters could be demanding. I had no intention of seeking unnecessary attention of an unpleasant kind by being known as Butterfly's friend. An appearance of conformity paid – so the class butt had to stay the class butt. All groups have their scapegoats and Butterfly was ours.

One Saturday afternoon, I had actually visited Butterfly's home, though naturally I did not breathe a word about that to any of the lads. I was glad to go there, for none of the others ever bothered to ask me. Butterfly's house turned out to be a suburban one just beyond the end of the Malone Road. It was sizeable compared with the house I lived in and had a nice big garden. Real middle class, I thought, but a bit gloomy and smelling of Jeyes' disinfectant. Butterfly's old man had money somewhere and, in the world I was familiar with, money brought admiration – you had prospered, so God was on your side. Of course, that was before I had turned fully into a red-hot socialist and thought it terribly wrong to have money wrung out of the downtrodden workers.

Butterfly's father was a stout man with a large moustache. He had a resonant voice that suggested self-confidence, yet the voice sounded a trifle gloomy and monotonous. I remember his telling me how he had started work as an office boy at five shillings a week. There's money in fruit, I thought, that's where it comes from. All those oranges and apples and bananas have brought in the money.

The father asked me what books I read. I mentioned a few and thought he would be impressed that I had dipped into writers as different as Forrest Reid – who lived somewhere in our city, it was said – Hardy and D.H. Lawrence. He too had looked at the work of these writers, but found them wanting in one way or another. Then he said, a trifle ponderously: 'In my view, Somerset Maugham's the greatest writer alive – and do you know why?'

'No, I don't,' I replied, wondering whether I should have added 'sir'. I wanted to be correct and amiable. He smiled. Then came the explanation.

'Maugham,' he said, 'understands human beings with all their foibles, yet he doesn't judge them. You ought to look at *Of Human Bondage* and some of his short stories. As for 'The Summing Up', I must have read it half a dozen times.'

Now my English master (whose lisping Oxford accent I had tried to imitate) had once dismissed Somerset Maugham in the withering phrase – the 'Austin Reed of literature'. Actually, I rather coveted the clothes I saw in our local Austin Reed branch, for their sports jackets and grey worsted trousers seemed exquisite. I knew there must be something wrong with my taste both in books and clothes. The English master was for me a hero of culture and I knew he could not possibly be wrong. So I nodded sagely when Mr Brown told me I should read Maugham. Snobbishly, I recalled that, after all, he had once been an office boy.

'Come and look at the flowers,' said Mr Brown, as if to indicate that the literary seminar had ended. I was not very interested in flowers because we had no garden at home, but I had manners enough to tell him that they were very nice. Then we talked about this and that, and laughed over a statement of a local MP who had said at Stormont that he was 'walking hand in hand with the floodgates of democracy'. Eventually, the conversation turned to the subject of Mr Brown's son. One sentence is still in my mind: 'I know I can rely on you to help Jim all you can.'

Jim! I found it hard not to laugh. Imagine anyone calling Butterfly *Jim*! I nodded gravely, feeling embarrassed. Mr Brown was not only a grown-up but a rich grown-up who gave people orders in his office. Fruit importers who had money and large gloomy houses in the suburbs and flower gardens with exotic blooms and who admired Somerset Maugham both impressed and revolted me. Mr Brown represented success.

I visited that house a few more times and, gradually, I came to have more respect for Mr Brown. He was a widower and I supposed that the melancholy I detected in his voice was because he had no wife to look after him and Butterfly – Jim, I should say. He always gave me fruit to take home and mother was pleased that I had made friends with nice people who lived in a nice area in a nice big house. At school, I kept quiet about these visits and even adopted an aloof attitude towards Butterfly.

The real bully in our form was McKittrick. People said his father had been a docker before he had gone into the hardware business and that he beat McKittrick for the slightest misdemeanour. McKittrick obviously had to get his own back on somebody. He was an average-sized 15-year-old, dark and brooding. When he smiled, you had to be on your guard. He struck without warning – and mercilessly. The more he hurt you, the better he was pleased. McKittrick seemed never to have heard of the schoolboy code of fair play that the majority of us observed. I had a bad quarter of an hour with him once, before I lost my temper and struck out. It led to a fight but, after that, McKittrick left me alone.

Fortunately for me, McKittrick slipped during the fight, so I came out of it reasonably well with only a cut lip. But he did manage to land several savage punches that had hurt. I thanked God for the metal tip on McKittrick's heel that made him slip. As I say, he left me alone after that punch-up, but he was still on the lookout for victims.

One day, Mr Phillips gave us quadratic equations to get on with while he marked test papers. McKittrick was sitting directly behind Butterfly. I had finished a couple of questions and felt I could take a well-earned rest without getting into trouble. I started looking round the class and making grimaces at one or two of my friends, just to see what would happen.

Then my eye caught McKittrick, who was in the act of jabbing Butterfly in the small of the back with a heavy ruler. Butterfly turned round and tried to focus his blue eyes on his tormentor. This gave McKittrick the chance to swipe at a big bottle of blue-black Stephens' ink standing on Butterfly's desk (like many boys indifferent at schoolwork, Butterfly was fully equipped with the impedimenta of learning: pens, ink, rulers, geometrical instruments). The bottle fell right between Butterfly's legs. He jumped up with a muffled scream. I saw the ink trickle down the dark-grey regulation trousers.

Mr Phillips looked up. His bushy eyebrows moved. He was clearly angry at being disturbed.

'Come up here, Brown,' he shouted.

Butterfly shambled up to the master's desk. He nearly tripped over an undone shoelace.

'Look at yourself, Brown, you useless creature,' said Mr Phillips in his hoarse voice, half-contemptuous, half-friendly. 'Just look at him, boys. Ready to join the army of the Great Unwashed.'

We all laughed.

'But, sir . . .' Butterfly began.

'But what?' enquired Mr Phillips wearily.

'But, sir, I was attacked, sir. It wasn't my fault.'

'You were attacked. Oh, indeed, and who was the aggressor, may I ask? Herr Hitler or Signor Mussolini?'

We all laughed again at the mention of these funny foreigners.

'Sir, McKittrick, sir. I think it was him.'

'So you *think* it was McKittrick. It's fascinating to hear you have started *thinking*. Come up here, McKittrick!'

McKittrick marched up smartly, his face as innocent as a whitewashed wall.

'Did you attack Brown, McKittrick?'

'No, sir. Certainly not, sir,' replied McKittrick in suitably outraged tones.

Mr Phillips ignored the reply and addressed the class. 'Did anyone see this alleged attack?'

I felt a shiver run through me. I looked down at the desk and the initials carved on it: W.L. As I gazed at the initials of some boy long gone from the school, I saw myself in the school yard near the bicycle shed, jacket off, facing McKittrick. I saw my friend, Dick Collins, holding my coat and books fastened by a leather strap. I heard Dick's enthusiastic voice as he jumped up and down and shouted encouragement at me, 'Let him have it! Destroy him, Robert.'

I talked silently to myself — 'You saw the attack on Butterfly. *Tell! Tell!*' But my tongue stayed as if paralysed, useless, inert. *Tell! Tell!* I remained mute. McKittrick might not slip a second time and he would knock the guts out of me. After all, Butterfly was not a real friend. I sat rigid and gazed at the initials W.L. William Long? Wilfred Lutton? Wesley Lang?

When we formed up in a jagged line to go into class after the lunch break, I heard a pathetic voice whisper down my neck, 'You saw him do it. Why didn't you tell?' Butterfly looked more dishevelled and forlorn than ever. I felt guilty. Had not Mr Brown invited me to his house and given me fruit to take home? Had he not asked me to help Butterfly all I could? I felt guilty, but also angry. The anger which should have been turned on McKittrick was deflected instead towards Butterfly. If he were not so stupid and useless, everything would be all right. Why didn't he stand up for himself, make an effort as I did? On impulse, I punched him in the ribs.

'I saw nothing,' I shouted. 'Nothing, I tell you. Butter-fingered Butterfly!'

A couple of days later, I went up to Butterfly and gave him a brown-papered parcel. It contained a big bottle of Swan ink I had bought out of my pocket money. 'This is for you,' I said. 'I shouldn't have hit you. Sorry.'

He smiled weakly, mumbled his thanks and ambled off.

He never again asked me to visit his home and I never let anyone know I had ever done so. Even today, I sometimes think of Mr Brown and his big gloomy house and the garden and the fruit and his interest in Somerset Maugham and the way he wanted me to help his son. Butterfly's almost inaudible words sound in my ears: 'You saw him do it. Why didn't you tell?'

If I could relive that incident all over again, would I have the courage to speak out? I'm afraid I don't know.

NINE

Waiting for Robert

Father was one of five children – John James, Robert, Henry, Elizabeth Ann and Samuel – born in the second marriage of a typical Presbyterian small farmer in County Monaghan. They moved two or three times, I believe, but for some years lived in the neighbourhood of Cootehill. A more prosperous and educated branch of the family had settled in the town of Monaghan – one of them was to become chairman of the county council, but we never had any truck with grand folk of that kind. Father's name, incidentally, was Henry and it was given to me as a second Christian name, though plain Robert suits me fine. My paternal grandfather looked the patriarch, white goatee beard and all. I do not know what persona he presented to his sons and daughter, but on the occasions I saw him I regarded him with awe. He was a rural Jehovah, thunder-voiced, or, if not quite that, one of the immortals from Mount Olympus who had lived and ruled despotically for hundreds and hundreds of years.

In fact, I am not sure whether grandfather was as stern as all that, but that was the impression I had as a small boy. I avoided him as I would have avoided a collision with a big puff-puff. Father himself had, somehow or other, struggled out of the harshly frugal parental nest – though it did not strike me as being one of singing birds – and attempted to make his way in the narrow Ulster world with only a national school behind him and an early-developed, un-Presbyterian taste for liquor, a liking he never lost. (One of his brothers, my Uncle George, was a lifetime teetotaller, and the others drank only occasionally, at weddings or around Christmas.) 'Many's the bit o' business was done over a wee drink,' Father used to say. Or again he would ask, 'Would you tell me a clever man that couldn't take a drink?' A rhetorical question, indeed, to answer which would have invited a cuff on the ear. Mind you, when I got a bit older, I wanted to say: 'Yes, Bernard Shaw — and he doesn't eat meat either! He's famous, too!' But I knew that Father had no use for Bernard Shaw, whom he regarded as immoral, partly because he had written an exposure of his parents. Father had once said, 'Imagine the oul' idiot makin' a laughin' stock of his own parents! He'll surely go till hell for it.' Apparently, at the age of 17, Father could down his whiskey with the best, or worst, of them. If success in business depended on a man's ability to drain his glass fast and often, then Henry Greacen's name would be inscribed far above that of Isaac Wolfson. Alas!

Father had tried farming without success. As his sister, my Aunt Liz-Ann — Elizabeth Ann — said, 'Harry's heart was never in the moilin' and toilin'.' That was only too clear. He wanted quick results. Crops would not grow fast enough or tall enough; prices in the market were never high enough; farming was a hard, dirty grind at which nobody grew rich. As a young man, he had tried his luck in one of those new-type creameries started by people like Sir Horace Plunkett and Æ (George William Russell) as the basis of an Irish Rural Co-operative Movement. This work was more to Father's liking. He enjoyed it and the prestige which came from being the manager of a creamery. He used to talk about a 'Father Poland' (that's what it sounded like but the name was probably Boland) he had been friendly with in those days, although Father was normally somewhat suspicious of those who 'dug with the wrong foot'. Perhaps the priest was something of a Graham Greene character. I know that Father was held in esteem in at least one of these jobs, for he always carried round with him a presentation gold-cased watch which had a copperplate inscription on the inside cover that referred, in a stiffly respectable phrase, to his qualities as a creamery manager. This watch was often consulted to know whether the pubs were about to open or shut. One of my early delights was to have him hold it to my ear so that I could hear the *tick-tick-tick*.

But Father was not a man to remain content with managing a small country co-operative. His eyes scanned wider horizons; he looked at the world, like the sage Dr Johnson, from China to Peru — or perhaps it was from China to Venezuela. (My father, as I mentioned earlier, was unwittingly subject to the contemptuous and derisive nickname — among my female relations — of 'Ven'.) He never travelled far, but, for all that, was more of a traveller than those who have actually viewed the Golden Gate. There was, after all, the nonconformist obsession with money to be reckoned with. If you made money you were, *ipso facto*, a good man, one whom the Presbyterian God had favoured. If not, why, you were little better than an RC (Father Poland excepted) who would do appallingly wicked things, like attending Sunday football matches or go dog racing at Dunmore Park! Thus, there was life on the one hand, the dream on the other: the unending grind at disagreeable chores, and the counter-feeling that race-tracks and whiskey (and, perhaps a bit surreptitiously, slyly, lovely women) were around the corner. Had not other country boys, forsaking plough and spade and hoe, made their way in the big redbrick city and ended up as pot-bellied aldermen who golfed at the weekend with elevated gents such as bank managers, solicitors and doctors?

During Father's lifetime I never understood him, nor did he understand me. We lived, for the most part, in a thick fog of non-comprehension. To me he was a darkly brooding, narrow-jowled, moody man who, to my disgust, chewed twist tobacco and spat out the liquorice-coloured juice, drank a great deal of noxious-smelling whiskey and believed that a man who had not made a fortune was 'no bloody good'. He lacked the gift for happiness or enjoyment. My mother and her sisters kept harping on the theme of his addiction to the bottle, and spoke with bated breath of the sinfulness thereof. I did not know so much about the sinful part of it – anything nice seemed always to be a sin – but drinking was obviously something that made a man miserable. Why does he do it, I thought, if he does not find it enjoyable, if it makes him sick? I had yet to hear of Sigmund Freud.

But Father being a good Prod in his heart (not that he was a kirk regular) was damned if he would do anything so fiendishly Papist or foreign as enjoy himself! My mother liked fun far more than he did, and delighted in what she called 'droll stories'. She liked innocent amusement, so long as it did not cost too much, for there were bills to pay. Pennies had to be counted – and even halfpennies. In the years when we ran the Kenilworth, we used to get a free cinema pass for displaying showcards of the current films. My mother and I, rigged out in our second-best clothes, would go off together to see films such as *Silent Hour*, which starred her great favourite, the very gentlemanly George Arliss, the very model of an English gentleman. Earlier I had been taken to see *Ramona* by Aunt Tillie in – of all places! – the Clonard, right in the heart of Rome, you might say. The mission bells were indeed calling!

Father came to a film once or twice, but he insisted – much to my chagrin – on leaving in the middle of the big picture, saying he could not make head or tail of it. Like most of his relations, he thought the silver screen a lot of high-falutin' nonsense, a veritable fraud perpetrated on decent people – Uncle George considered this wonderful never-never land nothing more than 'a wheen o' oul' shadows mugs pay to gape at'. Another time, I wheedled Ven into getting as far as the Classic, that palace of romance to my eyes. He hesitated at the box-office, decided against and pressed a half-crown into my sticky palm with the words, 'Better in your pocket than in some fat oul' showman's'. I could have wept. Excitement was what I hungered for, not a coin.

To an uncritical cinema-goer like myself, any and every film was vastly exciting. I could be as happy in the Pop on a Saturday afternoon, watching a western among the scruffy, smelly, jostling orange-sucking young plebs, as in one of those swish new establishments that impressed me far more than any cathedral had ever done. The Pop may have been rowdy and the noise a bit too much at times to allow one to hear the film dialogue properly, but it had the advantage of costing exactly one penny, merely 'a wing'. Matinees at posh places might cost as much as fourpence or even fivepence. All right for the nobs, but obviously the kind of place I could visit only as a very special treat. As I got a bit older, mere shootin' and killin' and ridin' on the range, with a dramatic chase before the villains were brought to justice, began to seem like kids' stuff.

The sophisticated world began to entrance me. What posh rooms – more like baronial halls than anything else – these high-class Yanks lived in and how they drank their cocktails with poise and charm! With what insouciance the elegant English actor could carry off a situation in which I would have curled up and died with embarrassment! How enviable were these lives that were played out against a Manhattan or Berkeley Square background! Nobody there worried about whether or not something cost sixpence, unlike the drab, damp, taxi-less, evening-gownless world where one queued for a fish supper (price fivepence) in Joe's steamy saloon near the Pop. I liked grandeur, swank, pretention, no doubt because such attitudes contrasted so violently with the horrible pinching and scraping that went on around me. The world symbolised by revolving doors that led into Grand Hotels of the Vicki Baum/Arnold Bennett type had a glamour far removed from the atmosphere of McMahon's Select Bar or Ross's pawnshop, with its aroma of camphorated clothes.

I was tired of existing. I cried out for life – or what I mistakenly took to be life. Father believed, as I developed into adolescence, that my head had been turned with nonsense I read in the boys' magazines we sold in the shop, and picked up from the gossip columns of the London newspapers. And no doubt it was. Not only that, but I was at the stage where I read any titbit I could find about sex, and viewed with delight photos of naked ladies I came across in journals devoted to the cult of nudism. But the world of high-life was only a temporary aberration, and soon I was to become too serious by half, and be filled with zeal for reforming the world. Nudist magazines were to be replaced by intellectual nourishment represented by the *Irish Democrat* (to which paper I contributed my very first article, 'A Youth's Views on Education') and those limp-cover books issued by the Left Book Club. But that time was not yet.

Ven and I were at loggerheads as usual. He denounced me for always having my nose stuck in a book, newspaper or magazine. My eagerness to understand the world around me (not just in a dry, academic way, but in a real human sense) left him cold. Nor did he forgive me for taking naturally to those uppish garments known as pyjamas – 'pan-jams' he called them contemptuously – introduced into our household by my Aunt Tillie, whom he loathed and I loved. I knew somehow that the lovely actresses would despise a boy who slept in his shirt, and the approval of ladies was for me far more important than that of Ven. Father still slept in the shirt he wore all day long. His ancestors had done the same thing, assuming they all had shirts to their backs, which I rather doubt. What was good enough for honest men was good enough for Ven. Why wear fancy clothes when you were asleep? The more he sneered, the more adamant I became. He complained that my shoes – he wore boots – had pointy toes and that I looked 'a regular show' in my white trousers – these were simply grey worsted pants, though not as wide as I would really have enjoyed having.

Nor did he like the classy, polite way I learned to talk at Methody, using big words, foreign phrases and schoolboy slang in a manner that obviously indicated a 'swelled head' and would never have passed muster anywhere near Cootehill. I started to be grammatical and say 'he's gone' instead of 'he's went', which showed that college affectation had insidiously crept in. Worse still, I began to pronounce English in a slightly Anglicised way. That was also wrong. The more critical Ven became, the more determined I was to make myself as different from him as I could, especially since these new directions had the warm approval of Aunt Tillie, who wanted me to be a gentleman like the McCreas, whom she said were 'all doctors and clergy'.

There was daily evidence of Ven's dislike for me and his feeling that, fundamentally, I sided with the feminine McCrea establishment, with its good humour, snobbery, conformity, hard work and relish in innocent amusement. Yet, at times, during a troubled boyhood – dark and haunted, yet not without an innate belief that one day I would live the life of Larry, far, far away from the Newtownards Road – a temporary bond would spring up between us, as it did in earlier days when I sat on his knee and combed his dark, grey-flecked hair. In the long, timeless evenings of July and August, I would take the beloved football I had obtained by collecting a set of cards from a boys' paper and off the two of us would go for a tram-ride that brought us to a destination such as Bellevue or Glengormley. We would hurtle through the still evening air, surveying the now inactive city from the top of, no, not a tram – a red chariot rocking its way ever onwards, that thrilled and pulsated with the energy of some elemental force. Those tram-rides were pure ecstasy. It was the route homeward that I feared, when he called at pub after pub for 'just a wee minute'. With tears in my eyes, we would come back to the shop, eyed by disapproving or amused neighbours.

Ven once went for about a week into a nursing home off the Lisburn Road, an institution that specialised in the treatment of nervous diseases. He had electric shock treatment. I went to see him there and, for the first time in my life, played table tennis, that very genteel middle-class game. Within a few weeks of coming out, he was, in my mother's words, 'at it again. Paralytic!' When she uttered words like these, she would first raise her eyes to heaven and begin to snivel, drying her eyes with her apron. I would go hot and cold, feeling a little angry, very afraid and thoroughly ashamed. Then would come the scenes that occurred regularly and made me as tense as an old maid who wakes up to find a man under the bed.

During these theatrical interludes, Ven would rant obscenities at Mother and even strike her, or, in a tantrum, throw his food into the fire, threaten to beat me 'within an inch of my life', or assert that mother and her relations had dissipated the fortune that he had made, and that he would have the law on the McCrea villains and leave them penniless. All these and more threats came out of an abysmally deep reservoir of alcoholic aggression, despair and self-pity. 'They ruined me, the McCreas have ruined me,' he would inform people who could not care less. Shaw remarked that home is the girl's prison and the woman's workhouse. It was certainly a workhouse for mother. 'Home Sweet Home' seemed an ironic phrase, or else one coined by people out of touch with reality. It was a place I was always glad to leave, and to which I returned with some misgiving. It was sour-smelling and affectionless. Fortunately, from time to time, I retreated to Aunt Tillie's where the atmosphere was always warm and cheerful, only shadowed by Ven's latest misdeed.

Home was where one slept and little more than that. Schoolmasters at least dispensed a rough justice. They could be respected, or most of them could. Their punishment was seldom unduly severe and seldom undeserved, whereas Ven was arbitrary and one never knew what might happen if he lost his temper. Like some of our politicians, he exercised power without responsibility. Authority – Ven's excepted – was not too bad, and after the first rebellion of youth and early manhood, authority in its various forms is something with which I have had little difficulty in coming to terms. Not for me the lifelong urge to be 'agin the government'. Coming from a household where civil war and alarms of one kind and another were to be expected, I began early to believe in Henry Miller's dictum: 'Peace, it's wonderful!'

Not that I was altogether a peace-at-any-price or *danegeld* boy in the incessant war against Ven, which was sometimes cold, sometimes hot. As in all wars, there came a crisis, a turning-point. It happened one summer day in 1935, when I was not quite 15. I had been out in the back yard, breaking up into sticks a number of wooden boxes in which goods had been delivered to the shop. This was something Ven used to order me to do when he was a bit high. I resented his manner of ordering it to be done, and the way his pale, dissatisfied face would press to the window to see the job was being carried out to his satisfaction. As a matter of fact, I rather enjoyed the task in itself, and I liked to do it well, always having had an instinctive desire to excel. It was, as I recall, a warm August afternoon, and soon I had broken up all the boxes. A little out of breath from the hurried exertion, I brushed up the wood chips and put them in the bin. I threw down the hatchet with satisfaction after a job well done. I was pleased with myself and hoped now to sneak past the old man and into the shop to ask mother's permission to go and visit Billy Davidson, a school pal who lived in the Malone Road end of town. This boy's father was a box manufacturer – I was a little flattered that a boy whose family actually had a skivvy found me interesting, and Aunt Tillie encouraged me to get to know such people. I had my way to make in the world, she said, and influential friends would be all to the good. Then an ugly face appeared at the window, glaring at me with bloodshot eyes. Speak of the devil – if it wasn't the 'oul' lad', and in a bit of a paddy, too! What eyes! Had he escaped from Purdysburn or what? Out he rushed like a bull stung by a wasp.

'I didn't tell you to stop,' he screamed. 'You fucking idiot!'

'I won't do any more. I've finished the job in any case. And I've got a friend to see.'

'You're a bloody idiot – you an' yer fancy white trousers, an' yer grand college chums. A lot of oul' cissies.'

'And you're drunk,' I retorted. 'You're talking through your headgear.'

'Drunk, you impudent pup,' he screamed. 'I'll show you who's drunk, you fucking half-blind get. You don't even know who your da is. He's down at the market sellin' oranges. Ask that oul' whore in the shop.'

I'll kill him, I thought, I'll kill him if he lays a finger on me, so help me God.

He had struck me in the past – and I was afraid he might smash my nice new glasses into my eyes and blind me. As it was, it was no fun being short-sighted, and it handicapped me badly at games. Words would get me precisely nowhere. Action now or never! I picked up the hatchet and lingeringly touched its slightly jagged gleaming edge with my left forefinger. I was atremble with fear and anger. Then I spoke, slowly, deliberately.

'Get inside, you dirty lying drunkard or I'll cut you open,' adding for good measure, 'Whiskey Ven.'

He opened his mouth to say something nasty, but, drunk as he was, he read the word that shone behind my lenses. The word was 'murder'. This was no play-acting and he knew it. Muttering incoherently, he turned, groped his way into the kitchen, and slithered into the swivel office chair. In a moment, he fell off it on to the worn linoleum.

Feeling ashamed and angry, I rushed into the house and out through the shop, not stopping to answer my mother's question as to where I was going. I ran wildly into the street, then turned left and ran. Past Kenilworth Street, past Fraser Street, past Cable Street, on and on, past Maidment's the greengrocers, on towards Connswater and the Holywood Arches. I glanced over at the Northern Bank where I carried the shop's weekly takings every Saturday morning. I carried my hundred pounds or more with dignity. Look at me now, a fugitive from Ven! The sun seemed to burn down as if to impede the progress of a malefactor. Old wives' tales came to mind. Had not Aunt Tillie once told me of the little boy who struck his parents, and how he died soon after of a brainstorm, and how even to this very day his fleshless hand stuck up out of his little grave. Oh yes, you had to 'Honour Thy Father and Mother . . .'. Yet how could one give honour where it was obviously unwarranted? Surely God was a just God? Nobody I knew could be asked to solve the dilemma, neither minister nor Sunday school teacher, for this was something which must, at all costs, be kept secret.

I went on and on, past grocers' shops and newsagents and pubs and butchers' shops and pawnbrokers and police barracks, until at last I came to sedate houses along the route to Holywood. I stopped running, for the chances were now less that a peeler would stop me and ask me to explain myself. How could a Methody boy explain that he had wanted to kill his father? It was inexcusable and would appal one of these dark-suited pillars of law and order. Or supposing the headmaster in College Gardens heard of this hou-ha? Supposing Ven went to the head to complain about insubordination – heaven knows, he had often threatened to go up to the school and disgrace me in front of my fine new friends. If I were expelled, what would become of me without having passed Junior or Senior? At life as a caulker in the yard.

Goodbye to my hopes of being a big man in London. London would callously close its gates to such a boy. These were my thoughts as I wandered, shirt sticking to my back, towards Holywood and the sea . . . Now in the open country, I climbed through a hedge and into a field. I wept bitterly for having wanted to kill Ven, for, despite everything, he was my father. 'God forgive me,' I prayed fervently. And I repeated the Lord's Prayer with a sincerity very different from the way I gabbled it normally before jumping into bed.

It was chilly when I returned, sneaking past the New Princess cinema, whose second house was just being let out. Tired, hungry and dishevelled I certainly was, but I felt strangely radiant and unafraid. I had purged my crime. Not only that, but at last I had done something: I had stood up for myself and would now take what consequences came my way. The shop was shut of course when I arrived, so I rattled the letter-box with as much confidence as I could summon up. My mother came to the door. Her eyes were red, and she looked much older than usual. I noticed the grey in her hair.

'Where were you, boy?' she asked. Her relief seemed to have an undertone of anger, a controlled anger, unlike Ven's.

'Out with a friend. Billy Davidson. We went to Holywood.'

'You look as if you've been through a hedge backwards. Why didn't you say where you were going instead of rushing out like a mad thing? I was worried to death about you, Robbie. First your father, now you . . . The Greacens are all mad! I never saw the like of them, not like my people . . .'

'You should've known I'd be all right, Mother. Honestly I was. I wish you wouldn't treat me like a child. I wanted to get away from Ven, if you must know.'

She began to weep into her apron, a sight that always made me feel guilty, but I was powerless to do or say anything. Something in me wanted to comfort her, but I could not or would not. What did I care about this crazy world of grown-ups with their tears and anger and admonitions, don't-do-this and don't-do-that! When I grew up, I'd be off and I'd never come back. Never, never!

I went into the scullery, poured out a cup of buttermilk and made myself a big 'piece'. I ate hurriedly, standing. Without a goodnight to Mother, I ran up the creaking stairs to the attic room where I slept. I didn't know if Ven had gone to bed or was still out; nor did I care.

Then I lit my candle with a Swift match — we had no electric light at the top of the house — and got into bed. I lay for a long time watching the shadows. Opening *Vanity Fair* I tried to read, but could not settle to it. Tomorrow was a new day, I thought. Perhaps I could relearn to honour Ven as I should. Perhaps not. It did not seem to matter much. Only a few more years and I would be out of the prison house, free to do as I pleased. I put out the candle and felt the darkness swathe me like a cloak — friendly and comforting.

About a week later, I was coming home from having had tea at the house of a school friend, for I was making every effort to cultivate the right people. Some book I had been reading stressed the need for contacts. I had every intention of making my way in the world and I had a contempt for those without ambition. For my part, I would have a shot at getting the best that was going. The idea of one man being as good as another — dear to many an average Ulster heart — was loathsome. I considered I was superior to most, and I wanted them to know it, too. Yet I sensed that the attitude caused resentment, even bitterness. Well, let it! I vowed that one day my achievements would outstrip those of the boys brought up on the Malone Road. In the past week, things had taken a turn for the better in the place I called home. Ven had been off the booze for three whole days!

At the corner of Templemore Avenue, I saw a group of people surrounding a navy-suited figure who seemed to have slipped into the roadway. A brown felt hat lay forlornly on the ground. As I approached I saw a man, red-faced and beefy like a cattle-dealer, holding in his clumsy hands a tradesman's bicycle with a big wicker basket above a low wheel. There was a sign under the bar that read 'Cochrane: Flesher of Quality'. I heard the big man's shrill, angry voice splutter out: 'If drunken eejits get in my road, it isn't my fault if I run them down.'

A weak voice from the ground: 'You . . . you . . . I'll . . . law on you.'

I came closer. Through my well-polished, steel-rimmed new glasses I realised with a shudder that the figure in the roadway was Ven. I thought of my mother's words — 'May Ven never come home alive this day!' — and how nearly they had come true.

I burned with anger and shame that I should be the son of such a man. How God had punished me and how I hated Him! But my anger found an easy target — it flared up against the red-faced oaf who held the bicycle in his rough hands like a mother grasping her only babe – as if his wretched tradesman's bicycle were studded with diamonds! Summoning up my every bit of courage, I pushed my way through the gawking bystanders.

'Look here, mister,' I said, 'clear off to hell, you fucking baboon. He's my father.'

Still burning with rage and shame, I pulled Ven from the gutter, shoved the brown felt hat on his head and dragged him home. When we got in, Mother started a tirade against drunkenness.

'Shut up, woman,' I said roughly.

Then I ran hell for leather up the stairs to my little room, where I fell sobbing on the hard but familiar bed. It seemed to me as if I had been crying on and off for hours before I at least came to my senses, and decided to have a wash. I carefully brushed and combed my auburn locks, looking at myself appraisingly in the cracked mirror, and was dreaming instead of the golden world I should enter in the distant future and in some distant place. The world of famous men and beautiful women beckoned to me . . . and I knew they were all waiting . . . waiting for Robert.

TEN

Not an Inch

Uncle George down in County Monaghan hardly ever wrote a letter. One day, however, we heard from him. He had a request. Could we board the son of a neighbouring farmer for a weekly sum? Uncle George assured us that the young man's family was most respectable and Orange to the core. I remembered having met this young man on one of my visits, though my memory of him had blurred. Mother was dubious about the idea, though she admitted we could do with the money. Where would he sleep? Father had a prompt reply: 'With your son, of course.'

This way he had of referring to me as my mother's son both irritated and pleased me, for implicit in it was a denial of his paternity. I cared not a straw whether I was his son. I was willing to settle for a father who might be more to my liking than the one I was saddled with. Father had sometimes said that my real father sold oranges at the market. I would answer, 'Why not? A lot better than being a candidate for an inebriate home, isn't it?'

This stung father as I intended. Mother hated this bitter exchange between us and would say sharply to me. 'Now that's quite enough. You know I don't like that kind of talk.' Anyway, several days passed while the pros and cons of taking in a boarder were weighed up. At last, it was decided that Tommy Gibson – that being the potential boarder's name – would be accepted. After all, if he proved troublesome, he could be got rid of.

I had mixed feelings about the arrival of a boarder. This Gibson fellow was some six or seven years older than me. My memory of him began to clear. On the occasions when we had met in the country, I had not particularly liked him. I sensed that he considered me the sort of townee who had little enthusiasm for fishing or shooting. On the other hand, I had not found Gibson positively objectionable, or I would have made my views clear when he was being discussed. I suffered a bit from loneliness as an only child, so that the idea of sharing my bedroom with someone had a certain amount to be said for it. His modest financial contribution every week would be of help in our finances and I could put up a plea for more pocket money. I needed more and more money for the second-hand books I was beginning to buy. Therefore I adopted a wait-and-see, neutral attitude to the plan to import a stranger.

Tommy Gibson turned out to be a presentable, not too countrified, fresh-complexioned young man in his early twenties. His eyes were grey and keen. He was of average height and stood erect, a trifle stiffly. Under a surface politeness, he had a challenging aspect. He talked about the need to preserve law and order, and keep dissidents in their place. Of his father he said: 'He's like yours – not worth a damn.' He had a commendable frankness. Tommy Gibson had started looking to the right in politics, a redneck in search of a leader. I looked to the left.

By 23 or so, Tommy had tried several careers. He had nothing in the way of school certificates, not, indeed, that he was stupid in any usual sense. He had often mitched from school and had left as soon as he could. Brought up among the stony small fields and lakes of Monaghan, he had handled rod and rifle since he was little more than a child. He was a hunter. On a visit to County Monaghan, I mentioned Tommy's name to an arthritic old man who remembered him: 'That Tommy Gibson could kill anything that moved – a real shot that same boy. I mind him as a wee lad comin' back at dusk wet to the skin and carryin' over his shoulder the biggest salmon you ever did see. Divil the keeper could catch that wee lad.' Tommy, I gathered, hunted alone. He wanted nobody's help or sympathy. So far he had been a lorry driver – for he had useful hands with machines – a farmer's boy and a garage mechanic in Dundalk. None of these jobs satisfied him. Besides, he had no liking for what we called 'the Free State'. Nor for freedom.

Tommy was a very neat fellow and could put his finger on all his possessions instantly. He imposed law and order on them. We got on reasonably well, although he annoyed me once by pointing a contemptuous finger at my books and saying: 'A lot of nonsense all that stuff. Where do you think that'll get you, boy? What do you want fillin' your head with soft drivel?'

'Books interest me,' I replied priggishly. 'I can learn from them. That's why.'

Tommy laughed sneeringly. I blushed and stayed silent. We would not become friends.

I never learned exactly where Tommy Gibson went every morning with his shining, carefully shaved face, in his tidy brown suit, stiff white collar and highly polished shoes. He had some vague temporary job.

I suspected he was up to something on the quiet, for he seemed never to be short of money. He wore a smart hat with a feather and the brim tilted at an angle detectives affected in Hollywood films. I sensed that Tommy had a secret ambition he preferred to keep to himself. Certainly he would not confide in a youngster like me, especially one not of his own manly kind.

Tommy was out most evenings. He once said something about drilling, for I knew he was a member of the B-Specials. He sometimes did physical jerks in the bedroom. One evening, my curiosity overcame my scruples. I knew Tommy had a cardboard folder containing photos, letters and comments, since I had once seen him placing a letter in the folder as I came into the bedroom unexpectedly. He then asked me to fetch him a glass of water and when I returned with it, the folder was out of sight.

It was far from being a practice of mine to sneak a look at anybody's private papers but, for once, the temptation was too great to resist. It would alleviate boredom, the feeling of flatness I often had in the period when I returned from school and before we had evening supper. I washed my hands carefully before the operation lest I should make the slightest mark, for Tommy had hawk-like eyes. A quick search put me right on target. The third drawer I opened contained the buff folder, an edge of which was exposed under a newspaper. I took it out as if it were an original Shakespeare Folio, noting the word 'Private' written in red ink in Tommy's childish calligraphy.

Opening the folder, I came on an assortment of photos of relatives and girlfriends, handwritten letters and programmes of sports meetings. I nearly closed it without reading anything, for I had a sense of shame about what I was doing. Then I saw an official-looking envelope.

Tempted, I decided to read the letter presumably inside the envelope and then call it a day. After all, Tommy might sneak up the stairs in those polished shoes of his, or Mother might come up for some reason and surprise me in the act of reading our lodger's correspondence. If she did, I would never hear the end of it.

Soon I was reading the letter that had attracted me. It was a reply to Tommy's application to join the police, the Royal Ulster Constabulary. The RUC was a body of men – each of them armed – highly esteemed by Protestants and disliked, even hated, by nationalists and republicans. The letter referred to a recent interview and pointed out regretfully that Tommy, although highly suitable in every other respect, was below the minimum height for entry.

Had he been merely half-an-inch below the required height, something might have been done because of his excellent record as a B-Special. As it was, they regretted . . . I was reminded immediately of the local political slogan – Not an Inch! Then I heard an urgent voice calling: 'Robbie, I want you to run a message for me.' The buff folder was hurriedly put away and I ran down the stairs to see what Mother wanted done. I forgot all about Tommy Gibson's ambition to be a policeman.

That night I slept soundly, as one always does when one has penetrated the secret of another. I had congratulated myself on my enterprise and cleverness. In the morning, I had just finished dressing when Tommy, an early riser, came into the room. He was frowning.

'Have you a headache?' I asked, trying to look innocent.

'Now look here, boy,' he answered. 'I'm going to ask you a question and I don't want a lie.'

I winced at the contempt in the word 'boy', but bit my lip. I did not at all like the rasp in Tommy's voice.

'How often have you been through my correspondence?'

'I don't know what you're talking about,' I stammered.

'You're a liar and the son of a drunken liar,' Tommy replied coolly. 'You damned well know what I'm talking about, you wee get.'

He opened the drawer I myself had opened and brought out the buff folder.

'Have you seen this before?' he asked.

'No.' He flushed.

'You bloody liar!' he said. 'You're only making things worse for yourself. How dare you read my letters, you impudent bastard.'

I kept quiet. Lies had failed. There was punishment on the way and I had got to take it. Not a whimper, that was it, no matter what happened. 'In future,' said Tommy, 'when you read someone's letters you should at least take care not to put them back *upside down*! They don't teach you much that's useful at that fine college, do they? I'm warning you that if you ever put a finger on anything of mine again, I'll break the glasses into your eyes. I'll bloody well blind you.'

He pulled the glasses off my face and threw them on the table. Then he struck me violently across the face so I could feel the hard metal of his ring cutting into my nose. Had he broken it? I made no attempt to defend myself.

'You impudent bastard,' he repeated. 'Get out of here before I really start to work on you.'

Blood streamed down my face. Some blobs of blood had got onto my collar and school tie. Fortunately, I got out of the house without being seen by Mother. I went to matron at school and explained I had fallen off my bike. She cleaned up the mess.

Tommy stayed with us for another two months or so. Never a word was spoken of our little scene. Mother accepted my explanation and told me I must be more careful on the bike or one day I would be killed. Father contented himself with the remark that I looked a proper eejit. I let it pass for I had enough of a wound for the time being.

Tommy, I discovered, was one of those who took delight in handing out punishment. He told me with satisfaction of how he had interrogated an IRA suspect. He took this man off to a lonely wood, having told his fellow B-Specials he wanted to talk to the man privately. He beat him up in a way that the man would have no visible scars in case a Nationalist MP tried to take up the matter. 'The police are too bloody soft,' said Tommy. 'I made the bugger talk.'

'What did you do?'

'Do you think I'd tell a nosey bugger like you?'

Occasionally I went out with Tommy. I knew he despised me but, now that I had taken my punishment well, his contempt had somewhat diminished. I liked to watch him in action. Even when he was wearing plain clothes, he stopped the traffic like a real policeman. People obeyed him sheepishly. To corner louts he would say 'Move on!' – and they would do so! Anyone other than Tommy would have been in for trouble. An open razor might have been flashed. But Tommy had an air of authority that all recognised.

Thwarted in his aim of becoming a policeman and bored by civilian life, Tommy joined the RAF. We heard that he was driving petrol lorries. How frustrated he must have been waiting for the war to begin. On the day he left Belfast for training, I helped him take his luggage to the Great Northern station. We shook hands without cordiality. Although younger, I was quite a bit taller than Tommy. I could not resist the comment, 'Height isn't everything.'

He smiled sourly and, as the train moved out, said, not unkindly, 'Nosey bugger.'

I never saw Tommy Gibson again. In 1942, news came that he had been killed in an accident in England.

Shortly after the end of the war, I found myself in a carriage of the Liverpool-London boat-train with a fellow Belfastman. He was a chatty, pleasant fellow who began to reminisce about his days in the RAF.

'Them was the days and no mistake,' he said, sighing and lighting a cigarette.

I discovered he had joined up about the same time as Tommy, and in Belfast, so I asked if by any chance he had come across Tommy.

'Don't say you knew that bastard. I'll never forget him.'

'I didn't know him all that well.'

'Lucky you,' said the Belfastman. 'Do you know that he once broke an aircraftsman's thumb for cheeking him?'

'I heard he was killed in an accident,' I said.

'Some accident,' said my companion with a smile.

'What happened?'

'Well, I don't know the details, but the long and short of it is that Tommy's lorry blew up somewhere near Wolverhampton. They called it an accident, but the boys wanted to get their own back. Mind you, he got a great funeral. Flowers and drums and all that. Yes, Tommy Gibson got a splendid military funeral.'

He winked and lit another cigarette. Perhaps it was only my imagination but there seemed something odd about the man's right-hand thumb.

ELEVEN

A Gentle Man

'As dacent a man as ever stepped in leather shoes,' said the man from Corrigan's garage in Castleblayney as he drove me out to Grigg. He referred to my Uncle George, who had a farm adjoining that of Aunt Liz-Ann, with whom I would be staying. Uncle George's land was mainly meadow and my aunt's hilly, her house perched at the top of a steep lane. These summer visits were a delight both in reality and in anticipation.

According to the amount of my luggage and how much money I had in my pocket, I would either walk the three or four miles out to Grigg or travel in comfort. The long climb up the narrow lane was not altogether to the liking of a city boy, especially in the dark, for I always remember arriving at Castleblayney station just as night was closing in. I slightly feared the darkness of this alien landscape, where bushes could look menacing. Crime in those days was minimal and it was not fear of being robbed that worried me, but fear that I might be set upon for not belonging to the right tribe. Yet, as the years passed, my fears grew less and less. It was odd that the Catholics of Belfast were enemies and those of Monaghan were friends.

Father spoiled it all for me by saying that my Aunt Liz-Ann had told him I was a nuisance and only kept her back from farm work. During my last two or three years at school, I would not go back despite repeated invitations. Then, when I was perhaps about 24 or 25, I paid a final visit. It was the last time I would see my aunt and uncle who had been so kind to me as a child and young boy.

On that occasion, I had a feeling of awkwardness. The distances had shrunk, her farmhouse seemed smaller than I remembered it, the collie dog's welcoming bark less resonant. Nor did I come alone. Patricia, my wife-to-be, came with me. I wanted her to meet some of my relatives. She made an immediate rapport with them.

Aunt Liz-Ann, as I recall her, was a little woman, a bit stooped but active as the day was long, busy with chickens and calves and pigs to be fed, occupied with milking and churning and baking and cooking. It was only years later that I realised how much work had to be done on a small farm for relatively meagre returns. Like most of my relatives, she had no time to be neurotic or wonder whether or not she was happy.

Aunt Liz-Ann had been left a widow with one child, a daughter, Sadie, who was perhaps 18 months older than me. Most of the time, Sadie and I got on well and I enjoyed meeting her friends, some of them fellow pupils at Dundalk Grammar School, to which Sadie commuted daily. She cycled into Castleblayney and caught the train there. The journey to and from school must not have been enticing in the depths of winter, but country folk were hardy and thought nothing of being soaked to the skin or wretchedly cold. We streetwise townees had our own kind of toughness, but traipsing up and down muddy lanes was not one of them. We would not shirk a fight, but a lengthy walk did not appeal to us if we could ride in a tramcar.

Uncle George towered above his sister (in fact, his half-sister) Liz-Ann. Much later, I wrote a poem about him:

> Sometimes he'd grip my hand
> In his rough bulbous gentle fist,
> Then guide me over fence and *sheugh*.
> I'd watch him out of big child eyes
> Half hope to see the beast run free.
> I'd hear the whole townland explode,
> The chuckle at his hunter's skill.
> Guns, harrows, ploughs his holy artefacts,
> His pulpit was his workshop,
> Toil his route to paradise.
> Sunday saw him dressed in navy serge
> Edwardian cut as in his youth,
> Knife creases made by mattress weight.
> In Bible mood he'd hold his peace
> Huddle close to the turf fire

Wrestle with John Knox's God.
He prophesied I'd live to see
The sun turn black at noon,
Earthquakes, meadows red with blood.
Each March I call to mind
His orchard massed with daffodils,
Their dance of life, their dance of death.

He liked to play practical jokes and these could frighten me, as when one night he wailed like a banshee before jumping out from behind a hedge. His images were simple, many of his phrases clichés – food and drink went 'down the red lane'; before leaving a house he would say he had 'to make tracks'. Interested in the supernatural though he was, I doubt whether he really believed in ghosts. Protestants usually did not and maintained that Catholics did. Certainly, though, he would not cut down a fairy thorn since that would bring bad luck.

Uncle George had a house of his own, thickly carpeted by dust and spartanly furnished. Here he sometimes slept but mainly he ate and bedded in his sister's well-swept house on the hill. From time to time, he would hole up in his bachelor establishment for days on end when the mood took him. No one knew why. Perhaps he had taken offence for some reason and was sulking. He belonged to that breed of northerner known as 'dour', so that he could sit in silence for long periods as if the world around him did not exist. Then his face would brighten and he would tell a story about some local event, a wake or a wedding. These wakes and weddings, I noticed, always took place among the Catholic community. Protestants did not celebrate anything except the Twelfth of July. Many of them were teetotallers and non-smokers and frowned on entertainment of any kind. They would no more play football on a Sunday than a Jew would eat pork. Yet when a few Protestants met together they could be jovial enough, even without alcohol. Cleanliness, tidiness, making money honestly – these were Protestant ideals.

Now, if Uncle George associated more with Catholic neighbours than others in the family, it was not because of any tendency towards their theology or liturgy. Like all of us, he had a strong suspicion of anything that came under the heading of Popery, which was considered a perversion of Christian truth as found in the Old and New Testaments.

I have the impression that, in those days, too much emphasis was placed on the Old Testament and the idea of a God of Wrath, rather than on the tolerance and forgiveness taught by Christ. Typically puritanical, Uncle George neither smoked nor drank alcohol, and I never heard him swear. He was, so far as I could find out, a total abstainer from wine, Woodbines and women.

Others in the family regarded Uncle George with amused tolerance. He worked hard, yet his enterprise bore little fruit. He was more indifferent to money than most Protestants, who tended to believe that a God-fearing life would bring prosperity. He was content to have a dry bed – two, in fact, one in his own house and one in Liz-Ann's – and to eat home-cured salty bacon, floury potatoes sauced by butter, scones and soda farls and potato bread, and to drink copious draughts of buttermilk and tea. Oh, I nearly forgot to mention porridge, which was eaten both for breakfast and last thing at night. Uncle George could not see why a man wanted whiskey and stout or fancy cuisine if he had on his table good country fare. He may well have been right and the city slickers wrong.

Uncle George once became angry with me for pointing a gun at the collie. The dog cringed under the table, moaning piteously.

'Never,' said Uncle George sternly, 'never let me see you do that again. Never point a gun at a person or a dog. It might be loaded.'

Another memory of a summer visit drawing to an end. The days had stretched into weeks. I had experimented with smoking and had lain under a tree watching the blue smoke curl upwards but then had a fit of coughing. It was a fruitful and lucky experiment that put me off smoking for life, all the more odd in that both my parents' and aunts' shops sold cigarettes and I could easily have helped myself to them. I used to go for cycle runs here and there, and occasionally meet other young people but, for the most part, I was content enough to loaf around or occasionally give a hand with the farm work. I hesitated to offer my services – not out of laziness, but because I feared that a townee would not do whatever job it was properly. But now field and lane and barn and orchard would soon be abandoned for the red trams of Belfast and the classrooms that smelled of chalk and polished wood and disinfectant. Heaven had lain about me for six weeks and I had buried myself in *Lorna Doone* and *Wuthering Heights*.

Uncle George got the trap ready and harnessed Bessie, the mare he loved more than many men love their wives. There seemed to be all the time in the world and I was in no haste for the end of the idyll. I wallowed in the sweet melancholy of adolescence and Uncle George was as calm as a lake surface on a windless day. I kissed Aunt Liz-Ann and cousin Sadie goodbye and off we went down the loanen. Soon we were trotting along the main road past Johnny McQuade's farm and heading for the station in Castleblayney.

Everything was going as harmoniously as a marriage bell until we met a neighbour coming in the opposite direction. This was a sour, grumpy man called Foxy Adair, a Protestant as it happened, a man somewhat unpopular in the district. Uncle George stopped to say hello and mentioned the train I wanted to catch.

'Well now,' said Foxy with an air of satisfaction, 'the wee lad won't get on that train unless that mare of yours grows wings.'

He put the enormous gold watch back in his pocket having delivered his bad news. Foxy Adair smiled knowingly.

Uncle George immediately took command of the situation as if he were the Iron Duke reincarnated and faced with a problem at Waterloo. He turned to me and said, 'Don't worry. You'll catch that train or my name isn't George Greacen.'

Bessie seemed to understand what had happened for she lifted her dainty hooves and ran as if she were going to meet her favourite stallion. Melancholy gave way to excitement. I wanted to prove old Foxy wrong, Uncle George wanted to prove him wrong – and so did Bessie. Just as we got to the bridge we heard the hiss of steam – there she came! Uncle George betrayed no emotion but simply urged Bessie to a final spurt. In we went to the station yard.

I jumped down, and ran with my ticket in hand as if it were a passport to the Garden of Eden. Within seconds, I had got into the train just as the whistle was blown and the train started to move. I saw Uncle George come lurching in with my suitcase, but by now the train was gathering speed. I waved to him and shouted, 'We've beaten old Foxy – thanks to you and Bessie.'

Victory was ours and it was sweet. What did it matter about the battered old cardboard suitcase?

TWELVE

A Gun in the Corner

Father's brother, my Uncle Robert, lived near Omagh in County Tyrone. He ran what was called a 'model farm' on the latest scientific lines, as might be expected from the brains of the family. He also worked as an inspector in the Department of Agriculture and his duties seemed largely to consist of going round the countryside advising farmers on grass management and milk production. Uncle Robert, wholly self-taught, was the only reader in the family. He read not only everything he could find dealing with his own special interests, but also books considered advanced at the time. He was the first man I heard use the word 'psychology'. I once heard him commend the verse of Ella Wheeler Wilcox and there was a book in my parents' house – *In Tune with the Infinite* – that had probably been a gift from Uncle Robert. He was, in fact, the kind of man who, in later times, would have had a brilliant university career.

His work brought him into contact with varied people in the farming community, some of whom valued his expertise, while others thought of him as being cranky. On a visit once to Uncle Robert's farm, I was to meet one of his neighbours, an acquaintance named William James Craig. Willie James, as everyone called him, was a bachelor in his early 50s, a thick-set man with legs like tree trunks, large, weather-reddened hands and hair the colour of a herring. He had decided political views for he was known as the staunchest of Orangemen in the area. So vehement were his views that he refused all contact with his Catholic neighbours. He neither smoked nor drank. Willie James was respected by Protestants, though few of them really liked him.

One day Uncle Robert took me to Willie James's farmhouse where he was delivering some medicine for a sick calf. This was not, strictly speaking, part of his work but he was a kindly man always prepared to help a neighbour. He did not share Willie James's narrow attitude, but that was neither here nor there when it came to giving assistance. Uncle Robert was frequently called upon to doctor animals and some farmers would swear — assuming a good Protestant *would* swear — that he knew more about how to treat sick animals than most vets.

Willie James kept his house scrupulously clean and tidy. This too appealed to the Protestant mind, with its insistence that cleanliness was next to godliness. Everything in Willie James's place was just so.

What seemed odd was that this big heavy man should be so dainty, even so old-maidish, in his ways.

'So this is your nephew Robbie,' said Willie James. 'He looks a right wee lad.'

I didn't altogether relish the informal 'Robbie' instead of Robert. My uncle was sometimes known as 'Old Robert' and I as 'Young Robert'.

The two men exchanged talk about animals, and presently left me in the kitchen while they went out to tend to the sick calf. I looked round with interest. It was a dull kitchen despite its gleaming oil lamp, the immaculate American cloth on the table, the clasp Bible on the window ledge and the well-scrubbed tiles. Then I saw the gun. It was standing in the corner.

This gun was different from others I had seen — shotguns that were used by the man of the house to shoot rabbits or rats or crows. This was a sturdy and short-barrelled job with a heavy wooden stock. I went over and picked it up, for it was unlikely to be loaded. I handled it gingerly, remembering Uncle George's rebuke when I pointed a gun at the collie. I tried to read, but could not, what looked like an ornate script engraved on the barrel.

At that very moment the door opened. Willie James scuttled over, snatched the gun out of my hands and put it in the corner.

'That gun's not to be touched by nobody but myself,' he said peevishly.

'I'm sure the lad didn't mean any harm,' said Uncle Robert, giving me a disapproving look.

'Maybe not,' said Willie James doubtfully. 'So we'll forget it and hope it won't happen again. What about a wee sup o' tay?'

Willie James bustled about like a housewife, though his movements could hardly be called graceful. Then he turned to me and said, not unkindly, 'Robbie, would you be interested in knowing why I'm so particular about that gun? It's a rare one, I can tell you.'

'Yes, I would, Mr Craig.'

'All right then. It'll be something you'll remember all your life.'

We sat down at the table – on which our host had placed a new-looking linen tablecloth – to cups of sweet tea and soda bread farls. Perhaps Willie James had baked them himself! He began his tale with a question.

'Have you heard of Colonel Fred Crawford?'

'I don't think so,' I replied.

Willie James turned to my uncle. 'Dear me, now, do they teach them anything at all in them schools in Belfast?'

The question remained unanswered.

'Well, I dare say you've heard of the UVF.'

I nodded and said haltingly, 'Ulster Volunteer Force.'

'Right you are first time,' said Willie James with approval. 'That lot of fellas was the heart of corn, so they were. None of your riff-raff or corner-boys. I was right proud to be one of them. The UVF took a solemn oath that they would never let the Shinners seize the north without a bloody struggle. An' if the English wanted to sell us out, which I wouldn't put past them, we'd take them on as well.'

He paused and then went on, 'Now you know you can't fight without guns, so what did Colonel Fred do but go over to Germany a wheen o' months afore the big war started in August 1914 and bring back 30,000 o' them wee lads.'

He pointed to the rifle in the corner in case we failed to take the drift.

'I don't suppose you know the name of the ship that carried them into Larne. Maybe even your clever uncle doesn't know or has forgotten.'

'Indeed, I know the name as well as I know my own,' said Uncle Robert. 'It was the *Clyde Valley*, wasn't it?'

'The nail has been struck squarely on the head,' said Willie James. 'This same *Clyde Valley* was the greatest wee ship that ever sailed in salt water. For 20 long years she had been carrying coals over from Lancashire. Now, of course, Colonel Fred loaded the guns first of all into the *SS Fanny*, another great wee ship, and got away from Hamburg without a paper to his name under cover of fog. The Royal Navy no less was after him but he gave them the slip and got as far as a sea loch in the Hebrides.'

Willie was beginning to sweat with excitement. He wiped his brow and went on. 'There he left the guns and the ammunition, and off he went to Glasgow where he met a good Unionist fella, a Belfastman who owned the *Clyde Valley*. Within hours the *Clyde Valley* had a Glasgow registration number and was under Colonel Fred's control. Next the bold Colonel sent a radio message to the *Fanny* to meet him off the Tuskar Rock.'

Willie James paused again to wipe his brow. Then he took up the story again.

'The name *Clyde Valley* was changed for the day to *Mountjoy II*. Then, off the Tuskar Rock the two wee boats were tied together and off they moved quiet as you please, having fixed the navigating lights to make them look like one big fat boat. They hirpled through the water towards Larne, and all night long the work went on.'

'What work?' I enquired.

'Are you listenin' at all?' asked Willie James in exasperation. 'Can't you see that they had to transfer the guns — wrapped in bundles of five in oilcloth — from the *Fanny* to her sister ship? When they finished the job, what happened then?'

Neither Uncle Robert nor I could answer that one.

'I'll have to tell you,' said Willie James, after a somewhat dramatic interval.

'They untied the *Fanny* and back to Scotland she went as fast as she could skip. The Royal Navy was searching for her and now, as you might say, she was searching for the Royal Navy. A few hours later she was intercepted by a Royal Navy corvette. Them Navy lads had the surprise of their lives, for not a single gun nor round of ammunition could they find in her holds. There were some red faces, I can tell you. Meanwhile, I need hardly say, the wee *Clyde Valley* was sailing, all innocent-like, into Larne harbour. Loyal hands soon unloaded the 30,000 guns and the four million rounds of ammunition, and they were on their way to Protestant Volunteers all over the north.'

Willie James looked lovingly at the gun in the corner. Then he poured boiling water into the teapot.

'I've never heard the like,' said Uncle Robert.

'Every word of it is true, as God's my witness. You see, when it comes to organisation, nobody can beat us. And do you know why? It's because we're in the right of it.'

He went over to the corner of the kitchen and picked up the Hamburg rifle.

'The Germans are the great craftsmen,' he mused. 'A pity we ever had to fight them.'

As my Uncle Robert and I plodded homewards through the twilight, I brooded on the story I had heard. I could imagine armed men lurking behind every Tyrone bush. From the meadows came the sound of UVF men drilling. I heard the distant crackle of gunfire. I heard voices raised in anger. I heard screams of pain as men fell mortally wounded.

I imagined we were in a foreign land – like the Tyrone countryside through which my uncle and I trudged our way towards home, yet somehow new and strange to my experience – where the UVF men had gone to take part in a fight against another enemy whose chief was called the Kaiser. German guns had been turned on Germans. It was all very confusing.

'Willie James is a big talker,' said Uncle Robert, breaking in on my reverie. 'Some would say he's only an oul' bletherer. Of course, he's never fired that precious gun of his in anger and I hope he never will.'

I began to wonder whether there would be war in my time as Uncle George had prophesied. Would there be darkness at noon? Would the green fields turn red with human blood?

Time would tell.

THIRTEEN

In Search of Bonar Thompson

Students of 20th-century British politics will know the name of Bonar Law, who served in Lloyd George's coalition during the First World War and formed a Conservative government in 1922. I understand that, though born in New Brunswick, Canada, Bonar Law had north of Ireland antecedents. All that concerns me with him, however, is the name Bonar. It came to have significance for me.

One warm summer day in about 1936, I was rummaging through the shelves of the little lending library (hired from Eason's, the wholesale newsagents) that was one of the sidelines in the newsagent's run by my Aunt Tillie and Annie on the Stranmillis Road, not far from the Botanic Gardens in Belfast. (My aunts, demonstrating the fabled Presbyterian thrift my father had so pointedly lacked, had worked themselves up from the rough-and-tumble of Broadway in the west of the city to the more genteel and cosmopolitan university area.)

Most of the books were detective novels, thrillers, romantic fiction – in short, rubbish turned out by literary hucksters. Then I caught sight of a spine – *Hyde Park Orator*. Intrigued, I opened the book to find an introduction by Seán O'Casey. I removed it stealthily and, putting it under my blue-monogrammed school jacket, crept upstairs with it to my book-lined room. The author was someone called Bonar Thompson.

Thompson proved to be a man from the Glens of Antrim who had lived through many a picaresque adventure. He had ended up, after a series of stop-gap jobs, as an acidly witty commentator on life with a capital 'L', at Speakers' Corner near Marble Arch. He wore a wide-brimmed black hat to symbolise his authority as 'Prime Minister of Hyde Park'. (Did he get the idea, I wonder, from the comedian George Robey, who advertised himself as 'the Prime Minister of Mirth'?) He had started a weekly newspaper called *The Black Hat*, which ran for nine issues.

Bonar obviously had much of the actor in him as well as the salesman's instinct. At one time, he had tried to make his fortune from selling contraceptives. Now he sold wit as a minuscule Bernard Shaw, except that he had abandoned socialism for what he termed nihilism. Thompson was the forerunner of the *Private Eye*-type of satire. This was spiced with his own cheeky brand of Ulster sauce.

At the end of his blarneying, Thompson took a 'silver collection' outside the gates of the park. This venue was forced on him by police regulations – though, of course, it diminished his earnings since only the truly thankful would follow him at the end of his spiel to reward him with a silver coin. Having read *Hyde Park Orator*, I decided that as soon as good fortune or clever management made a visit to London possible, I should make straight for Hyde Park to marvel at this genius of the soapbox.

Mother and my aunts often talked of Uncle Johnny who had gone to Liverpool, aged 14, to serve his time in the grocery business and who now – so they believed – was a thriving merchant in Birmingham. Time had eroded the family bonds for John McCrea and it was some years since they had had news of him.

Occasional letters and Christmas cards were despatched across the Irish Sea, but Birmingham sent no answering signal. Was he ill? Supposing he died and they did not hear of his death? Uncle Johnny had always been given a wonderful build-up. He was, in short, everything that father was not: the sober, industrious apprentice who, as a young lad, had gone forth to make his way in the world.

Now it was thought he had reaped his reward in cash and possessions, was a man respected by all and not least by his bank manager. Had not young Johnny been the bravest and most honest boy who had ever drawn breath? Had he not, until ill-luck came in the form of his wife's invalidism, been a generous and devoted brother?

In the late autumn of 1936, I saw an advertisement in *Belfast Telegraph* announcing a cheap excursion to Liverpool for football supporters. Here was my chance to get to Birmingham. I visited Thomas Cook's in Royal Avenue for the first time and asked them to make arrangements. To Birmingham would I go on pilgrimage to seek out the much-talked-about and long-lost John McCrea, grocer and Freemason, the Derry orphan who had prospered.

I called in at the Reference Library in Royal Avenue and did my homework. A scrutiny of *Kelly's Directory* provided me with the address in Birmingham – 219 Poplar Avenue, Edgbaston. I already knew his shop was in nearby Waterloo Road. I embarked full of zest for this would be my first visit to England, an unknown country. So far I had only been 'across the water', as we said, to Scotland.

I got to Liverpool and then Crewe and then Birmingham and, at last, I stood in Uncle Johnny's shop in Waterloo Road. I was just a tiny bit disappointed that he was not more welcoming to his nephew, whom he had last seen as a small child. But there he was, caught in the commercial act of bending over his bacon-slicing machine, white-aproned, chunky, full-cheeked and grey-haired. He turned out to be a sensible, right-minded small businessman of strong Conservative and anti-trade union views. Before I left to catch my train at New Street, he handed me a crinkled pound note. But, more important, he asked me to come and stay at his house the following summer.

I returned to Belfast a wise and more travelled boy than when I had left. I was pleased to be able to tell my pals at school of my visit to the English midlands, for at that time few had ventured outside the north of Ireland. The era of the package tour lay in the distant future. I spoke of the immensity of Crewe station with its multiplicity of platforms and silver curving tracks and signal boxes. What mattered most, however, was the invitation to return. Then, I knew, I would go to London for the day and on a Sunday so that I could see and hear Bonar Thompson, Hyde Park Orator extraordinary.

The months passed quickly from grey, short-dayed winter into spring with its promise – sometimes unkept – of warmth and long walks along the towpath to Shaw's Bridge with friends with whom confidences could be exchanged. Or I would go for a ride on my new Raleigh sports bike that had cost all of £4.19s.11d. I would push, push, push deep into the country, dreaming . . . dreaming . . . and usually with a Penguin book in my pocket. I was waiting as patiently as I could for the delights of suburban Edgbaston and visits to Warwickshire and Worcestershire that Uncle Johnny had promised. Though not particularly attractive, Birmingham was immense and I looked forward to exploring a city in which nobody would know me.

At school, boys began to talk of what lay in store for them. Some were worried since secure jobs, like money itself, 'did not grow on trees'. I had another couple of years to go and did not worry over-much about what would happen to me. I would survive somehow.

'I'm going to be articled in my father's firm,' Dixon would say.

His father was an accountant. How boring, I thought.

'Business for me, there's good money in it, and no more bloody exams,' Wilson would put in.

'I've always wanted to be a teacher,' Ferguson, a pale, studious boy, a swot, as we called him, would tell his friends.

I got used to hearing the question from adults, 'What are you going to do with yourself?'

I could hardly answer that I wanted to write. That would have been quite unacceptable, so I found a formula that went down well. I tried to keep a straight face as I said gravely, the 'Civil Service.'

It sounded respectable and gave the impression that I had given the matter some concentrated thought. There was the local civil service at Stormont and the Imperial in London, so if further pressed I would say with an air of grandeur, 'The Imperial, of course.' I imagined that Imperial civil servants lived a life of luxury, all Turkish carpets and soft lights.

For weeks before the end of term, I could smell the ripe odour of Birmingham's fruit market, not dissimilar to that in Belfast, but much vaster. This time I would not be travelling with a mob of Guinness-swilling football fans, but as a tourist. No adventurer set forth for the New World with more eagerness than I did for the English midlands, that I hoped would not be, in Hilaire Belloc's words, 'sodden and unkind'.

Uncle Johnny, a widower, was looked after by a housekeeper who also helped in the shop. I was given a bedroom in his Edgbaston villa that seemed to come right out of the catalogue pages of the Times Furnishing Company's showrooms in the centre of the city. Being a busy man, Uncle Johnny had not a great deal of time to devote to his Irish nephew, but he did do his best to show me the local sights and, on one Sunday, drove me into the lush Worcestershire countryside. I made some excursions on my own, to the zoo in Dudley which I reached after passing through dirty and foul rundown areas, and to Stratford-upon-Avon, a smiling, middle-class English town where I saw a production of *The Tempest* and ate Walls' ice-cream.

On another Sunday, I left Snow Hill station on a day trip to London where I hoped one day to settle, be a writer and live with a foreign woman to whom I was not married. Alas for dreams! I did live there for many years with the wife I married in Fisherwick Presbyterian Church in Belfast. But I digress. Arrival at Paddington brought me into the pre-war metropolis and an atmosphere that now is as historic as the fog-enveloped city of Charles Dickens. I walked through the broad streets, then into Bayswater Road and finally through chance and design got to Speakers' Corner in Hyde Park. Later I would have to take a quick look at Buckingham Palace or else be prepared to lie to my mother and aunts back home, for Buck House was the only building in London of any interest to them.

At Speakers' Corner they were all there in force – the Salvation Army, the Coloured Workers' League, the Independent Labour Party, the Peace Pledge Union, the Catholic Truth Society, the James Connolly Association and the indefatigable Dr Donald Soper. Tongues wagged, hecklers interrupted. *Words, words, words.* Then I caught sight of the object I was looking for – a black hat. This was perched on the head of a middle-aged man who had gathered a small band around him. There, indeed, was Bonar Thompson, the oratorical champ from the Glens of Antrim! I advanced to join his *al fresco* Bible class, which he addressed in an accent that still had traces of the Glens.

Thompson's style differed markedly from that of his fellow speakers. He was quiet, self-contained. In fact, he was not so much an orator as simply a good and persuasive speaker whose silver tongue was never at a loss for a pithy or caustic comment. He was a man who espoused no cause. Having abandoned socialism, he preached no gospel, religious or secular. He cast a cold eye on politicians and propagandists of all stripes, and served up a piping-hot commentary spiced with wit and humour, a man-in-the-street's GBS.

He undertook to talk about everything under the sun, but obviously enjoyed giving his anarchic version of the week's news. The Antrim man claimed to take his listeners behind the scenes, whether in the British cabinet room or Buckingham Palace. He was at home in both the Kremlin and the Vatican.

'Anthony Eden,' he confided, 'was the best advertisement the Fifty Shilling Tailors ever had.' Then he turned his attention to the police, who were apparently not among his closest friends. He told us how to recognise the policemen in plain clothes – 'By their boots ye shall know them'. He pointed out that London buses carried the notice: 'Spitting Prohibited: Penalty 40s' whereas in the British Museum a notice said: 'Spitting Prohibited: Penalty 20s'. The moral, he maintained, was that if one must spit, then it should be done in the British Museum.

Like many Irishmen of his generation, Bonar Thompson – despite coming from what he calls in his autobiography 'the poorest of the Ulster peasantry' – was extremely well read. He could quote from Shakespeare, Dickens and O'Casey at the drop of his own black hat. I was not alone in being one of his admirers. Michael Foot, a former leader of the Labour Party, has written in his *Debts of Honour* of Thompson. 'I learnt from him,' Foot tells us, 'much useful or, better still, useless knowledge which, as they say, stood me in good stead ever after.' Thompson died in 1963, after a hard and unrewarding life, aged 75. Characteristically, he chose a suitable epitaph for himself, bearing in mind the regulations of the Metropolitan Police. It reads: 'The collection was not enough.'

One by one the speakers on that pre-war Sunday afternoon got down off their platforms and stood on the flat earth before departing for another week. The captains and the kings of harangue – if not the art of Demosthenes – faded away in the anonymity of what was then the capital of the British Empire. I walked aimlessly in Hyde Park and gaped at the couples lying on the grass and clasped in that attitude of timelessness that enfolds lovers. They could lie more carefree than similar couples in puritanical Belfast, where even children's playgrounds were locked fast against Sunday pleasure.

Then a voice sounded beside me.

''ullo dear, lookin' for someone?'

The voice was husky and cockney. Behind it lay a suggestion of invitation and menace. I was overpowered by the odour of cheap perfume. I was speechless, never having been approached in that way before.

'First time in London, dearie?'

'Yes,' I stammered. 'How did you guess?'

The woman was heavily made up – blonde, coarsely over-lipsticked and with rouge on her cheeks. She looked middle-aged, but probably was under 40.

'Wot's your name, dear?'

'Henry,' I said, giving Father's name.

''enery . . . I've known some 'eneries in my time, I 'ave. Cheeky buggers, most of 'em. Like to come 'ome with me, 'enery?'

'I . . . I don't know. I've a train to catch at Paddington.'

She tittered.

'I can see as 'ow yer a busy man, love,' said the blonde.

Suddenly she came over and put her arms around me. She kissed me as I had not been kissed before.

'That won't cost you nuffin this time, love . . . Next time you 'ave ter pay for it,' she muttered. In a moment she was gone.

When I got back to Belfast I wrote in my diary: 'The visit to Birmingham was a great success – London even more so. Bonar Thompson was all I expected. As for London itself, it is everything I have imagined – and more.'

The dream of things to come now seemed to be taking shape. I knew that I would leave Belfast and never go back. The dream of living in London enchanted me. I knew in my heart that, come what may, I would follow my dream.

FOURTEEN

Tomorrow Evening about Eight

I came back from school, where I was in my last year, and put my bike away in the shed in the back yard. It was a bright, mild June day, almost cloudless in a way we seldom experienced in the north, where the low clouds – so low that one could nearly stand on a ladder and touch them – hardly ever disappeared. The school day had been like most school days, mildly boring, slightly tiresome. I was nearing the end of my school career. I had started, I hoped not too late, to make an effort in maths and physics but without any real interest in the subjects. I was rapidly developing a passion, an obsession for something else.

Mother came in briskly from the shop.

'I'm glad you're back, Robbie. There's a telegram for you.'

'A what?' I said. 'Who would send *me* a telegram?'

'Well,' said Mother, 'I hope it's nothing to do with politics. Politics only gets people into trouble. You must mind your lessons and leave politics to them that has nothing better to do.'

'Cut out the speeches, Mother. You're not on a soapbox down at the Custom House steps. I'm not either – not *yet*! Now where's the telegram?'

She fished it out from behind Granny McCrea's photo on the mantelpiece. I noticed my surname was misspelt – as usual. I ripped it open and read: COME TOMORROW EVENING ABOUT EIGHT STOP FORREST REID.

I jumped in the air – or at least I think I did. Then I hugged mother fiercely.

'You're very affectionate today,' she said, smiling.

'I've only one problem,' I said. 'I can't decide whether to be the next socialist Prime Minister or the Poet Laureate.'

'What a lot of fool talk,' she said, though still looking pleased. 'I don't know where you get all these strange ideas. It isn't from my side of the family. We're all sane.'

The implication was that some of father's relatives were not.

I showed her the telegram. 'I've never heard of this Mr Reid – I hope he's respectable and goes to church on a Sunday?'

'Respectable,' I said with contempt. 'The man is famous – everywhere except in his native city, that is. He certainly isn't a *petit bourgeois*.'

'You may know a wee bit of French,' said Mother, 'but that doesn't mean you have an iota of sense. Anyway, I hope this Mr Reid isn't a Sinn Feiner or a communist.'

'He's apolitical. He's a man who writes books.'

'Well, that's not as bad as I thought, but I've heard it said that these writer fellows are hardly ever sober. Now if he offers you alcohol, refuse it.'

I was in a daze. A telegram no less! An invitation from a famous writer! Though I never had much of a voice for singing I burst into song:

> You've heard of General Wellington, who won at Waterloo,
> But there's a good old Irishman I'll mention unto you,
> He comes from dear old Dublin, he's a man we all applaud,
> For he always finds a corkscrew more handy than the sword.
> He's good old General Guinness, he's a soldier strong and 'stout',
> Found on every 'bottle-front' and he can't be done without.
> His noble name has worldwide fame, for every heart he cheers,
> Good old General Guinness of the Dublin 'booseliers'.

'I wonder what your headmaster, Mr Henderson, would say if he saw you now,' said Mother, laughing.

'My dear old headmaster, Mr Henderson, wouldn't touch Guinness with a Lagan barge pole. Nothing for him – good Scotsman that he is – but the finest Scotch malt.'

When I had been at the elementary school, we were asked to write an occasional composition. To my surprise, this was the easiest bit of work we were ever given – so much easier than the tiresome columns of long addition sums, as if anyone other than grocers really cared what they added up, anyway. I delighted in words and tried to learn new ones, long ones, strange ones, rich and rare ones. I marvelled at the effect words had on others. Short, vulgar or obscene ones had an enormous effect as when someone called a boy a 'bastard' or 'wee skitter' or chalked the word 'fuck' on the wall of a urinal. Long, learned ones, like 'exasperation', drew exclamations of surprise, even pleasure, from the dour taskmasters who were our teachers.

A master once handed me back a composition and said, 'You write like Dickens.' From that moment I determined to be a writer in addition to whatever else I should become. For all I knew, the master was merely indulging in sarcasm. The speaker was either a Mr Harbinson or a Mr McCullough (the latter being the dark, sardonic vice-principal of the school). The face and name have vanished, the words remain. *Words, words, words* – how they could charm away the devils of fear and depression, especially when they were printed words.

Belfast, unlike Dublin, could hardly be called a city of wits and poets, though indeed we had a few dedicated spirits. The hand of Protestantism had grasped our community firmly and made it worthy if not virtuous, hard-working and thrifty. The 'Black Man' statue outside the grammar school, the Academical Institute, known popularly as 'Inst', symbolised the Victorian attitudes that, in the 1930s, still prevailed. (The statue, still there, is of an eminent divine, Dr Henry Cooke, and has been darkened by the elements – hence the name given to it.)

As I say, despite the inhospitable atmosphere, a few writers had managed to survive. There was Robert Lynd, the gentle essayist and convert to Home Rule, whose father had been minister at May Street Presbyterian Church. Lynd had found success in London. Rumour had it that he was a hard drinker who once said to a fellow boozer in a Fleet Street tavern, 'Do you realise that we are the kind of men our mothers warned us against?' My mother – simple soul though she was – had a point and I knew it.

Forrest Reid, then, was *the* literary artist living amongst us: a novelist and autobiographer who wrote for a minority, something perhaps of a cult figure. Sometimes, after the final ring of the school bell, I used to ride off on my bike to Smithfield – now long gone – to browse among the second-hand books in Hugh Greer's and rummage in the fourpenny and sixpenny boxes. It was there by some lucky chance or, more realistically, by a process of seeking and therefore finding, that I came across Forrest Reid's *Apostate,* in which he looks back on his childhood and youth. I read these words:

> Sunday became to me a veritable nightmare, casting its baleful shadow even over the last hours of Saturday. I hated Sunday, I hated church, I hated Sunday School, I hated Bible stories, I hated everybody mentioned in both the Old and New Testaments, except perhaps the impenitent thief, Eve's snake, and a few similar characters. And I never disguised these feelings. From dawn till sunset the day of rest was for me a day of storm and battle, renewed each week, and carried on for years with a pertinacity that now seems hardly credible, till at length the opposition was exhausted and I was allowed to go my own way.

This, indeed, was a soul speaking unto a kindred soul. I, too, had waged such a battle, and I too, in the end, had been allowed to go my own way. The street-corner evangelists would have consigned me to the flames of hell as readily as they would any Papist. I, who had been granted the opportunity to know better! At last I knew that in rebelliousness there had been at least one forerunner, a member of the writing tribe.

How thrilling it was to discover a writer whose pages had imprinted on them familiar names such as Mount Charles, the University Road and the Botanic Gardens, for it was precisely this area of Belfast, the immediate vicinity of my grammar school, for which I had the deepest affection. I turned the pages of *Apostate*, lost in a reverie of delight as paragraph after paragraph spoke to me.

This one, for instance:

> There was the beauty of an autumn afternoon in the Ormeau Park at dusk, with the dead leaves thick on the deserted paths, I had sat listening to a German band playing somewhere out of sight of the railings. Through the twilight, with its yellow twinkling of street lamps, the music had floated. The tune was the old Lorelei, but

into the plaintive twang of those instruments all the melancholy of the earth had passed. It was as if the very soul of the empty park had found a voice, and were sobbing out its complaint to the November sky.

The assistant in Greer's came up and gave me a hard look.

'You've been readin' that wee book a quare long time,' he said. 'It's gettin' on for closin' time. Are you thinkin' of buyin' it?'

'Yes.'

In this way, a new name came into my consciousness. Forrest Reid, one of my teachers told me, still lived in Belfast, out at Knock, he believed. Up to that time, I thought all writers lived in London or perhaps down south in Dublin. The teacher also told me that Reid had once gone out to a local shop in his pyjamas – such was the daftness of writers. With all speed, I ransacked the Public Library in Royal Avenue for Reid's other books, the novels *Uncle Stephen*, *Brian Westby* and *Following Darkness* (the last renamed *Peter Waring* a few years later) and read them avidly.

But the novels, unlike *Apostate*, disappointed me. They seemed, for all their lyrical charm and their fastidious sentence construction, to be too limited. Nobody I had read so far had written so sensitively of childhood and, more particularly, boyhood, but, outside the magic years of adolescence, Forrest Reid seemed to be at a loss. His adults did not ring true. At the time I sensed this but did not know why, for homosexuality was something I knew nothing about, not even the word itself. And yet, I had to admit that for me Reid was one of the great men – the only great man, perhaps – living in our matter-of-fact and all too Philistine city.

I looked Reid up in *Who's Who* in the Central Library. He had been educated at 'Inst' and Cambridge. The university in Belfast had conferred an honorary doctorate on him. He was a keen croquet player. Like our city, I was matter-of-fact on one point. I wanted his address and there it was in *Who's Who* – 13 Ormiston Crescent. Having lately acquired a Remington portable typewriter, second-hand at five pounds, I typed out, as best I could, several of my poems and a short story, and wrote a letter that started:

Dear Mr Reid,

Having read much of your work with admiration, I, a schoolboy
with the ambition to become a writer, am taking the liberty of
sending you some examples of my poetry and fiction.

Forrest Reid replied, in a remarkably neat hand, to the effect that he
had read my manuscripts with interest and that they showed 'promise'.
Would I like to call on him some evening so that he could discuss them
with me? I replied that any evening would suit me fine. Hence the
telegram.

On that memorable Tuesday evening, within a minute or two of
eight, I reached Ormiston Crescent. I got off my Raleigh sports bike
and walked gingerly past No. 13. He had said 'about eight' so I walked
to the end of the street and then back again to the pebble-dashed little
house that was No. 13. In my naïvety, I had supposed that a famous
novelist would live in a large house with a long drive up to the front
door. There one would ring the bell and be admitted by a butler
straight out of P.G. Wodehouse. 'What name shall I give, sir?' he
would enquire in BBC announcer tones. Then I would be ushered into
the study where the novelist himself, in evening dress, would be
clutching an extremely dry martini. He would offer me one and I
would refuse politely, explaining that I had a sore throat. But here was
a house smaller than the one inhabited by my non-famous Uncle Johnny
in Edgbaston – Uncle Johnny who had left school at 14 and now sliced
bacon and weighed out tea for a living. Life was full of surprises.

I rang the bell. Instead of a butler in tails, out came Forrest Reid
himself. A man in casual tweeds, he held a pipe awkwardly and peered
at me through thick-lensed glasses as if he were a sensitive, easily
frightened animal.

'Come in,' he said, politely.

In I went to make the acquaintance of the most important man in
Belfast.

He thanked me for letting him see my work and he talked about it.
Yes, definitely promising but rather derivative. Didn't I think so
myself? What writers had I been reading? Did I know the poetry of his
friend de la Mare? Had I read Yeats? I muttered something about liking
'Innisfree' and he smiled. Had I said something wrong? I mentioned
Swinburne and then proceeded to quote Tennyson. He corrected me

gently and I could have bitten my tongue. Literature, he told me, needed work . . . concentration . . . dedication.

I said I was a socialist. He replied that politics did not interest him. Politicians were loud people, vulgar, often insincere. The European situation was menacing. He said he loathed the Germans and their abominable Führer, who couldn't even speak German properly, and that – apart from Goethe – German writers of note had all been Jews. The room in which this conversation took place contained more books than I had ever seen in a private house. How was it possible for a man to gather, let alone read, so many? He made tea which we drank out of delicate china. No wine, whiskey or martinis were offered, so I was spared the embarrassment of refusal. 'Come again,' he said kindly, 'and do send me some more of your poems and stories.'

So it was that my first writer turned out to be avuncular and intelligent, but unlike any of my real uncles. As I rode home, I felt that somehow they were, in their rough, homespun way, more real as people, more manly. Forrest Reid was what? A private man, yes, a private man who allowed only a few to cross the threshold into his interior world. Belfast knew him not and he had no wish to know Belfast. But what had I expected from him? Some kind of lightning flash that would illuminate the whole of life? The boy who rode away from Ormiston Crescent was a somewhat different one from the boy who arrived with glowing face and high hopes on a close June evening.

True, I went back two or three times to the little house, and its book-lined study always fascinated me. Perhaps I warmed to Reid's vast assembly of books more than I warmed to Reid himself. He seemed to be hiding away in a world beyond my reach. In later years, we exchanged a few letters and he kindly contributed to a couple of anthologies I edited. He sent me a warm note of congratulation on my marriage, an institution, I imagine, for which he had scant regard. But soon after these visits, I found new literary gods. One of these was the Viking god reincarnated as Wystan Hugh Auden.

Yet all these years after meeting Forrest Reid, I find pleasure in recalling that I knew, however slightly, the author of *Apostate*. Nor do I forget that the young Reid once saw Oscar Wilde – an unlikely figure among the linen merchants and the shipyard workers of Belfast – climb up and sit beside the coachman on the box seat of a carriage. Culpable escapism no doubt, but I cannot help longing in this noisy, polluted age for the placid days of Forrest Reid's boyhood when the Linen Hall still existed and the inner suburbs were almost rural and 'the few horse trams, their destination indicated by the colour of their curtains, did little to disturb the quiet of the streets'.

FIFTEEN

The Goddess that Failed

I spent my childhood and adolescence in Belfast. Self-righteous young Presbyterian and would-be sensualist, I walked those everlastingly damp streets. There I was first visited by the creative impulse, wayward, undeniable, long before I had written a line of poetry. Listen. Suppose it is a spring evening, the lamps not yet lit, mysterious, full of tender whispers, the shadows massing, and the trees along Botanic Avenue quivering gently in the silk air. I have been out walking alone, thinking the long and unfulfillable thoughts of youth, gaping at girls but speaking to nobody, stirred by a young melancholy, half-wistful, half-divine.

A red tram, with an open upper deck, clangs along and I enjoy its boisterous show of noise, its shouting that it is alive though factually it is inanimate. A policeman in his dark-green uniform clumps by, revolver on hip, a reminder that we live in a bitterly divided society. A group of respectable citizens pass, talking in a subdued way, indistinct, afraid to speak up as if they were afraid to be overheard and reported to some secret police force.

I bounce along brimming over with life, floating 'down the rivers of the windfall light'. I am in love with being in love. Years later, I would read and recognise myself in the words of André Gide, who says that, in the spring, 'the ardent adolescent, tormented by an unknown restlessness, leaves his scorching bed to go in quest of the mystery'.

This evening our work-a-day town wears a wanton and brash beauty. Warehouse and factory chimney and ship funnel and gasometer are seen as if for the first time and they are out of time. Now, outside the prison of school, I tell myself I, yes I, am young and alive. The gift of life is wonderful and one cannot be too grateful for it. I repeat my name inwardly and it seems strange, foreign, exotic. But what of my future? Would anyone be interested in my thoughts, my images, my word rhythms? I could but try.

An artistic vocation is one thing, a career quite another. I did not know what to do with myself so far as a career was concerned, for the only thing I cared for was thinking my own rebellious and ecstatic and lonely thoughts, and strolling over bridge and quayside and through the markets, watching life flow round and over me. Well, well, they told me there was no career in writing down such daftness . . . who would read such stuff . . . no security for one's old age, no pension. No, there was positively no career in letters – unless one became a postman, ha-ha! Not like working in a nice bank, or teaching in a nice school (such good holidays, you know) or doing one of the other thousand and one jobs guaranteed to make even the most eager and daring spirit mediocre. Obviously I was not going to become a good citizen, a respectable elder of the Presbyterian church and so on; I would be a dead loss to myself and everyone else and a sore disappointment to my schoolmasters, who assured me I could be as conformist as the next boy *if only I tried*.

I had sat for a Bank examination and been let down by my lack of knowledge of the mathematic sciences; and if I but knew, perhaps, some of the subversive but to me very natural ideas that crept into my examination essay had rightly led an examiner to realise that my talent, unlike that of the young T.S. Eliot, would not flower best at the receiving side of a polished mahogany or oak counter. I cannot recall the precise reason why I failed to make a début in the assured world of Marine, Accident or Life Insurance: once again my naïvety told its own tale to an astute businessman. Oh well, I thought, I would just have to go to the local university, until penny-a-line journalism would receive me, for one or two local editors had been vaguely encouraging, saying they might have taken me on but for anticipated wartime shortage of newsprint. Snags, frustrations, too young here, too old there, too clever, not clever enough . . . yet in the end, I felt, with a little bit of luck, something would turn up, even if it was not exactly what I had longed for.

The 1930s ended on 3 September 1939, not on 31 December of that year. We were at war with Germany, a fact Chamberlain announced unheroically, undramatically, tired resignation in his voice. 'A low, dishonest decade', in W.H. Auden's words, was over. On that Sunday when war started, it thundered and lightning'd in the hills ringing Belfast. The voice of God or the vast bass rumble of Aryan man asserting world supremacy? *Ein Volk, Ein Reich, Ein Führer*! How well we knew that voice which had often invaded our homes through the air waves.

Were the street evangelists, with their hoarse cries, right in suggesting that anti-Christ was upon us? 'Prepare to meet Thy God' might be more than a biblical quotation scrawled on brick walls. Had my Uncle George – farmer, philosopher, prophet of doom, isolationist, bachelor, misogynist, tinkerer with agricultural machinery and red-nosed introvert who launched a thousand silences – been right after all in his prophecy that civilisation was on the way out?

On that still-remembered Sunday of 3 September 1939, I went to church to please my aunts who were worshippers at Fisherwick, a massive Presbyterian church of unusual dignity. I pondered the words 'Thou shalt not kill', for now I knew that in the Ulster Protestant community the killing of Germans would be considered praiseworthy. Yet I could not help wondering whether Christ had not preached pacifism and – to the dismay of some of his followers – the quiet acceptance of foreign domination. I felt that such doubts I should keep to myself. Our community was not one that welcomed criticism of its values. It continued to live under siege and was inclined to equate criticism, however well meant, with betrayal.

Here I was, rapidly growing out of my teens and in love with life, and in love with love, and awakening to both sensuous and sensual delight. This surely was no time to hug the death-wish that reflected the collective unconscious. I kept telling myself that in the end life could, *must* conquer. Rumours abounded. It was said that a bomb existed which, dropped on the City Hall, would destroy the whole city, a prefiguring of the atomic destruction visited upon Japan several years later.

I had read and been told about the war of 1914–18 and tended to assume that history was about to repeat itself. I expected mass hysteria would slowly develop. Would I too succumb in time and join the war-dance in the black-out? To me the only answer was that if I kept on writing I might be able to remain detached and sane. Writing seemed to be a necessary therapy which, if frustrated, would lead to mental numbness and inner death. As T.S. Eliot put it, 'I would not know what I thought until I saw what I wrote'.

That September was a painful and critical month for me. This was partly due to depression caused by the outbreak of a war I had long known to be inevitable and partly due to my own trauma at the time. Irene, goddess of peace, had said 'No', and I felt as if my emotional structure was crumbling. 'No' shouted the angry gods, as the leaves fell heedlessly from a brooding sky. I wandered restless, apparently defeated before the struggle had started, hurt and rebellious but drained of energy, obsessed with futile sexual fantasies and doomed to non-conformist frustration. Under the shadow of Cave Hill and Divis, along the towpath to Shaw's Bridge where hardy swimmers still plopped Adam-naked in the cool Lagan, around the big tinsel-laden stores in the city centre, in the dusty second-hand bookshops of Smithfield, back and forth from the Stranmillis Road to Belgravia Avenue off the Lisburn Road (where my old school friend, Leslie Baxter, lived), feverishly intent on long-forgotten enterprises of work and play I hastened, while the world cocked its ear and waited for the crunch of bombs and the moans of the injured. Or I would go up the Antrim Road to Brookhill Avenue and glance at the dignified, if nondescript, brick house inhabited by my beloved blonde Irene. I consulted a doctor who diagnosed my complaint as 'nervous dyspepsia'. As for my chronic catarrh, he advised me to emigrate to Canada as soon as I had the opportunity. O God! O Montreal!

Irene may merely seem a figure of speech to conjure up the Greek goddess who failed to preserve peace in 1939. In fact she was a real – only too intensely real – person and I have not changed the name. She was a tall, slight-breasted girl, greatly interested in literature but neither doomed nor buoyed up by literary aspiration. She had read some of my poems and articles with approval and, to my delight, expressed the opinion that some of them were up to publication standard. She introduced me to the BBC weekly, *The Listener*, which printed poems that did not necessarily use rhyme schemes. Irene and I discussed poetry from Wordsworth to Dylan Thomas and Louis MacNeice, and as my admiration for her blossomed, so did my love. She was my pale shepherdess. But now she had cast me out of her life in favour of a man who, I understood, was an engineering student.

Most men thrive when they are 'believed in' by women they respect; and it is a heavy blow to find that belief arbitrarily withdrawn so that the world of reality is no longer cushioned by affection. Then one sadly realises that one's only friend in this harsh world is oneself. All the more poignant, at the outset of life, to find a flower and later see it wither in one's hand. Yet the life-will somehow asserts itself and the caravan of ego moves ruthlessly on. Nevertheless, the shock to the personality can take years to wear off. I cannot even now be sufficiently exhibitionistic to explain the hows and whys of Irene's repudiation. That it did happen must be sufficient for the purpose of this narrative. And so I enrolled reluctantly in the Faculty of Arts of Queen's University, Belfast, for war had shut all the other doors into the great world I longed to enter. I wrote, wrote, wrote. Words formed into oblongs and squares and diamonds that were poems. Could words in some magical way call back mankind to love and reason? It seemed doubtful but one could at least try to pass on to others the intensities and depths in being alive. Despite the near-suicidal fits of despair that came unbidden, life was still worth going on with.

Irene's defection, apart from depression and 'nervous dyspepsia', prompted me to write a poem I simply called 'Love' and which appeared in the Queen's University magazine I was later to edit during a brief and less than brilliant undergraduateship.

Love is a wet autumn night
and a youth who walks alone,
whose damp hair is plastered unheeding
like rain-swept leaves on the sullen ground.
It is tears in the eyes
and a woman's automatic politeness,
sorrow for everything and not knowing
why it matters so much,
and getting wet, and not caring,
and walking and walking – alone
– walking aimlessly unloved.

It was in the autumn of 1939, or the beginning of the 'phoney war' winter, that I met Roy McFadden at a discussion group meeting of the local branch of the Peace Pledge Union. He and I had much in common

– as indeed we still have. The passing of time has deepened rather than diminished our friendship. Roy had an appealing shy intensity and smouldering anger against all merchants of death and their apologists. His mother, whom I had come across shortly before I met him, told me of a son who intended to qualify as a solicitor, wrote poetry and opposed the war. Odd, I thought. We exchanged specimens of our work and recognised in each other a wish to write poetry because it was essential to our well-being and not because it was a pleasant hobby to while away the dull, wintry Ulster evenings.

Poetry mattered and life mattered; and we felt anxious to communicate to others, however few they might be, this urgent sense of the inner reality behind the outer reality. Roy's inner reality still rests in that he is a poet; and his outer reality consists in his day-to-day work as a solicitor: an inner and outer world. He manages to fit together the two sides of his personality, and so create for himself a satisfying and vital lifestyle. In the days when I first got to know him, he was looking for that inner-outer synthesis. His poetry had, I remember, a Keatsian loveliness; it stirred me and yet it only half-appealed. I say 'half-appealed' because I was then beginning to be overwhelmed, almost obsessed, by the idea of contemporaneity. What of the new heroes in my poetic firmament, Eliot, Auden, Spender, MacNeice? Pylons, not daisies! Contemporary ugliness seemed to have its poetic uses, for did not Day-Lewis write of 'sour canals'.

I introduced Roy to another new friend of mine, Leslie Gillespie, a Queen's University Honours English student, also a keen writer but one more interested in prose than verse. A stocky, Germanically fair, slightly tough-looking young man, Leslie enjoyed the battles on the football field in a more robust way than I ever had. He had a great admiration for Ernest Hemingway, whom I only mildly saluted, and whom, I suspect, Roy probably loathed.

I had met Leslie at Queen's. Since his surname began with the same initial as mine, we had been placed in the same history class. It was at Queen's that I truly realised that history was about the dead – at Methody figures like Napoleon, Wellington, even the most distant figure of Cromwell, seemed as real to me as Churchill and Stalin. Leslie, in fact, was the first person I had met who expressed the wish to be a writer above all else. He wrote mainly short stories, while I wrote poems. Each of us thought the work of the other was good, remarkable; indeed at times we may have even used the word 'inspired'. His belief in the value of my early writing was of great assistance in my gaining self-confidence. If I was a fool – and there seemed to be increasing evidence for that view – then I had found another of the same kind. If I was not a fool – and the occasional letter of acceptance encouraged me to think I might not be – then he and I would go to London and conquer it together. Thus we laid the basis of a firm literary and personal friendship.

He was an extrovert, I, an introvert. It was fortunate I met him for I was in a phase of suicidal despair when Leslie suggested we should spend a few days cycling round the countryside during the Easter vacation, and I was glad to fall in with the suggestion. The war seemed very far away – and indeed it was – and the blonde Irene who 'never wanted to see me again' (and had thereby induced the despair) appeared less of a goddess as Gillespie and I cycled round the Antrim glens and ate our tins of baked beans, fried eggs and bacon at youth hostels, and talked ourselves hoarse and to sleep in the early hours – our main topics being (in big capital letters) Life, Death and Being Writers.

In time Roy, Leslie and I formed a trio (later joined by John Gallen) of eager young men turning out poems, critical articles and short stories in a rather sceptical and, at times, even hostile environment. Hostility spurred me on, although I found indifference devastating. During the next couple of years the Queen's University literary magazine, *The Northman*, was at our disposal, edited as it was by John Gallen and myself.

I do not know whether the thesis-writers will ever try to gain PhDs based on the literary events and atmosphere of Belfast in the early 1940s. These had an exhilarating tang and led to perhaps more good work than might have been expected in the circumstances. True, the 'three Gs' and Roy incurred dislike in some quarters (especially among their immediate and somewhat Marxist-orientated elders) and a reputation for a certain arrogance. Who were they to set themselves up? They were 'angry young men' long before that catchphrase had been invented. What was worse, they had assumed a strangely noncommittal political attitude in the middle of a war which was, so we were told, being fought to ensure the survival of civilised human values. It was all very reprehensible.

I am far from wishing to apologise for the attitude of my early adulthood. I enjoyed the struggle with older and wiser heads that shook sadly and knowingly. Some offence was taken, too, by the undergraduate body at the university which disliked the supposedly cavalier way in which John and I, aided and abetted by Roy and Leslie, decided to make *The Northman* into a journal of reasonable literary quality – 'Ulster's only literary magazine' as we called it in showcards displayed by local booksellers. Eventually John and I were ousted from the editorship, but not before we had introduced into the pages of *The Northman* work by various non-Ulster writers then making their name. Among these were Henry Treece and Alex Comfort. Local contributors included Denis Ireland, John Irvine, J.H.Scott and Harold Brooks. We reprinted a furious attack, contained in a letter to me, on a pamphlet I had recently edited, *Poems From Ulster*. This came from an irate St John Ervine, who lived in the far reaches of Devonshire.

Time passed. The phoney war ended. Bombs fell on Belfast – despite the forecasts from wiseacres that we were too far away and too unimportant to be worth the attention of the Luftwaffe – and de Valera sent up the Dublin Fire Brigade to help in rescue work. For myself, I was busy with a number of activities, the least important of which I considered to be my academic ones, with the result that I never finished my degree, although I was later to acquire a Diploma in Social Studies at Trinity College, Dublin. Poems and reviews of mine began to appear in the Dublin *Bell* and the London *Horizon* and elsewhere. Wrey Gardiner, editor of the then influential *Poetry Quarterly*, gave me a lot of encouragement. Through my contact with Wrey, I met the versatile scientist-writer Alex Comfort (then a militant pacifist reading medicine at Trinity College, Cambridge) and the two of us were soon hard at work editing an anthology of contemporary verse for Wrey's brave little wartime venture, the Grey Walls Press. This emerged in 1941 as *Lyra: A Book of New Lyric*, for which we were lucky enough to obtain an introduction by Herbert Read.

I scamped my university work, though I did pass a few exams. My studies were pushed aside as I tackled each new literary venture, whether in actual writing or editorial. Throwing myself into the literary life, I joined the local PEN club and one way and another got to know various writers and would-be writers. It was at a meeting of the PEN club that I first met the novelist Michael McLaverty, who had just published his fine lyric novel, *Call My Brother Back*.

Then in his late 30s, the short but stocky Michael, his hair already receding and brushed flat over his head, could seem almost shy. He had little in the way of jovial banter but in a real exchange of views one was struck by the aptness of his remarks and, most of all, by his evident sincerity. His words were considered and came out in a slight nasal tone. He was a professional in the sense of aiming high artistically but I could not imagine him writing deliberately for money. He supported his family as a teacher. I always supposed that Michael taught science as he had an MSc from Queen's University but former pupils have told me that he largely taught poetry and geometry. Perhaps when headmaster he could teach whatever he pleased. Later, the journalist and fiction writer Jack Holland, a pupil of McLaverty, told me of Michael's great love of geometry and of the encouragement Jack got from him for his writing as a schoolboy. I always think that behind every good writer there is a good teacher. I got to know Michael well despite the gap in our ages – some 16 years. From time to time I visited him and his wife, Mollie, in their home at Deramore Drive off the Malone Road. They were very hospitable. There I would drink Michael's sherry and listen to him speak of books and authors for I was still at a stage when writing seemed glamorous, magic, and had yet, really, to come across the spite and malice writers often delight in. Michael impressed me by saying he sometimes lit the open fire with old copies of *The Times Literary Supplement*. In those days I revered the *TLS* and like most provincials was over-respectful of its anonymous reviewers. Michael helped me realise that the *TLS* was as fallible as anyone else.

Michael, as I said, at that time had just published *Call My Brother Back*, the most satisfying of his eight novels. Originally entitled *Waste Ground* (a title put paid to by the protests from his London publisher), the novel had the ill luck to appear in 1939, just before the outbreak of the war. A year earlier or a year later would have ensured more publicity for his début. A few years later, *The White Mare*, a collection of short stories, was published by Rowley's Mourne Press. The short story indeed proved to be Michael's métier.

I certainly valued Michael's warm friendship and the kind comments he made on my work. A chat with him would always raise one's spirits for, as I said, he was entirely free of the envy and malice only too readily found in the literary world. I was always amused by his suspicious attitude towards Dublin which, in some ways, differed little from that of a typical Orangeman. He showed no interest in Dublin's Augustan beauty or its literary ghosts or its easy-going relaxed character. He tended to think that the city was a trap for the writer who would squander his energies and ideas in tavern talk.

Michael had some recognition from the critics both in these islands and in America, but not as much as he deserved. His books are perhaps too quiet in tone in an age when serious writers shout obscenities or even tendernesses from the rooftops.

A regular feature in the literary landscape was the university flat of Sam Hanna Bell and Bob Davidson. Saturday evenings there could be fun, when the clans gathered to drink, and discuss books, politics and the theatre, and listen to records, and make a pass at whatever girls were available. As the evening progressed, and the bottles of Guinness were emptied, the discussion would become more and more animated, if possibly less and less factually accurate. Hanna Bell was a fiction writer who later joined the Northern Ireland BBC, as did my friend the playwright and man of letters John Boyd. A schoolteacher, John encouraged me to read widely. It was he, I think, who introduced me to Joyce and Lawrence. Anyone might turn up at the Davidson-Bell ménage, for they had acquired a reputation as good-natured fellows who kept open house to all-comers interested in left-of-centre politics and the arts.

Because I was a few years junior to them, Bob and Sam may well have regarded me with just a grain of suspicion as a young man who threw his weight about rather more than could be justified. For all that, I cannot remember more than a couple of disagreements. I recall with gratitude their kindness and hospitality to a sometimes moody and cantankerous young man.

Belfast, in its own small way, in the early 1940s established a rather more cosmopolitan atmosphere than in the immediate pre-war period. One of the 'soldier-poets' I met in Belfast was Drummond Allison, who had been a contemporary of Sidney Keyes and John Heath-Stubbs at Oxford. Drummond went to some pains to locate me and get in touch. I believe he discovered my whereabouts from Wesley Lutton, who worked in that cultural hive, Dave McLean's little bookshop in Howard Street. We took a great liking to each other, visiting theatres together and drinking foamy-headed glasses of Guinness in the bars, discussing writing and sex. I liked Drummond for the almost ingenuous way he told me of his envy for me because my poetry was being published more widely than his. Also, it seemed to him that, despite my living in a faraway province of the United Kingdom, I seemed to have been admitted to at least fellow-travelling status by a group of new London poets. All this was news to me, for I had thought I led an isolated, even insulated, life, made bearable only by the dropping through my letter-box of copies of *The Bell* and *Horizon* and letters from Wrey Gardiner or Tambimuttu. I envied Drummond's life at Oxford.

Drummond's mother sent me a copy of his book, *The Yellow Night*, his only book of poems. He had signed his name and written an inscription on a gummed slip before going abroad on active service. She enclosed a note to say that Drummond had been killed in the Italian invasion. It seemed unbelievable that a life of such promise and gaiety – for in our few meetings I had sensed in him a true joy-in-living, despite his dislike of army life – should have ended. In later years I have sometimes talked about him to that scholarly poet, John Heath-Stubbs, in the Queen's Elm in Chelsea or the Catherine Wheel in Kensington. Heath-Stubbs and I could hardly be more dissimilar in background and interests, yet every time I see him my first image is of laughing, brave Drummond Allison and myself riding on top of a bus across the Albert Bridge arguing about the merits of W.H. Auden. Even now, over half a century later, I feel strongly that Allison's death left a gap in post-war English poetry.

At this period, perhaps the most well-known literary meeting place for writers and artists was Campbell's coffee house opposite the City Hall. Upstairs there, one could look down, possibly in both senses, on the Common Man jumping on and off tramcars.

Imagine a sunny morning in Campbell's during the Second World War. Belfast has been gashed by the Nazi bombers, khaki-clad figures and their War Department vehicles are everywhere. Civil Defence workers are no longer laughed at for their inactivity. Like London, Belfast is learning to 'take it'. The Yanks are here, some said 'over-paid, over-sexed, and over here'. They have started dating local girls – 'Say, whaddya do about sex?' Through the windows of Campbell's, one looks across at the City Hall erected in the full flush of Victorian prosperity by the Protestant bourgeoisie. Its statues and gardens I have known from childhood. The City Hall indeed, like the poor and the war profiteer, is something one puts up with. After the war, perhaps, change may come . . . but will the war *ever* end?

But let us return to Campbell's. In comes the soldierly, full-figured and genial-faced Denis Ireland, the essayist and wit, whom some people still call Captain Ireland because of his service in the First World War. He is closely followed by his friend William Conor, who sports a bow-tie that suggests his vocation as a painter. A few minutes pass before the arrival of Richard Rowley – the pseudonym of a businessman called Williams who has started a publishing firm, the Mourne Press, which is devoted to making writers like McLaverty and Hanna Bell better known. The conversation is crisp, wryly humorous in the throwaway northern fashion. It tends towards practicality rather than abstraction. 'How much did they pay for it?' Denis Ireland asks, apropos of some literary merchandise broadcast by the Belfast regional station of the BBC.

Then Denis launches into yet another funny story, something about 'hogwash' and Sam Goldwyn, and a Hollywood character who told Denis after some allegedly stupendous event, 'You ain't seen nuthin' yet'. Denis knows the USA from the time he used to visit the States on behalf of the linen firm run by his family. With some care he avoids politics, though we all know him to be something of a white blackbird, that is, an Ulster Protestant – Presbyterian, in fact – with strong nationalist sympathies, a sort of throwback to the radical Presbyterians of the late 18th century who supported the demands of their Catholic fellow countrymen for reform. Yet even if he did get on to politics, it would not ruffle anyone here, for Campbell's is an island of tolerance in our bitterly divided community. Dissent is permissible and nobody will drench you with coffee for not saying 'the right thing'.

As the minutes pass, more and more faces appear in the upper room. Friends, acquaintances, rivals look in for a 'wee bit of crack'. Over there stands Joe Tomelty, playwright and manager of the Group Theatre, later to appear in the film version of F.L. Green's novel about the IRA, *Odd Man Out*, and later still to be the victim of a cruel motoring accident that will effectively end his career as writer and actor. But now he is talking with some animation to Sam Hanna Bell, whose realistic short stories of Ulster life have been published by the

Mourne Press under the title *Summer Loanen*. F.L. Green, the best-selling novelist, an Englishman living in the city, limps in, leaning heavily on a stick, chalky-faced behind enormous spectacles. Green, one understands, had a leg severely injured, I never discovered how or where. Everyone remembers Diana Wynyard in the film of Green's *On the Night of the Fire*.

Green starts twitting me about the so-called 'Ulster Renaissance' and then tells me about his latest fiction project. 'I'm writing,' he says, 'what you and your friends should be writing, about the real dramas going on here. You people ignore what's going on on your own doorstep.' He gives me a ticking-off and warns me against the lures of 'that God-awful place London with its literary cocktail parties'. Laurie Green does not fit in at all with the angry young men, but we find him stimulating. A touch of cantankerousness goes down well in these parts. Plain speaking passes for integrity.

Over in a corner, a couple of young painters are arguing about paintings recently exhibited by CEMA – letters that stand for Council for the Encouragement of Music and the Arts, and the forerunner of the Arts Councils that now exist in Belfast and Dublin. Who is that gentleman whose elegance contrasts with the shabbiness of the arty brigade? Why, none other than Gerry Morrow, a member of that remarkably talented theatrical and literary family. I know his more extrovert cousin quite well, 'Larry' Morrow, who writes witty profiles in *The Bell* in Dublin where he works as a radio journalist. The scribes talk about war aims and how the city ought to be rebuilt in a contemporary architectural idiom. The company includes two or three who hope to write the Great Ulster Novel. The conversation turns to the latest offering at the Group Theatre – Ibsen's *Ghosts* with Allan McClelland playing the lead.

Lunchtime approaches. The writing men, the arty-crafty boys with long hair and their short-haired girls drift off in search of food or, more likely, drink. Food these days is rationed, but with an agricultural hinterland people here mostly do rather better than their counterparts in the big English cities. One can always go down to Dublin for a substantial pre-war meal, anyway. The air is heavy with cigarette and pipe smoke, for nobody yet knows the dangers of smoking. I am, fortunately, a non-smoker because smoking irritates my throat and makes me cough. I sit lost in a dream until a buxom waitress bustles round me collecting cups and crumby plates. 'Wake up, you,' she snaps. 'If you've no work to do, other bodies have.' The customer is always wrong. I'm surprised she does not add the clichéd phrase 'Don't you know there's a war on?' This is the way sloppy service is excused.

Down the stairs I go and out into the flowing tide of humanity. A couple of books under my arm, I saunter along. My feet, if not my head, bring me to the Central Library in Royal Avenue. My mind crowds with images. I think of all the things I want to do in the next few years – assuming I don't perish in the next blitz (hundreds are already dead and there are empty spaces where bombs fell). One takes one's chance and hopes for the best. As the Chinese say, we live in interesting times.

I think of the poem I have written about Irene – 'Love is a wet autumn night'. But I reject the words. The sun is shining and the city is full of pretty girls. The autumn seems a long way off. As I cross the road an American jeep flashes past. It misses me by inches. A coal-black GI shouts at me in a Deep South accent, 'Hi, bud, mind ya step!' I follow a dream in Royal Avenue, Belfast, even in the middle of a great war. Even without Irene.

SIXTEEN

Going South

I can sum up my reasons for going south to Dublin in a word — escape. I was dissatisfied with my personal life in Belfast. I felt oppressed by the general narrowness and philistinism. I wanted new doors to open, new opportunities. I wanted to qualify as a social worker so I would have something to fall back on if I did not succeed as a writer or journalist.

I persuaded my McCrea relatives to finance me at Trinity College, Dublin, where I was prepared to work for a Diploma in Social Studies. This in fact I did, for as I said earlier, I never had any difficulty with exams provided I did a minimum of work for them; and this to date is my sole academic qualification — a small one to be sure but better than nothing I suppose. It seemed to me that social work might be both interesting for me and valuable for others, though indeed since taking the diploma I have engaged in practical social work only in the most marginal way. Even that amount of direct contact with the grimmer facts of life have provided me with a measure of experience that I might not otherwise have had.

When I left Belfast for Trinity in the autumn of 1943 I knew that it was goodbye for ever to the River Lagan. The time had come to venture from home and kin, and from the people who, with all their faults and maddening ways, I loved to the point of heartbreak. Father had rejected me; so had Irene. I decided to leave and never go back except for brief visits — and so it has turned out. I went up to the Antrim Road and had a last look at Irene's house, standing solid and four-square in an area that had been severely bombed. It was with a feeling of loss, yet buoyed up, too, by the unshakeable optimism of early manhood, that I took my leave of Belfast. Dublin represented to me the kind of life I had once craved on the Newtownards Road as an adolescent — a triumphant yes.

Dublin's contrast appealed to me: the wretchedly poor but spirited people of the slums and the elegantly tweeded Anglo-Irish ladies; the splendid glass of the shops in Grafton Street and the broken fanlights in Mountjoy Square. One noted, too, the Dubliner's ready assumption of his city's — and therefore his own — importance. Wartime Dublin was the most fascinating city in these islands, a beacon of light in the European gloom.

The 'Emergency' in Dublin did not take me by surprise since I had already sampled it during brief weekend visits. I had made friends with the Salkeld family, since Cecil Salkeld had published a poem of mine in a hand-set limited edition of 250 copies. Cecil's mother, Blanaid Salkeld, who had once acted at the Abbey Theatre and also wrote poetry, welcomed me to their house in Morehampton Road, Donnybrook.

Cecil had studied in Germany before the war and brought home to Dublin a German wife, Irma. He was a new experience for me, for I had not met before a man who had grown up in an atmosphere where the arts were taken seriously and professionalism encouraged. I learned that Cecil had been something of a prodigy, having exhibited at the age of 16. Now he seemed to spend much of his time in bed, reading, writing, chatting to his many callers, talking of his plans. Sometimes he did get up and set to work, especially in the weeks leading up to an exhibition by the Royal Hibernian Academy, of which he was an associate member.

I would call at his house, walk up the stairs to his room at the top, sit on a chair by the master's bedside and listen to his witty and informed comments on the arts, politics, religion and philosophy, interwoven with current gossip. Eventually Cecil would lift himself slowly out of bed, dress quickly and then head, myself in tow, for his local, Reddin's pub. Cecil, more than anyone else in Dublin, became my guide, philosopher and friend. Being still touched with that northern puritan spirit, I would ration his company, remembering I had a lecture to attend or notes to study.

Years later in 1969, I was to read Kate O'Brien's comment on Cecil shortly after his death: 'He was a man of too many gifts — none of them sufficiently strong to control him . . . He seemed to me to have a contempt for life – which in a man so gifted was especially sad. The invalidism of his later years was deplorable, but must have been an expression of wounded pride, a refusal to compete . . . Yet he must be said to have had a good life.'

That Cecil had been showered with gifts was indeed true though. At the time I knew him, I did not sense in him a contempt for life. He did refuse to compete in a race in which he felt that the prizes went to industrious mediocrities and time-servers. Painting was the art for which he had a training and his style was easily recognisable, even to a layman. He dabbled in writing and I remember seeing quite a creditable play of his performed by a group of enthusiastic young actors. It was called *A Gay Goodnight*, a phrase lifted from W.B. Yeats, in which 'gay' is used in the original sense. Cecil knew everyone in the arts in Dublin. Once, in the Bailey, he pointed to a man and told me, 'That's Liam O'Flaherty.' But O'Flaherty was too drunk for Cecil to approach him. I was very disappointed not to meet the author of *Skerrett* and *The Informer*.

It was around this time that my first collection of poems, *One Recent Evening*, was accepted by the London-based Falcon Press. Headed by a young army officer, Peter Baker, Falcon Press was later to join forces with Wrey Gardiner's Grey Walls Press. The Yorkshire-Irish typographer and poet Séan Jennett left Faber and Faber to join the house.

It was thrilling to sign my first publisher's contract and dream of the day the book would actually be on sale in the shops. As it happened, *One Recent Evening* sold well, for it came out bang in the middle of the wartime boom. My next volume, *The Undying Day* (1948) – handsomely designed by Jennett and containing, I believe, better work – sold wretchedly, probably not more than a hundred copies. Poets obviously do not live by poetry alone.

A close literary and personal friend around this period was Valentin Iremonger, a contemporary who worked in the Department of Education. He and I liked each other's poetry and we liked each other. Val took a keen interest in the theatre and acted in the amateur group which performed Cecil's *A Gay Goodnight*. He introduced me to Mary O'Malley who, years later, started the Lyric Players' Theatre when she went to live in Belfast. I remember Val, his face plastered with make-up, playing Mosca in Ben Jonson's *Volpone*.

Val and I would sometimes go together to Geoffrey Taylor, who had succeeded Frank O'Connor as poetry editor of *The Bell*. Taylor, formerly Phibbs, had once been one of a *ménage à trois* with Robert Graves and Laura Riding in London but, by the time we knew him, he was a very respectable man-of-letters. Taylor really encouraged young poets and, instead of merely sending a rejection slip, would write letters of instruction and encouragement. Or Val and I would go on visits to the painter-poet Freda Laughton whose husband, John Midgley, son of the northern politician, was serving with the Inniskilling Fusiliers in India.

Together Val and I planned various projects, some of which were translated into reality. One that came off was a selection of our most militant poems – together with some by Bruce Williamson – in a paperback volume we called, rather cheekily, *On the Barricades*. This came out under the imprint of New Frontiers Press and carried Val's address in Tritonville Road in Sandymount. Our blurb ran as follows: '*On the Barricades* has literary – and not political – implications. Its three authors – Robert Greacen, Bruce Williamson and Val Iremonger – give proof of a new vitality in Irish writing, a vitality the older generations will not acknowledge. Here they raise and defend their first barricades against the low standards, facile half-truths and lack of integrity that have for too long rotted the Anglo-Irish spirit.' It seems odd to me now that we should have laid such stress on Anglo-Irishness since Val came from Catholic Irish stock and Williamson and I were Belfast Protestants. Though Val was a fluent Irish speaker, he often railed against Irish language activists.

I carried on the imprint more or less on my own for some time and tried to break into publishing. I got together an anthology, *Irish Harvest*, in which were assembled stories, articles and poems by the established Irish writers of the time as well as the newcomers. This venture was backed financially by Maurice Fridberg, a Jewish Dubliner who had done well in bookselling in London and who hoped to set up as a publisher in Dublin after the war. This he did, in fact, using as colophon an hour-glass. His first venture was Frank O'Connor's translation of Brian Merriman's *The Midnight Court*, the 18th-century classic. I still have a copy of the book which bears the inscription, 'For Robert – my first publishing effort – with every good wish. Sincerely – Maurice. 1.9.45.' I did risk my own money in a venture that actually made a profit. This was a children's book, *Ivan and his Wonderful Coat*, written by Patricia Hutchins and illustrated by the painter Nano Reid. Just after the war, children's books were in short supply and great demand both in Britain and Ireland, and I had no problem in selling every copy. In fact, I did not print nearly enough.

But I was not commercially minded. Had I been so, I might have established myself as a fringe publisher. Publishing in Dublin, unlike today, was then only a minor activity and there was room for an energetic newcomer. Val Iremonger and I had set our sights on higher things than making money. We began to collaborate on putting together an anthology of modern Irish verse. Night after night, we sat in front of a huge turf fire in the sitting-room of Val's home in Sandymount and debated the merits of this and that poem, this and that poet. We read incessantly both books and magazines in which living poets had contributions, and together decided, with the minimum of friction, who and what ought to be in. News leaked out that we were in the anthology business and it was confidently asserted in the Dublin pubs that the project would come to nothing. Although we had the ear and eye of T.S. Eliot, through an acquaintance of mine in London, it seemed, after a promising start, that our labours might be in vain. Eliot asked us to make a few revisions in the manuscript we submitted. I went over to London and met the great man himself in 'Uncle Tom's cabin' in Faber's, then in Russell Square. He was fatherly and encouraging. He accepted our revised selection and the anthology, *Contemporary Irish Poetry*, appeared in 1949. Val and I had concocted a fighting introduction, but Eliot dropped it. Here are a few of the unpublished (or unpublishable) sentences:

> Few people really believed that Ireland would succeed in preserving her neutrality: consequently as the problems to be solved in Ireland were similar to those in any other country, it was obvious that it was no use burying one's head under the wool-blanket of the Celtic twilight. Ivory Round Towers, even if complete with the green-whiskered wolfhounds of Banba, Deirdre of the Sorrows, the harp that once and the dying fall of the mellifluous and kingly Gaelic, would hardly provide cover against the assault of tommy-gunned, jack-booted airborne divisions.

Patrick Kavanagh refused to be included in the anthology. Val and I did everything we could except fall on our knees to ensure his inclusion. His peasant stubbornness triumphed. His ploy was to demand a ridiculously high fee that Faber simply refused to give. It was Kavanagh's way of saying no and perhaps hoping for more publicity than if he had been included. A critic in the *New Statesman*, then the most powerful of English weekly reviews, assumed we had left him out for unworthy reasons. I had to write to the paper giving the real facts. Neither Val nor I quarrelled with Paddy because of his obstinacy, but we were bitterly disappointed by his refusal to co-operate.

Frank O'Connor, like Val Iremonger, lived in Sandymount and I went to see him there. He was going through a bitter, irascible phase, and was no doubt angry at being penned up in wartime Ireland.

He had kindly accepted a poem of mine for *The Bell* and written a favourable comment about it as well. When we met, I had no idea of what kind of man he might be – I had only read a few of his short stories in *Guests of the Nation*. He surprised me by the vehemence of his anti-Catholicism, not just his anti-clericalism. Yet he exuded vitality and charm and I came away with a sense of exhilaration. His fellow Corkman Seán O'Faoláin, whom I met about the same time, turned out to be very different: slightly academic but forceful, self-controlled and with an air of sophistication new to me. He took me to tea in a place called Anne's Teashop and I remember one of his questions was 'What are young people in Belfast thinking?'

The very first fan letter to come my way was from a lady called Mary Devenport O'Neill whose address was in Kenilworth Square. We began to correspond and I discovered that she herself, middle-aged, was a poet with a volume to her credit and that some of her verse plays had been performed. Her husband, she wrote, was a civil servant in the Department of Education. When I was invited to visit the O'Neills, I called at her husband's office, and he and I went by tram to their home. This proved to be the first of several visits.

The O'Neills lived in a middle-class style unfamiliar to me. I was impressed by the spotless linen tablecloth, the solidly furnished and spacious rooms, the silverware, the excellent French wine. Lunch was served by a uniformed maid.

Joseph O'Neill, a tall, ruddy-complexioned man, kept quiet and it was obvious I was his wife's guest. Mrs O'Neill – she always remained Mrs O'Neill in those more formal days – turned out to be a lively woman, even a bit confrontational in attitude. She reminisced of the days, evenings rather, when she had run a 'Thursday At Home' attended by famous writers in that very house. Yeats she had known particularly well. She became his consultant when he was writing *A Vision* – a fact recorded in a notebook of Yeats' now in the National Library of Ireland. She told me that Æ (George William Russell) – simple in manner yet a great man – used to tease the ageing, somewhat pompous Yeats by calling him 'Willie' and persisting in pronouncing his name as 'Yeets', much to the annoyance of the Nobel prizeman.

Mrs O'Neill, though naturally influenced by the ideas and ideals of the Celtic Twilight, had wide horizons and was well aware of the work of Proust and Pound, Auden and MacNeice. She felt that Irish writers on the whole were still too concerned with 'the mist that does be on the bog'. This chimed with my own view and she urged me to say so in public.

Joseph O'Neill remained silent while this discussion was in progress, but later he counselled caution saying that a young man ought not to antagonise his elders by being too opinionated. But I, being 'young and foolish' and outspoken in the northern fashion and emboldened by the impulsive Mrs O'Neill, not to mention the two glasses of Châteauneuf du Pape, paid no heed to his advice. I wrote a fiery letter to *The Irish Times* that resulted in acrimonious replies from the Dublin *literati*. On the other hand, my attack on the old-fashioned literary moulds drew applause from some of my own contemporaries in Dublin.

Some years were to pass before I began to realise that Joseph O'Neill was himself a significant writer and a man of intellectual distinction. O'Neill, born in Tuam, County Galway, in 1878, spent his boyhood on the Aran Islands. His upbringing in a house where Irish was spoken made him keenly interested in the revival of the language and its literature so that, after graduating from Queen's College, Galway, he became a student at Kuno Meyer's School of Irish Learning. Later he studied at the University of Freiburg in Germany where he formed a close friendship with Oscar Bergin.

At the age of 30 he gave up his Irish studies to become an inspector of primary schools and, in the same year, married Mary Devenport – also from Galway – who had been a student at the National College of Art. In 1933, he was appointed Secretary of the Department of Secondary Education, a post he held until he retired in 1944.

O'Neill's literary career started with poems in the *Freeman's Journal* and articles in the *Irish Statesman*. It was probably the association with men such as Æ, Yeats, Lennox Robinson and Austin Clarke on those Thursday evenings in Rathgar that led him to attempt more ambitious projects. Five novels with London imprints were to appear, the first in 1934 and the last in 1947. His *Land Under England* is a political and psychological allegory of a young Englishman caught in a horrifying world under the Yorkshire countryside. This turns out to be an area where the inhabitants are non-human automatons descended from the last Roman soldiers to occupy England. It is a fascinating novel in the tradition of Aldous Huxley's *Brave New World* and the science fiction of H.G. Wells. In 1935, when it appeared, it had relevance to the rise of Hitler and the Nazi attempt to conquer Europe. Æ wrote a preface to *Land Under England* in which he claimed that O'Neill had 'elevated the thriller into literature'. Æ went on:

> . . . how was I to know for all the torrent of picturesque speech and prodigality of humour, that, within that long head and long body, there were other creatures than those he exposed to me? . . . How was I to know that he had it in him to imagine and write *Land Under England* . . .?

For a time, I assisted Peadar O'Donnell when he took over the editorship of *The Bell* from O'Faoláin. I was the successor to H.A.L. Craig, whom everyone knew as Harry, a big fellow with an enormous shock of fair hair. Harry, the son of a Church of Ireland rector, lived for years in rooms at Trinity, though I think he left without a degree. He used the college as a convenient and relatively cheap place to live. I remember that, outside his door, there stood a vast array of milk bottles that had not been washed out. He was full of energy and used much of it in speaking and canvassing for the Labour Party. Sometimes he would hand me a galley proof for *The Bell* in the Trinity dining hall and ask me to read it for errors. I found Peadar a most erratic employer but a very pleasant one – one could keep whatever office hours one liked. Peadar was a marvellous speaker, both in public and private. He was full of ideas and plans that sounded absolutely convincing. His defect was that he lacked the patience to carry most of them through. Had he been able to do so, I think his impact on Irish public life would have been enormous. His own literary work is significant, all the more so since he split his time between writing and political activism.

It would be tedious to list the various writers and artists I got to know in Dublin. Nano Reid was one of the painters I knew fairly well, though at the time her talent was only beginning to be recognised. The White Stag Group, as they called themselves, were people who had come to Ireland to avoid being involved in the war in England. One of these, Nick Nicholls, painted and wrote poems. A poem by Nicholls, 'The Bone and the Flower', led to controversy when it appeared in *The Bell*. Its symbolism was taken to be sexual and, in the middle 1940s, anything that even hinted at sex came under suspicion. The poem began:

> Wound in the seed, the rose's tongue,
> Among flowers, the chatter of light and shade . . .

Sexual in tone or not, there seemed to me to be a good deal of Edith Sitwell's influence in it.

Pearse Hutchinson, then beginning his career, was a friend of a friend of mine who came from Armagh. Sam Harrison and I met Pearse a few times but never got to know him well. He must have been in touch to some extent over the years, since I have a postcard from him from the International Labour Office building in Geneva. I expect he was visiting Sam in Switzerland where Sam spent many years. Pearse's inscription runs:

> Friedrich Hölderlin
> hated committing sin,
> but, although he never
>   visited a bad house,
> he still ended up in a madhouse.

The publication of my second volume of poems, *The Undying Day*, in 1948, brought me my first experience of betrayal — at least as an adult. A northern Protestant, whom I considered a friend, attacked it bitterly in a Dublin newspaper, to the astonishment of those who knew us both. For some time my wife, Patricia Hutchins, and I had been thinking of leaving for London. It was difficult to make a living in Dublin from freelance writing and occasional part-time jobs in publishing. The day after the review appeared I said to Patricia, 'Let's go.' Val Iremonger used to say that Belfast was a good place to have come *from*. Dublin seemed to me to have been a good place to have lived *in*. London appeared to be the right place to go *to*. I was still following a dream.

SEVENTEEN

Encounters with Kavanagh

In 1942, I was living in Belfast but managed to get a travel permit to visit London where literary life, somewhat fragmented, still went on. Stephen Spender had published a poem of mine in *Horizon*, of which he was poetry editor. *Horizon*, started by Cyril Connolly, was, perhaps, the most notable magazine to keep the cultural flag flying during the war. Spender kindly invited me to stay in his flat in Maresfield Gardens. One day he said, 'Do you want to meet Connolly?' Something of a rhetorical question. He went to the phone and arranged that I should present myself at the *Horizon* offices.

Connolly, as ugly a man as I ever saw, made a few clever flippant remarks in keeping with the style of his *Horizon* editorials. I was constrained, as I had not been with Spender, aware of being a provincial. He asked if I knew John Hewitt. I said I did. Then he went to the shelves, loaded with review books despite the wartime shortage of paper, cloth and skilled printers.

He handed me a copy of Patrick Kavanagh's *The Great Hunger* which had come out in a Cuala Press limited edition. 'Five hundred words,' he said. Before we parted, he asked me, 'What should a writer aim at?' I mumbled something about telling the truth but sensed that this was not the right answer. 'He should aim at writing a masterpiece,' said Connolly. I went out into London's bomb-scarred streets pleased and chastened.

I can still recall the excitement with which, in the Liverpool boat-train, I opened the elegant little book in its blue binding and read: 'Clay is the word and clay is the flesh . . .' It was clear even to a 21-year-old that a harsh but vital new wind was blowing from County Monaghan, a part of Ulster I knew well. Vivid in memory were those summer holidays I had spent with relatives near Castleblayney.

The stony fields and the people who sweated in them came before my eyes as I read and re-read Kavanagh's masterpiece. The cruel narrowness and frustrations of these small farmers – peasants indeed, though they would have resented the name – seemed real as people in books seldom were. This was raw, disturbing work, quite different from the handful of lyrical and pastoral poems by Kavanagh I had come across. It was different by far from the essentially urban and middle-class attitude of Irish poets of the time. It hit some nerve untouched by, say, Joseph Campbell or F.R. Higgins. Yet powerful as *The Great Hunger* seemed to me, I did make one or two minor criticisms of it in the *Horizon* review.

It was rumoured that the gardaí had confiscated copies of the book and threatened the author with prosecution. I never discovered whether this was a fact or just one of those stories that mushroomed in Dublin pub mythology. But I searched diligently through the poem for lines that might have caused the police to think that poets were as dangerous as parachutists. Was it the veiled reference to masturbation that set off alarm bells?

> He sinned over the warm ashes and his crime
> The law's long arm could not serve with 'time'.

Were the respectable Civic Guards acting on instructions from still more respectable members of the Catholic *bourgeoisie* outraged by some image like this?

> Maguire spreads his legs over the impotent cinders
> That wake no manhood now.

As I wrote my *Horizon* review, much exercised by Connolly's parting shot that the aim of a writer was to produce a masterpiece – but were mere reviews exempt from Connolly's Law? – I hoped I would be able to convey something of my excitement to the magazine's mainly English – and sophisticated – readers, who would be unlikely to have any knowledge of the mores of the small farmers of County Monaghan. I myself, city-bred and a Protestant at that, had had only fleeting contacts with the people about whom Kavanagh wrote.

I said – here I quote – that *The Great Hunger* was 'a poem well worth reading both for its value as poetry, which is simple and direct, and its value as clinical evidence, complex and indirect'. I suppose I had picked up the word 'clinical' from W.H. Auden. I had a few reservations as to the poem's value, however, and later was to learn that the notice was not nearly enthusiastic enough for Kavanagh, though he never once referred to it during the several years I knew him. He felt aggrieved, perhaps, that Connolly, in whose distinguished magazine he had published a section of the poem, should have commissioned a review from a young Protestant 'eejit' from the Black North, instead of from some established English critic whose word would carry weight. It is possible that Connolly was intent on a bit of mischief.

It was my witty fellow Belfastman, the journalist H.L. ('Larry') Morrow – sometimes unkindly nicknamed 'To-morrow' – who introduced me to Kavanagh in Dublin's Pearl Bar. Kavanagh greeted me with his native caution, but a torrent of abuse – and here he could be devastating – did not descend on the shy young man who had done his best to be scrupulously fair. On subsequent meetings – when Kavanagh realised that I did not bark or bite and rarely argued with my seniors – our relationship thawed into more than acquaintanceship, if a trifle less than friendship. I doubt whether friendship came easily to Kavanagh. Life had taught him to be on his guard.

He and I never met by arrangement, but central Dublin is small and compact, and in those less crowded days we would bump into each other in Bewley's coffee house or in a bar or just in the street. He used to prowl round the streets like a hungry wolf and get especially restless before the evening papers appeared. Paddy, as I soon came to call him, devoured news of all kinds – politics, racing, gossip. For him, the world had dwindled into a parish not unlike his own native Inniskeen. He wanted to know the latest titbit about Churchill or Roosevelt – one of his poems is about Roosevelt – or Hitler, though his own world now seemed confined to the writers and journalists he consorted with in the Grafton Street-O'Connell Street area, and to whom he reacted strongly, positively and negatively. His usual greeting to me was, 'Hello, Rob, what's new?'

From time to time, as our acquaintance grew, he would call me a 'Protestant bastard'. This would have been offensive from anyone else, but he would say the words in affectionate tones, almost as if he envied my background. It was a signal that he liked me, for he had a ready stock of vulgar phrases to describe some impeccable Catholic bards who had incurred his wrath! A careless word, a tone of voice, could irritate him. I think his over-sensitivity must have lost him much goodwill. One of Paddy's often repeated tags of abuse was 'an ould bags'.

So far as Austin Clarke was concerned, I think Kavanagh distrusted rather than hated him. Clarke in the War years, a grey eminence in a black hat, had not fulfilled his early promise and nobody could guess at the important work that lay ahead. On the occasions when I met Clarke, he struck me as unhappy and frustrated, fed up with the literary hack work he was forced to do for a meagre living. In the period I am talking about, writers could not travel easily outside Ireland. Censorship laid its dead hand on creativity, the reactionary element in the Catholic Church held sway and it was exceedingly difficult for writers to break into the British or American market. All that contributed to the despondency of Clarke, Kavanagh and others, and was partly responsible for their irritability and willingness to attack each other on the slightest pretext.

The name Brendan Behan I first heard from Kavanagh's lips. They had once been friends. Kavanagh denied this in a court case for libel which he lost and in which the *Leader* magazine was vindicated for its profile of him. The counsel for the defence, John A. Costello, had confronted Kavanagh with a copy of one of his books affectionately inscribed to Brendan, who had done some house-painting for him. By the time Kavanagh had talked to me of Behan, their days of friendship were over and he described Behan in picturesque language. Among other things Behan was a 'drunken bowsie'. The name Behan stuck in my mind. In a few years' time that name was to be known throughout the English-speaking world.

Sometimes I would see Kavanagh strolling along Lower Baggot Street or Grafton Street, stopping to gaze in shop windows, accompanied by a young man called Arthur to whom he talked in a kindly tone. Arthur, whoever he was – and no description of his background was ever forthcoming – uttered not a word. Arthur's clothes and demeanour suggested a middle-class provenance. Could he have been the offspring of some benefactor?

At other times, I would run into Kavanagh and his brother Peter, who taught at a Christian Brothers' school. The two of them occasionally lunched at the Trinity College buffet. Trinity College itself, of course, had been blacklisted for Catholics by the Archbishop of Dublin, Dr McQuaid, though a sizeable number of Catholic students defied the ban. Peter's ideas and opinions seemed almost identical with Patrick's. At the time, I think he was engaged in research on the Irish theatre for a PhD. He had the education, Paddy had the genius. Peter, too, was combative but could be a pleasant enough fellow when in high good humour. I used to speculate as to whether Peter bore the relationship to Patrick that Stanislaus Joyce did to his elder brother, James.

I would sometimes ask one of the pair, 'Where's your brother?' only to get the off-hand answer, 'How do I know?', as if to suggest that the bond between them was not strong. My impression was that, even if the two brothers had a falling out from time to time – as seemed likely – each was highly defensive of the other. Indeed, since Patrick's death, Peter seems to have devoted much of his time and money to republishing his brother's prose and poetry. I contributed a short memoir to Peter's life of the poet.

In the preface to Kavanagh's *The Complete Poems*, Peter writes a letter to the dead Patrick:

> A year or two ago I might have discussed your funeral, trying to decide which group was the most offensive, those who came or those who stayed away. There were a few genuine friends in attendance, of course . . . Much talk of you since you have gone – at least half of it bitter and the remainder begrudging, Still, I suppose one should not complain. Perhaps they mean well. It is hard to say.

Peter Kavanagh goes on to say he has 'been whacking away on my own', publishing Patrick's papers, beginning, as arranged between them, with their correspondence, *Lapped Furrows*, followed by *November Haggard*, a selection of uncollected prose.

Peter complains that, for *The Complete Poems* and the other books, not a penny was contributed by anyone but himself – 'and this in a world of Cultural Committees, Arts Councils, fellowships and the rest'. He recalls that when, in 1952, Patrick asked him if he would help in starting a journal he (Peter) 'threw everything I owned into *Kavanagh's*

Weekly, knowing I would ever see it again'. He adds, rather sadly, 'I am merely stating the position so that you may know the way things stand – not much different, I'd say, from when you were around.' This preface makes for melancholy reading. That a poet of Kavanagh's stature should be neglected is scandalous. Yet there may be another side to it all – simply that Patrick and Peter Kavanagh, hurt by the slings and arrows of the world of Irish letters, turned savagely on their critics. I am confident that a younger generation, both in Ireland and elsewhere, will assess Patrick Kavanagh on his achievement as poet and, to a lesser extent, prose remembrancer of the Monaghan years.

He was a big, shambling creature – a Dr Johnson, as it were, reincarnated as the son of a small farmer and cobbler in Mucker, Inniskeen, County Monaghan. Money problems oppressed him, as they did Johnson. City slickers patronised him. A countryman to his dying day, Kavanagh fitted uneasily into urban life, yet many years spent in Dublin with some brief excursions to London made him unwilling to return to what we glibly call his 'roots'. A displaced person, he enjoyed his role as a character, and his loud, husky, south Ulster voice boomed dogmatically on subjects large and small. He inveighed against writers who had been formally educated or had made reputations he considered inflated. It did not surprise me to know that Robert Farren, the poet he despised most, put much emphasis on metre and grammar. Kavanagh would have loved to have been present when Dylan Thomas remarked sarcastically, in a room full of American professors, 'Isn't education wonderful!'

Kavanagh surprised me one day by appearing at breakfast at the guest house I was staying at. This was an establishment run by a Mrs Kenny at 19 Raglan Road in Ballsbridge. Here he remained for perhaps six months. It was a somewhat genteel place and peaceful but for the eager bells of the nearby Church of Ireland, which shrilled out even the quarter-hours. (One thinks of how maddened Ezra Pound had been by the bells of St Mary Abbots in Kensington, pre-First World War.) Kavanagh, as might be expected, enjoyed outraging the residents. He would clump into the dining-room as if he were returning from footing turf in a bog, march heavily as far as possible from the others – schoolteachers, clerks, students, a violinist in the Radio Eireann orchestra – and, without a word, open a newspaper noisily. Friendly to me outside, he usually ignored me in the house. I tried to stick up for him, but the teachers and sales reps refused to believe that such a man could be a poet, let alone a significant one. They refused to condone his breaking of the conventions. Fifty-odd years ago, doing one's own thing aroused hostility.

Raglan Road apparently came to have an emotional resonance for Kavanagh. One of the loveliest poems in *The Complete Poems* is called 'On Raglan Road' to be sung to the air 'The Dawning of the Day'. The first quatrain runs:

On Raglan Road on an autumn day I met her first and knew
That her dark hair would weave a snare that I might one day rue;
I saw the danger, yet I walked along the enchanted way.
And I said, let grief be a fallen leaf at the dawning of the day.

In a note, Peter Kavanagh writes:

This ballad, originally published in *The Irish Press* under the title 'Dark Haired Miriam Ran Away', was written about Patrick's girlfriend Hilda but to avoid embarrassment he used the name of my girl-friend in the title.

Stories about Kavanagh abounded during the 1940s when I knew him. They have been embroidered and grow more colourful as time passes. One I remember hearing was his alleged remark to the editor of *The Standard*, a Catholic weekly in Dublin (it employed Kavanagh as film critic) on the death of a bishop. Kavanagh was reputed to have said, 'Now the ould bastard knows there is no God'. Yet Kavanagh, in my presence, again and again emphasised his belief in God and in Mother Church, and his contempt for atheists and agnostics. He liked to shock, so the story about the bishop may well be true. He would not listen to a 'dirty story', much less tell one. He liked women to be what then was called 'womanly' and remarked of a girlfriend of mine that she was 'a real woman'. No higher praise could he give. As for poets then writing, the only one I heard him commend without reservation was W.H. Auden. He kept quiet about Yeats whom he probably thought more 'Anglo' than Irish and given too high a place in the pantheon. I think he had the faintest touch of snobbery, to judge from various remarks. He spoke kindly of Harold Macmillan, whom he had met at the family firm of publishers in London. 'A real gentleman,' he called him.

Kavanagh, I believe, liked to consider *himself* 'a real gentleman', one who was free of the shams and hypocrisies of the lower middle class, 'the lace curtain Irish' of American usage. That may be why he was so contemptuous of the people in the Ballsbridge guest house. He despised the way they opted for 'correctness', their sheep-like acceptance of the social conventions. He might well have endorsed the D.H. Lawrence of 'How beastly the bourgeois' and execrated 'Willie Wetleg'. I'm sure he would have approved of Frieda von Richtofen as being 'a real woman'. He hated all establishments, literary, political and ecclesiastical. I was once in a group with him when someone quoted, 'Whatever is, is right'. Kavanagh in a flash said, 'Whatever is, is shite'.

Savage indignation lacerated Kavanagh as it lacerated Swift – and, despite his remark about excrement, he had a squeamishness, even prudery, that was a bit Swiftian. He tried to discipline his strong emotions but then out would come some ill-considered remark that caused offence or laughter, according to the company.

Kavanagh's autobiography, *The Green Fool*, published in 1938, must have made him feel on the verge of a breakthrough into literary recognition, but the book had to be withdrawn because of a libel action by Oliver St John Gogarty. 'Stately, plump Buck Mulligan' had taken exception to Kavanagh's remark that the woman who answered his knock on the door had been Gogarty's mistress. As a result, *The Green Fool* did not get back into print until 1971, four years after Kavanagh's death. This has not met with the approval of Peter Kavanagh, who says, in the preface from which I have already quoted: 'Recently *The Green Fool* was re-issued but since you stated many times that this book was part of your juvenilia it is hard to know the motive behind the present edition.' However, I am inclined to think that the *Irish Press* reviewer was not so far wrong in writing: '*The Green Fool* has Traherne's mystic vision, Hemingway's stark simplicity, Thurber's fantastic humour; and it is one of the few authentic accounts of life in Ireland in this century.'

I lost touch with Paddy Kavanagh when I left Dublin for London in 1948 but the green fool – and genius – remains vivid in my memory. The child or fool in him ensured the freshness, the originality of his writing, its freedom from influence and artificiality.

Some recognition did come to him before he died in 1967, aged 62, after a losing battle with cancer. Anthony Cronin was one of those younger fellow writers who championed him. Fortunately, Kavanagh had a splendid second phase as a poet and I was glad to hear that well on in years he had married – and happily, I hope. When I wonder about his life, as I have often done, speculating on whether it contained more misery than happiness, I keep remembering that he wrote, 'Great poetry is always comic in the profound sense.' He echoed W.B. Yeats, who believed in an ultimate gaiety. Kavanagh was much more than a local poet, a parochial poet, yet it is hard not to identify him with his early years in Monaghan where his native black hills forever look north towards Armagh as he tell us in 'Shancoduff':

> My hills hoard the bright shillings of March
> While the sun searches in every pocket.
> They are my Alps and I have climbed the Matterhorn
> With a sheaf of hay for three perishing calves
> In the field under the Big Forth of Rocksavage.

Would he, I wonder, have been less the poet he is if he had never looked south, first to Dublin and then to London? Would he have been a happier man?

EIGHTEEN

A Foothold in London

Without 'connections' – and being a northern Protestant in a predominantly Catholic country where the bishops reigned supreme, as they no longer do – it seemed that my best chance of a career lay in England. Patricia, too, was intent on a career. In today's terms she was a feminist and I think a bit inclined to the belief that anything a man could do, a woman could do better. She had just finished the manuscript of her book, *James Joyce's Dublin*, for the Grey Walls Press in London, a small publishing company run by our friend Charles Wrey Gardiner. Publication came in 1950 when we were settled in London. The blurb stated:

> . . . the writer's aim has been to outline the topographical and 'documentary' aspects of Joyce's work; to stress his skill in conveying the essence of his period.

Sixty-four plates included a series of Dublin in late Victorian and Edwardian days as well as several portraits and facsimiles of letters written by Joyce. It was a handsomely produced book that has become a collector's item. While Patricia was writing it, Wrey came over and stayed in our flat in Lower Baggot Street, in central Dublin. I remember he went out to Howth. Later he wrote a poem about that expedition in which he recalled me as being 'the cold boy with the warm heart'.

London did not prove a strange place for Patricia and myself. She had grown up partly in England and partly in County Cork, and knew London quite well. Her mother was a Londoner who had moved to Ireland when she married into an Anglo-Irish family and then had returned to the Home Counties after her husband's death. Patricia, interested in documentary films, wrote frequently for *Sight and Sound*, the journal of the British Film Institute. She impressed me by speaking of how she had met Alistair Cooke, a keen film buff in his early career, at a party in London, for even by that time I was one of Cooke's fans.

I too had some London friends and a great number of acquaintances. Since the age of 20 I had been contributing poems, articles and book reviews to various English magazines, among them *The New English Weekly* (to which T.S. Eliot contributed), *Horizon*, *Poetry Quarterly* and others whose names would only be known to survivors or scholars of the 1940s. Since I was always a letter-writer, missives went to and fro to contacts – writers, editors, publishers. These contacts had been made through a diligent study of what I came to think of as my literary bible, *The Writers' and Artists' Yearbook*. Apart from the addresses of editors and publishers, I had learnt from it always to keep a copy of one's manuscript and that the editor's decision was final. In the war years, letters crossing the Irish Sea to England used to be opened and then resealed by the censor with a band across the envelope indicating the censor's number. I never remember anything being scissored out.

Patricia's sister, Peggy Hutchins, demobbed from the WAAF, lived in a house in Redcliffe Gardens that could claim to be in Earl's Court or Chelsea, according to the snobbish inclinations of the tenant. There we moved, together with a goatskin rug – a wedding present from Patricia's brother Dick – into a house presided over by an eccentric, elderly Anglo-Irishwoman, Miss Kirkwood, and her two cats, Whisky and Brandy. A large house, it harboured a variety of tenants. One of them, an amiable sort of retired army captain, advised me on where I could get the best beer and Algerian wine, Finch's in the Fulham Road.

On the name plate outside the front door I saw an intriguing one: Charles Rousseau. This proved not to be a descendant of the Rousseau who had – erroneously, I think – declared that 'man is born free and is everywhere in chains' and despatched his five illegitimate children to a foundling hospital. In fact, his name was more likely Smith or Robinson. He seemed to have no fixed employment (nor had I, to be honest) but what he could do was provide Irish Sweepstake tickets at a reasonable price. Lotteries were then illegal in the UK. Patricia and I declined M. Rousseau's services.

Our rooms in Redcliffe Gardens were sparsely furnished. I, however, had furniture, stored in Birmingham with a firm called Chamberlain and Jones, which had come from my Uncle Jack's house in Edgbaston. I also had some money in the bank from the same source, a timely godsend. Patricia and I did not greatly care for the Birmingham furniture since it did not reflect our taste, but we were glad to have it until we moved into more attractive quarters. The important fact for me was that at last I was no longer visiting London, staying in hostels or boarding houses or with friends, but actually living in the great city ghosted by Dickens and Thackeray, Dr Johnson and David Garrick, where history had been made century after century, and the Labour government was replacing an old exploitative system with what one hoped would be a Brave New World, though not one on the lines of Aldous Huxley's pessimistic novel.

I walked through the streets of London with delight – the Chelsea of Carlyle and Whistler, the great print factories in Fleet Street, the Bloomsbury of Virginia Woolf, Keynes and Lytton Strachey. I got a reading ticket for the magnificent library in the British Museum, I drank pints of bitter with friends in Soho at a time when there were still gaping wounds inflicted by Hitler's bombs and doodlebugs. I enjoyed exploring what Margaret Drabble in *The Middle Ground* speaks of as 'the old and the new side by side, overlapping, jumbled, always decaying, yet always renewed'. To which she adds the rhetorical question: 'London, how could one ever be tired of it?' echoing the well-known sentiments of Dr Johnson (himself not a Londoner by origin).

While looking round for a job in such places as small ads in the *New Statesman*, I freelanced; poems of course but also book reviews and articles for wherever I could find space. *Tribune* was useful as a market. This was the left-of-centre weekly associated with the fiery Welsh orator, Aneurin Bevan, whom I admired, as opposed to the increasingly right-wing Ernest Bevin. For a time George Orwell had been literary editor of *Tribune*, so it certainly was not pro-Communist. I had contributed a few times while Orwell was there but, to my regret, never had a letter from him. The then literary editor was Bruce Bain, whom I knew fairly well and who once came, with his girlfriend, to visit Patricia and me in West Cork. Bruce made a name for himself later as Richard Findlater, drama critic and author of *The Unholy Trade*, a controversial book on the theatre. Earlier he had tried his hand as a poet but the Muse did not smile on him.

Poetry Quarterly welcomed my poems and book reviews. One day I went with Derek Stanford to Printing House Square because Derek had an introduction to the editor of *The Times Literary Supplement*, Alan Pryce-Jones, who struck me as charming but a bit precious. Pryce-Jones explained why they then observed a policy of anonymity, declaring that sometimes a vicar in an out of the way rectory would prove to be an expert on the most unlikely subject though his name might mean nothing to scholars. I merely tagged along with Derek but I it was who got books for review, mainly on Irish matters. I remember reviewing a book on Maria Edgeworth by P.H. Newby, Arland Ussher's *The Face and Mind of Ireland* and Terence de Vere White's biography of the politician Kevin O'Higgins. There were probably too many claimants for books on poetry or of poetry for Derek to have got into the sacred column of the *TLS*.

In the war years Soho's publand had been the great stamping ground for artists, writers and their assorted hangers-on. After the war, it attracted fewer of the Bohemian crowd. Even so, in the 'French' pub and other hostelries Tambimuttu, the Sinhalese editor of *Poetry London*, held court or, more exactly, he sponged on anyone willing to buy him drinks, as I found out to my cost. Julian Maclaren-Ross, author of incisive and witty short stories, made an elegant figure with his cigarette holder, supercilious air and anti-publisher sentiments. He lived extravagantly in hotels and often spent an advance long before the book was written. I was to meet him in the company of Anthony Thwaite years later when I reviewed for *The Listener*. Much to Thwaite's chagrin Maclaren-Ross was demanding instant payment for some work he had done and Thwaite had to point out that he had no control over the payment system of the BBC.

Wrey Gardiner I used to visit in his Crown Passage eyrie in Westminster when he had gone from Essex to join forces with one Captain Peter Baker, MC – my first book publisher – of the Falcon Press. The typographer Séan Jennett, who was dubbed a 'Yorkshire Irishman', had much influence on what was actually published. It was through acquaintance with him that I first heard that Faber might be interested in the anthology of contemporary Irish verse that Val Iremonger and I were compiling.

Wrey Gardiner was my first literary contact in England and I remember the man with affection. Away back in 1940 I had sent some poems to a magazine located in Devonshire whose address I found in *The Writers' and Artists' Yearbook*. Months passed and I assumed that in wartime conditions the magazine no longer existed or that the editor was in the army and I would hear nothing more. Eventually I got an acceptance from a Charles Wrey Gardiner in Billericay in Essex for a publication called *Poetry Quarterly*. I was to discover that Gardiner lived in his mother's house, named Grey Walls, and from there he had started or continued a publishing business on a small scale.

As it happened, I corresponded with someone living a short bus ride away from Billericay. This was Alex Comfort, a Cambridge medical student who was at the evacuated London Hospital. The correspondence with Alex had started when I read poems of his in the Hogarth Press anthology, *Poets of Tomorrow* (1940). These struck me as outstanding, so I wrote to the 20-year-old author at Trinity College, Cambridge. The note in the anthology told me that he was a Christian pacifist and hoped to be a medical missionary. Apparently he had already published a travel book, *The Silver River*. It seemed as if he was destined for a career of distinction but for the possible vagaries of war. That he was a pacifist appealed to me for I had been converted to that philosophy while still a schoolboy, mainly by the arguments put forward by Aldous Huxley in *Ends and Means*. It was Huxley who put a stop to my brief flirtation with Marxism and the rightness of my position was confirmed by the notorious Hitler-Stalin Pact of 1939.

Alex Comfort was a young man of tremendous mental energy. In addition to his medical studies – at which he excelled – he wrote poems, fiction, critical articles on literature and politics, and found time to correspond with and encourage his young pen-friend across the Irish Sea. Together, we persuaded Wrey into letting us compile a selection of poems by contemporaries. I managed to get over to England (the excuse being to deal with legal matters after the death of my uncle, John McCrea, in Birmingham) in 1941 while we were still gathering poems for the book. I made my way to Billericay where I met Wrey and Alex. I remember Alex sitting down at a table and writing a letter to Herbert Read asking him for an introduction. He dashed off the letter in a matter of minutes, whereas, had I done it, I would have agonised over it for days. Alex exuded the confidence of the scholarship winner who knew exactly what he was about and abhorred any waste of time. In the parlance of that era, his motto was:

'Do it now'. I asked his advice on various sexual matters that perplexed me and got direct answers and instructions to read a book by a man called, I think, Van De Velde.

Wrey Gardiner proved to be one of the most complex men I ever met and in almost every respect the opposite of Alex Comfort, who said to me early on that Wrey's trouble was that his mother had spoiled him. At the time I met him, Wrey would have been about 40. His father died when he was an infant so that he was left, an only child, in the midst of elderly relatives. Since the family was comfortably off, there was no pressure to adopt a career. He left Oxford after a few terms, then went to France after an unsuccessful marriage and remained there for some ten years. A second marriage broke up in the mid-1930s. By this time Gardiner was working at his writing. Leonard Woolf of the Hogarth Press took some interest in a manuscript but decided not to publish it. Back in England, before the war started, Wrey pursued what he hoped would turn into a literary career based on interest rather than the need to make a living.

Though keen to be recognised as a poet and prose writer, Wrey did not reveal himself as the Bohemian he undoubtedly was but had the *persona* of an English gentleman – quiet, somewhat diffident, good-mannered. Derek Stanford, who was right at the centre of literary activity in the 1940s and knew Wrey better than most of us in the *Poetry Quarterly* – Grey Walls circle says that Wrey 'was only knowable by degrees . . . first because he kept his guard up until he learnt one was not hostile, and secondly because he largely existed in a world exclusively his own'. Stanford sees him as having a naturally solipsist temperament so that even though he wrote no fewer than five autobiographies, he still remains an elusive figure. Wrey detested the mass of mankind, whom he classified as philistine, and cherished only those he considered to be the tiny creative élite. His womanising was another clue to his character. I met one of his mistresses but failed to keep track of the various women in his life and his tribe of children. Sometimes he seemed so vague that I wondered if he ever confused their names. Yet he was a man whom I would never have imagined being deliberately unkind. On a few occasions when he was supposed to meet me for lunch, he did not turn up – simply a lapse of memory with no slight intended.

Alex Comfort told Wrey that he 'must go with the young moderns' and that is precisely what he did, with *Lyra* setting the tone of the new direction. In this volume Alex and I gathered together new poets like James Kirkup, Vernon Watkins, Norman Nicholson, Clifford Dyment and G.S. Fraser. Herbert Read spoke of the poets included as being 'profoundly pacifist', despite the fact that several of them were soldiers. He himself, after all, had been a young soldier in the First World War and had written in prose two vivid accounts of trench life, *In Retreat* and *Ambush*. Poet, art critic, chronicler of war, Read was a writer who commanded our respect. Like Alex, he was committed to the philosophical anarchism of a non-violent nature. Herbert Read wrote:

> I feel that they are all pacifists in the poetic sense. They have realised that the world of poetry is a world of peace: not merely a recollection of emotion in tranquillity (which is the valid individual aspect of the problem) but even more the reconstruction of the mind on tranquil foundations.

He went on to say that an image of this attitude could be found in Alex Comfort's poem 'The Atoll in the Mind' where

> . . . a beautiful metaphor, perfectly controlled and extended, describes with poetic subtlety the essential nature of this recovery.

Indeed, this poem by Alex is a good example of the striking poetry he was writing at the age of about 21. Its concluding lines are:

> I find the image of the mind's two trees cast downward
> one tilting leaves to catch the sun's bright pennies,
> one dark as water, rooted among the bones.

I have probably only a dozen copies of *Poetry Quarterly* on my shelves, many other copies having been lost, lent or perhaps filched. They range from Spring 1942 to Summer 1951, and it is interesting to notice how the format changed from being somewhat amateurish to highly professional. That change was due to the typographer Séan Jennett, who increasingly came to influence Wrey and later to work for the two firms, Grey Walls Press and Falcon Press, when they came to share offices and staff. Séan managed to give offence to various people, including myself and Val Iremonger. He did help us to have our selection of Irish verse brought to the attention of T.S. Eliot, but vigorously disputed some of our choices and forced us into scrapping our introduction. Val was a Dubliner, I a Belfastman, and we felt we knew more about what was going on in Ireland than a man who had never lived there, despite his Irish parentage. Séan overrode decisions made by Wrey in the case of Derek Stanford and Derek's friend John Bayliss. John's novel *Chiswick House*, set in the 18th century, was accepted by Wrey and apparently the poet Nicholas Moore (then widely known but now almost forgotten) praised its 'peculiar dreamlike quality'. John went off with the RAF to India but when he returned in 1946 he found that Jennett had vetoed it. Derek Stanford's *Freedom of Poetry*, an analysis of the work of David Gascoyne, Sidney Keyes, Alex Comfort and others, a pioneer series of essays, was mauled in manuscript by the same grey eminence.

To some extent I have anticipated. By the time Jennett came on the scene, the Grey Walls Press had moved to London. Nicholas Moore and Wrey formed a kind of partnership, sharing profits and expenses. They found offices in Vernon Place in Bloomsbury. It was from here that Alex Comfort and John Bayliss edited a hardback volume entitled *New Road*, the first of a series. Kathleen Raine wrote an article in it with the menacing title: 'Are Poets Doing Their Duty?' She thought that:

> . . . the poets of the last generation – Auden, MacNeice, Empson, Michael Roberts, Day-Lewis, Robert Graves, have one great merit that the younger poets on the whole lack. That is, an adult and responsible attitude towards society.

I hope we took those words to heart! A surrealist section was edited by Toni del Renzio which interested me since, like most of my contemporaries, I knew little of the impact of surrealism in the non-anglophone world. Derek Stanford, I see, mentioned me in his essay, *The New Landscape*, though at that time we had not met. He wrote:

> Examining the word-structure of such poets as Nicholas Moore, Robert Greacen and Alex Comfort, we find that their speech has a kind of cellular growth about it, in direct antithesis to the

formulated measure and advance of classical prosody, and different
from the loose colloquial speech of the Auden, Spender and Day-
Lewis of the '30s.

In London Wrey added to his contacts, as he could not easily have
done in a small town in Essex. Nicholas Moore seemed gradually to fade
out so far as partnership was concerned. In came a new and very
different personality. Peter Baker, a rather brash young man, had a
distinguished record in the war, having won the MC. He was as thrusting
as Alex Comfort as a person but I should guess he possessed only average
intelligence. He had money to invest but probably not as much as people
thought. He had persuasive powers and, I think, ambit:on that far
outstripped his ability. Anyway, Peter Baker and Wrey joined forces.
Their premises were in Crown Passage, off Pall Mall. Peter Baker's drive
seemed to ensure that if the books were of high quality both in literary
and production terms, these two publishing firms would prosper and
eventually take their place with publishers such as Faber and Faber,
Jonathan Cape, Chatto and Windus, and the Hogarth Press.

Before the publication of my second collection, *The Undying Day*, by
the Falcon Press, Peter Baker took me out to lunch at Prunier's, the
famous French fish restaurant. Very different from most of the poets,
critics and publishers I had met, Peter struck me as uncouth but good-
natured. I recall to this day the ostentatious way in which he pulled out
his wallet crammed with fivers (and a fiver in 1948 could really buy
things) to pay the bill. Unlike Wrey Gardiner, he was clearly not a
gentleman. On the other hand, I should have been glad of his company
had I been walking through a dark alley in the East End.

Peter Baker had big ideas. He went into politics and became Tory
MP for Norfolk South. He wrote about his vision of Conservatism in
a book called *Confession of Faith,* though I wonder if any of his authors
would have liked to be dubbed Tories. He published books with more
zest than discrimination, bringing into his board of directors money
men and industrialists. Peter diversified. We young writers were
astonished to hear that he dabbled in aeroplane parts and, more
excitingly, in whisky blending. I think Peter was not unwilling to have
the occasional dram.

When in 1950 Peter Baker became the youngest member of the
House of Commons, it looked as if the sky was the limit. I think Peter

succumbed to *folie de grandeur* or what the ancient Greeks called *hubris*. He could see no end to his expansion of interests until he became the tycoon of his dreams. The dreamy, impractical, anti-Philistine Wrey Gardiner no doubt felt everything was in order. After all, he knew nothing of business and never in his life had had 'a proper job'. I remember how he said to me jokingly: 'I am a Gardiner who doesn't garden and Peter is a Baker who doesn't bake.' He was publishing, in the Grey Walls imprint, Henry Miller and F. Scott Fitzgerald (then just being rediscovered), Raymond Radiguet, Ramón J. Sender, and selections from the classics as far back as Edmund Spenser, with prefaces mainly by notable poets and critics. There seemed little to worry about except the women in his life and the children he had fathered.

But the poetry scene was changing. New Romanticism had run its course. The Movement poets and critics of the 1950s were declaring that the 1940s had been a notoriously bad decade for poetry. Sales of *Poetry Quarterly*, which had so bravely flown the flag for poetry throughout the war years, were falling off. In 1953 *Poetry Quarterly* came to an end with its 55th issue.

Back from a holiday in North Africa in 1954 – he had crossed the Sahara in a bus, he told me – Wrey got bad news from his bank manager. The Falcon Press was in deep trouble. In Crown Passage he discovered that he was the only director who had not resigned and that the 17 companies that formed the organisation were over half a million pounds in debt. What had happened was that Peter Baker had forged signatures giving the impression that funds of £100,000 were available.

The media publicised Peter's trial, thanks to his war record and his being a Tory MP. He pleaded guilty and was given an unduly severe sentence of seven years' imprisonment. Theoretically Wrey might possibly have levered Grey Walls Press out from the octopus Peter had created, but it was not practicable. The whole publishing empire had to be wound up. I felt angry when a bookseller said to me that he was sure Wrey had been implicated in the shenanigans. I was certain that he was too innocent – or simply too unbusinesslike – to have known anything about it.

When he sold the house in Billericay, Wrey bought property in London and turned himself into a landlord. An autobiography appeared in which he wrote of this unsuccessful venture. Though to an extent fictional, friends of Wrey's such as Derek Stanford and Muriel Spark can be discerned in its pages. The title was hardly one that would cause a stampede to the bookshops – *The Answer to Life is No*. His fourth wife was the widow of Julian Maclaren-Ross, so that relationship kept memories of Fitzrovia green. He was deeply upset when she died.

I tended to lose touch with Wrey in his last years. He drank heavily and I had enough problems of my own by then. Because I lived near Notting Hill Gate I sometimes saw him going into the 'Hoop', more likely than not to meet his great comrade-in-arms John Gawsworth, two sad, lonely poets who felt that due recognition had not come to them. I now feel slightly guilty that I did not see more of Wrey in his declining years. He was a man whom I very much liked and to whom I owed a great deal. I would like to think that a few of his poems or some passages from his prose will live and that he will be rediscovered one day. He died in 1981 but a year earlier, on his 80th birthday, the Enitharmon Press printed six Gardiner poems in an edition of 100, with a charming frontispiece drawing of him by Nina Hamnett.

Many years after Charles Wrey Gardiner's death, Derek Stanford was visited, as it were, by Wrey in a dream. He has written a poem in memory of a man who for us is unforgettable:

Old friend, most dear, what do you ask of me?
Dreams have, we know, their own economy
entire unto themselves; but you were there

behind a coffee-stall with some young Mimi,
sharing with her a new anthology
without a penny and without a care.

You seemed content in Pluto's company;
said it was warm behind the coffee-stall
but, yes, you'd have a sandwich and some tea.

There, on the London pavement, at your ease,
you reassured me everything was well.
'I am,' you said, 'a heavenly pensioner.'

Old friend, old patron, my first publisher,
had you some purpose in contacting me?

My first collection of poems, published in 1944, is dedicated to 'K.D.'
— that is to say Kay Dick. A poem written in Dublin begins:

> I send you greetings, Kay, now in this exiled time
> From this careless Augustan city of grace and slums
> Where in Merrion Square the whispers of death
> Gauze over the rhododendrons and the parched grass.
> I greet you from a neutral country in a neutral hour . . .

When I first came across Kay, later to be a distinguished novelist, she
was manager of a Staples' bookshop and hoping to publish a number of
young poets in a series to be called the Westminster Poets. This never
happened but in my case her friend, the literary agent Kathleen Farrell,
got a contract for me from Resurgam Books, later to become the
Falcon Press.

Wrey Gardiner described Kay just as I found her:

> Kay is tall and wears a shirt open at the neck like a man in
> summer. She bends forward slightly towards you as if she would
> dominate you with her blue eyes like the small flowers you find
> on the very cold heights of mountains, but which soften in certain
> eerie lights. Her beloved period is the Nineties and she lives on
> her nerves and books.

Kathleen, he said, ran about their elegant Belsize Park flat like 'a nice
homely squirrel intent on the efficient harvesting of the moment'.

Kay seemed to me, a young provincial, an exquisite *grande dame* of
letters in the Virginia Woolf mould. I stayed in their finely appointed
flat on a visit to London and could not quite believe that outside their
oasis a beastly total war was in progress. Not least I found another
member of their household fascinating in his supercilious and
aristocratic way. That was Hamlet, their dachshund, with his sad
Elsinore eyes. Kay wrote letters to me in Belfast and Dublin, always in
green ink and full of encouragement and delightful London literary
gossip about writers known and unknown, among them their friends
William Sansom and Daniel George.

Another person who put me up for a few days (on the floor, under
a leaky roof, not quite up to the standard in Kay and Kathleen's flat)

was Reginald Moore, editor of *Modern Reading*, the most popular of the wartime magazines and one to be found on every railway station bookstall. At one time it was reported to have reached the phenomenal circulation for a journal of that kind of 100,000. Reginald had a particular interest in the short story and published many of its leading exponents: Frank O'Connor, Fred Urquhart, William Saroyan, Graham Greene, V.S. Pritchett, H.E. Bates. He told me he had written a novel which appeared just as the war started and that the war had won.

Reginald once inveigled me into playing a sort of cricket in the alley at the back of his flat. *He* won. A keen sportsman, after the war he was involved in sports publishing with John Arlott. (Arlott, by the way, in his time had written and published poems, but then cricket and poetry can co-exist, as in the case of Alan Ross and Edmund Blunden.) Moore and Arlott founded the Sportsman Book Club. When I stayed with Reginald, his wife Elizabeth Berridge was busy writing short stories. Later she developed into a novelist and book reviewer for *The Daily Telegraph*.

I had come across Reginald – a great encourager of young writers – through Maurice Fridberg, a Dublin-born Jew, then running a bookshop in London. He returned to his native Dublin after the war, starting up in publishing. One of the books he brought out was a translation from the Irish of Merriman's *The Midnight Court* by Frank O'Connor. In my copy I find this inscription: 'For Robert – my first publishing effort – with every good wish. Sincerely, Maurice. 1.11.45.' The beautifully produced little book – a minor classic of the middle 18th century – must today be a rare collector's piece. Maurice has gone and it is for me a reminder of a gentle, kindly man.

Maurice Fridberg engaged in various business ventures for he was by nature an entrepreneur and brimmed with ideas. He once said to my wife: 'Robert is a great little businessman.' I could not decide whether he was paying me a compliment or merely indulging in irony. He was the financial backer for *Irish Harvest*, an anthology of stories, poems and essays, edited by me, and published under the imprint of New Frontiers Press. Maurice wrote short stories, he took photos, he gave money to charities, Jewish and non-Jewish, he emigrated to Israel but finding life there not to his liking came back to Dublin. An enthusiastic man, he tried his hand at all kinds of commercial ventures that prospered for a time and then folded. I think that what he most wanted was to win recognition as a short story writer. I wonder now if, when he called me a great little businessman, he was not perhaps thinking of himself.

Soon after coming to London, I made an appointment to meet, at her offices in a lovely Georgian house in Portman Square, the young woman who edited the *Poetry Review* for the Poetry Society. This organisation was founded in 1909 for the promotion of poetry and the art of speaking verse, and was sponsored by eminent figures in the literary world such as the classicist and translator Gilbert Murray, Robert Graves's father A.P. Graves, Edmund Gosse and Arnold Bennett. Over the years most notable British and Irish poets had been contributors of poems, book reviews and articles. The problem was that from time to time the Society and its journal fell into the hands of an obscurantist clique. Then a revolt of Young Turks had to be mounted which might or might not succeed.

Of this young woman I was to meet I had heard much in her praise. I heard how she had championed the younger poets and was fighting our cause against the opposition of the elderly deadweights on the committee who controlled the Society. She had encountered quite vicious opposition, perhaps all the more so for being such an attractive woman. Her charm, intelligence and spirit had won over everyone to whom I spoke. The reader may have guessed the name – Muriel Spark. When we met, she already knew something about me for she had accepted poems of mine for the journal. I was impressed but not surprised by Muriel's good looks, smart appearance, poise and frankness.

It was generally known that she had a close relationship with a man called Howard Sergeant, an accountant from Lancashire who wrote poems and ran a 'little mag', *Outposts*. Howard I found agreeable enough, though I felt his talent was minimal. Apart from his undoubted expertise as an accountant, I did not take his literary ambitions all that seriously. Years later he became a great anthologiser and poetry publisher. Muriel has made some acerbic remarks about Howard and others in her autobiography, *Curriculum Vitae*, though she admits that Howard 'danced so beautifully' and was 'fairly manly' – though that 'fairly' is rather faint praise. She found him 'an extremely jealous man' and 'rather too interfering'. Above all, she found a fault in him that I had discovered at an early stage and that was his 'deficient sense of humour'. For that lack alone, she tells us that she would not have married him.

Curriculum Vitae details the intrigues that went on behind the closed doors (and outside them) of that elegant Georgian house devoted to the Muse. Jealousy, hatred, faction-fighting and what used to be called bitchiness – no longer so frequently used because of political correctness – are not unknown in the literary world. These negative factors do exist, as in all professions, but it is also fair to say that kindness and generosity are by no means absent. It may simply be that writers express their feelings, negative and positive, with greater passion than the usual run of humanity. I remember Muriel once saying that her best friends and worst enemies were writers. She had a point.

One day, when having a stroll with Derek Stanford in Kensington Gardens, he expressed to me a tentative interest in Muriel. By that time she had put what she terms the 'madness and frenzy' of the Poetry Society behind her, as well as her relationship with Howard Sergeant. Now Muriel tells us she is a great preserver of documents – correspondence of all kinds, appointment books, cheque-books, everything that comes one's way. A partial exception to that rule is apparently the letters Derek wrote to her in the 1950s and yet over 500 such letters survive. Muriel says they add up to 'a social history'. I am not surprised since I know and admire Derek's devotion to letter-writing.

It is not my purpose here to unravel or attempt to unravel the strands that went to make up the relationship that existed for some years between Muriel and Derek. That is their business, not mine or anyone else's. I can only bear witness to what I saw and heard as an outsider. Indeed, their subsequent parting surprised Patricia and me, and the bitterness that ensured saddened both of us. We had both imagined that Derek and Muriel were an ideal couple and I often wondered what kind of wedding present we should give them. Derek's scholarly interests in literature and religion combined with Muriel's wit and intelligence made them highly welcome visitors to our flat.

Towards the end of 1951 Muriel and Derek came round to see us. Her news was that she had written her first short story, 'The Seraph and the Zambesi', based on her experiences in Africa as a young married woman, and had entered it for *The Observer* Short Story Competition. Hitherto her literary work consisted of poems so far as creativity was concerned. We thought little more about the matter. She even told us how she had scrounged typing paper from an art shop in

South Kensington, just beside the arcade. Stories had to be submitted under a pseudonym and hers was 'Aquarius'. Shortly before Christmas 1951 I opened *The Observer* to see who had won the first prize. Muriel's name came first out of an entry of 6,700. Patricia and I were thrilled.

Winning even such a prestigious competition and becoming known internationally as a fiction writer do not always happen to the same writer. Thinking of Muriel as a poet and critic, I did not realise that she had the potential for the creation of character, dialogue, atmosphere. Nor was her ascent to a high rung on the literary ladder all that easy. Later she had a serious breakdown somewhat similar to that of Evelyn Waugh. (Muriel was to follow Waugh in deciding to convert to the Roman Catholic Church. Her maiden name, Camberg, indicated her Jewish father, and with an English mother she was hardly a typical daughter of Edinburgh.) Derek helped her enormously during the period of breakdown and this she acknowledges. He sought out financial assistance for her treatment from Evelyn Waugh and Graham Greene. At the time I thought that Derek's support would cement their relationship.

I also recall Patricia taking food round to Muriel when she was living in Vicarage Gate in a rooming house named Eras House. She was only a short distance from St Mary Abbots Church and its churchyard where there were still Victorian graves to be seen. There was a little garden tucked away, an oasis of quiet right behind noisy Kensington High Street with its large department stores. Muriel and Derek, in the best romantic tradition, were great frequenters of this and other graveyards. Muriel tells how on fine days when she was not working she used to go there to write poems and eat sandwiches.

I owed a lot to Muriel and Derek, not only for their stimulating company. They introduced me to Erica Marx of the Hand and Flower Press who was looking for someone to write an appreciative study of Noël Coward. This I did. The book, *The Art of Noël Coward*, was beautifully produced and illustrated. It got well reviewed and made me more money than any other book. Muriel got me a job, short-lived though it was, with the publisher Peter Owen in Old Brompton Road. Peter, a frugal man, used to boil an egg in the office for lunch while I went out to a restaurant in South Kensington. But my stint with Peter Owen gave me some insight into small-scale book publishing. I contributed an essay on Wordsworth's politics to *Tribute to Wordsworth*, a symposium on Wordsworth by several hands to mark the centenary in 1950 of the poet's death. I also wrote a piece about my maternal grandmother for a magazine, *Forum*, that Muriel edited but which folded after two or three issues.

Some time after the break with Derek, Muriel came round unexpectedly bearing a bottle of expensive wine (she was always generous when in the money). She was recovering well from her illness and had made a lot of new friends, some of them influential and among them David Astor and Philip Toynbee. For a literary aspirant, these were the sort of people worth getting to know. After a long chat and a glass of her French wine I said I would see Muriel off and find a taxi for her in Kensington High Street. As we waited for a taxi, she took a piece of paper out of her handbag and wrote something on it. As the taxi drew up she handed it to me and said: 'Robert, give me a ring sometime. I'd like to introduce you to some of my friends.' I kissed her on the cheek and she was off. I never phoned her, since I felt that keeping in touch with her would be disloyal to Derek. Nor have I ever seen her since that day.

Muriel Spark began her literary career as a poet and rightly thinks of herself as a poet. The satire, the verbal economy, the comic element, the eye for social nuances, above all the fantasy and even the occasional nod to perversity and necromancy are so intertwined as to form a poetic 'vision of reality', to use Yeats's phrase. Her characters are many and varied, eccentric and *farouche*, but of them all there is surely one destined to live. That character was plucked from Muriel's memories of her schooldays at James Gillespie's High School for Girls which, in Muriel's own words, is 'to this day one of Edinburgh's best-known schools'. Her 12 years there were well spent if only because they brought her into touch with Miss Kay, the prototype of her character Miss Jean Brodie.

The formative period in my creative writing life was the 1940s, the first half of which saw the most terrible war in human history with its disruption of life, its mass carnage and organised brutality, its movement of populations – against all of which we poets beat our wings in vain. With the war over our life-affirming structure of neo-romanticism began to crumble. New poets arrived on the scene styling themselves 'the Movement', a term coined by J.D. Scott, literary editor of *The Spectator*. Poets like Kingsley Amis and his close friend

Philip Larkin, D.J. Enright and Elizabeth Jennings were included in anthologies that signalled an about-turn, an anti-romantic and rational view of life my colleagues and I could not accept. Robert Conquest spoke of their 'negative determination to avoid bad principles'. By the end of the 1950s the Movement itself came to an end, as do all movements, whether with an initial capital 'M' or not.

As a poet I seemed to have fallen into a vacuum. I reckoned that the Muse, like the lovely wanton she is, had forsaken me. However, two decades later she came back. Captain Fox — about whom more later on — came to my rescue. Unlike her, Captain Fox never deserted me. Yet even without my early love, Irene, or the consoling embrace of the Muse, I had acquired a foothold in London and there I intended to stay.

NINETEEN

The Retreat from Moscow

W.H. Auden spoke of the 1930s as 'a low dishonest decade'. Towards the end of the 1930s I, as a schoolboy, came under the influence of a master (not at my own school) who was a convinced Marxist and, for all I know, a card-carrying member of the Communist Party. He talked of how widespread the Communist faith was in England and especially at Cambridge which, we learnt years later, nurtured a group of upper-class traitors. My teacher friend took me to see Clifford Odets's play *Waiting for Lefty*, and Soviet films like *The Battleship Potemkin*. The Spanish Civil War raged and I thought vaguely of running off to fight for the Republic but common sense prevailed.

All this was heady stuff for a boy of rebellious temperament and sympathy for the underdog. The events in Russia in 1917 were tailor-made for me, as those in France were for the young Wordsworth, who believed that it was bliss to be alive in such stirring times and that 'to be young was very heaven'. Unhappy at home, I turned my thoughts outward in the last years of the 1930s from provincial, sectarian Belfast where the political scene was characterised by the centuries-old clash between the Orange/Unionist and Green/Nationalist/Republican tribes.

While still at school, I had published an article in the *Irish Democrat* on the shortcomings of grammar school education as well as poems about the Spanish Civil War, quite oblivious of the fact that creative work needs to be grounded in lived experience. Someone put me on to the *Sunday Worker* in New York. I sent them reports of politics in Ireland which they published and I got books in return for my efforts. Like others I came to know, I thought of Stalin as an avuncular old fellow who worked ceaselessly for the well-being of the Soviet Union.

But the honeymoon with Marxism and the USSR was to end somewhat abruptly. I found that I could neither excuse nor condone the Nazi-Soviet Pact of 1939. How could we come to an agreement with our avowed enemies? How could the massacre of Guernica be so quickly forgotten? My schoolmaster friend tried to show me how naïve I was and to give me some conception of *Realpolitik*. All in vain, for my doubts about the validity of Communism had been growing thanks to the works of Aldous Huxley and Eugene Lyons's *Assignment in Utopia*. Huxley's *Ends and Means* – an enquiry into the nature of ideals and into the methods employed for their realisation – opened my eyes to new and startling realities. In brief, Huxley maintained that means determine ends. I still believe that is true.

In 1941, after Hitler invaded Russia, so tearing up his pact with Stalin, I wrote a long poem, partly lyrical, partly satirical, published in the Belfast University magazine. It contained the couplet:

Red star and swastika are fellows
That turn all whites to greasy yellows

The magazine was normally stocked in the local Communist-run bookshop and copies of that issue were duly delivered there. Some time later a student called at the bookshop to see how many copies had been sold. A stony-faced assistant in the shop handed the young man a bundle and declared: 'We don't peddle anti-Soviet propaganda.' I did not, however, turn, in disillusion with Communism, to some form of right-wing reaction but, still believing that constitutional Socialism would lead to a just society, placed my faith in a Fabian approach, on the lines approved by Bernard Shaw and the Webbs.

That was my political background in Belfast. Forward now to my early days in London. An advertisement in the personal small ads column of the *New Statesman* caught my eye. An editorial assistant was required by a non-party political body. I applied, stating my somewhat meagre qualifications. A reply came from one Andrew Boyd, editor with the United Nations Association, then in Maiden Lane behind the Strand and within sniffing distance of Covent Garden's fruit and vegetable market and Opera House.

Boyd, a Wykehamist, turned out to be a fair-haired, spectacled young man slightly older than myself. After army service he had been in book publishing. On our first meeting we adjourned from his office room to the pub a door or two away. I explained in more detail what I had to offer. After a couple of pints of bitter, he said that as far as he was concerned I could have the job, but I would have to appear before a committee. As preparation for this ordeal he gave me a sheaf of pamphlets, brochures and circulars published by the United Nations Association, outlining and publicising the activities of the United Nations and its various Agencies. (UNA was the successor of the League of Nations Union.) The interview proved fairly painless. One man asked if I was a good mixer. Naturally I said yes. Another asked me to say which I thought was the most important of the UN Agencies. I plumped for UNESCO and gave reasons which I hope he found convincing. I realised that perhaps the answer some would have given might have been the Security Council.

I took my dear little Remington portable – bought for a five pound note in Belfast in 1940 – into our editorial room. Andrew and I produced an illustrated bi-monthly magazine, booklets and leaflets. We sent out press releases and formed an excellent working relationship. Sometimes we went out to lunch together, our favourite eating place being Fortes in the Strand. Neither of us talked about our background or personal matters, only of books and politics. We visited each other in our homes a few times.

I realised with dismay that Andrew was on the look-out for a more interesting job and one with better prospects. I was unwilling to see him go elsewhere. Eventually he left for the BBC monitoring service in Caversham where his knowledge of Russian no doubt was useful. After the BBC he went on to *The Economist* where he stayed until his retirement.

The only UNA publication I can find on my shelves is a pamphlet called *World Front: 1950*, the authors being given as Andrew and myself, though my memory is that Andrew wrote most of it. The subtitle is: *A Survey of the United Nations at Work*. We mentioned that our national headquarters at 11 Maiden Lane would, during 1950, be moving to 29 Queen Anne Street in Mayfair. In *World Front* we surveyed UN work in Indonesia, Kashmir, Palestine, Greece, Berlin ('The Blockade that Boomeranged'), Korea, the Italian Colonies – and that's only half of it!

'The Association', we said with pride, either real or assumed:

> works ceaselessly to present the real facts about UN and world
> problems to the British people, through local meetings in every
> part of the kingdom, film shows, discussion groups and publications
> (over 1,300,000 books, pamphlets, leaflets and posters were issued
> in 1949.

I note that our illustrated magazine, *United Nations News*, published every two months, sold for sixpence.

Since he left UNA, I have met Andrew Boyd on a couple of occasions. I remember a lunch we had when he was at *The Economist*. I had wanted to meet him to ask his advice about teaming up with people who ran a magazine called *Eastern World*. There would have been some financial involvement and I could not decide whether I was more in demand for my expertise or for what paltry amount I could add to their funds. I held on to my rapidly diminishing savings. Then in 1995, at an *Irish Times* dinner held at the elegant Royal Dublin Society, I was seated next to the distinguished writer Ruth Dudley Edwards. In the course of conversation it emerged that she knew Andrew well, partly because of his help when she was writing a history of *The Economist*. A small world indeed.

Through Ruth as a go-between, I have received a witty and friendly letter from Andrew telling me of the death of his cat and a projected trip to the West Country. Nor has he forgotten that narrow street off the Strand. When I am in London, Andrew has promised me a lunch in Maiden Lane at Rules restaurant, a more elegant place than Fortes in the Strand.

Andrew's temporary successor was UNA's Information Officer Leslie R. Aldous, a keen member of the NUJ. A man with a sense of humour, he had an encyclopaedic knowledge of the United Nations in all its aspects. Our committee did not think him suitable as editor. I did not apply for the job because I felt too inexperienced. In recent years I have seen photos of George Orwell's NUJ card, signed by none other than Leslie R. Aldous, father of the chapel branch to which Orwell, Andrew and I belonged.

There was a surprising number of applicants for Andrew's post. While they waited to be interviewed, several of them sat in the editorial room and it was interesting to try to size up the various would-be editors. The committee decided to appoint a man called Stephen W. Pollak. Originally from the then Czechoslovakia, this man had been a member of the Communist Party. He had taken part and been injured in the Spanish Civil War, so that he limped and carried a walking stick. Interned in India during the 1939–45 war, he returned to Czechoslovakia and there met and married an Ulster woman. He broke with the Communists, got to England and wrote an apologia entitled *Strange Land Behind Me*.

Pollak and I did not get on particularly well, partly because of the difference in our backgrounds. He used UNA facilities to further a business venture and I felt this was wrong. (I must confess, however, that I did write the odd personal letter in office time on UNA headed paper.) We moved to Mayfair, a very different and, for me, a less congenial ambience than Covent Garden. Costs of paper and materials rocketed. There were cutbacks and what is now called downsizing. I was made redundant in the early 1950s. As it happened, I never found another job on a magazine. Twenty-four October ceased to be of any real importance for me as United Nations Day. Once again I simply thought of it as – my birthday. By this time I had almost wholly retreated from Moscow, though I did not yet understand the extent of Stalin's criminality which had been responsible for the death of millions and untold human suffering. I should have listened more carefully to the voice of George Orwell.

TWENTY

Peace in Our Time?

I remember vividly the reports of Neville Chamberlain's return from Munich in 1938 after meeting Adolf Hitler. He declared that there would be peace in our time and quoted from Shakespeare – 'Out of this nettle, danger/I pluck the flower, safety'. Left-wingers attacked Chamberlain for not standing up to the German dictator, but there were many who felt relieved that we had at least a respite from the conflict that increasingly seemed inevitable.

It is difficult now to recall the tension that occurred just over a decade later. The war against the Nazis had been 'won' and with the assistance of the Soviet Union, and yet the new threat was that Western Europe might be overrun by Stalin's hordes. Patricia and I were so conscious of this threat that we decided not to buy a house but simply to rent a flat so that when the new war came we could make for Patricia's childhood home in County Cork in neutral Ireland.

Among my letters I have one written in Paris, and dated 2 October 1951, which begins: 'Cher Monsieur Greacen, Je doute fort de pouvoir me trouver à Londres pour la conférence que vous organisez.' The writer goes on to say that he would have been glad to have met Monsieur Alex Comfort since he had great intellectual sympathy with him. For personal reasons he must stay in Paris in October and November. He expresses his solidarity with us, says he is no longer an academician and sends his best wishes. In a PS he tells me that he of course signs the appeal. The signature is that of Albert Camus who, in 1957, won the Nobel Prize for Literature.

The appeal which the famous French writer was willing to endorse was known as the Authors' World Peace Appeal (AWPA). In 1950 I read a short letter in *The Manchester Guardian* from A.E. Coppard, a man with a considerable reputation as a short story writer but who had been more widely esteemed in the 1920s and 1930s. Coppard pointed out the danger that existed of war between Britain and the Soviet Union, and appealed to all writers who felt that such a war would be disastrous, to write to him, on a postcard, in Essex. I knew little about Coppard but I had read a few of his stories in anthologies and remembered having read one called 'The Higgler'. Coppard acknowledged my postcard and said a group was being formed and information about it would be sent to me.

At the time I was working with the United Nations Association and my work brought me into close contact with what was happening in the political world in Britain and overseas. I voted Labour, though I may say that in my entire lifetime I have never voted for a successful candidate either in England or Ireland. Certainly, I was strongly in favour of any action that would help prevent another war. The bomb sites that still existed in London reminded one daily of what war meant and in addition there was the spectre of the atom bomb which had devastated two Japanese cities. Andrew Boyd was more cautious in his reaction to the Coppard letter. I shuddered when I thought of Dresden and Coventry, Hiroshima and Nagasaki, and the 20 million deaths suffered by the Soviet Union. War was unthinkable. As Einstein said, it might put us back in the Stone Age.

I got an invitation to a meeting in a flat in Kensington. There I met a number of fellow writers who had answered Coppard's appeal. A new movement came into being on that evening, the word 'appeal' being part of its name. The person most in evidence at the Kensington gathering was John St John, a pleasantly mannered, smiling young man who worked for a publishing house called the Naldrett Press. John radiated charm and bonhomie. His friendliness was infectious. Someone told me that John had been at Wellington where, like many public schoolboys in the 1930s, he had turned Communist. At that inaugural meeting in Kensington, I overheard a snatch of conversation. 'What would your attitude be if war did come?' someone asked St John. 'Revolutionary defeatism, of course,' he answered briskly.

A.E. Coppard, a late-middle-aged, gypsyish looking man, could have been the perfect model of the pre-war writer-in-a-cottage who had evidently prospered. I did not know until years later that Coppard, born in London, had come from a miserably poor family and had worked in a variety of jobs before becoming a full-time writer, the money prizes won through his skill as an athlete had supplemented his literary earnings. The stories show his sympathy with odd men out, casualties of the social system. At committee meetings when AWPA had become established and where we discussed the possibility of a delegation of writers visiting Russia, Coppard used to insist that what he wanted most to see was the Moscow football team, the Dynamos, playing a match. He gave the impression of being healthy and of having led an outdoor life. Nor did I guess at any time that he had not had a fairly conventional education.

Among those present at the Kensington meeting was Alex Comfort, medical doctor as well as prolific writer, and then working on research into senescence at University College, London, for the Medical Research Council. He it was who had crossed swords, as pacifist and philosophic anarchist, with George Orwell during the war. Alex was given to verbal aggression, while his grasp of a wide variety of unrelated subjects usually unnerved his opponents. Not that he ever held grudges or indulged in malice. He specialised in straightforward intellectual combat that compelled admiration even from those who did not agree with him. I felt that he had in this respect a resemblance to that intellectual fighter from Dublin, G. Bernard Shaw, with a dash of H.G. Wells thrown in. Alex used to define himself as 'a biologist' and his philosophical stance as 'scientific humanism'.

It may have been Alex who suggested me as a committee member. Meetings were held in the offices of a publisher, Malcolm Kirk, in the Old Brompton Road near the Zetland pub. Among those on the committee were the Australian Jack Lindsay (friend of Edith Sitwell), the playwright and Scot Roger McDougall, Anthony Thorne (novelist), the redoubtable Naomi Mitchison (sister of the scientist J.B.S. Haldane), Montagu Slater, known for having written the libretto for Benjamin Britten's *Peter Grimes*, a writer of educational textbooks called Ronald Rideout, John St John, Ronald Mason (author of a novel, *The Wind Cannot Read*) and Pearl Binder, wife of a Labour MP, Elwyn Jones. All of us had books to our credit. While I remained a member of AWPA, the composition of the committee changed slightly from time to time but most of those I have mentioned remained active.

After a time I was persuaded to join John St John as joint secretary of AWPA which meant that our affairs, under the general guidance of the committee, were conducted by a Communist and a non-Communist. I came to have a considerable affection for Johnny, valuing his good humour, integrity and willingness to sacrifice his leisure time. Unfortunately I could not share his views on the rightness of Soviet policy. Later, at the time of the Soviet invasion of Hungary, Johnny resigned from his Communist Party membership, like thousands of others whose dream had been shattered by Soviet intransigence and brutality.

AWPA put out a bulletin outlining our aims and activities. Several sub-committees were set up. One of them did research into the violence and xenophobia to be found in some 'comics' and books for children. We organised discussions and readings from their work by members. One of these was given by Compton Mackenzie at the Institute of Contemporary Arts, founded largely by Herbert Read. We were kept busy preparing for the conference to which Albert Camus referred in his letter. The conference was well attended and Paul Eluard, the French poet, came to it. Support among writers continued. We were proud to announce that our aims were being endorsed by Dylan Thomas, C. Day-Lewis, Christopher Fry and Edith Sitwell. The press in general, particularly *The Daily Telegraph*, took a jaundiced view of what we were up to. To them we were a bunch of Reds, a Communist-front organisation similar to the British Peace Committee, though we kept pointing out that only a minority of committee members were Communists. John Cousins even called himself a Conservative, and others were strictly non-party political.

There was an interesting case of witch-hunting across the Atlantic involving Aldous Huxley. I am indebted for the facts to David King Dunaway's *Huxley in Hollywood* (1989):

> By the fall of 1952, the only film project Huxley had left were short sketches he hoped to adapt for his compatriots Vivien Leigh and Laurence Olivier.
>
> One reason for his dearth of work is found in the 7 November headline of COUNTERATTACK: FACTS TO COMBAT COMMUNISM – LEADING AUTHORS STILL BELIEVE IN 'PEACEFUL COEXISTENCE' HOAX. Huxley's name appeared first on the list.
>
> Huxley's trouble had started when, at the request of old friend

Naomi Mitchison, he had signed this statement: 'We believe that differing political and economic systems can exist side by side on the basis of peacefully negotiated settlements . . . We condemn writing liable to sharpen existing dangers and hatreds.' Co-signers included C.E.M. Joad, Edith Sitwell, Christopher Fry, André Maurois and Albert Camus.

'These deluded authors have helped Stalin,' the professional anti-Communists yelped. To an industry which saw nothing undemocratic about John Wayne's monthly expense account of $13,000, talk of internationalism sounded red: this was definitely graylist material. Despite COUNTERATTACK's note that the statement's sponsor, the Authors' World Peace Appeal, was an 'assertedly non-Communist group of 750 famous writers', a small, neat check was added to Huxley's growing file, alongside another petition he had signed on behalf of Friends of International Freedom.

Entries in an old diary have reminded me of certain AWPA events. On 18 June 1952, I took the chair at a meeting held at Pearl Binder's when the theme was 'The Writer's Responsibility', the speakers being Naomi Mitchison and C. Day-Lewis. Naomi said we lived in a house 'with the drains up and smelling' and she spoke of the greater power of the writer in a small community such as her own in Argyllshire where she was a county councillor. She did not think too highly of AWPA sub-committees or panels since she considered they took writers away from their real job which was writing. Day-Lewis referred back to the social and political commitment writers had in the 1930s and how it all seemed to have been in vain, yet we had to do something about the situation. Communists and pacifists, he felt, needed to find common ground. He asked AWPA members to work one day a week or even one week a year for AWPA. At the end of the meeting I remember Naomi speaking of how she did much of her writing in buses and trains, especially on the Circle Line on the London Underground. She also said she liked the 'privilege' of being rude to journalists. Day-Lewis said to me in a whisper: 'Dangerous.'

Another diary entry deals with a meeting on 27 June 1952 at Naomi's flat in King's Bench Walk on the eve of departure to Russia of an AWPA delegation. A press conference was scheduled for 17 July and a meeting in that evening to report back to our members. Naomi said she would keep a diary for general reference, and that she would take a typewriter for the use of all. At an earlier gathering she said she would bring some Penguin paperbacks for the Russian hosts, as well as books she thought suitable for translation into Russian.

Alex Comfort brought up the question of the magazine *News* which he maintained did not always create good feeling. He suggested that the party from London should see the editor of *News* and *New Times*. How orthodox did writers in Russian have to be? Who decides whether a manuscript should be published? Naomi and her fellow Scot Douglas Young thought they should call on the British Embassy in Moscow. This idea was opposed by Coppard and Edmund Penning-Rowsell. St John, in shirt-sleeves and wearing braces – for it was a hot evening – sat puffing his pipe, while Naomi passed round a huge dish of cherries and a plate of chocolate biscuits. The cherries, appropriately, were as red as cherries can be. She had a big notebook on her knee into which she wrote furiously.

The handsome Richard Mason, obviously not deeply committed to any 'ism', said little except that he would write an account of the visit for *World Books Bulletin* which had a circulation of a quarter of a million. He also expressed surprise that I was not going with them (for various reasons I had declined the offer). A.E. Coppard, venerable and white-haired, declared: 'I love England. I'm not going abroad to run down my country although I prefer some aspects of Soviet policy to that of British.' Doris Lessing, dark and full-figured, said only that she had passed through Russia when five years old in 1924. Her father, who had been working in Persia, 'loathed *those Bolsheviks*'. (Her italics.)

Douglas Young, bearded and in sandals wanted to be 'au courant' with AWPA activities and peppered his remarks with foreign phrases, some of them in Latin. He sounded more like Thomas Carlyle than James Boswell. After all the talk, Coppard handed John St John an envelope containing, so he said, a five pound note. He looked at me and said: 'You are a witness that I gave him an envelope.' I did *not* say: 'An envelope yes, but how do I know whether there was a five pound note in it?' A man who loved England and admired the Moscow Dynamos could be trusted. Before we dispersed, someone remarked how the temperature was just right in view of the expedition to Russia. To this day I remember the redness of those cherries.

As arranged, the public meeting for the returned delegates took place on 17 July 1952 in Friends House in the Euston Road. Coppard, as the oldest member of the party of writers, spoke glowingly of the Soviet Union and the Russians – delightful people, full of goodwill! The queue for Lenin's tomb on Sunday lasted from 3 p.m. to 6 p.m. At 6 p.m. there was still a half-mile queue. This worship of Lenin did not impress me but perhaps it went down well with the comrades present.

Naomi revealed good Scots common sense in her remarks. She pointed out that events seem different to people at different stages of history. Perhaps the Russians did not know the true facts about the United States' actions in Korea. They were not interested in the British liberal point of view. She thought the standard of living was higher than it had been on her visit during the 1930s. Naomi said she hoped more groups from Britain would visit the Soviet Union but that she would also like to see delegations going to the USA. She auctioned a bottle of vodka to raise funds for AWPA. It was bought for five guineas by Douglas Young. Alex Comfort made the comment: 'This is the first time in the history of Friends House that a bottle of vodka has been auctioned!' Quakers, after all, are not primarily known as vendors or consumers of alcohol.

I increasingly was having misgivings about AWPA. I felt that too many decisions were being made because of pressure by the small group of Communists on the committee who invariably put forward the same point of view. The others tended to be individualistic. Naomi, Alex and I frequently made objections that went unheeded. I decided therefore to resign from the committee and wrote a letter to that effect while remaining an ordinary member of AWPA as I still believed in our fundamental aim, the promotion of good relations between the UK and the Soviet Union. I felt very much at a loss for a certain camaraderie had grown up between all of us.

Since the 1950s I have not engaged in any political activity, though I have never lost interest in politics in the UK, Ireland and the world at large. Politics, I came to believe from my brief experience on the fringe, is not for the idealistic. Young people have always had the hope that they could change this nasty old world of ours with its exploitation and inhumanity. But they reckon without the deadweight of tradition, human inertia and wickedness.

Despite my growing sense of despair over the prospects for peace, I supported the Campaign for Nuclear Disarmament and, later, the

Northern Ireland Peace People, who bravely brought together Nationalists and Unionists in their struggle against sectarianism and violence. Peace in our time? We must hope for the best.

I would like to commend to my fellow Ulstermen and fellow Irishmen some words spoken by King George V when he came to Belfast in 1921 to open the Stormont Parliament:

> I appeal to all Irishmen to pause, to stretch out the hand of forbearance and conciliation, to forgive and forget, and to join in making for the land which they love a new era of peace, contentment and goodwill.

TWENTY-ONE

The Reluctant Teacher

Bernard Shaw, whom I regarded in my youth as the wise old man of the tribe, declared that: 'Those who can, do. Those who can't, teach.' Who was I, an innocent young provincial, to doubt the greybearded sage? Had he not, despite his feckless father, climbed up to a top rung on the theatrical and literary ladder? I also took Shaw's advice in regard to public meetings and school debates and said something even when I really had nothing to say.

As a schoolboy I often heard that teaching was a fine profession, a noble one in fact, and that it promised security as well as short hours and long holidays. What kind of work could be more appealing, especially in an era yet to emerge from the depression of the '30s? My school-friend Leslie Baxter regarded teaching as a vocation. He was little concerned with pay and security. He simply loved teaching. His Senior Certificate results were excellent, so he went with some confidence to the interview for admission to a teacher-training college. The worthies who questioned him returned the verdict: 'This candidate is unsuited to the profession of teaching.' It may have been for the best since Leslie was too gentle to control the sort of boys I had encountered at primary school. He was not defeated. Instead, he went to the College of Art in Belfast and spent his adult working life as a grammar school art master.

Through my sister-in-law, Peggy Hutchins, who at the time, after service in the WAAF, was running an agency that found flats for clients, I met a young man called Dick Easton. Dick had been at Trinity College in Dublin, like myself, and again like myself nursed literary ambitions. He was a bit of a professional Irishman, complete with brogue and that great capacity for talk and beer-drinking guaranteed to impress the more gullible type of Englishman. He had a job teaching English to foreigners at the City of London College. This kind of work was to become a growth industry in the next couple of decades. Dick asked me if I would like to teach for a month at their summer school. I hesitated but he blarneyed me into deciding to give it a go. Had I not published books and been a contributor to lots of magazines? 'You'll find it a piece of cake,' said Dick.

The first day was absolute hell, but I persevered. Colleagues were kind. Give them dictation, use this and that textbook, explain the tenses, write lists of useful phrases on the board and so on. At the end of the month I realised that here was work I could do at least adequately. Practice and an exchange of views as to methods with other teachers would, I believed, make me into an effective if not dedicated teacher of English.

A new profession had opened up for me but I did not adopt it straightaway. I was grateful to Dick Easton and sometimes wished I could take life as easily as he did, but my Ulster puritanical background forbade me. Dick told me of how an admiring female student had said to him: 'Oh, Mr Eastman, you are a caveman!' I cursed my restraint. Fellow teachers numbered among them the usual literary aspirants: Henry Cohen, who wrote under the name Roland Camberton, had published two novels and won the Somerset Maugham award intended to give young writers the opportunity to travel abroad; the folk singer Sydney Carter, later to write the popular religious songs, 'Lord of the Dance' and 'One More Step'; and F.A. Voigt, political journalist and for a time co-editor with Helen Waddell of the journal, *The Nineteenth Century*.

Voigt and I crossed swords in the pub opposite the college where a number of us gathered after lessons to chat and drink beer. The middle-aged Voigt struck me as a disappointed literary man. He ably defended right-wing views with which I had little sympathy, being at the time inclined to believe that Kingsley Martin's articles in the *New Statesman* constituted Holy Writ. I remember arguing for what I called a 'general settlement' with the Russians. Voigt rightly kept demanding what the precise nature of such a settlement should be. I could not tell him.

Henry Cohen was friendly and amiable, whereas Sydney Carter was quiet and withdrawn. I once told Henry about the rigours of my Presbyterian childhood, expecting sympathy. 'That's nothing,' he said, 'compared with being brought up as an Orthodox Jew.' At the time I knew nothing of Jews, Orthodox or otherwise. Living in London would bring me into contact with a wide spectrum of Jewish people ranging from the Orthodox to the atheistic. Henry was hoping to go to Spain and I think he did so but I cannot remember any book resulting from his visit. He had two books published by John Lehmann: *Scamp* and *Rain on the Pavements*. *Scamp* remains on my shelves and I see there is an inscription: 'To Robert – Fraternally – Roland Camberton. March 1954.' For some years Henry and I kept in touch, and when I last saw him he was working as a courier in London. Perhaps it was not for nothing that people said that winning the Somerset Maugham award was 'the kiss of death'.

For several years, I think about four, I taught for a month every summer at the City of London College. In 1954 I heard that a Mr Joyce had brought a number of his students from Trieste to the college. I was excited by this news for the Mr Joyce in question proved to be Stanislaus Joyce, the younger brother of the author of *Ulysses* and author of *My Brother's Keeper*. I introduced myself and explained that my wife had written *James Joyce's Dublin*. From notes made at the time, I learn that on 21 July 1954 Stanislaus Joyce came to tea and stayed to supper at our flat in the Boltons.

He told us that it was half a century since he had been in London. Our conversation ranged from wines obtainable in Trieste to details of James Joyce's life. The bald Stanislaus Joyce looked like the stereotypical German Herr Doktor. He said he was going to Dublin for a few days, though he loathed that city. About a week later I went round one evening to his hotel, the Austin, in South Kensington, and stayed till midnight. When I went up to his room he told me he had just finished writing a letter to T.S. Eliot whom he had met earlier at Fabers in Russell Square. Then two of his students arrived and we all went down to the lounge.

Stanislaus Joyce spoke of his annoyance with an American woman who taught English in Trieste and objected to English pronunciations. He said that it was he who had given *Stephen Hero* its title and this had been taken from the ballad 'Turpin Hero'. He half-sang this and other ballads. I was amused by his impression that in Ireland everyone now spoke the Irish language. He was worried that English might not be understood any longer! I assured him that, despite all the efforts of de Valera, the

Anglo-Saxon tongue had not been banished as St Patrick had banished the snakes. Joyce was courteous and amiable except when Catholicism or Dublin came up. He felt safe so long as he was with a Belfast Protestant like myself and an Anglo-Irishwoman like Patricia. We found this rather amusing.

On another occasion he talked of his sporting life and in particular his interest in rowing. He had had a bit of trouble with his heart and hoped in London to have cardiac examination. He read aloud a 7,000-word review of a book entitled *James Joyce and My Ireland*, fiercely attacking it. Where could it be published? he wanted to know. I suggested that he send his essay to *The Partisan Review* in New York since they tended to publish long pieces, unlike English journals. What happened to his review in the end I have no idea. I liked Stanislaus Joyce and felt that he had been hurt by James's neglect of him, especially when James had become the great literary lion in Paris and no longer needed the adoration and practical help that had been so freely given him by his younger brother.

As time went on I began to realise that book reviews, articles, occasional broadcasts and poems brought in little hard cash. Patricia made a few pounds now and then from her writing. She and our daughter Toosie (Arethusa) used to spend most of the summer in our house at Ardnagashel in County Cork. The successive flats we lived in in London were expensive to rent. We sub-let rooms in them for this activity was one in which the Hutchins women were adept. Years on, financial pressure increased because we were not living within our means. Later still, with every bill paid and no overdraft at the Midland Bank, I decided I would never be in debt again – and I never have been.

Through Dick Easton, then, I got a toehold into teaching. My next move was to acquire classes at the City Literary Institute in Stukeley Street near Holborn Tube Station in the nebulous subject called 'the art of writing'. This was not in calligraphy, as one acquaintance thought, but an attempt to teach adults how to write stories, poems, articles for the press – any literary form, in fact, except plays. At the 'City Lit', where I had been engaged by the principal, A.C.T. White, a VC, and at other literary institutes dotted over Greater London, I dealt with a mixum gatherum of would-be writers. It showed me just how wide the gap was between the amateur and the professional. Occasional students showed promise, but few of them seemed ready for the hard and lonely slog that writing entails. One man insisted that I was wrong to condemn clichés. Another said that all Dylan Thomas's poems were unintelligible. I read out Thomas's haunting 'Fern Hill', explaining its meaning as best I could and he agreed that there was 'something in' Thomas after all. But perhaps the most satisfying experience of my entire teaching career was when I was asked by a shy and stammering young man, at the end of the class, to tell him what was meant by a 'split infinitive'. I told him and gave him a few examples. He went off as if he were walking on air, having discovered the secret of the universe.

In May 1996 I read an obituary of a former class member at the 'City Lit'. John McArthur (1901–96) was the son of Glaswegian parents who moved to London when he was a child. He qualified as a medical doctor, became a malariologist and was working on research in that field in Borneo when the Japanese invaded. For three years his wife, son and he were either together or separately prisoners of the Japanese, who destroyed most of his manuscript notes. They also seized an early prototype pocket microscope he always carried. He wrote descriptions of this ordeal which I read out to the class. These were not brilliantly written, for writing was not McArthur's forte, but all who listened to them marvelled at their author's lack of bitterness or self-pity.

McArthur kindly asked me to visit him. He told me with enthusiasm of his pocket microscope project. He said that the drive behind his invention was simply that as a student he could not afford to buy a microscope. He therefore had designed an instrument which would be cheap as well as easily portable. The *Guardian* obituary states that McArthur 'for over half a century remained dedicated to the continuing development of his pocket microscope which, barely larger than one of the flat fifty cigarette tins common in the 1930s, was the first major advance in microscope design for a century'. One of McArthur's microscopes was carried across Antarctica by Sir Vivian Fuchs on the Commonwealth expedition in 1957 since the design resists the effects of extreme temperatures and condensation better than conventional microscopes.

I met a wide range of London residents – clerks, secretaries, accountants, doctors, small businessmen, teachers, booksellers, nurses – some of them English, others Scottish, Irish, Welsh and foreign, in the years when I taught 'creative writing', though I came to doubt very much if it *can* be taught. Real writers find their own way sooner or later and perhaps the most that can be done is to give them a push forward. A myth exists that writing is easy; anybody can do it. I have sometimes heard the lament: 'I could write a book if only I had the time.' I am too polite to answer: 'Well, take the time. Do it. Don't just talk about it.'

The most talented writer I came across was an electrician from a working-class London family. He had been a Communist and at one time had been a friend of Ted Willis (Lord Willis), who was gradually making a name for himself. Harold, a nice, idealistic man, was lacking in ambition. He wrote a number of superb short stories in which the dialogue rang true. I remember how Harold and I, after a couple of pints one evening in Marylebone Road, shook hands solemnly, wished each other luck and even continued existence, on the eve of John F. Kennedy's showdown with Khrushchev in 1963. We met, as usual, in the writing class a week later as if nothing had happened.

For some time I was a writer who did a bit of teaching. Gradually I became a teacher who did a bit of writing. Remembering my City of London College summer work, I applied to various private schools wearing the hat of a teacher of English to foreigners. I found it easy enough to get such work but to be paid adequately was quite another matter. These schools exploited their tutors, some of whom were exceptionally well qualified, a few of them PhDs. Why were they doing such ill-paid work? It was a puzzlement. Once again one came across would-be and failed writers. 'Those who can, do. Those who can't, teach.' Was the old Dubliner right after all?

Fortunately in 1962 I got work as an EFL (English as a Foreign Language) tutor with West London College (later Hammersmith and West London College). This was run by ILEA (the Inner London Education Authority), so salaries were much higher than in private schools. Students' fees were much lower. The Welsh head of department engaged me, I think, because I had brought along a couple of published books. He never even looked at my references. I stayed at the college, working at different branches, until my retirement in 1986.

The staff at West London College consisted of men and women with varying backgrounds and academic achievements. I was pleased to meet Anthony Dickins, a Cambridge man, who had been a friend of

Tambimuttu, the Bohemian editor of *Poetry London*. Linton Stone, a Dubliner, had worked in journalism in Dublin and wrote successful textbooks, some of which I used with students. Sally Mellersh radiated cheerfulness and goodwill. Harper Reekie, whom I would have called a Scot, described himself as a Pict. Jim McCarthy made witty if cynical remarks about both staff and students. My colleagues – bar one or two – were invariably helpful.

Not so long ago I got a phone call from a friend and former colleague, Cliff Williams, to tell me he had been at the funeral of Richard Trudgett. Trudgett had been lecturer-in-charge at the South Kensington branch where I worked for three years. He and I became friends for we had literary interests in common. Trudgett was a good if harsh critic, and had published a collection of poems shortly after the war. He and I sometimes went to poetry readings in the house of the poet and art critic Edward Lucie-Smith in Chelsea.

One day Trudgett gave me the manuscript of a novel he had written. I thought it publishable and sent it to a friend who was a literary agent but in the event the novel did not find a publisher. I think Trudgett's pride was hurt. At any rate our relationship deteriorated and in the end I was glad to go to another branch, away from the rows between Trudgett and others in the tiny staff room. In all fairness he was forced to work under bad conditions, with tutors and students traipsing in and out, not to speak of phone calls. I remember an occasion when Trudgett and McCarthy almost came to blows over the ending of a word. One said it ended in 'er', the other in 'or'. The word in question is conjurer/conjuror.

Trudgett despised the work we did but in his capacity as lecturer-in-charge could be very exacting. He once accused me of leaving a class two minutes early. I showed him my watch which pointed to the exact time the class was due to end. It was sad to lose a friend, and to see a talented man become so embittered as to squander his energies on trivialities. Was it due to failure as a writer or to some deeper cause or secret trauma? I shall never know. However, on the day I retired, he shook hands and wished me well with the parting words: 'You have stuck to your last.'

This teaching was nearly all language and very little literature. Most of the students wanted to learn English for purely commercial reasons. Who, for heaven's sake, was Will Shakespeare or George Orwell, D.H.

Lawrence or Dylan Thomas? I was more surprised to find minimal interest in Eng. Lit. among my colleagues. For Linguistics I could not have cared less, as the phrase went. In July and August I did find work teaching 20th-century literature with the Educational Interchange which brought groups of foreign teachers of English to London for talks on British history, education, language and literature. These groups came from France, Germany, Greece and sometimes Latin America, and this gave me an opportunity to talk about Joyce (James not Stanislaus!), Yeats, Hardy, Anthony Powell, Beckett, just to think of a few random names. It was a relief from teaching the use of the Present Perfect and explaining for the thousandth time the difference between 'its' and 'it's', and 'quiet' and 'quite'.

Through meeting Walter Mahon-Smith, an Irishman then living in London, I began to run a weekly Eng. Lit. class in Ealing at the Questors Theatre, the Redgrave Room to be precise. For two hours once a week I could talk as much as I liked about books and writers, and get paid for it (not awfully well, I'm afraid). This class brought me into contact with a delightful set of people, many of them retired professionals. One was a Church of England priest who was always able to put me right on theological points that might arise in literary texts.

Walter Mahon-Smith turned out to be a kind of father-figure. One of the kindest men I have ever met, he helped me in all manner of ways, not least as a recruiter of class members, for the local council judged the success of a class by its attendance. Walter came from the west of Ireland where his family had been landowners. Some of them turned Protestant in order to hold on to their stony acres. Walter gave not a button for Orange or Green, or the fanatics in Ireland who live in either 1690 or 1916 instead of Time Present. He told me he had been a film reviewer for *The Irish Times* but otherwise never spoke of how he had managed his life. I assumed that he had a private income.

Walter had a number of endearing characteristics. He had a great love of neckties, of which he owned a large collection. Newspapers delighted him and these he bought with the delight of a sailor on shore buying drinks all round. 'My only vice,' he remarked. Always conventionally dressed, Walter faced the world as the epitome of the Irish country gentleman of the Edwardian era before anyone had heard of de Valera and Michael Collins, and the big event of the year was the

Horse Show every August at the Royal Dublin Society, run by the Anglo-Irish upper crust.

After retirement from whatever work he had done – journalism perhaps? – Walter came to London to be near his grown-up son and daughter. He settled in Ealing, once known as 'queen of the suburbs', and started the Ealing Forum to provide classes in the arts and discussion groups for older people with time on their hands. A letter about the Forum published in *The Irish Times* led me to contact Walter in the hope that I might run an Eng. Lit. class. So it proved. Walter and I, as well as our good friend Meg Watkins, often lunched together. He always had entertaining stories to tell of the west of Ireland.

On a visit to Dublin in the 1980s I spent an evening with a writer reputed to know all about the city, its 'characters', celebrities and wits.

'Do you know my friend, Walter Mahon-Smith, who now lives in London?' I asked.

'Yes, of course. You mean the man who went to prison and then wrote *I Did Penal Servitude?*'

'You must be joking or mistaken.'

'I assure you I am not,if you are speaking of Walter Mahon-Smith.'

The bookseller Eugene Mallon found me a copy of *I Did Penal Servitude* right away. Extracts from it had appeared in the monthly magazine *The Bell* under the editorship of Seán O'Faoláin. These apparently created a stir and the publication of the book a sensation. Walter, indeed, as a young man had spent a year and nine months in prison – the sentence was for three years – for embezzlement when working as a bank clerk. He had stolen money to pay off gambling debts.

Walter's account of his prison experience is detailed, possibly a little too detailed. It shows the deep human sympathy with other prisoners one might have expected from such a sensitive man. The harshness of prison life is not glossed over, yet one senses it is not exaggerated. Not least moving is Walter's account of his experiences after release. Who wants to employ a jailbird? By the time I read the book, Walter was a very ill man. I would have liked to meet him for a last time if only to say how much I had appreciated his help and friendship, but his daughter said he was no longer in a fit state to see anyone.

The years as a teacher and lecturer brought me into contact with colleagues and students I could not otherwise have met. On visits to Spain, France and Germany I found welcome and hospitality from those

I had known in the classroom. I regret that I never took up an invitation to visit Istanbul. Teaching of course, like any job, was not always pure bliss. Out of every 20 or so students one or two gave me more trouble than the others put together. A persistently ill-behaved French girl forced me into bad, if understandable French, followed by pretty lucid English: 'Get out of my class and don't come back!' She never came back. Day after day I had to listen to complaints about English weather, English food and the general shortcomings of Anglo-Saxondom.

Mr Akagi was my first Japanese pupil, though not my last. Most Japanese wrote down conscientiously every word I said as if they were reporters for *Hansard*. Mr Akagi, an early middle-aged man who worked for Mitsubishi in the City of London, did not write anything down. I travelled out to his house in Wimbledon once a week where we studied the *Times* editorials and financial pages. He advised me to invest in the building industry just as a Turkish jeweller once urged me to buy gold. I foolishly asked someone in the Midland Bank for advice. He told me *not* to buy gold. The Turk was absolutely right. As for Mr Akagi, after visits over a period of three years, I knew no more about him, apart from the fact that he had served in the Japanese navy, than when we had met. I may say that he was scrupulously polite and insisted on paying for cancelled lessons. I hope he ended up a rich businessman.

Well, then, did Bernard Shaw get it as wrong about teaching as he did about conditions in the Soviet Union? What was the old Dublin sage himself but a lifelong teacher? How, too, did he come to make such sympathetic remarks about the Fascist leaders hellbent on war? Perhaps I am just being nasty about a fallen idol. Yet Shaw was not so far off the mark when his heroine in *The Millionairess* declares: 'Money is power. Money is security. Money is freedom.' Teaching, he might have pointed out, was not an occupation that impressed bank managers. Even so, like writing poetry, it has its own rewards.

TWENTY-TWO

The Acid Test

I have already spoken of my early years of marriage, first in Dublin and then London. Patricia and I spent at least ten happy years together. Then we began to drift apart. We separated in 1962 and divorced, on the grounds of my desertion, in 1966. A few years later Patricia and our daughter Toosie went back to Ireland to live at Ardnagashel, Patricia's ancestral home near Bantry Bay in West Cork. Toosie still lives there and has a job in that area. Patricia died, as the result of a stroke, on 26 November 1985. The day she was buried, St Andrew's Day, I wrote a poem about our relationship. The last four lines run:

> I remember our time of roses, promises,
> The silvered sea at Ardnagashel,
> Earrings of fuchsia in the hedgerows,
> Hope arching, like a rainbow, over all.

Towards the end of Patricia's life we became very good friends. This was because she wrote me a letter in which, at long last, she acknowledged that some of the blame for the failure of our marriage was on her side. From then on I was happy to act as literary adviser – as I had done during our married life – and welcome her to London. Just before her fatal stroke I got a postcard from her giving me the dates of a visit and her acceptance of my invitation to stay in my flat near Notting Hill Gate. She was to have given a talk at the Tate Gallery on Ezra Pound, a poet in whom she had been interested for many years. Her biographical study, *Ezra Pound's Kensington*, appeared in 1965.

Dozens of times I have asked myself: why did our marriage fall apart?

I used to blame it on Patricia's conversion to vegetarianism shortly after we married. For a year before our marriage I often enjoyed Patricia's delicious Sunday roast. Then came her renunciation of flesh of every description. Even fish was 'out'. She stuck rigorously to a vegetarian regimen for the rest of her life. I resented her bringing up our daughter as a vegetarian. I felt I had little in common with Patricia's vegetarian friends, who no doubt disapproved of me as an unrepentant carnivore.

There were deeper reasons than this for frustration. As I advanced into my 30s I became depressed and irritable. I experienced a sense of having lost direction. The success I aimed at and believed to be within my grasp had not come about. Nagging questions assailed me: where was I going, if anywhere? Would I spend the next 30 years in relatively ill-paid teaching and writing? Had I been wrong not to qualify in some lucrative profession? In short, would I fail as my father had done?

I sought the advice of Alex Comfort. We lunched at an Indian restaurant near University College where he was researching senescence and he gave me the name of a psychiatrist he recommended. I consulted this man but could establish no *rapport* with him. Next I went to a Harley Street therapist called Peter Fletcher, whose book on emotional problems had impressed me. Fletcher was helpful but too expensive. I told him this frankly and he suggested I should see a Dr Joshua Bierer who ran a 'day hospital' in St John's Wood.

Within minutes of meeting Dr Bierer I knew he was the man I had been looking for. A Viennese Jew who had studied under Alfred Adler, the one-time associate of Freud, the stocky, bearded Dr Bierer reminded me of an amiable Old Testament prophet. I sensed that he could guide me back to discover the true self I seemed to have lost. I kept thinking of Shakespeare's 'To thine own self be true . . .' but what was this self? I knew that when I found it I would be faithful to it.

Joshua Bierer believed in stressing the social element in treating patients. He did not think they should be isolated from human contact; he experimented with LSD (lysergic acid 25), the hallucinogenic drug which at that time had no meaning for the general public nor was abused by addicts. For some emotional problems LSD could be an effective therapy.

Dr Bierer had started a number of clubs for his patients in which he encouraged them to develop social skills. Realising that I had been trained as a social worker, he recruited me as a part-time assistant in one of these clubs which used a church hall near Victoria Station. I met a wide variety of people there, both professional and working class. Only once did I fear attack from an aggressive patient. Sometimes I was regarded as a doctor, despite my denials, and consulted about medication. I would ask: 'What does your doctor advise?' and, when told, reply: 'I absolutely agree with him/her.'

Joshua Bierer was a remarkable man, a dedicated and witty pioneer. It was my great good luck to come across such a healer. Nor have I forgotten the help given me by his associate, Dr Joyce Martin, for it was on her suggestion that I agreed to have the LSD treatment that many feared. The series of 12 LSD 'trips' that I underwent, though under strict medical supervision, caused me acute emotional distress since they made me relive various painful experience in my life as baby, child, adolescent and adult. Yet from the process of abreaction involved, I derived lasting benefit.

On one LSD occasion I remember ideas bubbling up so that my mind could not cope with them in their abundance. I had the image of creativity as being like a huge reservoir that could never be emptied. Halfway through my life I discovered that inner self which so long had eluded me. Father's failure no longer disturbed me. I would set out to 'climb every mountain, ford every stream'. I knew I was a winner.

TWENTY-THREE

Three Englishmen

Mad dogs and Englishmen
Go out in the mid-day sun.
The Japanese don't care to
The Chinese wouldn't dare to.
Hindoos and Argentines
Sleep firmly from twelve to one
But Englishmen detest a siesta.

Not quite poetry but certainly tuneful verse that is cogent and witty. The song has a special resonance for me and I love to hear it sung by its author in the clipped diction that became his trademark. I'm referring, of course, to Noël Coward; 'the Master', as his disciples call him.

When I was trying to make my way in London as a writer, two friends called unexpectedly one day, the novelist Muriel Spark and the poet and critic Derek Stanford. Each had been asked to write a study of Coward's writings and they both refused, pleading ignorance of the theatre. Would I do it? I said no.

But next day I went to the Kensington Central Library and took out everything of Coward's I could find. As I read *Hay Fever* and *Blithe Spirit* I decided to have a go. I wrote a synopsis and sent it to the publisher who wished to commission the book — Erica Marx of the Hand and Flower Press. She decided I was the man for the job. We met and she gave me a generous advance. All I had to do was to write the book.

I discovered that it was with his third play, *The Vortex*, that Coward had scored his first success in London as a young man of 25. New York also acclaimed this play which reflected the shallowness that characterised upper-class English society after the First World War. *Hay Fever* further added to Coward's reputation for wit. It looked as if he was London's belated answer to Dublin's Oscar Wilde.

Success followed success in the 1920s for the actor-dramatist-entertainer born in 1899 into a modest family in the London suburbs. *Bitter Sweet* in 1929 showed that Noël Coward could tackle not only straight drama but was capable of writing 'book', lyrics and music for a revue. *Private Lives* and the patriotic spectacle *Cavalcade* in the Drury Lane Theatre made the name Coward a household word.

By the time I began my research on the man and his work, Coward was in his 50s. His star no longer shone so brightly. True, he had continued to be prolific with plays such as *Present Laughter* and *Blithe Spirit* in addition to the wartime films *Brief Encounter* and *In Which We Serve*. Coward might have made friends in high places – one such being Earl Mountbatten – but a younger generation was not only 'knock, knock, knocking at the door' but threatening to break it down so that the kitchen sink could be dragged in. The stage was being set for the arrival of angry young men with rough manners and names like John Osborne and Brendan Behan.

Now my job, as I saw it, was to mount a sort of rescue operation, to produce a study of Noël Coward that without being bland would point up his strong points – the crisp dialogue, the unerring sense of theatre. I intended to look at his work from the stance of a poet and literary critic, rather than as a man of the theatre which I manifestly was not. I outlined the plan in writing to Coward and he told me to go ahead with his blessing.

When I had done some of the initial spadework I met Coward's secretary, Cole Lesley, whose name Coward had changed from the more prosaic Leslie Cole. After this vetting, the Master invited me to lunch at the Ivy, the famous theatrical restaurant near Leicester Square. Asked what I would like to drink, I said 'a dry sherry' only to find that Coward reacted as if I had uttered a four-letter word. 'Not very enterprising,' hissed the Master, who insisted that I should drink vodka. So vodka it had to be.

But in a moment he switched on the charm and regaled me with anecdotes about writers he had known. Arnold Bennett he mimicked with what I imagine was considerable accuracy, making dramatic use of Bennett's stammer. Having stunned me with vodka and stories, he took me off to a rehearsal of Shaw's *The Apple Cart* in which he was to play King Magnus, in the Theatre Royal, Haymarket.

My wife and I were duly present on the first night which an old diary informs me was 11 May 1953. When the play ended, we climbed a winding staircase right to the top where we saw a brass plate with the inscription 'Mr Noël Coward'. In we went to a dressing-room overflowing with people and flowers. Coward, his face still bearing traces of greasepaint, looked worn out, his slight figure wrapped in a flowered dressing-gown. Fame, it was obvious, had its price.

It would be idle to pretend that Noël Coward is a great dramatist, yet his best plays do reflect many of the social changes of this century. His gift, I believe, was that so frequently as playwright, actor, song-writer and entertainer he could provoke laughter. Egotist he may have been, as what creative artist is not? Yet he possessed the insight to say of himself:

> Ever since my life began
> The most I've ever had
> Is a talent to amuse.

The book I wrote was called *The Art of Noël Coward*. Among the illustrations is an unpublished – at that time – facsimile extract from Coward's *Future Indefinite*, a reproduction of a Coward painting and a photograph of the Master in a thoughtful mood by Dorothy Wilding. Paper, binding and jacket were exquisite. My book got good reviews, a particularly favourable one appearing in *The Sunday Times*. The book sold well, largely because it was about a celebrity of international stature. As a young writer in his early 30s I felt proud of what I had done, and not least proud of having been driven down Piccadilly and past Hyde Park Corner in his little car fitted out with tartan upholstery by this half-sentimental, half-astringent, effervescent, self-mocking genius.

Here are the final two paragraphs of the book:

> Enjoyment of life runs through most of Noël Coward's plays, stories and miscellaneous writing. In a time of death-wish and despair he believes it is good to be alive. He delightedly triumphs over the bores, the killjoys and the silly men and women who mis-

manage their own lives and keep interfering with those of other people.

Bitter sweetly, the boat of his remarkable talents tilts from one side to the other; for many years now it has carried the imagination, laughter and emotion of the young and the not-so-young. It is always excellently equipped, unhesitatingly navigated; what the future of its voyage may be we cannot know. The wind which carries along a particular kind of genius has its own and unpredictable will.

The only book I have written which also came out in an American edition is *The World of C.P. Snow*, published in 1963 at the height of Snow's fame. In it I analysed the factors that contributed to Snow's outstanding success as a novelist, scientific administrator and social critic. In doing so, I drew mainly on the novels but looked also at Snow's other writings such as *Science and Government* and his address as Rector of the University of St Andrews. I also dealt with F.R. Leavis's boorish attack on Snow at Downing College, Cambridge, when the angry don declared that 'Snow is portentously ignorant'. I cited several writers in Snow's defence: the novelist William Gerhardi, the playwright Ronald Millar, and the distinguished scientist Professor J.D. Bernal. The controversy certainly helped in obtaining reviews of the book and stimulated sales.

I met Snow, both as Sir Charles and later as Lord Snow, on many occasions, mostly at the Savile Club and once in the House of Lords (he was not a success as a politician, despite his sharp political sense). Once in the Savile he had gathered into his circle a number of writers and intellectuals, including Kingsley Martin, editor of the *New Statesman*, then the most notable British weekly review. The conversation came round to the atom bomb. Everyone there believed that the atom bomb would be used within a period of five to ten years. I felt a fool when I said I thought it would never be used since it was too terrible to contemplate. I am reminded of how another expert was absolutely wrong. In Belfast in the 1960s, John D. Sayers, editor of the *Belfast Telegraph*, assured me that never again would the north of Ireland erupt into violence. Experts!

Snow was a genial, big man, obviously delighted with his success as novelist and administrator – and director of the company, English

Electric — and a living example of how, despite the barriers of social class, a boy from what was then called 'humble circumstances' in Leicester could make his way into the establishment, albeit that of the Left. Snow exemplified the triumph of the meritocracy. He approved of what I had written about his work. I quote from a letter dated 30 November 1962:

> I have now read your book with the greatest delight and satisfaction. It has given me nothing but pleasure and I am grateful to you. I can't write at length, since I am not yet in full circulation. I expect you heard that my heart stopped during the operation. I am perfectly all right, and they did a good job on the eye, but it has been something of an experience.

Snow's reputation for novels like *The Masters* has to some extent slumped but I believe it will rise again for he tackled territory in academe and business and the civil service of which few other English novelists have had inside knowledge. Influenced by Trollope, of whom he wrote a study, C.P. Snow eschewed modernism and formalism. His concern with the nature of power, whether at the level of a Cambridge college or at government level, and with ethics in science and technology, is still relevant as we travel towards the 21st century. If for nothing else, Snow will surely be remembered as the man who coined the phrase, 'the corridors of power'.

W. Brownlow White of the *Belfast Telegraph* invited me to review books for their literary page. Since he and the editor liked what I wrote, he then asked me to contribute a series of profiles of contemporary writers. One of these was of Anthony Powell whose pre-war satirical picture of the Bohemian world in Chelsea and Bloomsbury I had admired. Post-war, Powell was engaged on a highly ambitious sequence of novels with the overall title *A Dance to the Music of Time*, so called because of Poussin's famous painting. In these novels — 12 of them in the end — Powell's narrator, Nicholas Jenkins, surveys a wide spectrum of English life, extending through literature, painting, music, politics, the City, publishing, the army, and involving almost every social class. Powell ranges from the aristocracy — Lord Erridge, for instance — down the social scale to drop-outs and frauds. Yet out of the host of characters the most memorable is the power-hungry, ludicrous and eventually sinister Kenneth Widmerpool. He is as central to Powell's gallery of characters as were Scrooge and Mr Pickwick to that of Dickens. Widmerpool is one of the immortal creations in English fiction.

When I wrote in the *Belfast Telegraph* of Powell's sequence, it was far from complete. In any case I got a letter of appreciation from Powell and an invitation to lunch at the Travellers Club in Pall Mall. I found that Powell had spent some time in Belfast as an army officer during the war and that was a link with him. A more relaxed man than C.P. Snow, Powell, with an army family background and educated at Eton and Balliol College, Oxford, possessed the easy manner that was indicative of social security. He also had something of that mischievous humour one finds in his novels. I recall that he once told me gleefully that he had written 'Scotch' in a review instead of 'Scots' or 'Scottish' with the express intention of irritating his readers north of the Border.

After Malcolm Muggeridge became editor of *Punch*, he invited Powell to be his literary editor. Powell included me in his panel of reviewers. I think it was his sense of mischief that meant I was given for review a book on Persian art, a subject of which I was blissfully ignorant. Reviews mostly ran to only 150 words or even less, yet it was remarkable how much content could be packed into this word limit. The payment staggered me in its generosity. I think this was the only instance of my being over-paid in half a century of book reviewing.

After a visit to the *Punch* offices near Fleet Street where I collected books, Powell sometimes suggested we should go for a drink to a quiet pub in the Strand at the corner of Chancery Lane, gin for him, sherry for me or lager in hot weather. He was unfailingly entertaining about fellow writers. On only one occasion did I find him a bit grim. This was the day on which the *London Evening Standard* had headlines screaming of the flight to the USSR of Burgess and Maclean. I felt sure that Anthony Powell, wearing his military hat, would willingly have shot the pair of them as traitors and with all the more relish since they came from the same upper-class milieu as himself.

It has not escaped the notice of humankind that good times never last. Muggeridge either left or was ousted from the editorial chair at *Punch* and went on to be a television guru. Powell also went. Like the gentleman he was, he recommended me to H.D. Ziman of the *Daily Telegraph*. For many years Powell wrote a lengthy weekly review article for that newspaper. Whenever I met Ziman he would say: 'Well, I don't think I have anything for you' but I never remember an occasion when he sent me away bookless. Once I wrote a hasty, careless piece for him and felt ashamed of it. This was the only review of mine he praised. Perhaps it had a spontaneous quality I had not reckoned with.

As the years went on and I no longer frequented the *Punch* offices, I saw Powell less often. We corresponded and I read with enthusiasm each successive volume in *A Dance to the Music of Time* series and then the four volumes of memoirs to which he gave the general title *To Keep the Ball Rolling*. I wrote in 1988 to congratulate him on being made a Companion of Honour. He replied, sending me a card reproducing the portrait of him by Rodrigo Moynihan. This revealed an older and frailer Anthony Powell than the middle-aged, vigorous man I used to watch leaping on to a bus in the Strand after our pub sessions. As I write, he is alive and, I hope, in good spirits at the age of 92. I sometimes turn over in my mind the words of his narrator Nicholas Jenkins, who may well have been Powell's *alter ego*: 'All human beings, driven as they are at different speeds by the same Furies, are at close range equally extraordinary.' Quite so.

TWENTY-FOUR

Enter Captain Fox

W riter's block has often been held up as the bane of the writer, the negative disease that cuts off the flow of language. I never suffered from this complaint so far as prose was concerned. Poetry turned out to be a different matter. Disappointment with the reception of my second collection of poems, the fizzling out of the neo-romantic phase that flourished during the war years, the pressures of day-to-day living . . . all these effectively silenced me as a poet for about 20 years.

My friend Derek Stanford, a born and bred Londoner, and always a stimulating companion, often accompanied me on expeditions to editorial offices where we competed for which of us could carry away the greater number of review books. This was partly because books could be sold for half the retail price to an off-Fleet Street bookseller. Then Derek decided to leave his native London for a quieter life on the South Coast. Worthing, Brighton, Hove were not all that far away but living in such places meant that our meetings became less frequent. We kept in touch, however, in the old-fashioned way by writing letters, a habit that the telephone seems to have rendered obsolete. This reminds me that I once told Derek I sometimes felt I was living in the 19th century. 'That's nothing compared with me,' he said. 'I'm living in the Middle Ages.'

In my letters to him in Sussex I spoke of the people we knew, the books I happened to be reading and the trivia one can share with a friend. Then I had an idea to make my letters more lively. I invented a character called Captain Fox. Derek responded to this invention and soon I was getting postcards from him telling me of the activities of that gentleman in southern England. Captain Fox provided us with private jokes. One day it occurred to me that this was no laughing matter. I sat down and wrote a poem simply called 'Captain Fox', sent it to Robert Nye, in Edinburgh who, as poetry editor of *The Scotsman*, got it into the books page of that newspaper. Scottish readers were the first to be alerted to the existence of this character. On a visit north I met Robert Nye who advised me to write a series in which the Captain would be the central figure. I did so and when I had about 20 poems posted them to Peter Fallon who ran the Gallery Press in Dublin. In 1975 Fallon published a volume entitled *A Garland for Captain Fox*. At last I was back in the poetry business.

But what was Captain Fox all about? I should say right away that he is *not* myself and does not reflect my own values. I based him on a man I had been introduced to by the psychiatrist Dr Joshua Bierer, a sophisticated Englishman who had served in the Royal Navy before becoming a BBC drama producer. That at least provided a starting point for the character to whom I added new layers of background and experience. Fox represents a version of 20th-century man, wily as his name suggests, sometimes an adventurer, sometimes a philosopher, a man who can appreciate Rilke yet also deal briskly with a would-be assassin. Fox comes across as the quintessential gentleman yet his father had been an NCO. Various critics have attempted to define him. Derek Stanford has seen him as 'the James Bond of poetry'.

The 35 or so Captain Fox poems in my *Collected Poems* (1995) were singled out for comment by various critics. I think that of them all Rory Brennan got nearest to what I was trying to do when he wrote in the *Irish Independent*:

> Fox is a gun-runner, a bon vivant, an informed amateur philosopher, a user of women, a world traveller, a holder of numbered bank accounts, a spy, most likely a murderer. But behind the tales of deals and plots hangs a tapestry tinged with metaphysical doom. The Captain with his debonair betrayals seduced us into a shoddy admiration of evil.
>
> Thus Greacen exposes the fellow-traveller in all of us, for Fox is a figure that underwrites the glib codes of late 20th-century capitalism (or what you will) by which we comfortably pretend to live. Though it smacks of the barracks and the gaming-table, and not at all of the pulpit, here, in fact, is poetry of a high moral order.

Imagine Fox had been a real person, as indeed he is to me, and not a creature I invented, how would his death have been reported in one of the broadsheets? It would surely read something like this:

> Captain Horatio Fox, CBE, soldier and philosopher, has died suddenly in Germany at the age of 56. Born in Cologne, where his father was serving in the British Army of Occupation, he was educated at various schools in Germany and England. Commissioned pre-war into the Green Howards, he was assigned to 'special duties' during the Second World War. Later he was engaged in a number of business enterprises, in Zürich and elsewhere, and was awarded the CBE for undisclosed missions undertaken at the request of the War Office. A man of wide cultural and intellectual interests, he found time from his numerous practical tasks to contribute to philosophical thought. His most notable publication is Reflections on Wittgenstein and it was mainly because of his monograph that the University of St Andrews bestowed on him an honorary doctorate.

Then there would follow an appreciation of Fox by a public figure or academic. Let us say that this has been written by an academic I shall call Professor Helmut Bachmann of the University of Zürich. It would run:

> The sudden death of Captain Fox has come as a great blow to his many friends in the German-speaking world. Others are more qualified to write of the Captain's outstanding qualities as a man of action, but I should like to say a word about this remarkable man's interest in pure thought. I met him some years ago when he was engaged in running a travel agency in Zürich and what particularly struck me was the rare combination of the practical and theoretical in his nature.
>
> This would not be the proper place to attempt an analysis or even a summary of Fox's contribution to philosophical enquiry. Suffice it to say that his main speculations in that field centred on Hegel, and towards the end of his life, on Wittgenstein. His volume on Wittgenstein, slim though it is, has given rise to many animated discussions among Swiss, German and Austrian academics of my acquaintance. I understand that a consideration of Fox on

Wittgenstein is currently being prepared by Dr Mathias Hoffmann of Vienna.

Nor should one forget Fox's brilliant commentary on Robert Musil's encyclopaedic novel, *Der Mann Ohne Eigenschaften* (The Man Without Qualities).

There is a little story which, it seems to me, illustrates the essential Britishness of Captain Fox. It has often been related in the senior common room of Swiss and German universities as an example of English upper-class wit. A dear colleague of mine, impressed by Captain Fox's views on Erastianism as well as his easy command of the German language (he spoke it with a slight Berlin accent) said to him: 'I assume, sir, that you have spent many years at one or more of the great British or European universities. May I ask which ones you have honoured with your presence?' 'Yes, indeed, I've been to a university,' replied Fox without a moment's hesitation and in the odd drawl he sometimes affected. 'I had a weekend in St Andrews in Scotland when I went there to receive my honorary doctorate. But I must admit that I spent most of the time on the golf course.'

The death of Fox has extinguished a bright and intellectual flame. Had he lived to complete the large-scale work of Hegel of which I have been privileged to read a fragment, Horatio Fox would undoubtedly have acquired a worldwide reputation as a philosopher of weight and originality. Yet, for all his lightly carried learning, Fox, a modest man, could well have cried like Goethe's Faust:

The impossibility of knowledge!
It is this that burns away my heart.

Fox brought me back to poetry but when he died of poisoning by his enemies, I had to go on without him. I found a new theme in my childhood and boyhood, and drew portraits of family members and friends, as well as those 'characters' that for years seemed to have been forgotten. From the worldly-wise ambience of Captain Fox I travelled back in time to the Ulster in which I grew up. Even so, memories of Captain Fox kept returning and out of these I fashioned new poems. Fox is dead. Long live the Captain!

TWENTY-FIVE

Danger: Poets at Work

Some months after the publication of *A Garland for Captain Fox* in 1975 I ran into that singular character Eddie Linden at a poetry reading in London. 'Wee Eddie', as he is generally known, rarely misses a literary event. I have often seen him on such an occasion shouting in his Glaswegian vernacular, '*Aquarius, Aquarius*'. In other words he was seeking customers for the literary magazine he edits. Eddie is the protégé of the blind poet John Heath-Stubbs, one of the most learned writers of my generation. My link with John is that he knew Drummond Allison, a casualty of the 1939–45 war. They were close friends at Oxford. In passing I may say that John Heath-Stubbs is not only a poet-scholar but a fine cook. I speak as one who was a guest of his on a Christmas Day long ago.

Wee Eddie, a Hiberno-Scot whom I once called 'a Catholic Paisleyite', told me in his inimitable 'Glesca toun' voice: 'There's a wee poet frae Donegal who wants to meet ye. He's a great admirer o' yer Captain Fox.' Eddie had not been mistaken and I did enjoy meeting Matthew Sweeney, a native of the Inishowen peninsula who explained how he had just missed being born in the city of Derry. I forgave him the oversight.

'What about coming round to my flat in Pembridge Crescent and reading a few of your poems?' I suggested, adding, 'Don't tell Wee Eddie because he would drink me out of house and home.'

Matthew Sweeney thought this was a good idea. He would bring a couple of friends and I would invite others. I stocked up with some bottles of golden Somerset cider to see us through what I feared might be a couple of sticky hours with temperamental young poets. I need not have worried. Everyone behaved well. Comments were sensible, informed, constructive. Nobody got drunk if only because I deliberately did not provide excessive alcohol. Nobody walked out in a huff. Nobody smashed a glass on the skull of a critic. We had a break and I asked smokers to go into another room because I cannot stand cigarette smoke. Did anyone in there smoke pot? I didn't ask. The evening was pronounced a success, so we fixed another date. That went well, too. The workshop just 'grow'd' as the slave girl in *Uncle Tom's Cabin* said of herself.

We were never imaginative or pretentious enough to give our group a name other than the Pembridge Poets. Matthew acted as recruiting sergeant or chief whip, and drew on his large acquaintanceship among young hopefuls, English and Irish. I brought in a few older writers. I suppose I represented a kind of father-figure since I had published two collections of verse before most of the workshop young men were born. I say 'men' advisedly though we tried hard to bring in women too. The daughter of a well-known Anglo-Irish earl came a few times but must have found us wanting in talent or critical acumen for she soon disappeared.

Guy Carter, a young English artist, became one of our staunchest supporters, though he was the only person in the group who ever declared himself a true-blue Tory. He simply had to tolerate a bunch of Leftist radicals and anarchists but did so with grace. I think he disapproved of a poem of mine called 'Queen of the Bucket Shop' which showed some disrespect to a lady he admired. Whatever Guy's political views, we were all delighted when he won second prize in a British mini-saga competition in which one had to tell a story in exactly 50 words. The competition attracted no fewer than 80,000 entrants.

The Pembridge group met regularly, every fortnight or three weeks, for about ten years. Attendance would sometimes be as high as 15 and rarely less than six. Cider was our preferred drink for a few years but then we went up-market with wine. For some reason it was said that criticism of poems read was more kindly towards the end of the evening.

James Sutherland-Smith, a poetry competition winner, became the self-appointed scourge of sloppy versifiers. His fearless criticism gave him the reputation of a Judge Jeffreys. One cowardly poet used to phone me and ask: 'Is Sutherland-Smith coming this evening?' Putting on a metaphorical black cap, James once declared: 'This is the worst poem I have ever come across.' Being reasonably diplomatic – or cowardly? – I oiled the troubled waters. But in all fairness to him, James could be generous. When he said that a poem was 'a splendid piece', we knew that no higher praise was possible.

Guest writers of some note came from time to time, and read from their work. No criticism then was permitted. They were always treated with politeness if not enthusiasm. I remember the Irish writer Dermot Healy coming to read a short story – except that the story turned out to be rather long, so long in fact that a South African present fell asleep and snored loudly before Dermot had finished. No reflection on Dermot's skill of course. Nor did he take offence.

We started to have readings open to the public (but minus critical comment). These were held in pubs wherever we could find a room at a cheap rent. Then we used a fringe theatre at Notting Hill Gate above the Prince Albert (here I was nearly locked in for the night) and finally a bookshop in Church Street, Kensington. Poets who came to read included Gavin Ewart, Brian Patten, John Heath-Stubbs and Dannie Abse. But it was Stephen Spender, the 1930s survivor, who drew the biggest crowd.

Following my return to Dublin, Matthew Sweeney transferred group meetings to his flat in central London. But after ten years a certain tiredness sets in, old-timers disperse and the real poets among the members – like Matthew – are too busy with their own writing and commitments to be bothered carrying on. It was fun while it lasted. I made some good friends through these cidery and then vinous evenings near Notting Hill Gate. More important still, some of us, in James Sutherland-Smith's immortal phrase, managed to write 'splendid pieces'.

TWENTY-SIX

Flowers in Bloom

The past decade is too near in time for me to see it in perspective. I shall summarise. Like every other decade, it brought its problems and its satisfactions. In 1986 I had to retire from teaching, having been allowed to stay on for some months after my 65th birthday. It was an odd feeling that I should be leaving my colleagues, some of them friends, and forsaking the classroom and language laboratory for ever. Also in 1986 I was elected to Aosdána in Dublin, having been sponsored by Benedict Kelly, novelist, critic and fellow Ulsterman. Walter Mahon-Smith used to say that Ben was the only writer in Dublin of whom never a malicious word could be heard. A born storyteller, Ben is widely known throughout Ireland.

Aosdána is a society of artists, established by the Arts Council in 1981, to honour those whose work has made 'an outstanding contribution to the arts in Ireland'. It also encourages and assists members to devote their energies fully to their art. Membership consists of not more than 200. To be considered for membership, a candidate must have produced a body of original and creative works in one or more of the following forms: literature (poetry, fiction, drama), visual art (painting, sculpture, printmaking, photography, film or video) or music. He or she must have been born or have been resident in Ireland for five years, and must not be less than 30 years of age. Members of Aosdána are eligible to receive from the Arts Council an annuity, called a *Cnuas*, for a term of five years to assist them in pursuing their art full time. This *Cnuas* is renewable at the discretion of the Arts Council. So far as I know, there is no comparable scheme in operation in any other country. It was brought into being in Ireland by the former Taoiseach (Prime Minister) Charles J. Haughey who, to a large extent, was assisted in the working out of the details by the poet and biographer Anthony Cronin. I have reason to be grateful to both of them and all the more so since, though born in Ireland, I spent most of my adult life in England.

I ran into unexpected problems with my flat in Pembridge Crescent and moved, not altogether willingly, to a flat in a large, impersonal block in Chelsea. This did not prove satisfactory. What to do? The answer was to move back across the Irish Sea to Dublin. Living there would be no hardship, no Siberian exile. It was one of the best moves I ever made.

Through a series of contacts I found a flat in Ballsbridge, a pleasant inner suburb, near the RDS (Royal Dublin Society), membership of which means one can use their magnificent library and reading room. My landlady turned out to be Beatrice Behan, widow of the playwright Brendan Behan. I had known her as Beatrice Salkeld many years earlier, in the 1940s, when I used to visit the house of her parents and grandmother, Blanaid Salkeld, poet and one-time actress at the Abbey Theatre. Beatrice's father, Cecil Salkeld, painter and wit, had been a kind of *guru* in my life, opening doors for me in Dublin's Bohemia. One day years later, not having seen Beatrice around for some time, I knocked at her bedroom door. I kept knocking because I could see a light in the room. At last I entered, only to find her lying in bed, dead. I stayed on in the house until I was offered a flat in Sandymount, only a short walk away from Ballsbridge.

Here, at my desk of Irish cherry wood, I can look across the road to the Star of the Sea church which is mentioned in James Joyce's writing. Sandymount has literary resonances: Yeats's birthplace, for instance. Frank O'Connor, the short story writer from Cork, lived for a time in Strand Road as does the Nobel prizewinner Seamus Heaney. Words and seagulls fly through the Sandymount air.

Since my return to Dublin I have continued writing. Unlike teaching, one can go on writing till one drops. In 1990 John F. Deane of Dedalus Press published my collection of poems, *Carnival at the River*, mostly based on memories of childhood and youth. It was favourably received. Lagan Press in Belfast brought out my *Collected Poems* in 1995. I never had a book that received such acclaim in Ireland, England and the USA. This acclaim was followed by the *Irish Times* poetry award, the most prestigious prize in Ireland. Just past my 75th birthday I had the pleasure of being presented with an engraved silver plaque and a substantial cheque by the President of Ireland, Mary Robinson, at a widely attended gathering at the Royal Dublin Society. This made me feel that perhaps I had not spent uncounted hours in vain struggling to find the right simile and metaphor.

I have just referred to my age. Like most older people I cannot believe that so many years have slipped away and I am aware of having achieved only a fraction of what I had in mind as a boy. So much wasted time! So many opportunities I failed to take! So many wrong decisions! I think of Henry Reed's delicious parody of T.S. Eliot: 'As we get older we do not get any younger.' But even old age has its compensations, and older people, thanks to improved living conditions and better medication, increasingly lead productive lives. Prejudice on age does exist and must be resisted like any other prejudice. The journalist William Rees-Mogg put it well in an article in *The Times*: 'Ageism should have no more acceptance in our society than any other species of apartheid.'

Poets are supposed to die young but not all of us are as obliging as Keats and Shelley. Robert Frost, W.B. Yeats and Thomas Hardy kept working into old age. Hardy, at 85, published a collection of poems and carried on for another three years. The violinist Yehudi Menuhin discussed his personal and professional life with vigour when, at 80, he sat in the psychiatrist's chair for a radio interview with Professor Anthony Clare. John Gielgud, the actor with 'a golden voice', is still working at over 90. Alistair Cooke at 89 continues to send vivid radio despatches from the United States. He once told how the BBC tried to get rid of him and of his refusal to go.

These are random examples from the creative and performing arts but in other fields, too, men — and of course women — defy the years and go on achieving. Activity of whatever kind, mental or physical, seems the best way of coping with the ageing process. Pablo Casals remarked when he was 93: 'Work and interest in worthwhile things are the best remedy for age.'

Since my own working life as a college lecturer ended some ten years ago, I have been able to reflect on the considerable experience of life I acquired one way and another. I have looked back on my life with its frustrations in childhood, its years of promise as a young man eager to make his mark, the setbacks that crowded in during my late 30s and early 40s, and then the renewal of ambition and hope as I neared 50 and which has continued to this day.

I have learnt various lessons, some of them a bit late for effective action. But one thing I have learnt is that events rarely turn out as one expects. As Robert Burns warned us, the best-laid plans, the most fervent desires may not come to fruition. Yet doors open and opportunities arise that cannot be foreseen.

In a poem I tried to recall the time of hope in springtime, the time of uncertainty in high summer, the time of serenity as the leaves begin to fall:

THE CALL

for Jack W. Weaver

I can state it plainly now:
It has not been what I expected.
Away back in my boyhood
I dreamed in the twilight,
Lost in book,
And as the light faded
Heard a voice from a garden
Calling me softly
To a dew-drenched Eden.

I spent fresh mornings there
An eager apprentice
Active in the sun.

In the null years
The garden grew rank,
I strayed from it
Into the mute forest
of naked trees.

Yet the dream came back.
I returned to a garden of sorts,
Weeded, planted.
A few people visited.

FLOWERS IN BLOOM

Now in late autumn
There are flowers in bloom
Though the evenings are chill.
Yet I must repeat:
Things are not what I expected.

TWENTY-SEVEN

Never Go Back, Boy!

'Whenever you go back to any place,' she said and I marvelled at the phrase, 'across the planets of the years, nothing is the way it was when you were young. Never go back, girl.'

— Seán O'Faoláin, *The Planets of the Years*

When I return from time to time to the damp Belfast streets of childhood, youth and early manhood, they no longer glitter like patent leather. They are sleazier, more littered. The lights are less bright. All changed, if not changed utterly. And not just because of the 'Troubles', which have brought destruction and tragedies too frequent to record to Belfast and the north of Ireland. Even before the latest outbreak of civil strife, the process of change was well under way — flyovers, blocks of flats, new hotels, high rises, fast food, Chinese restaurants. Even so, many of the old buildings still remain intact if put to different uses. My aunts' newsagent's shop on the Stranmillis Road is still a newsagency.

The vivid faces of the generation before mine have all gone — Mother, Father, Aunt Tillie, Uncle George, Tommy Gibson. All dead as, indeed, are some of my contemporaries, one or two of them younger than myself. I walk, a kind of exile, in a city of ghosts. As my late friend, the poet and writer, Clifford Dyment, put it:

The end is death!
I cry in terror.
In the end, death,
Agrees the mirror.

Ghosts – and memories. An image that comes to mind is of a doorway in Royal Avenue, a short distance from the Grand Central Hotel. It was a wartime evening, with army officers and their girlfriends coming and going to and from the hotel. I had been bored and depressed. Life seemed to consist wholly of blackout and drizzle. I went into a scruffy, ill-lit café somewhere around Rosemary Street. There I got into a bantering conversation with a buxom, dark-skinned girl called Peggy who wore gypsy earrings and had been unsparing in the use of powder and rouge. She spoke in that harsh type of local accent that lends itself to easy mimicry and laughter. I felt we could continue our conversation in a less oppressive atmosphere.

'Would you like a drink?' I asked, a trifle apprehensively, for I carried in my mind the idea of the Demon Drink.

'Well, I've never had one before, but I don't mind if you don't mind.' We went out into the drizzle and searched for a bar.

For a girl who had never had a drink before, Peggy showed a remarkable capacity as a learner. She consumed several gin-and-limes with consummate ease. I drank a couple of bottles of Guinness and felt well on the way down the slippery path. The dark brew went slightly to my head. Peggy told me about her dear old granny up the Crumlin Road and how careful she had to be 'with all them Yank soldiers about'. She surprised me by telling me she hated the police. This, in our small, in-grown community, signalled the fact that Peggy did not belong to my own tribe.

After our drinks we went out and, without speaking, looked for a doorway around Smithfield. The streets were unpeopled in the black night, all solid citizens were at home listening to the radio and drinking cocoa. Peggy kissed me with abandon and pulled me vigorously towards her. I arranged to meet the dark-locked Peggy a few days later, thinking she might assuage the ache in my heart Irene had caused. We were to meet in the pub. I arrived punctually but, after a few minutes, I had a feeling she would not turn up. I drank glass after glass of the dark beer as I waited – in vain.

Two or three weeks later, I did catch a glimpse of Peggy. She was strolling along arm in arm with a soldier – an American private, First Class. I accepted my defeat with philosophic calm. After all, Peggy was no Irene, no inspirer of high endeavour, no Beatrice for a would-be Dante. Hundreds of Peggies roamed the streets, hardly distinguishable one from another. In the whole wide, mad, cruel world there was but one Irene.

Irene, goddess of peace, had been a symbol of light in a dark and threatening world. The flesh-and-blood person who once existed for me becomes less and less real as the years blur the image. Have not most of us, one way and another, had an Irene in our lives? She is the girl we once saw in a train and loved instantly, but never even spoke to. She is the person we have lost. For poets and dreamers, because they trade in images and magic, the Irenes, the Maud Gonnes, are not so much women as enchantresses.

In *Poetry and Truth*, Goethe tells of his Irene who, in actual fact, was called Gretchen. He says:

> It was at this time, too, that a friend urgently invited me to an evening party . . . We met quite late; the meal was most frugal, the wine just drinkable . . . When at last the latter gave out someone called for a servant. Instead there appeared a girl of uncommon and, indeed, in that environment, of incredible beauty.
>
> 'What do you want?' she asked, after she had saluted us all in the friendliest way. 'The maid servant is ill and in bed. Perhaps I can help you.'
>
> 'There's no wine left,' said one of the company. 'If you were to get us a couple of bottles, it would be very nice.'
>
> 'Oh please do, Gretchen,' said another. 'It's only three steps . . .'
>
> From that moment on the image of this girl followed me wherever I went. It was the first lasting impression which a being of the other sex had made on me. Since I could neither find nor even seek a pretext to see her in her house, I attended church for her sake. I soon found out where she would sit and so I gazed my fill during the long Protestant service . . .
>
> The first stirrings of love of an unspoiled youth takes on a decisive spiritual collaboration. Nature seems to desire that one sex should apprehend in the other that which is good and beautiful in sensuous form. And so to me, too, there was revealed through the vision of this girl and through my love of her a new world of the beautiful and the excellent.

For Irene's sake, I too – so recently a devout young Leftist and rebel against religious authority of all kinds — attended services at the virginally white Christian Science Church near the university. Like Goethe on his Gretchen, I too gazed my fill on Irene during the long service.

Illusions, delusions, romantic will-o'-the-wisps die hard. When I go back home — ah, but is it really home any longer? — I still on solitary evening strolls keep an eye out for the figure of slender, willowy Irene. Whether she is alive or dead or, if alive, where she may live, I do not know. Perhaps I am still following a dream. And I think of the youth who, half a century ago, eased his heartache by writing:

> Sorrow for everything, and not knowing
> Why it matters so much.

❂ Contents List ❂

Leading and Managing Groups in the Outdoors

❂ Contents

Contents

LIST OF DIAGRAMS AND TABLES

Preface to the 1st Edition

Aspirant leaders wishing to take groups sailing, canoeing, hill-walking, skiing, mountain-biking, caving or climbing can find any number of handbooks or skill manuals to aid them in acquiring technical knowledge about the activity of their choice. What they could not, at one time, find anywhere in the U.K. under one cover, was a compact volume on the subject of leading, handling and managing a group of people in the outdoors - which is what leaders do for a substantial proportion of their time spent with groups even when engaged in environmental studies, ecological projects or field work. The reasons for this lack are significant and complex. Historically, the rising tide of accidents to school-led parties in the late 1950s and early 1960s tended to put the focus on the technical aspects of leading groups in new qualifications simply to cut down on the number of accidents. The leadership dimension may have been *neglected* at one time because leaders were simply unaware of it. It may have been *ignored* because such matters were felt to be less important than the business of acquiring the technical skills. It may have been deliberately *avoided* because of an aversion, common in this country, to anything with the suspicion of a 'psychology' or worse, a 'pedagogical', label on it. So the apparently low profile of the subject was partly to do with attitudes, but also partly due to the fact that such information was rather inaccessible and scattered about in a wide range of magazine articles, conference reports, occasional pamphlets and specialist journals.

This book is an extended version of an article first written in the early 1970s. It has been revised from time to time and now attempts to collate some of the relevant material available elsewhere on the subject in order to make it accessible under one cover. One of its main purposes is to introduce aspirant leaders in the outdoors to leadership theory and practice by indicating the main themes and sub-headings rather than by running the risk of overloading them in attempting to cover the subject too comprehensively. There is much that could have been included to extend this book further; the difficulty was knowing where to stop. The earlier shorter version of this book in Langmuir's "Mountaincraft and Leadership" was a treatment of the subject at level one. The present version might be conceived of as grade two. To go further would begin to approach "degree" standard which the majority of leaders do not really need as it would be probably more suited to the specialised needs of the management development trainer or those in the specialist 'therapy' field. Those wishing to delve deeper will find a suggested bibliography at the end.

The intention is also to raise levels of awareness about the skills involved in the leading and management of groups of people - an area of outdoor practice that has been neglected over the years.

No claims are made to be fully comprehensive. A thorough coverage of human behaviour would require more than a lifetime of experience and study. We, most of us, only manage to scratch the surface of this vast subject. But scratch it aspirant leaders must if their groups are to have worthwhile experiences.

The script may be repetitious in places but it is necessary. Leadership material is of that sort which attempts to describe the intangibles in a system which is open-ended, fluid and infinitely variable. It is therefore less predictable. Human behaviour does not always follow regular logical patterns. More often than not it is messy and untidy. It is not always easy to demonstrate the inter-connectivity that exists between different aspects. When the link is one amongst many alternatives, it is often not easy to identify the correct one. So it may be difficult to achieve an appreciation of some of the inter-relationships in material of this nature unless links are specifically demonstrated sometimes by being repeated.

Events conjoin to bring the subject of leadership into greater prominence and create a climate more receptive to material on the leadership of groups in the outdoors. The Sports Council issued a Report in August 1991 entitled "Leadership in Outdoor Activities" which spelled out the need for more and better leaders in the outdoors. A survey conducted by Dale Johnson in the mid 1990s revealed that providers of leadership training for the various Mountain Leader Training Boards felt least confident in delivering the 'soft' skills. There is no doubt that the fashion for management training courses has also made 'people' skills a necessary requirement which has made it more generally acceptable and less of an esoteric subject to be shunned. Outdoor and adventurous activities now feature in the National Curriculum as an option in the P.E. Curriculum. National Vocational Qualifications (NVQs) in the Outdoor Industry, as they came on-stream, also tended to give the subject of outdoor leadership a sharpened relevance.

What I have to say about leaders - not leadership - may be somewhat challenging in some quarters in this country (U.K.). I have used "his/her" and "s/he" in an attempt to help break down the gender stereotyping so prevalent in the outdoor world. It causes a bit of awkwardness in composition at times but the device is needful for an area where outdoor leaders are predominantly male. Numbers in the text, (e.g.[1]), relate to references found at the end of the book.

Preface to the Second Edition

It seemed timely to update this book as a reprint was imminent. Much has happened since it was first written - not least the appearance of AALA on the scene to keep us all in order following the Lyme Bay tragedy. NVQs, which were a hot and, arguably, unsavoury topic in the early 1990s, are lower on the horizon and the Local Skills Councils and Skills Active are now the rising stars in the drive to raise standards. But Governing Body Awards are still an essential part of the leader's toolkit. It is to be hoped that currently on-going discussions with the Health and Safety Executive (HSE) about the Working at Height regulations reach a sane conclusion in what could otherwise become a nightmarish and unworkable situation.

The unwelcome and growing trend towards risk avoidance and 'blame' litigation makes the task of the outdoor leader harder and less pleasant than it was formerly, whilst the declining health of the nation, particularly in the young, makes the need for active, life-long recreational activity more vital. Now more than ever does the leader need to 'have it all sorted'. The times seem to be drawing the National Governing Bodies (NGBs) into closer cooperation as moves within Skills Active seek to define 'generic' coaching skills.

An extensive updating has been undertaken, particularly in the area of risk management which is all the rage these days. We always did it but didn't need reams of paper to prove it! The chapter on aims has been expanded and a plea made for greater attention to be paid to environmental issues and ways of integrating them into programmes.

There is an introduction to the latest theories about how people learn which has made great advances recently and has given a higher substantiation to learning in the outdoors. Other 'goodies' like 'leading adult groups' may be found useful. A section on the legal framework within which leaders outdoors operate, seemed needful in these litigious times. I have again tried to avoid overloading aspirant leaders but the attempt to do so grows daily more difficult as society becomes more complex.

This book should be seen as one that is essentially for the practitioner. It is neither intended to be an academic treatise on the subject of leading, nor does it claim to be the definitive, final word about good practice which is always moving on and happily continues to be the subject of robust opinions. The book is the author's attempt to provide some notion of what leading groups can encompass and require.

Acknowledgements

I am most grateful and much indebted to all former staff members of Ghyll Head Outdoor Education Centre over the years whose contributions in discussion helped in the generation of ideas, in particular to Sue Gillard and Greg Care. Elsewhere, and at a later time, to Chris Loynes for his very useful suggestions, and to Shirley Payne for her editorial help, hard work and ideas freely given in the final stages of putting the first edition together.

A special thank you goes to Lyn Noble, a former Principal of Derbyshire's White Hall Outdoor Education Centre, for his humorous illustrations. His long experience in outdoor education gives him that insight and feel for situations out-of-doors which gives his artwork a sharpened, sometimes delightfully mischievous, and 'chuckleful' relevance.

Very many thanks too, to Fiona Exon at the IOL Office, for all her hard work in re-formatting and putting a second edition all back together again ready for printing.

Introduction

The title of this book is about the leading of groups in the wide context of the outdoors for a variety of purposes. Although it tends to deal with the more 'adventurous' types of situation, it has much to offer leaders involved in less 'heady' situations. It is relevant to groups on a ramble in woodland, a stroll along a beach or river walk, a coastal trek along cliff tops, a natural history outing, a day on upland moors or more rugged mountains, rock-climbing or canoeing, sailing or caving, and most demanding of all, the setting up of self-led, independent, unaccompanied expeditions or journeys. It will be noticed, however, that some of the detailed descriptive examples illustrating fundamental concepts and principles about leadership have featured, but not exclusively, those situations in which expedition leaders and leaders of groups in upland country find themselves. This is partly because it is in the nature of these two activities that they are characteristically conducted as group activities, arguably more so perhaps than most other outdoor activities. This is also partly to do with the fact that, unlike many other activities such as caving, canoeing and possibly sailing in certain situations, walking activity takes place in an unconfined environment which requires a greater range of skills and leadership to operate effectively. But it should be no hard matter for leaders, whatever their activity interest, to pick out the elements which are universally applicable to any leadership situation. Leaders of outdoor study groups, field studies or ecological projects may also find them of use for no matter what the purpose of any day spent in the outdoors, the environment is the same and the ever-present imperatives imposed by the natural environment on human endeavour, requiring modifications in behaviour and care, still apply. That said, it is one of the hopes of this book that environmental content will figure more strongly in leaders' thinking than it has hitherto. It was never more needed than now.

For long enough, ideas about what constituted a suitable syllabus content for the training of leaders, instructors or coaches of outdoor activities such as canoeing, sailing, caving, skiing and various mountain activities in the U.K., have placed top priority on high standard technical skills practically to the exclusion of all else. I daresay enthusiastic teachers of geography, geology, biology, botany and the like have been equally keen, under pressure from tight curriculum time, and the need to ensure that syllabus material is covered, to put the scientific content of the day first and group needs second. But in the context of leadership, where a group of people interacting with each other is involved, a concentration on reaching high levels of technical skill and/or knowledge alone are inadequate. No matter how highly skilled, if a leader does not have the ability to manage properly a relationship with the group, and at the same time enable the members of the group to manage their own relationships with each other, then that leader is likely to be less effective. Situations charged with negative emotions caused by poor leadership may become as fraught with potential danger as if the group was unskilled, poorly equipped or out of its depth - which, in a different but very real sense, it would be.

It is arguable that a leader with lower level technical skills and higher level leadership skills will do a better job than a leader with higher technical skills and lower inter-personal skills who is more motivated to deliver high achievement, but who is more likely to end up with an unhappy group. A leader with lower level technical skills and higher level leadership skills, is more motivated to have a group whose morale will be high, but might be less likely to deliver a high level of achievement. In all of this much depends on what criteria are used to judge success and what the aims of those in the situation are.

Consistently high levels of achievement and a contented group require a leader to be equally accomplished in both sets of skills.

Leading is an holistic activity; it is whole - signals come in, responses flow out. All the aspects of leading and managing are blended together, almost seamlessly, and working together. Breaking everything down and reducing it into its component parts is a necessary evil in a book of this nature. Having to fragment means that one of the unavoidable illusions created by any book such as this dealing with the skills, is the impression of a mass of material sub-divided into watertight compartments, any one of which a leader may be required to recall from time to time. What such books cannot easily convey, is the need for all these items of skill and knowledge to have been so well absorbed that they no longer exist in isolated compartments. It is necessary for them to have meshed with all the others in an integrated manner similar to the way in which tapestry threads interweave to form a pattern or picture. This mingling of threads underlines the fact that each of them has a related connection with all the others. The nature of these interdependent relationships must be understood by the leader for a special reason. When faced by situations, minor or major, requiring particular skills, the interaction of all the influences (e.g. weather, nature of the terrain, group morale, abilities of members of the group, suitability and condition of equipment worn or carried) which bear on the situation should have taken place in the leader's mind, almost intuitively and spontaneously to the point where the key factors in the situation will have become identified. Identifying the key factors from a mass of background detail is a crucial leadership skill. It is these factors which influence judgements and subsequent decisions. The ability to scan them analytically and quickly to select from the tool-box of skills the appropriate one to deal with a situation, should be an important aim for all aspirant leaders.

This book does not set out to tell leaders how to "get it all together" so that all that has been learned can be applied exactly in the right sequence, pitched at exactly the right level, delivered at exactly the right moment in the manner most appropriate for a group in the course of a day in the outdoors. Depending on one's experience and point of view, it is either a very simple or a very complex business.

Technical competence in the various outdoor skills and the professional knowledge about the specialised outdoor environments (river, sea, lake, cave, cliff, moor or mountain) pertaining to them that leaders must have, are expertly dealt with elsewhere in other manuals. In the context of this book they are important not only because they are essential to carrying out the job efficiently, but because research shows that competence and knowledge are key strands in a leader's power base, making authority more credible. The focus of this book therefore takes technical competences as read, but sets them aside for the moment to concentrate on those other kinds of competences required by leaders.

" *Identifying key factors from a mass of background detail is a crucial leadership skill*".

The chapters that follow attempt to describe the various parts comprising the integrated nature of the task when the job of leading a group is being carried out. They are also concerned with the leader's ability to handle ideas. Ideas are not solid, concrete things like the contents of a rucksack. When the contents of the rucksack are pulled out, they are visible. It is not necessary to imagine what they are or what they look like. If they are damaged, imperfect, too heavy or unsuitable it is fairly obvious. Ideas being of the mind, have to be created by an effort of will. To be able to push ideas around, sort them out, modify them and shape them into some sort of framework that feels right for you, is not easy. The various concepts and models found in these chapters are tools to assist leaders in their thinking about leadership.

It is important to be aware that ideas and thinking 'drive' everything else.

❂ Chapter One ❂

What's it all About - Aims and Values

The outdoors has many facets, many features, which we find intriguing, attractive, useful, challenging, beautiful, off-putting even - but you name it and someone, somewhere will be 'turned on' by it. There is something in the natural environment to suit all tastes and we all have our own favourite preference which we value individually. Ever since people began to go voluntarily into the wilder parts of the outdoors in this country about three hundred years ago, human activity in it has been characterised by an infinite variety of reasons for being there - sailor, scientist, explorer, naturalist, mountaineer, caver, canoeist, artist, poet, aesthete, mystic, hunter, farmer, industrialist and developer. Each followed the aspect of it they were interested in purely for its own sake. It is only in the last hundred years, as the industrial revolution changed the communal/rural lifestyle into the urban jungle, that society has seen the outdoors as a marvellous medium for developing the young - in so many different ways - that it has become necessary for anyone intending to do this type of work to make choices and decisions about which particular way they will do it and how and why.

Making a Difference

Most people who lead groups in the outdoors do so out of a hope or conviction that they will make a difference in the lives of those they lead. That difference may come about for any number of reasons - through increased physical skill, the acquisition of new knowledge, a new caring awareness about the natural environment, improved social skills, better communication skills and teamworking, enhanced feelings of self worth (feeling good about yourself), greater self confidence, lifted horizons, new insights and so on. All of these 'differences' have their own particular values attached to them. These differences can be something that is added to a person or something that is removed (like a chip on the shoulder). Increased effectiveness does not always depend on new skills or knowledge, but often on removing or lessening the influence of something that is preventing progress.

Ask the average person to say what their values are and they will probably find it quite difficult on the spur of the moment and begin asking questions to discover what you are driving at - "what do you mean? Values about what?" Until they are given a few cues to set them going, there is often a kind of mental block, for values tend not to be readily accessible when starting from 'cold'. Putting to them a situation needing preferences or priorities to resolve will soon set them off. Values are contentious things about which people can get very emotional because values are the essence of a person - what they believe in and stand for. As a subject of study it is both fascinating and challenging, whilst for others it can be a necessary but boring topic. Therefore, the more in-depth treatment of this subject is placed in an Appendix at the end of the book so that the impetuous activity types can get more immediately into what they will regard as the meatier and more relevant chapters of this book. The Appendix can be by-passed and read later or it can be read now as a more general introduction to values.

Judgements, Choices and Value Conflicts

In pursuing any activity in the outdoors with a group of people, the party leader has one characteristic value conflict or big paradox to resolve - the management of risk (see chapter 7). At first glance this might appear to be a purely technical and practical problem. The leader has to find the right balance between what is dangerous and what is safe. If the leader is engaged in encouraging a novice group to take up an outdoor activity purely as a recreational pastime, the matter may be as simple as that. "Is this white water too technical for the skill level of the group or that cave passage too committing?" As the group becomes more skilled and able, it continues to be a matter of judging whether their skill is equal to the challenge that is contemplated. This simple line of approach to 'recreational activity training' used to be quite common but may, hopefully, have been superseded by methods a bit more sensitive to the wishes and needs of the participants.

But if the leader sees him/herself as working in the sphere of social education or outdoor learning, the problem is not quite that simple.

Many forms of work with groups in the realm of outdoor learning contain an added element which is based on the belief that confronting challenges, making judgements and taking decisions about them and overcoming them by coping with the element of risk and uncertainty which is attached, is personally developmental for the participant. The straight-forward practical problem of getting the balance right between danger and safety may thus become overlain with strong ethical or moral overtones. In a nutshell, the problem is that what is perceived to be 'dangerous' may be equated with what is seen to be 'exciting' and what is perceived to be 'safe' may be equated with what is seen to be 'dull'. This then may be taken a logical step further. If a session is to be 'developmental' for a student, it has to be exciting because it is believed that a student has to be extended or stretched by challenge in some way for development to take place. So there may arise the dangerous belief that an activity can only be exciting if there is an element of danger present. If it is safe it will be dull, undemanding and therefore 'non-developmental'. So, it is maintained, danger is developmental and safety is not.

In everyday life this is not necessarily true of course and is, admittedly, oversimplifying the matter. But at the heart of the problem of resolving this particular value conflict, lie the most fundamental questions to do with philosophic considerations involving values:

- Why are you doing it?
- Why are you saddling yourself with a group that will be a severe restriction on your own freedom to follow your own thing?
- What is it all for?
- What are you hoping to achieve?
- For what overall purpose is the group really being taken out into the mountains, or down a cave, or onto a river, along a stream, a beach or a wildlife habitat?
- Just what is it all about?

Values will be embedded in the answers to all these questions. The hardest question, and the most important one to answer is that most difficult of personal questions - **"what am I all about?"** - for it is usually the case that when a person with authority over others gets them to do some kind of activity, the way that activity is conducted constitutes a projection of that person's personality which may even extend into the sphere of moral activity. A simple illustration will make the meaning of this point clear, as when a leader behaves immorally in seeking to make others become like him/herself. This is the likely scenario. When a leader decides to take young people into the countryside because "it is 'good' for them" (for whatever reason), this decision will be informed by that leader's belief about what is 'good'. The leader's concept of what constitutes 'good' is a moral judgement. In this instance it is often likely to be a case of, "If it did me 'good' and made me what I am, it must be 'good' for others too." The mistake here is in assuming that the needs of others are exactly like one's own and that all one has to do is repeat one's earlier experiences to create similar effects with others. If you do not know what your values are in this context, you may be unknowingly trying to mould others in your own image. To do so would be immoral. Knowing about your own values and what 'you are all about' greatly reduces the possibility of trying to mould others in your own image. You may have got as far in your thinking as hoping to make 'a difference' in their lives. Now you need to spell out to yourself, "what kind of difference?"

Unconscious Nature of Values

To find answers to the question, "what am I all about?", the vast, inner world of ideas, values and aims must be conscientiously explored. The search requires thought and energy similar to that required to discover the immense, external, physical world of the mountains, the sea and all their flora and fauna. The working model of the world carried inside one's head is a complex structure of ideas, impressions, beliefs, attitudes, prejudices, underpinned by values - all of which shape and determine our behaviour and how we deal with the outside world or other people. We can call this model a working hypothesis, which is only 'true' for the time being until it is changed or modified by new or different experiences acting upon it. This 'values model' affects all of one's actions and reactions. The process by which this complex of ideas is acquired, is often largely unconscious. Few of these processes operate out of a state of awareness. Many leaders are not likely to be aware that they have adopted many of the values that they hold. They may not be aware that there is a choice and that it is possible to choose which values they will adopt. They may not be aware of what range of choice exists. It is a very useful and revealing exercise for example, for leaders to identify and describe the authority model which they prefer to work under and to describe the style of control they use for preference when vested with authority themselves. Are they similar or, if different, why?

The Need for a Philosophic Basis - The 'Why'

Whilst in the past much thought and emphasis has been given to the *'what'* of leadership (technical skills and knowledge etc.), insufficient time has been given to the *'how'* of leadership (processes). Still less time has been given to providing leaders in training with a range of ideas about the *'why'* of leadership (reasons/motives). This could be interpreted as 'brain-washing'. It is crucial to be quite clear here, that:

the intention would not be to tell leaders what they

ought to think, but rather what they ought to think <u>about</u>.

It is important that leaders develop their own philosophic frameworks, but it is unfortunate that they are sometimes left to develop one in isolation, without any assistance from those who direct the work of leaders in training. A particular set of values is required that is focused on the working needs of leaders.

Time should be set aside in training to provide a range of ideas so that a leader does not have to begin this process in a near vacuum. This would be most beneficial. If future leaders can be helped to become aware that there is a range of choices in these matters about which they have to begin making conscious decisions, they receive a booster start in what is a difficult, essentially self-directed, often very slow, process.

It is important to understand why it is vital for leaders to develop a philosophy (which is all about values):

the reasons one has for doing things

determine the whole way in which they are done.

To illustrate the point, the leader who takes groups out in order to train them to become hill walkers or canoeists, will treat the whole process in a way markedly different from the leader who takes groups out in order to have a different or more informal environment in which to improve working relationships with the group. With the former, "things" are the priority, with the latter, "people" are the main emphasis. These standpoints which favour either 'things' (embodying values to do with achieving a task or developing skill and becoming proficient) or 'people' (embodying values to do with good working relationships) are the two main positions or standpoints (orientations) from which to approach the leading of young people. To risk labouring the point, it should be apparent that it is doubly important for leaders to be aware which orientation is their natural preference or inclination. Without this awareness, leaders will tend to be inflexibly stuck with a particular attitude, unable to move away from it when necessary. For the first-mentioned, activist leader in the example just given, techniques and proficiency, ascents and achievement will be the main aim and end, whilst for the 'relationships' leader they will be a means to other ends concerned with effective relationships and personal development.

"A booster start in what is a difficult....often very slow process"

The programme of the former will concentrate on the acquisition of proficiency in the skills deemed necessary in the long term for many different types of situations, whilst the second will be concerned only to impart the minimum of skills necessary for the immediate particular situation so that they do not overshadow the main aim of improved relationships. For example, to include capsize drill in a first time, 'taster' sailing session with a novice group using dinghies could be a pure waste of time. It could be a valid thing to do if the session was so set up that the capsize was a problem to be solved as part of a team building exercise! The way in which the leaders in each situation present the 'content' of the day and conduct it, will be quite different. Leaders need to be aware of how and why they are operating in the way they do, because only then does it become possible for them to see whether aims are in harmony with style and practice (see 'style pitfalls' in chapter 4). If they are not in accord then progress along the lines aimed for will be retarded or blocked.

To be operating in a particular way, without knowing why, can be acceptable sometimes. There are leaders who can work intuitively in this way quite successfully but they can tend to be unwilling to challenge what they find. An intuitive style can be a recipe for poor quality leadership as when leadership practice becomes an extension of a leader's own personal motives for pursuing that particular activity. No censure is intended for a leader having such a personal set of motives. Indeed they are a vital element in the generation of his/her motivation to lead others. It would be abnormal if a leader did not possess such "springs for action". But it is important that such reasons are not allowed to impinge too heavily upon operations with a group.

Most leaders probably have two sets of motives and aims. The personal set is about what the outdoors means to them. The other set should be more selfless and concerned with what the leader hopes to achieve for, and with, a group of other people. The act of identifying one's own commitment to one's preferred activity confers certain benefits - only then is it possible to be able to discount or set aside these personal aims when leading. Days out which are driven by motives inappropriate for the group, whilst they may not necessarily harm the group in any way, are more prone to unproductive outcomes. Leaders not in touch with themselves may perpetrate acts of selfishness and insensitivity which can leave their groups diminished and devastated, rather than enlarged and uplifted.

Leader training which includes a better balance between the 'technical' and 'people' skills will make this less a matter of chance.

The Process of Acquiring Values

Young leaders entering this field may find the business of sorting out aims for themselves a difficult process. It is all very well to say that you must have aims to guide an outdoor programme, but where do these aims come from? What generates them? How does one know which aims to choose? How can one be certain if the right aims have been picked? Being certain about what you are doing is a fundamental need in leaders and one of the function of aims (values) is to provide that sense of certainty. So there is a bit of a chicken and the egg situation here sometimes. How does one actually go about the business of choosing aims and where does one start? They aren't picked out of the air like butterflies - that's for sure.There is no easy answer but I'll try to give some indication of how it tends to work.

The short and unhelpful answer is that for most people it takes time. The amount of time varies greatly between people. A young person grappling with this tricky area often approaches it in a very mechanical fashion. Indeed 'going through the motions' may be the only way possible for some leaders initially - perhaps only by doing this do the implications reveal themselves to become more obvious and known. Information about aims is gleaned by reading, listening, copying - a shopping list, so to speak. But then it can only be applied in a very clinical fashion. There may be very little or no conviction, no beliefs driving the choice. It is after one has bounced around life for a while, or conversely has been bounced around by life, that values begin to emerge in one's consciousness. They develop perhaps as a result of discussion and argument, or of lessons learned by experience, or from discoveries or comparisons made with other leaders. It is bound up with the process of deciding about the meaning of one's own life, even its purpose! There is also the matter of deciding which values are aimed **for** and which values are used for aiming **with**; and what is the difference between aims and objectives?

Perhaps the best place to start is with yourself. You would not be coming into this line of work if you did not already have some convictions about its benefits - probably already experienced by yourself. Those for whom it just seems to be a good idea - best of luck!

The following brief description of some of the phases to be found in this process, as it relates to the outdoors, are deliberately simplified in order to highlight essentials. It should be noted that the phases do not necessarily occur in the order in which they are described here. Elsewhere the holistic nature of outdoor experiences has been noted and how the splitting of it up into its constituent parts is a somewhat artificial practice (chapter 5).

The Physical Phase - and Physical Values

There is a time when the emphasis is on the joyful exploration of new ground both externally (geographically) and internally (physically and mentally). The poet, Wordsworth, experienced this:

"......... For nature then
(The coarser pleasures of my boyish days,
and their glad animal movements all gone by)
To me was all in all".

And:

"........................ the leaping from rock to rock".

It is a time for discovering personal capacities by testing oneself against the environment and great store is set by the satisfactions to be gained from physical achievement, high skill levels and endurance. This is often during youth when physical capacities are at their maximum. But in these days of early retirees, the phase can occur much later on because the opportunity had not presented itself, or was not taken, earlier.

The Environmental Phase - And Environmental Values

A deep interest in the environment can develop at any time but, for some people, the time when the faster pace of youth slows down will have a significant effect in this respect. Or, holidays with your young children often alters the focus of your previous interest outdoors as you show them the micro natural wonders all around them. More time becomes available to be interested in other things such as phenomena in the natural environment. Greater interest is found in the flora, fauna and geological aspects and why things are the way they are. Interestingly, Wordsworth found a way via the natural environment of bridging this phase to the social phase. How many leaders have been inspired to take groups into the outdoors by his words in the 1798 poem, 'Matthew', I wonder?

"Books! 'tis a dull and endless strife"

or

"Come forth into the light of things
Let Nature be your teacher "

and

"One impulse from a vernal wood can teach you more of man
Of moral evil and of good than all the sages can."

The Social Phase

There comes some time a realisation that, with groups, the pursuit of outdoor activities for their own sake, an approach which is called '**autotelic**', is not necessarily everything and there comes an understanding that:

> **the effectiveness of work with young people**
> **depends more on the quality of the**
> **relationships that are formed,**
> **than upon the width or depth to which**
> **outdoor activities are pursued.**

The concern for the quality of relationships and the needs of the individuals in the group becomes the more dominant focus. It can then matter less to the leader whether it is two or three peaks that are ascended or even if the summit is reached at all. It will be more important that the group is enabled, the modern 'buzz' word is "empowered", to exercise a greater degree of initiative and decision-making in the creation of its own experience rather than implement some plan of the leader. It is only when a person is empowered or feels in control that their values are being actively called upon. Values are not really called upon when passively following a programme dreamed up by someone else because the programmer's values are driving everything. The exception is when an adverse reaction to the leader's plans provokes rebellious feelings and a desire for an alternative (also value laden) option. Demands are only made directly upon personal values when people are involved in making judgements, choices, decisions and living with consequences.

"One impulse from a vernal wood...."

Personal Philosophy Changes with Time

Once a philosophic basis for leadership has been identified it is important to recognise that it is not static. It can be affected by changing personal circumstances, such as changes in work situation (which may entail different kinds of groups and aims, different equipment, even different activities), or marital status, or parenthood - which brings different perspectives to bear on one's viewpoint. The periodic review and evaluation of aims is a useful habit to acquire.

Fresh Outlooks for Changing Times

There are leaders whose thinking may not have progressed beyond the stage of, " I got a lot out of it and I hope they will too". Up to a point, that is a valid point and acceptable, but in pursuing that narrow line exclusively, the group may be denied valuable learning opportunities. Is it not the case that, 'I got a lot out of it' because I was doing it unled and independently finding out for myself? Is it equally not the case, that individuals who only ever experience being led in a formal group will never get out of it what I got?

This attitude sometimes receives reinforcement from the media which ought to know better, and from poorly informed sectors of the community who seem to believe, for example, that leaders only involve groups in activities in order to teach them how to become proficient and therefore safe participants! The dramatic facade of the physical activities is an outward show that tends to mesmerise and mislead the lay observer (and seemingly, the media) about the true nature of the underlying rationale.

Outdoor practice has greatly changed in range and complexity since the early 1960s. Then, a reaction to the post war austerity years gave rise to a hedonistic outlook which, in the outdoors, was activity-oriented in its pursuit of enjoyment. The activity was done purely for its own sake - unless it was an Outward Bound course. Now the greater diversity of types of people participating in some kind of activity outdoors has produced a wider range of rationales to support their involvement and there is much less opportunity, or justification, for the simplistic outlooks and single-minded approaches of earlier times.[1] The participants can no longer be described exclusively as 'white, middle-class, able-bodied and conformist'. Every type of race, colour, class or creed and many ranges of disability are now catered for in the outdoors which requires of leaders, a level of ability in the soft skills, awareness, sensitivity and empathy, arguably once deemed less necessary.

If leaders have not thought about such philosophical matters, there will be something lacking in the way they approach their groups and any activity outdoors. It is emphasised that these ideas will colour and shape all subsequent behaviour in their leadership and in what they plan and do. Discussing ideas with others and exchanging opinions will help, but the amalgam of values arrived at must necessarily be a personal act.

Paradoxes and Value Conflicts

In attempting to reach a philosophy about the whys and wherefores of leadership, the aspiring leader will feel the contradictory pressures of a paradox touched on at the start of this chapter - safety versus danger. The leader will be aware of the weight of opinion emanating from a safety-conscious, over-protective, risk averse society seeking to impose safety values even more strongly now that we are subject to a Health and Safety Executive (following the Health and Safety at Work Act of 1974) and subsequent to the lessons and outcomes of the Lyme Bay canoeing tragedy of 1993 and the establishment of an Adventure Activity Licensing Authority. Many safety posters, pamphlets and leaflets, guidelines and regulations, whilst giving much good advice, can act to put the leader in a safety strait-jacket if the guidance is too prescriptive. The regulations of Local Education Authorities often reveal a detailed effort to guarantee the safety of pupils by an attempt to seal off all possibility of mishap. This attempt, though understandable, is ultimately unsustainable. No code of practice can possibly envisage all the potentially accident-causing combinations of circumstances that could arise with groups in the natural environment. We cannot guarantee absolute safety but we can do something about guaranteeing good practice. So it is important that all relevant basic safety precautions are observed and notice taken of the various National Governing Bodies' advice. Parents do have a right to expect that all reasonable care will be taken with their children and that, apart from cuts, bruises, bumps, sneezes and minor fractures, they will be returned to their homes better educated and in one piece.

However, there has to be a general acceptance that involvement in outdoor challenges may entail some risk and uncertainty. There has to be an awareness that for such activities the total elimination of risk is not feasible, as it is not in ordinary life, and that with such outdoor activities there is the possibility of either physical or psychological harm despite the fact that all reasonable precautions may have been taken by leaders obliged by law to exercise more than just "reasonable care" (see legal section in chapter 7). There are times when participants have to be dependent upon their own skill and have to take responsibility for their own actions. This is as it should be - otherwise how do they ever become independent adults particularly in an age when children are more over-protected than ever before and are less familiar with the natural environment than they ever were before. Because of the nature of some activity situations, the leader will be unable to assist. Even in relatively easy situations it is virtually impossible to intervene to help an individual in the middle of running a rapid, surfing down a wave or perhaps negotiating some awkward section of hillside, whether walking or mountain biking.

*"Apart from cuts, bruises, minor fractures....
better educated"*

❂   Countering this whole body of opinion concerned with safety, is another set of values -the ethics and traditions of the various outdoor sports. Many of the basic attractions of these sports have to do with the spice of danger, the calculated risk, testing one's nerve, finding one's limits, venturing into the unknown, freedom and spontaneity. There are other aesthetic attractions of course such as beauty and solitude, but these pose less serious problems for the leader for they are not usually directly at variance with the safety values, though they can sometimes conflict with them. Being with an over-large group, a perennial feature of unsound practice at one time, can reduce the impact of these aesthetic attractions such as peace, solitude, scenery and the impact of the grandeur of the mountain environment or the 'wilderness feel' of a river gorge running through unspoilt countryside.

Getting the Safety-Danger Balance Right

❂   The leader then has both a practical and a moral problem in maintaining the right balance between danger and safety. This requires finding the balance between, on the one hand, excitement, pleasure, interest, spontaneity, enjoyment and freedom; and on the other hand, too much discipline, regimentation, monotony and the sterile rigidity that comes from over-planning and over-preparation. A leader should always try to be aware if the balance is being tipped in one direction or another - whether towards unjustifiable danger through the leader's arrogant over-confidence or towards too much safety through an anxious lack of self confidence. Nowadays leaders are required to think less in terms of finding a 'right balance' and more in terms of managing and minimising the risks by various means (see chapter 7) - to reduce the level of risk to an acceptable level. But, however one describes it, it amounts to the same thing in practice. It should be borne in mind that the idea of a 'right balance' is not a fixed thing. It flexes and changes according to the circumstances of the group's age, ability, experience, weather etc.

It may have been a surprise for some to find this chapter discussing risk management in association with values. It serves to underline the important fact that they are indivisible and interlocked. It is like the old song about ♫'Love and Marriage' -♫ you can't have one without the o....ther!♫

❁   A leader has to know when it is permissible to prevent the considerations of safety from intruding too strongly on the party to the point that they detract from the intended experiences such as when you want to allow them to find things out for themselves.

❁   A leader also has to know when it is necessary for such considerations to be paramount over all others. This is sometimes to do with an appreciation of the limitations of activities. Activities are characterised by their own peculiarities of situation in that the extent to which a leader can safeguard all of a group all of the time, is variable. So, in some situations the consequences of mistakes would be serious, in others, not. For the more serious situation the best a leader may be able to do is provide a structure that ensures the safe conduct of the activity, e.g. a one-way traffic circulation system for surfing canoeists, board surfers and/or skiers will help prevent collisions; a system of signals will help to control a flotilla of boats. Some situations are not immediately dangerous, but a potential for disaster is present and foreseeable so some provision of a safety structure becomes necessary such as the need for a ban on unaccompanied swimming in running or open waters whilst at camp, where it would also be advisable for there to be a policy that anyone wishing to leave the site must inform the leader and get an O.K.

❁   A leader needs to manage the safety factors so that they are a discrete background of good practice working to ensure feelings of excitement, interest, curiosity, exploration, adventure, achievement and a general enjoyment of the outdoors without unnecessary risk.

Environmental Attitudes and Their Effect on Aims

Traditionally, the safety-danger conflict has seemed to be the chief basic, practical, issue for leaders to need to address. But increasing pressures from an ever growing population escaping to the outdoors for a 'fresh air fix' is causing wear and tear on the finite resources of the natural environment on such a scale, that lip service to environmental issues is no longer enough. It may come as a surprise to learn that taking groups out into the natural environment has long (mid 1980s) been regarded in some quarters as part of the problem, not part of the solution!

**Environmental concern as an issue must
now, more than ever before,
be moved up to lie in equal importance
alongside safety and danger in the consideration of aims.**

One interesting integration of outdoor activities and environmental issues is to be found in the concept of 'eco-adventure' being pioneered by some outdoor and field study centres in which adventure activities are used in a special way, as the sugar on the pill, to make environmental awareness/involvement more attractive to youngsters and easier to become a regular feature in a programme.

A Report issued by the Sports Council in February 1992 called "A Countryside for Sport" highlighted the problem and the implications of unchecked usage of the countryside, the need to plan for what it calls "sustainable participation" and "the long term need to maintain the natural resource". Stated baldly, this means that the capacity of the natural environment in the U.K. to cope with the passage of people over it, is finite. The activities of too many people can literally destroy the environment. It goes without saying that if too many of these 'participants' are people uncaring about the natural environment, the process is inevitably accelerated.

One would not wish to see this kind of criticism leading to a form of group outdoor involvement more prevalent now than it used to be - namely the increased phenomenon of 'on-site' activities where the group never gets beyond the perimeters of the provider's property. On-site activities have a justifiable place but it is desirable that individuals experience some of their time in the outdoors in its proper free setting. Ironically, the results of one instance of bad practice within the world of outdoor provision may have contributed to a certain reduction in groups using the outdoors. Following the Lyme Bay tragedy, the regulations of 1996[36] which designated certain activities to be within 'the scope' of the regulations may have induced some providers to go down this path. But the extent to which these regulations increased this development of on-site provision is uncertain. Meanwhile, Tourist Boards provide a counter to any possible reduction in outdoor usage by their on-going intensive promotion of the outdoors generally.

The traditional attitude of many outdoor users to the environment in regarding it mainly as a kind of playground or testing place for the self, as mentioned earlier in the 'physical phase', can place them in the uncaring category. In some adventure or survival courses and even in some types of personal development courses based purely on challenge, the outdoors is also seen as an adversary or antagonist to be conquered and overcome because the priority is believed to be the benefit that accrues for the individual. Much lower down on the list of priorities is the effect on the environment. Such an exploitive rationale will encourage attitudes which induce the participant to see the environment as a rival or a competitor, as something to be dominated, subjugated to the human will. Competitive or exploitive behaviour has a place in the world but the natural environment has probably reached the point of being the inappropriate place for outdoor participants to practise it. The so-called 'honey-pot' locations are the prime examples. It behoves leaders to adopt new ways of presenting the natural environment to their charges in ways which accentuate the idea of working with, rather than against it (see Cooper [25]). The current trend towards minimal impact camping is a start only.

Leaders need to instigate a process to change attitudes by incorporating in their aims and practices, values which embrace the ideas of reverence for, protectiveness towards and harmony with the natural environment [2]. The competitive, exploitive approach too often entails violation and desecration. A desirable shift in aims would be to replace it with the gentler, more respectful, cooperative ethic which would be conducive to reduced wear and tear.

Outdoor leaders' attitudes to the environment run the whole range from seeing it as a playground for purposeful activity; an amusement park for fun or reward; a hostile type of jungle to be beaten or a battlefield to be won; a proving ground either for self-esteem or status; a metaphor for learning; a sacred place to be treated with affection, awe and respect. Industry and commerce tend to see it as a pantry and storehouse of goodies to be plundered in the pursuit of progress and profit. We all need to remember it is our life-support system. It is the only one we've got.

Traditionally, attempts to instil 'right' attitudes in young people about environmental issues depended on rather formal academic studies which were a turn-off for many who saw it as too 'school' related. It was not appreciated that youngsters needed fun and play in the outdoors, and to experience happiness as a foundation for the development of affection for it, before they could come to embrace more adult concepts about respect and conservation. As mentioned earlier, an important trend is how ways are being explored which manage to combine activity and environment in the development of eco-awareness.

Values Need Clear Thinking

An interesting sidelight on values was provided at an Outdoor Forum Conference in December 1997 organised by the English Council for Outdoor Education, Training and Recreation. An episode there may help to focus thinking about values. People were asked to say what were the values of outdoor learning. The more they talked, the more they became confused by the question. Did it mean benefits (outcomes) to the participants in terms of 'course content' learned or from the 'process' of being involved as a part of a group; did it mean 'aims'? Some wondered if these were the same thing; some thought they were different. Others thought it could even mean 'methods' or 'approaches'. People confused qualities, attitudes, awareness and understanding (states of being) with trainable skills (states of knowing and doing). With qualities and certain kinds of attitudes we are touching on the immutable 'genetic' part of our characters. But with the other elements we are dealing with the 'nurtured' bit of our personalities, that is, the alterable attitudes, awareness and understanding and trainable skills that are capable of change, enhancement, development, and the physical skills and knowledge that can be taught, learned, instructed and trained. Different kinds of values are involved in all of these aspects, aims, outcomes, methods, approaches etc (see Appendix 1).

Knowing what values classification is applicable to which aspect helps avoid confusion.

❂ Chapter Two ❂

Personal Experience

***There is no substitute for actual personal experience
and
there are no short cuts to the gaining of it***

The quality of the leader's personal experience is going to be a crucial factor in how well, or badly, a leader carries out the task of leading. Considerable demands can be made on powers of judgement, decision-making and many other capacities. To be effective, these judgements and decisions must be able to call upon a sound foundation of solid, personal, experience.

Motivation and the Quality of Experience

If an aspirant leader pursues an activity merely to gain sufficient experience to scrape through some assessment or college course of study to win a qualification, then it is necessary for that person to think very deeply about whether or not to continue with the idea of leading groups. A considerable amount of experience is necessary and if the acquiring of it is going to be regarded as a chore rather than a pleasure, it is suggested that the reasons for taking on the training are inadequate and that the enterprise should be abandoned.

The chances of becoming an effective leader are greatly reduced unless a considerable amount of time is spent on accumulating personal experience without a group in tow. Such an acquisition will be adequate when the background of personal experience is sufficiently extensive to enable accurate assessments to be made of most situations likely to be met and therefore sound decisions regarding action to be taken.

These assessments and decisions will then have to be tempered by knowledge of what a particular group can take, is capable of doing or even wants to do. If it is a new group about which the leader's knowledge is less complete or certain, safety margins must be greater.

✿ A comprehensive experience of the activity means that:
The leader will be able to distinguish between real and apparent or perceived danger.

The distinctions are not immediately obvious and some examples will help in the business of recognising which is which.

Real Danger

A group member would be in a position of real danger in a situation where that person would have to rely on his/her own powers because the leader would be powerless to help if things went wrong:

For example, if a group was scrambling along a sharp, horizontal, rocky ridge and the leader was unable to reach one of them in trouble because other members were blocking the only way back, this would be real danger.

A simple matter like running downhill is a situation of real danger. If a person loses control of the rate of descent, a leader will be unable to intervene or assist even if fairly close to the person out of control.

In traversing under crags heavily populated with climbers, there would be a real danger from stone-falls. Canoeists, cavers, sailors and other outdoor sporting enthusiasts will doubtless be able to identify parallel situations of 'real danger' in their own chosen fields - a fleet of dinghies hit by a squall, canoeists crossing a tidal race, skiers suddenly hitting an extensive icy patch in a 'gun barrel' type situation, having to cross a major piste or going off-piste.

Perceived or Apparent Danger

'Apparent danger' is when a person *feels* a situation is dangerous though the danger is a lot less than it is *perceived* to be. An apt illustration which happens occasionally, would be someone protected by a rope from above whilst descending an awkward few metres of rock in an exposed situation on a hillside in order to gain easier ground. Fear of falling could cause the person to feel in real danger even when the rope provided security. A canoe novice doing capsize drill for the first time might have similar feelings. Abseiling with the protection of a top rope is another example. Fear of falling on a steep hillside would be unfounded if the angle of the slope provided enough friction to prevent a slip becoming a fall.

"....decisions will then have to be tempered by knowledge of what a particular group can take, is capable of doing or even wants to do"

Sometimes leaders make more of a situation than is necessary and end up presenting their groups with an exaggerated impression of a situation which has exactly the opposite effect to what they are trying to achieve. Leaders who attempt to make their own jobs easier or who try too hard to show how caring they are, in trying to settle fears or worries in their groups by dwelling on the hazards and how to cope with them, may heighten the perception, or feeling, of danger rather than reduce it. Inexperience, particularly in the young, renders a person unable to make an accurate assessment of the degree of danger present in the hazards of an actual situation. But youngsters are not idiots and can usually see or feel when a situation is fraught with danger. On entering a cave, for example, they may not be able to discern all the elements that make up the danger, they may not be able to tell how serious it is or how to cope with it, but they are aware that it is potentially dangerous. Telling them about claustrophobia beforehand however may not be very helpful. Some people are 'incidents looking for somewhere to happen' and well-intentioned advice on what to expect and how to cope may trigger the behaviour one is trying to prevent. It is very easy to hype up the perception of danger to abnormal proportions (see section on coaching and supporting). It is worth pondering how far such advice in attempting to allay fear and surprise, may subtract something desirable, and even vital from the experience.

These days preparatory explanations which specifically contribute towards reducing the risk of harm may be necessary as part of risk management. But a balance should be struck in order that some opportunity is left open for students to experience the 'first-time ever' novelty of situations uncluttered by too much information which can detract from the thrill of discovery when all is revealed. Certain aspects of the attempts to prepare the kids for what is coming so that some won't be frightened, alarmed (psychological harm?) are misplaced, for in doing this it diminishes the newness, novelty quality or freshness of the experience and therefore the surprise impact of it - there is no 'unexpectedness' about it. They have in effect been told what to expect, what to feel and how to feel it - they have been robbed to some extent of the opportunity to experience it for themselves. Is that what we want? Coping with uncertainty is held to be one of the key assets of this kind of outdoor learning experience. Are you doing them a favour by reducing the uncertainty factor for them?

Then there is the, "they think it's all over" syndrome. Moving from a more dangerous to a less dangerous, apparently safer situation can lull the inexperienced into relaxing their guard as tiredness is setting in and allowing their movements to become sloppy or clumsy. A well known situation is towards the end of a hill walking day when descending and everyone is satisfied that they have 'done it' and it is all over bar the shouting. The skill of descending rough ground is a skill not possessed by most city youngsters used to flat even surfaces. Anyone can walk uphill, but descending uneven sloping ground is quite a different matter. Canoeists entering calm water after a sustained stretch of white water need to guard against a relaxation of watchfulness. Running before the wind after a stiff tack to windward can feel less dangerous unless one is aware of the ever present possibility of a gybe.

Self Knowledge

Leaders also need to know what their own technical strengths and weaknesses are so that they can recognise and avoid situations where they will be more concerned for themselves than the party. Risks taken with parties in such situations are unjustifiable.

Leaders can do much to reduce these 'fear for oneself' symptoms by going out and deliberately exposing themselves to unfamiliar situations. Until a leader has discovered, for example, how it feels to be stuck in a 'stopper', capsized from a canoe in a rapid or from a dinghy in strong winds, lost in a mist or not quite certain of one's exact whereabouts (the two are not quite the same thing), there is something quite important lacking in a leader's experience and knowledge about self. Is experience on scree or steep ground sufficiently practised to the point where there are no longer worries about personal ability to cope with the terrain? Has a planned bivouac been carried out in order to be better prepared one day for the unexpected, enforced bivouac with a group? Has really foul weather been experienced? Having learned the wrinkles of camping high in the hills and discovering the only way to cook in rough weather is inside the tent will alter one's attitude to Duke of Edinburgh expedition training and the standards of skill expected of students. All these familiarising experiences enlarge the leader's confidence base and push back the boundaries of the unknown. It is important to have pushed back the personal anxiety threshold because anxiety in a leader is highly infectious and quickly spreads through a group. Fear of the unknown is one of the prime causes of anxiety. Knowing from experience roughly what to expect in the situations outlined above has helped many a leader through a tough spot.

Depth of Experience Develops Judgement

Leaders also need sufficient depth of experience to enable them to recognise those exceptional situations when the text book answer should be disregarded because it is unsuitable to a particular set of circumstances. For example, recommended techniques for descending scree can only be generalisations that will work most of the time. But a time will come when the configuration of a particular scree-shoot, which for some reason you just have to descend, will not allow any of these methods to be used. It then becomes a question of using past experience to help judge what needs doing, what should be guarded against and applying intelligence to the best way of doing it with the means at hand. Mountaineers have a rather vague term for this. They call it having 'mountain sense'. Mostly it is strongly conscious and insistent, but there are times when it is intuitive and almost subconscious in nature. It probably has its roots in past experience where from a store of minute observations made about conditions, events or people over the years, some detail about the present is different or unique and of acute significance to the present situation.

I remember a day with a group arriving at the summit of High Street in the Lake District. High Street is a very broad ridge 828 metres high with the feel of a high plateau about it. It was a day of darkish haze, of the sort experienced when easterly winds bring air laden with continental, industrial pollution. Whilst having a lunch break the quality of the air around us seemed to be changing. It seemed to become much darker and denser. For no reason I could identify, I suddenly felt 'exposed' and vulnerable - a dangerous place to be in. We hurriedly packed and left the top. Fifteen minutes later we heard a tremendous bang above from the area we had just vacated - lightning had hit it! I had had no prior experience of such conditions. Nor was there any of the sizzling or crackling around metal objects that the books talk about as warning signals.

Experience Needs to be Diverse

"*There is experience and there is experience*", said some now forgotten sage. What he meant was that it is possible to have had fifteen years' experience which may sound quite impressive. But if those years have been spent learning more or less the same thing over and over again, it hardly compares with the richness of fifteen years spent in a whole variety of contexts and situations.

Experience has to be supported by the essential skills, and practice in them. Experience alone does not necessarily develop skill, but practice does. Experience provides a kind of database for judgement to fall back on when comparisons are needed for making risk assessments or safety evaluations of many sorts.

Experience, no matter how extensive, is not enough. There are other considerations of a more formal nature to be included in the leader's catalogue of needs which are to do with the actual business of leadership and how it will be conducted.

Leading Experience for Trainee Leaders

One of the difficulties for trainee leaders is trying to grasp how everything they have learned about leading theory fits together and works on a practical day out with a group. It is a bold leader these days who, in effect, jumps into the pool in order to learn how to swim. There is nothing to beat experience gained as an assistant leader to a group. It is strongly recommended that trainees do all they can to get themselves helping different leaders too. That way a number of personal styles will be observed in action and this will be an invaluable reservoir of information and experience for future use. Once a leader begins leading groups it is amazing how infrequent is observational contact of a leader of another group.

Finding opportunities to work as an assistant leader may be difficult for some. One way is to get in touch with a local outdoor centre, school or club, but first establish that it operates with groups likely to be similar to those you expect to lead - similar not just from the activity point of view, but the types of group you are likely to be dealing with and whether they come from a background of school, youth club, or voluntary organisation. The age range would need to be checked too.

Whether or not the training course of your chosen training agency or National Governing Body requires you to keep a log book of experience, it is a good idea to do so. In it the act of writing is an opportunity to reflect on your experiences and whatever useful or memorable lessons can be drawn from them (see chapter 8 and reviewing). To learn requires one to think. Learning only takes place after thinking. The leader who stops thinking is dead.

❁ Chapter Three ❁

Ideas About Leaders and Leadership

Distinctions to Clarify Confusion

The term 'leadership' is capable of many widely differing interpretations. The resultant confusion tends to hinder a proper understanding of the subject. It is important, in this chapter, to make clear distinctions between:

> **leaders as individuals:** how they are, or
> what their qualities and attributes are

and:

> **leadership:** which is what leaders have
> to do and how they can do it.

Two or more people constitute a group. When they depend on each other to achieve their goal and, in order to do so, influence one another, that act of influencing means that leadership exists in the group. Influence takes many forms. In a group of two, emotional blackmail or bullying might be used instead of reason and persuasion. Influence may exist because the influencer has the power to punish or reward or has a legitimate right to make demands (train conductor asking for "tickets please" or an outdoor leader asking the group to "keep together")

It is only when different kinds of managerial techniques (described later) are used to respond sensitively to the people in the group that the leadership function is properly exercised - which here is to help a group to enjoy safely the achievement of its agreed aims or objectives.

To make meanings clear, each of these concepts, leader and leadership, will now be considered in greater detail.

Ideas About Leader's Power Base

People often confuse 'leader' with the term 'leadership' by asking the questions,

> ⊙ **"How do you become a leader?"**

or

> ⊙ **"Where do leaders get their power from?"**

The authority that forms the basis of a leader's influence; is it inherent in that person or acquired? Is it self-assumed or given? The way in which that 'influence' shows itself may or may not be a clue. Some leaders have the authority to make demands, give commands, reward or punish, some have not. Some leaders appear to have a legitimate right to make demands on others whilst other leaders appear to have to cajole, persuade, even bribe to get their way and some can only exercise their leader function by the use or threat of physical violence. Classically, leaders influence the followers more than the followers sway or manipulate the leaders, but the reverse is often true. Leaders are commonly supposed to control events, but what are people to think when events patently control leaders sometimes? They are then constrained to look at other examples for enlightenment.

A study of the sources of power does not clarify the distinctions to be made between the two concepts, leader and leadership. But knowing about the nature of a power-base helps an understanding of the way leaders with particular sorts of power-bases work and why they might succeed or fail. It also serves to give a better idea about where outdoor leaders fit into the power-base picture.

One clichéd distinction often made in an attempt to clarify matters is that leaders are the people who lead and leadership is what they do.

Leadership is doing the right thing. Management on the other hand, as we shall see later, is doing it right.

Genetic - Born - Natural - Charismatic

The classic example of confusion is found in the saying "leaders are born, not made". The implication is that those who exercise leadership, do so *naturally* either because of some inherited, privileged position in society (the elder brother or the aristocrat) or because of *inherited* qualities of personality, i.e. traits.

"Leaders are commonly supposed to control events, but what are people to think when events patently control leaders?"

It is all a matter of luck and genetic inheritance. In this 'great man, great woman' category come the royals, aristocrats and the elite class idea subscribed to by English education for 150 years and nurtured by the Public Schools. Aristotle subscribed to the idea of **'genetic'** or natural leaders in believing that *"from the hour of birth, some people are marked out for leadership and others to be led"*. This suggested that leaders succeeded by virtue of their inherited traits, through force of personality or because they were highly motivated to become leaders and possessed the necessary energy and charisma. Motivation and energy are prerequisites for leaders in any situation. Charisma is not vital, but properly used is a great asset. It is traditionally acquired through an unusual power, insight or vision which is communicated with a fervour experienced as inspirational by the recipient.

> Max Weber, the German social philosopher, defined charisma as a:
>> *quality of individual personality, by virtue of which (the*
>> *leader) is set apart from ordinary men and treated*
>> *as though endowed with supernatural, superhuman,*
>> *or at least specifically exceptional qualities.*

These traditional opinions are very enduring and contribute in large part to a general misconception that, "*You either have it or you don't, and if you don't, there is not much you can do about it*". The mistaken implication being that no amount of coaching or training will make any difference to the leadership skill of the aspirant leader.

Charismatic leaders inspire and require a high degree of devotion from their followers. Weber also argued that the moral fervour of such leaders is likely to bring them into conflict with traditional morality and normal reason. Such leaders, Adolf Hitler was one although his 'fervour' in the moral sphere was immoral, also tend to by-pass traditional forms of organisation and often display a revolutionary disdain for established procedure. The almost paranoid belief in the rightness of his cause was a factor contributing to his charisma. Tony Blair's messianic fervour also affected his judgement and view of reality and arguably drew him into an illegal war with Iraq. But whatever charisma he may or may not have possessed, it certainly did not ensure the whole country was behind him. Far from it... Some types of charismatic leaders would appear to be eminently unsuitable in the outdoors for the supervision of developing young people! Interestingly, Isobel Hilton in an article "*Breaking up is hard to do*" in '*The Independent*' Newspaper of May 11th 1991 found similar, but less disturbing, parallels in the style and nature of Mrs. Thatcher's leadership. The charismatic kind of person should not be confused with the eccentric character such as Barbara Woodhouse, the dog trainer, or Patrick Moore, the astronomer, who differ in many respects and will often provide memorable leadership and valuable insights. Most 'pop' idols can be charismatic but some are completely lacking in leadership qualities, although they may be role models for the young.

Some leaders are 'inspirational' in that they manage to convince people, especially in confused times, that they know where to go and how to get there - they offer deliverance from unpleasant circumstances and the promise of better things to come. They articulate a general feeling about aims and goals which ensure everyone is with them and highly motivated. It is about ideas, emotion and role models. Such leaders may or may not be charismatic though they usually are. General Sir John Hackett believed,

Leadership is getting people to do things willingly.

Sir William Slim thought 'morale' was,

a state of mind, a force that will move people to make
sacrifices without counting the cost. It is founded on the
spiritual because only they can stand the strain; on the
intellectual because humans are swayed by reason as
well as feeling; on the material which is last and least
important because the very highest kinds of morale
are often met when material conditions are lowest.

All seem to agree that the one trait that really counts in the leader is that of being straight - consistently just, honest, unbiased and fair. No amount of ability or cleverness can compensate for its absence. Integrity is all.

There is another version of leader to be mentioned in this category before leaving it. Seniority gets priority. The idea of 'seniority' is sometimes applied to the process of promotion - *'waiting to fill dead mens' shoes'* is how it is commonly described - or 'it's Buggins' turn'. It too is a form of inherited leadership. It is not genetic but is based on the idea that long experience provides the necessary qualification to inherit the senior post and become a leader. Bureaucratic institutions often work this way which is why some of them are not very effective since people are, arguably, often promoted up into situations beyond their abilities to perform greater acts of incompetence. The bureaucrat's experience must be backed up by confident and sensitive relationships skills to be effective.

Designated

The leader concept becomes further confused by the fact that some people such as headteachers, directors of nursing establishments or foremen are appointed leader roles without the benefit of leadership training, when authority, higher up the hierarchy chain, invests them with the authority to exert influence over others lower in the chain. They are not natural but '**designated**' leaders who may, or may not, be adequate leaders. The criteria, one of which might be the idea of 'seniority', governing the process of their selection may have very little to do with their leadership ability. Reference by subordinates and others to such people can often be derisory or cynical and they are seen as having been "promoted to a higher level of inefficiency". Derisory or not, there may well be grains of truth there. Being good at the respective jobs of teaching or doctoring does not necessarily mean that a person will make a good headteacher or a hospital manager. Nevertheless, those so designated have responsibility and authority by virtue of the position or office they hold, and are, or should be, accountable for the exercise of it. Recognising this fact, it was interesting to note that the topic of leadership became a high agenda item in the National Association of Head Teachers quite recently (e.g Secondary Leadership Paper Number Nine-July 2001). In the TV 'Dad's Army', Captain Mainwaring appears to have become platoon commander by virtue of being the local bank manager! He is an example of a leader relying on rank and authority but little else. He has the trappings of power but little real respect or influence. His group are a forgiving lot but it is knowledge of the military hierarchy and its penal back up structure which prevents their falling apart, as well as the binding sense of common cause in the defence of their country.

Selected

Pre World War Two, officers in the Armed Services often fell within the 'designated' category - it was even legitimately possible to 'buy' your way in by purchasing a commission - leadership for sale! But now their appointment is characterised by a rigorous process of **selection** to identify those with the qualities deemed to make the best leaders for the requirements of military situations. These qualities are seen as natural leadership traits, but often just as much the product of a public school education, which are then developed by further training.

This is a process of selection based on a kind of merit or worth which differs from working skill. But it is important to note that though the Armed Services believe they are selecting the 'best' leaders - and for their purposes they are, where good or bad leadership can mean the difference between life and death, it is expedient to pose the question, "Best for what?" There is no leader who is 'best', in an absolute sense, for all circumstances - the magic of Churchill's personality would not have worked in France in 1940.

In the matter of accountability, which itself is a useful and revealing criterion by which to gauge the nature of leadership, leaders in an hierarchical system, like the Army, may tend to feel more responsible to the superiors above them but less so to those they lead or manage - unlike the next type of leader normally accountable to those who put him there. But in both cases, strong personalities may end up ignoring those impositions.

Elected

A further category of people such as M.P.s, Chairpersons and Shop Stewards are '**elected**'. They earn their positions because of some worth which is perceived by those electing them. It may be their career history, their skill in articulating and communicating, or their achievements, or their personal charismatic qualities that are the important factors here. It is thus a worth or ability that may not necessarily be relevant to a leadership role. Their tenure of office will depend on the maintenance of that perceived worth or the popularity of decisions made - neither of which needs necessarily to be underwritten by sound leadership. However, you cannot fool all of the people all of the time, and the leader who would be long-lived needs to keep this in mind! The medieval Christian church may have managed to fool Christendom for an amazing thousand years about the nature of the universe, but even it could not sustain the myth for all time.

Contingent

Contingencies, or special circumstances, tend to throw up leaders so we may call these '**contingent**' leaders. It is sometimes referred to as 'situational leadership'. Leadership here is sometimes seen to be vested in, or to arise from, a person having the specialist knowledge or skill to solve the problems presented by particular circumstances. A qualified first-aider coming upon the scene of a vehicle collision will be able to enlist and coordinate the assistance of those standing around who do not know what to do. However, attempts to order them about after the emergency is over may be resented and resisted. The example of Winston Churchill's elevation to power at the start of World War Two might be seen simply as contingent, but is not. It was his qualities and personality that fitted the situation rather than his skills and knowledge. At the risk of causing confusion, we might call this charismatic-contingent! So here there is a blurring of the classifications which is a timely warning against being too ready to stereotype leaders into single categories. In this way there are probably as many sorts of leader as there are leaders for none of them is a strict stereotype in real life, being a mix of a number of elements which may change in response to situations and people.

Sometimes it is **any person** whose skills and knowledge render them most able to satisfy the needs, wants or ambitions of the group members at a particular time. It is not always the 'designated' leader upon whom this contingent mantle falls and this can cause anxieties about status and over-sharp reactions in those designated leaders unprepared for the appearance of this phenomenon. We are accustomed to perceiving the leader as the one who is in control of events, and from our parents we are used to perceiving control as the giving of instructions or commands. A common attitude, if the leader is not in control, is how can they still be the leader?

Leaders need to be aware that because of the vagaries of situations, leadership can move around the members of a group. A group member voicing what everyone feels at the time, is taking a leadership initiative and may not even be aware that that is what they are doing. By supporting and harnessing that initiative, leaders resume a leadership role again. If the initiative is inappropriate, then reason and influence have to be applied to persuade the spokesperson, the potential rebel or the group itself, otherwise.

Leaders need to be aware when the initiative is with them and when it is not and they need to be aware when it needs be with them and when it does not.

Contingent leaders labour under the disadvantage that they are rarely able to operate outside the very limited range of conditions contained in the circumstances that gave them power. Churchill and the Tory party's displacement from power at the end of World War Two has a contingent feel about it. The story about "The Admirable Crichton" in which the butler and his aristocrat master reverse roles when they are shipwrecked and marooned as castaways on a remote tropical island is a better example of the rise of a contingent leader. After rescue, the butler is sufficiently aware to see that he must revert to his subordinate role.

Outdoor Leaders

Leaders of groups in the outdoors are different in being essentially self appointed in the sense that they are not designated or elected in the first place by others. Leaders of groups in the outdoors tend to come to their leading through a belief that taking groups out into the hills, onto the water or to do field studies, is a good thing. They are primarily self-motivated. Having come **voluntarily** to be in this situation they may be assumed to be well motivated too - a prerequisite in any leader. Their previous outdoor experience gives their power base a 'contingent feel' which will require to be complemented substantially (and legitimised), usually by formal training, in order to escape the restricting limitations of the contingent leader and to attain the wider, flexible and more dynamic perspective provided by modern leadership theory and practice. Leaders operating from an outdoor centre, although self selected in the sense of having chosen this line of work, would of course have been selected and appointed too. A freelance solo operator, though self appointed, has to reverse the process to succeed - careful advertising is needed to persuade people to select them, in effect by vote.

The outdoor leader's situation has other noteworthy and different features:

In industrial situations, the group process is used as a means to give a team a competitive edge in the achievement of its ends, task or goal. The work of the outdoor leader is unique in that the process of group interaction and cooperation itself is often the task in order to facilitate the personal and social growth of the members in the group.

And whilst the group may find itself competing against the environment occasionally or even itself, it is not usually competing against others.

The outdoor situation is also distinctive in that compared to a whole gamut of situations researched by authorities on leadership, the outdoor leader is usually an older, adult person leading a group of younger people. S/he is not normally part of a peer group, a project team or a firm of colleagues as in a business. So age is recognisable here as a component of the leader's authority. This gives it a 'parental' complexion which is also recognised and supported by law which regards adult leaders of the young as acting '*in loco parentis*', i.e. in the place of a parent, and from the legal point of view, they even have to take more care than the 'reasonable care' a parent would take (see legal section in chapter 7). This legal imperative may be felt to put the use of power-sharing methods characteristic of some leadership styles under some handicap and difficulty, but this does not have to be the case - it depends how it is done, how it is introduced and developed (see next chapter, 3, on styles of leadership).

Being the adult amongst younger ones also gives the outdoor leader's experience, skill and knowledge of the outdoors a greater prominence. It is very obvious where the technical expertise lies in the group.

"And whilst the group is often competing against the environment or itself, it is not usually competing against others"

Together, age and perceived expertise combine to give the adult a status in the group which will make any exercise of power-sharing a more complicated business. With ten to twelve year olds all that is needed to harness their enthusiasm is the power of suggestion and a kind of enlightened despotic parentalism. With teenagers going through all the anti–authority trauma there is much more work to be done to achieve credibility.

To review this section so far, it will be apparent that the origin of a leader's authority often affects the way that authority is used. It is important for leaders to be aware of the nature of that origin of their authority so that they operate appropriately. It is important too to appreciate the difference between 'authority' and 'power'. You may have authority invested in you, but you may not necessarily have the power to influence or control a group. Real influence, as opposed to a domineering style of bullying (and real respect which is a part of the equation) comes from the quality of the leader's relationships with the group members.

It may hearten aspirant leaders to know a generally accepted fact - that those who have the energy, drive, self confidence and determination to succeed will usually become leaders because they work hard to get leadership positions.

Leaders and Leadership - A Distinction

The fore-going brief review of types of leader is useful in showing how concepts of leadership have become blurred by too close an association with the various ways that people become leaders. One is erroneously taken to be synonymous with the other.

Thus there are clear distinctions to be made between the concepts of 'leader' and 'leadership'.

- ❂ The **leader** is a person with certain qualities or traits exercising a definite and particular role in relation to others.
  - ❂ a **role** is a set of expected behaviours associated with a person's position in a group - the role of a follower might be to listen and obey, for example. There are other kinds of roles seen in groups which will be looked at later.

- ❂ **Leadership is a set of identifiable behaviours, functions and skills** which is used, not only by the leader, but sometimes by other individuals in the group, which are intended to influence the others in order to achieve particular aims or goals. Within these sets of behaviours it is possible to identify particular **skills which can be acquired through training** - of which more will be said later.

But before moving onto those behaviours and skills, it will be useful to look closely at other attributes associated with the leader.

For those who find a flow-chart type of presentation more comprehensible, here it is with 'leader' and 'leadership' side by side for comparison. Its inclusion provides a useful opportunity to make a point expanded on later in chapter 8 about learning:

people have predispositions that incline
them to learn in many different ways.

Put another way, we do not all learn the same way. So far from being an unnecessary addition, this diagram may mean more to some of you than the preceding explanations earlier.

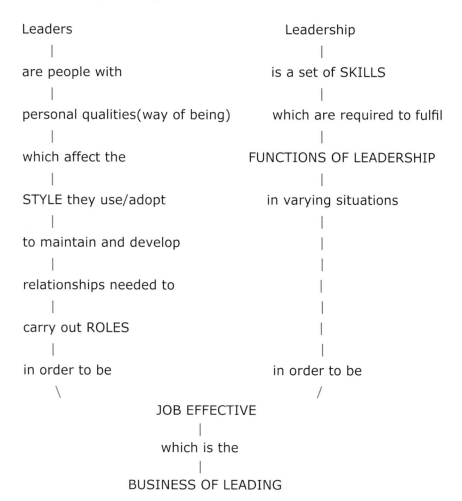

```
Leaders                               Leadership
   |                                     |
are people with                    is a set of SKILLS
   |                                     |
personal qualities(way of being)   which are required to fulfil
   |                                     |
which affect the                   FUNCTIONS OF LEADERSHIP
   |                                     |
STYLE they use/adopt               in varying situations
   |                                     |
to maintain and develop                 |
   |                                     |
relationships needed to                 |
   |                                     |
carry out ROLES                         |
   |                                     |
in order to be                     in order to be
      \                               /
              JOB EFFECTIVE
                   |
              which is the
                   |
          BUSINESS OF LEADING
```

Leader Qualities

"Leaders are neither born nor made - they grow" [3]

Whilst the acquisition and possession of leadership skills may be a prerequisite for effective leading, they do not result in 'instant leadership'. Those skills by themselves, however, will be insufficient unless a range of particular personal qualities are present to drive them. It is these qualities which give colour and substance to the quality of maturity possessed by a person. The degree of acquired wisdom and personal maturity, which is not necessarily dependent on age, is closely linked with the extent to which a person may be effective as a leader.

The manner in which qualities are shown varies greatly in people. It is the way in which a quality is used by a person which gives it either a good or a bad characteristic. The courage, tenacity and single-mindedness in Winston Churchill during the period 1940-45 was admirable and totally suited to the times, but the tenacity and single-mindedness of Margaret Thatcher in the 1980s was viewed more ambivalently. Clearly, qualities are coloured by a person's set of values and beliefs and are affected by their behavioural habits such as having a 'short fuse' or being 'laid back'. Qualities in leaders thus come in mixtures of the good which may help, and the bad which may hinder. Amongst the qualities which might be seen as more desirable in a leader are warmth, enthusiasm, courage (both physical and moral), integrity, patience and humility. Higher key qualities would be competency and potency (see below). But any quality displayed or used excessively can be a mixed blessing. Later we will look at particular stereotypes of leadership styles, but at the risk of causing confusion, it should be said at this point that the combination of qualities in a leader and the manner in which that leader uses them, means that there are as many styles of leadership as there are leaders. I have used the phrases, 'leadership styles' and 'styles of leadership' in an attempt to indicate two rather different but seemingly similar things. If the distinction is not yet clear, hopefully it will become apparent later in this and the next chapter.

Competency

The competency referred to here is not about being a perfectionist. Perfectionists can be severe trouble because they are focused on performance. An unaware perfectionist can be completely oblivious of the difficulties members of the group are experiencing and fail to give understanding and support at critical times. Perfectionists tend to elevate too far, the standards of the system in which they are operating, so that the delivery of goals or outcomes for the group may be put in doubt or at risk.

There is a different type of competency relevant here which is of a general nature almost related to one's outlook on life, unlike a more specific competency which applies to a particular skill. It is of that basic kind in which a person is neither inhibited by past precedents, traditions or past mistakes, nor is deterred by fears of failure or pessimism about the future, but who deals freely and effectively with the present here and now. It is the 'can do' mentality.

Potency

Potency is that crucial quality derived from the development of the other qualities and which links style (see later in this chapter) and skill. It is the capacity to be powerful appropriately to the circumstances and people of a particular situation; to be assertive without being aggressive. It is the capacity to cope confidently with uncertainty and the unknown - which for outdoor leaders is probably the most important test of all. The most effective leader is one who is experienced by a group as being potent. This is not the same as being bossy or pushy!

More Qualities for Outdoor Leaders

It is stating the obvious, but essentially a leader has to want to be a leader. The wanting creates the energy and motivation required of the leader to do the job thoroughly especially at those times when personal energy levels are low or when, for example, it is the challenge of the fifth wet day in a row that must be met.

Because the outdoor leader's situation has special characteristics and particular differences (see earlier sub-section) there are certain qualities or attributes of personality that might be deemed as more advantageous for such leaders to possess.

Enthusiasm has already been mentioned. Its presence could be expected in a self-motivated person, but the ability to transmit this feeling and 'infect' others with it, is essential to those leading the young. Enthusiasm is one way of raising levels of motivation in others. Enthusiasm is more particularly useful if combined with empathy when the youngsters are innocent volunteers and especially if their morale needs to be lifted when conditions deteriorate to become hard, miserable, or uncomfortable. Insensitive enthusiasm, however, feels like a steam-roller! As I write this, I am reminded of a day in the hills when it was so wet and windy that my friend and I decided to put our upper half clothes in the rucksack and walk wearing just ex WD anoraks (windproof but not waterproof), trousers and boots. Getting wet was a miserable process. But once soaked through the realisation that we could not get any wetter was somehow a release from gloom and we spent the rest of the descent singing our heads off, morale high. Energy output was enough to keep the cold at bay. I am wondering whether a leader could motivate a group to do this voluntarily?

A sense of humour is allied with enthusiasm. It is the capacity to be humorous and the ability to inject humour into learning situations. It is difficult to decide whether a capacity to be humorous is a quality or a skill - the one seems to blend so subtly into the other that the boundaries between capacity and ability are quite indistinct. It is certain that skill with humour can be acquired and improved upon with practice, but there does seem to need to be some underlying, inherent prerequisite for a person not only to see what is funny in a situation but also make humour out of it as the cartoonists do. There is no better way to overcome the moodiness, the apathy, or the negative attitudes that are sometimes found in teenagers. A skilful combination of enthusiasm and humour can come close to being charismatic.

It is important to distinguish between being funny, acting the clown and providing fun however. People sometimes think they are being funny by taking a rise out of others and calling it a joke. The wise leader will avoid committing this type of error. In groups, the practice of making jokes at someone else's expense should be discouraged. Any joke that has to be paid for by someone's discomfiture can lead to undesirable repercussions which have a disquieting habit of erupting at the most inopportune moments.

Clowning around can be a useful tool for the leader. With some groups it can make him/her appear more human or approachable, less of a stuffy, distant adult - it is a means of breaking down barriers. With the wrong sort of group it could have the opposite effect. Providing it is not overused to the extent that a group ceases to take him/her seriously, and providing it is used with discrimination, acting the clown can help relationships.

Some of the things that leaders have to do are not very interesting for young people. Induction processes, briefings, safety preparations, the checking of gear after use for example, may all be a bit dull. In these kinds of situation, the ability to think 'laterally' can sometimes be a way of lightening the heavy stuff or even introducing a feeling of fun. If the conventional can be given the appearance of the unconventional or unusual, it often jerks people out of the 'hypnosis of routine' in such a way as is likely to intrigue and hold the interest. The use of cartoons in this book sometimes emphasises a point in a lateral way.

Any of the above-mentioned qualities can cause a leader to be regarded as 'a bit of a character', someone who is 'off-beat' and whose company is stimulating. With such people the occurrence of possible problems with leader-group relationships is greatly diminished.

Personal Style

The unconscious or intuitive manner, i.e. the leadership style, by which a person combines personal qualities with the range of leader skills is uniquely distinctive to that person and is the **personal style** of his/her leadership. It will tend to be this way until the person begins consciously to think about it. The person is locked into a particular kind of leading behaviour because of an unawareness of other alternatives. Sometimes the personal style will suit the situation, sometimes it will not. Leaders need to be able to escape from their preferred or natural style by having available alternatives.

The use of the word 'style' here denotes the unique manner in which a person leads. It is partly derived from an inner state of 'being' - it is subjective and personal.

'**Style**' is used later in chapter 3 as a term to portray distinct, identifiable ways of leading which are objective and exist in their own abstract rights. These different styles of leadership can be consciously chosen and adopted to suit appropriate circumstances.

A leader can do much to acquire a wider range of leading behaviours and skills. Conscientious leaders will find that there is as much material here to get one's head around as there is on the technical aspects of their preferred outdoor activity or ecological study.

The cultural traditions of Britain seem to have been less fertile ground for this body of knowledge. There seems to have been a general resistance to its acceptance, growth and development, particularly in the outdoors. Preoccupation with the technical aspects of an activity, and fears that any 'digressions' would result in "a fall in standards" seem to be elements contributing to this stance. The 1980s saw a welcome waning of this attitude. There was a very basic chapter on leadership in the MLTB's handbook 'Mountaincraft and Leadership' (1984). In the mid 1990s, the situation showed signs of improvement with intense research interest focusing on leadership. The second edition of the Basic Expedition Training Award (BETA) included a section on leadership. The national newspapers deluged the public with an unprecedented torrent of articles on leadership because it was seen as a life saver for failing companies in industry and commerce. The world of industry and commerce, began to appreciate the value of managers having good relationship skills and a variety of leading styles which seems to have precipitated a growth in management training courses. Corporate companies discovered the value of team bonding by means of team building courses. The school curriculum acknowledged the cross-curricular importance of personal and social development even if it was not able to do much about it because of the pressure of league tables. Some of the content of leadership, such as the understanding of self and others, is to be found in both management training and personal and social development. It is, or ought to be, a basic element of 'citizenship', a 'buzz' word in the early 21st century school syllabus.

It is sometimes not appreciated that the processes of managing, teaching and leading have a common core of fundamental similarities in the skills and the knowledge about people that each requires.

It is only when technical skills are used equally in combination with leader skills and relationship skills that effective leadership can happen <u>consistently</u>.

❂ *Chapter Four* ❂

Leadership Models and Leadership Styles

Five Elements to Consider

In looking at leadership models and styles it may help to keep in mind throughout, that up to five main elements may be involved. In the models which are described later, some or all of these features may be present. In no particular order they are:

- ❂ the task - some aim or goal that will be done or is being done.
- ❂ the group - considered as a whole.
- ❂ the individual - considered as a person in his/her own right or as a part of the group.
- ❂ the environment - terrain, water state, weather.
- ❂ situational conditions - other special conditions prevailing.

A number of 'models' about leadership have been proposed over the years. They are regarded as significant in the development of thought about leadership training but have only gradually become better and more generally known in the outdoor world since the middle to late 1970s. They are very helpful and useful, but it is stressed that they should only be regarded as aids to help leaders to think and develop their own ideas about leadership. They should not be regarded as tablets of stone about leadership. These thinking devices are essential for the formulating and honing of a personal conceptual framework of ideas about leadership.

This chapter looks at four leadership models. There are many more that could have been included but it was felt that those illustrated would suffice as an introduction and avoid possible confusion. Anyone wishing to explore further is referred to the reading list at the back of the book.

Even so, there may be a risk of confusing the reader with four models, but it is taken because one of a number of models is more likely to 'click' or 'press a button of comprehension', whilst only one or two might not mean very much.

Also included is a model about groups. It seemed needful since leaders are as nothing without them.

Action centred leadership - John Adair [4]

This model conceives of three main aspects that a leader will have to keep in mind continually and cope with if a particular task or goal is to be achieved.

All three areas should be regarded as interlinked in that an over concentration on one will be to the detriment of the other two.

If the needs of the task are made paramount to the extent that the needs of the individuals or the team are ignored or overridden for too long, it is less likely that the task will be achieved. A single-minded concentration by the leader on the task is likely to result in a breakdown of communication with the group. Also possible is the alienation of some or all of its members and the loss of their willing cooperation in the achievement of the goal.

Diagram 1. Adair's three circle action-centred leadership

" A single-minded concentration by the leader on the task is likely to result in a breakdown in communication"

Trying to push on when the group needs a rest, or a stop to eat, or when someone has developed a bad blister would be typical examples of this kind of situation. Unless the leader has a very good reason for wanting to push on and can convince or persuade the whole group of the rightness of the case, the situation will eventually grind to a halt until the neglected element is given its due consideration and dealt with.

Conversely, concentrating too much on individuals in the group could mean that the attainment of the goal is put in jeopardy or never achieved.

This model is comprehensive in its visualisation of the scope of leadership tasks. It is not static but dynamic, because it offers a way for leaders *continuously* to sustain their leadership in a variety of different situations.

The model also provides one way for a leader to identify which of the three areas most requires immediate attention in a situation where priorities are always changing and shifting. It works 'reactively' on the "fly in the ointment" principle by visualising the three circles as pots of ointment any one of which, at any time, is likely to have a fly in it that needs to be removed! It can also be used 'proactively' as a check list for looking ahead and ensuring one is on the right track.

Leaders could also use this model to decide the longer term priority area of their focus when setting up a particular outing or project.

The central part of the diagram where all circles overlap represents the ideal when all three components are working in balance and harmony.

A check list follows on the next page, for those who find them useful, itemising the various roles and functions relevant to task, group and individual.
Be aware that it is possible for anyone, individual **or** leader, to take on these roles at any time.
It should not be assumed that the list applies solely to the leader.

GROUP ROLES AND FUNCTIONS

Work/Task Functions:
Member behaviour required for doing group tasks.

Building Functions:
Member behaviour required for building and maintaining the group as a working unit.

Task Roles

1. **Initiating**: Proposing tasks, goals, or action; defining group problems; suggesting a procedure.

2. **Informing**: Offering facts; giving expression of feeling; giving an opinion.

3. **Clarifying**: Interpreting ideas or suggestions; defining terms; clarifying issues before the group.

4. **Summarising**: Pulling together related ideas; restating suggestions; offering a decision or conclusion for the group to consider.

5. **Reality Testing**: Making a critical analysis of an idea; testing an idea against some data; trying to see if the idea would work.

Maintenance Roles

1. **Harmonising**: Attempting to reconcile disagreements; reducing tension; getting people to explore differences.

2. **Gate Keeping**: Helping to keep communication channels open; facilitating the participation of others; suggesting procedures that permit sharing remarks.

3. **Consensus Testing**: Asking to see if a group is nearing a decision; having a 'straw poll' to test a possible conclusion.

4. **Encouraging**: Being friendly, warm and responsive to others; indicating by facial expression or remark the acceptance of others' contributions.

5. **Compromising**: When his/her own idea or status is involved in a conflict offering a compromise which yields status; admitting error; modifying in interest of group cohesion or growth.

Negative non-Functional Roles by Group members:

A look out should be kept for member behaviour that does not contribute to the solution of either the group's task or the smooth working of the group process.

1. **Aggression:** Deflating other's status; attacking the group or its values; joking in a barbed or semi-concealed way.

2. **Blocking:** Disagreeing and opposing beyond 'reason'; resisting stubbornly the group's wish for personally oriented reasons. Using hidden agenda to thwart the movement of a group.

3. **Dominating:** Asserting authority or superiority to manipulate group or certain of its members; interrupting contributions of others; controlling by means of flattery or other forms of patronising behaviour.

4. **Out-of-focus Behaviour:** Making a song and dance about one's lack of involvement; 'abandoning' the group while remaining physically with it; seeking recognition in ways not relevant to the group task.

5. **Avoidance Behaviour:** Pursuing special interests not related to task. Staying off subject to avoid commitment. Preventing group from facing up to controversy.

6. **Passivity:** Another form of avoidance behaviour which is serious and unconscious. It is not about 'doing nothing', but using energy to avoid all kinds of feeling, thinking and doing, which may range in severity from mild to severe depression, from silence to extreme violence. The subject is a whole chapter on its own and it must suffice here merely to flag up its existence and refer the reader to books on Transactional Analysis for further enlightenment (see suggestions for reading at end of this book).

Adair's Model Environmentally Amended

In the context of the early 21st century however and the greater concern about global warming, pollution and the dodgy state of the natural environment, (see chapter 1 and 'environmental attitudes') it would seem appropriate to make this model into the shape of a four-leafed clover by adding another circle to take account of the needs of the environment. Memories of older people, photographs, old surveys are important, otherwise it becomes impossible to track changing states. As youngsters we tend to take what we find as the 'natural state', unaware of how it used to be. In the 1940s, the top of Helvellyn was still all moss covered, for example - now it is a stony waste. A number of important geological sites have been almost literally hammered to extinction by specimen hunters. National Parks are botanical deserts compared with, say, parts of the western seaboard of Scotland. National Park Authorities under legal obligation to maintain public access have felt the need to slow down human impact on the environment by constructing footpaths high up the popular routes on the hills and by comprehensive sign-posting lower down. Where footpaths were once the width of the boot they are now replaced by 'mountain motorways' visible from miles away. We might not like this 'spoiling' of the wilderness feel, but it would appear necessary.

The impact of recreational and educational users of the countryside is everywhere increasingly apparent. The scars of footpath erosion, the destruction of sensitive sites, the over-use of particular places for popular activities are examples of a growing need for leaders to temper their usage patterns with discretion and try to consider viable alternatives [1].

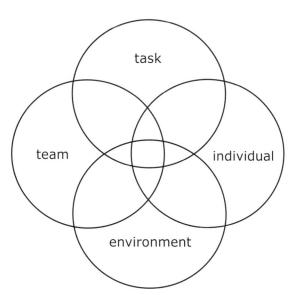

Diagram 2. Adair's three circles environmentally amended to four

Needs of Task - Individual-Group

The description of the Adair model is not complete without a further list of the needs of the task, the individual and the group referred to in diagram 1 earlier. It is not quite the same as the other list although there are some similarities. The two complement each other. This one is included for completeness:

Task Needs

Define the task.
Make a plan.
Have competence in all skill areas.
Have neccesasry equipment.
Give information/ teach skills.
Allocate work and resources.
Control pace/maintain standards - quality control.
Check performance against plans.
Adjust plan as needed.
Bring it to a close.

Individual needs[5]

In order of importance, with the most immediate first:
Physical: food, water, sleep, shelter, warm and dry.
Safety: feel safe and secure.
Social: feel liked and belonging.
Self-esteem: status and recognition of worth.
Sense of indentity: purpose, achievement, have values.

(The leader needs to be aware of, know about, understand, recognise, encourage and make allowances for these needs in the group.)
Give status to individuals.
Recognise and use individual ability.
Train the individual.

Group Needs

Plan group composition.
Encourage participation/ motivation.
Set standards.
Maintain discipline.
Facilitate communication.
Build team spirit, cohesion and trust.

Resolve interpersonal differences and conflicts.
Relieve tension.

Build group morale.

Co-ordinate group activities.
Give sense of purpose.

Praise and motivate.
Appoint sub-leaders.

Train the group.

Environmental Needs for the Four Circle Model

- ✹ active respect and care for the environment (e.g. observance of country code);
- ✹ reduce to a minimum the impact of the group;
- ✹ recognise and avoid sensitive areas;
- ✹ sustainable usage - avoid over-use of an area;
- ✹ 'leave only footprints, take only photographs': bring all litter and human waste out;
- ✹ on-going educational campaign to publicise and raise awareness of important issues;
- ✹ public protest and action to counter the fearful combination of the vested interests of corporate developers and power politics.

Greater Need for Environmental Themes in Outdoor Experiences

The state of our only life support system, our planet, has pushed environmental issues up the agenda for everyone. There is a need for our young people to be informed and aware of the environmental and wildlife havoc we are still wreaking on it, and the need for them to feel sufficiently strongly about it to be active on protest, and/or, conservation fronts. This requires the world of outdoor learning to give it a much higher profile than it has had. I suspect more than half of outdoor learning is currently still devoted mostly to programmes of outdoor activities either as an end in itself or as a means to other objectives like social education. Learning **through the environment** i.e. using it as a learning resource, is no longer enough. Whilst the environmental and field study centres have done much to promote learning **about** the environment, there has to be a greater emphasis on learning **for** the natural environment - the looking after it aspect.

How this is achieved is crucial. Dry, boring lectures or talks about it to young people won't work very well, won't inspire the level of necessary concern and alarm. Compelling them to work on active projects with similar aims in mind won't work either unless they have been genuinely persuaded and enthused by other means. To be effective with young people there has to have been laid down a foundation of affection for the environment so that it is cared about. One way of doing this is ensuring early experiences were such fun and enjoyable that a lasting residue of good, happy, memories was embedded. This emotional attachment creates an energy reservoir which serves as the jumping off point for positive environmental attitudes and active participation. The John Muir Trust Leader Scheme is a fine example showing the way on this front (details from JMT, 41, Commercial St, Edinburgh, EH6 6JD. Tel: 0131 554 0114). Steve van Matre's books, listed at the back of this book, on Acclimatisation for ideas to use in this respect are very good. Many of the traditional field study or environmental study centres are showing how to combine traditional outdoor activities effectively with environmental themes.[29] The current buzz phrase describing this seems to be 'eco-adventure'!

Outdoor learning programmes have to represent in effect a concerted publicity and information campaign to bring about public attitude changes that will feel strongly enough to challenge the continuing devastation of the planet by global corporations. All is meaningless and lost otherwise. Economic policies based on the concept of 'growth' are causing untold harm. A new economic ethic is needed. Not everyone feels sufficiently empowered to confront problems at the macro global level; but one really useful aim is to show youngsters what they can do at a more local micro level especially in areas at risk.

Control and Power - Tannenbaum and Schmidt [6]

This is a useful model for looking at the different ways a leader can handle power and control in a group.

It sees leadership as a variety of roles lying on a line in a range between two extremes. At one end is maximum intervention - as by a dictator who asks all the questions, gives all the answers, makes all the decisions and gives all the orders - the 'command and control' style. At the other extreme there is a minimum of intervention - as when delegating jobs to others.

As one moves further up and along the continuum line in diagram 3, the leader progressively decides, or should do, to give up more actual control whilst the people in the group receive more responsibility and therefore more power/control over what is happening. The leader has to decide which particular style is the most appropriate for a situation.

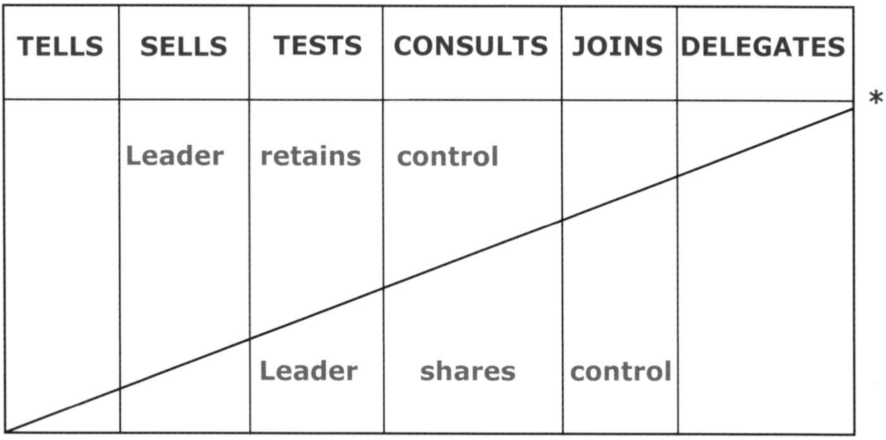

TELLS	SELLS	TESTS	CONSULTS	JOINS	DELEGATES
	Leader	retains	control		
		Leader	shares	control	

Diagram 3: Tannenbaum and Schmidt's
continuum of Control and Power

This model emphasises the idea that leadership is an interactive, two-way process. As the relationship between the leader and the group develops it becomes possible, or necessary or desirable, for the leader to use alternative ways of exercising power.

At times the group's reaction to the leader will determine what style is adopted, e.g. are they showing signs of aggressive independence or are they in a meekly dependent and conformist mode. The group's resistance to a leader's direction or suggestion would indicate a need to change to a consultative mode to find out what the problem is. At other times, because situations can change so rapidly from moment to moment, it might be the nature of a particular situation which is the deciding factor. "It's going to pelt down with rain in a minute. Stop whatever job you're doing and get your anoraks on." Although leaders may have a preferred style that is a reflection of their personality and comes naturally, it will not always be the appropriate style to use in particular circumstances. It is very important to be able to 'mix and match' to suit circumstances. An inability to be flexible with regard to the style of leadership that might be best suited to a situation, would be a serious limitation on a leader's effectiveness, credibility and possibly tenure of office. "OK, this guy has broken his leg. We're over half way up Snowdon in a strong wind. What do you think we should do?" - consulting might not be a wise move in the circumstances - unless... it is a very experienced and competent group also up to the hard physical job of the stretcher carry out.

A number of useful options are demonstrated in this model. They should not be regarded as fixed entities in any way but as part of a continuum where one element fuses imperceptibly into the next. Be aware that the continuum is not always moving forward - it can go, or need to go, into reverse gear (see below 'adjourning' section in this chapter).

A brief explanatory note about the various alternatives now follows.

Tells

The leader assesses the situation, the group and the resources available, selects a course of action and tells the group what to do (assertive). Reasons may or may not be given. "OK. This is how it is going to be and this is how we will do it". "I want you to...."

Sells

The leader chooses a course of action as before but this time gives reasons and explanations (persuasive) to highlight the advantages of the plan and to persuade the group about its rightness. "I want you to do this because...., so that.... If we don't do this now, then such and such will happen".

Tests

The leader identifies and outlines the problem or situation giving some of the relevant background information and possible options. "This is how it is and I think we should do so and so." "How do you feel about it?." There will be some discussion but it will be confined to answering objections rather than an open-ended debate before going ahead with the intended course of action.

Consults

The leader presents the problem and background thinking as before but then asks the group for ideas and comments with the possibility that the intended decision may or may not be modified. The leader reserves the right to impose his/her own decision. "This is how it is. Do you have any ideas on what we should do about it or any useful comments?"

Joins

The leader presents the problem and perhaps some of the relevant background information and thinking together with some suggestions for possible solutions. The leader then asks for ideas and help and joins the group. The final decision is likely to be a consensus, a joint one - or a majority decision, the result of a real sharing and exchange of views. "What should we do?" "Shall we take a vote on it or keep talking further until we have ironed out the disagreement bits and reached a workable compromise?"

Delegates

The leader either identifies the problem or responds to problems raised by the group or one of its members. The problem is given to the group for them to solve and arrive at a decision. The leader is committed to following their decision and will be available if necessary for consultation. "Will you three sort that out?" "We can't move on until you have sorted this out between you and decided who is carrying what in their sacks."

If the leader is not to be available then the leader can be said to have abdicated the leadership role in that situation. The position is as represented by the * asterisk outside the continuum in diagram 3.

Sometimes a leader may be perceived by the group to have abdicated, in effect by default, as in the case when a leader is unable to give a lead or does not know what to do. If this situation has happened before, too often for the group's liking, and the leader is unable to or will not delegate to someone else, the situation may deteriorate to the point where it is ripe for the usurpation of power. If this vacuum occurs in a crisis situation it may be filled by a 'contingent' type of leader. There may even be some situations where it is politic for the leader to simulate indecision in order to have the group, which has problems with the 'authority thing', get to grips with a problem where anything the leader said would be seen as an intrusion.

Sharing control is the mark of a more mature leader and is conducive to the development of more effective groups. Put another way, it leads to the development of more effective people in such groups. But leaders do well to remember that the extent to which people may benefit from such methods will also depend on the skills and resources available, the age of the people in the group or their maturity and the length of time the leader and the group have been, or will be, together. According to Tuckman[10] (see later in this chapter) one definition of group maturity is their capacity to set high but achievable goals, which requires the necessary motivation to achieve them, and a willingness and ability to take responsibility. Their 'education and experience' will be other important factors with a bearing on the situation. He reminds us however that this maturity can vary and may be determined by the type of goal chosen, i.e. some apples are sweeter and more easily eaten than sour ones. Too much responsibility at too early an age in a person's life or too soon in a group's existence, or responsibility for problem solving that is very complex or difficult for present experience and capacities to cope with, can undermine confidence. If the way a group handles its power is not discretely monitored or even at times supervised, the abuse of power by bullies or over-domineering members can appear which may destroy belief in the democratic process as a credible way of doing things. Just as importantly, it may also deny the development of other members' potential.

As a warning footnote to this section illustrating the effect of a misjudgment about leadership style, it is commonly accepted that Hitler's ferocious style of 'command and control' and insistence on deciding everything, so rendered his immediate aides and generals impotent as to contribute in a large part to Germany losing the war. By contrast, Churchill began like that but allowed the reins to loosen progressively thus enabling the initiative and creativity of his team and the allies to operate to good effect.

Situational Leadership - Hersey and Blanchard [7]

This model looks at the leadership situation in terms of choices or orientation options, the orientation (a focus or mindset) being either 'tasks' or 'relationships'. It holds that a certain sort of situation is best served by a particular style of leadership. A leader, trying to discern the appropriate style of leadership to be used in a specific situation must:

a) assess the relative importance of a specific task. i.e. importance might be measured by how difficult or complex the job is: or how vital or soon its completion is to the well being of the group.

b) take into account the quality of the relationships and behaviour in the group. i.e. how well they get on together, including their skill level and cooperative capacity and whether or not those relationships would be requisite to the achievement of the task.

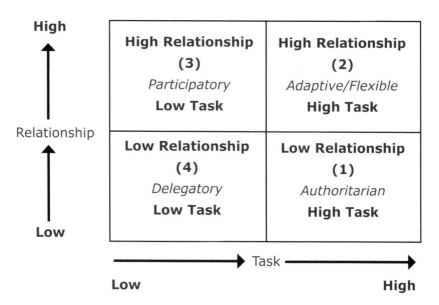

Diagram 4. Hersey & Blanchard's grid of task/relationship orientations

For example, a leader confronted with the need to improvise an emergency evacuation of an injured member of a party (high task) of fractious novices (low relationships - i.e. (1) in diagram), would be authoritarian because it would be the style most suited to getting the job done quickly. But it would be vital to explain what was needed in order to ensure problems did not arise because the group did not realise the significance of what it was being asked to do. "Trust me" would not be enough to engage their cooperation. Such a style would be a less appropriate choice for a highly experienced, trained group of friends (high relationships). In the former instance the leader would be authoritarian and directive, whilst in the second case, where both task and relationships are high [(2) in diagram] it would be more effective to be less directive and take a greater account of the group's skills and resources (more relationship-orientated) by being more flexible and adaptive and sub-delegating without renouncing overall control.

1. High Task/Low Relationships

This category is well illustrated in the early stages of a group's life when the members are uncertain of each other, not too sure about the leader and a bit hazy about the objective. The important thing is to get things (the task) moving by feeding in much information and perhaps imparting a lot of skill. In this situation the leader will be doing a lot of telling and directing and staying in charge. Personal feelings and group needs will be secondary to the achievement of the task. Emergencies would come into this category.

2. High Task/High Relationships

In this situation the leader will be active and visible but not necessarily directive. A lot is going on, as, say, in the 'storming' phase of a group's life (see later in this section for 'Tuckman on Groups'). Questions to do with 'why' rather than 'what' are being asked so reasons and explanations are required in order to persuade and convince. Good relationships are as important as getting on with the job because at this juncture, if the relationships become too fouled up, the task falls apart too. The leader's role tends to become political and diplomatic in essence, particularly when conflicts, a feature of this phase, have to be resolved positively.

The leader has to be flexible in order to be able to adapt to a variety of conditions or situations.

The sustained exercise of a single leadership style here might well be disastrous.

3. Low Task / High Relationships

Here, roles have been assigned to, or assumed by, group members with the skills and ability to undertake them. Control of some things is moving naturally away from the leader. But it is important that, with the removal of this cohesive influence, group harmony is maintained so that the various parts continue to work well together.

To avoid becoming too distant from the group, it is now possible for the leader's focus to move away from the task, and concentrate more on the needs and wants of the group and the individuals in it.

*"Control of some things is moving naturally away
from the leader"*

The leader will thus participate on a level nearer to the group by joining, sharing, testing and consulting as in the 'norming' phase (see later in this section for 'Tuckman on Groups'). On some expeditions, leadership never gets beyond this phase because of the leader's need to feel his/her skills are being fully used: some leaders also like to feel their groups are always dependent upon them. This is a limiting attitude and can be considered as unjust or selfish in that it blocks the development of responsibility, creativity, initiative and confidence in others.

4. Low Task / Low Relationships

In this situation, the leader is concerned to allow his/her role to become low key in order that the group is able to become self-functioning to the extent that it, or individuals in it, can see what needs to be done, set up tasks, take most of the decisions, and carry them out. The leader will be mostly delegating, consulting a little, supervising a lot and monitoring all the time. A typical example of this sort of situation would be a group well on the way to self-sufficiency as, say, with an established, fairly well trained and experienced group, preparing to go on a semi-unaccompanied expedition as part of the training for the Duke of Edinburgh Award. I am aware that there is a possibility of confusion developing here. Within the expedition group there will need to be high relationships in order to carry out a task that may be simple at times and complex at others. So how does this fit into the category of 'low task/low relationship'?. The distinguishing feature here is that it is the relationship between leader and group that needs to be less involved, looser or 'lower'.

A simpler example would be telling a group to set out chairs for a meeting. The task is simple and consequences not serious if they mismanage it, nor are high degree skills and cooperation required. Also, for the purposes of this model, it does not matter whether the task is delegated by request or command. Once it is delegated, the involvement of the leader with the group is decreased.

✪ The Hersey Blanchard model can be improved by the inclusion of two qualifications:

1. The response to a situation that is **planned** for may well differ from the response if the **same** situation is **unplanned** i.e. is confronted unexpectedly. The lack of any opportunity to stage simulations or full rehearsals may mean a group is unprepared both psychologically and in terms of skills - sailing is full of those situations. The leader may have the equipment, but the impact of the unexpected will impose a greater burden and probably constrain the leader to be more directive but alert to the need to boost morale and motivation.

2. Similarly, in the matter of relationship behaviour, a distinction needs to be drawn between the quality of relationships that **is actually present** in a group and the kind of relationship behaviour that **would**

be required (and may not be present) to complete a task. If the required level of relationship skill in the group is inadequate for the proposed task, a more directive style may be needed to compensate and provide the means to attain the necessary teamwork for the achievement of the task - even for more adult groups.

Conceptual Limitations Caused by Uniformity of Groups and Settings

One other important lesson to do with groups is highlighted by the Hersey Blanchard model.

In their normal working situations, most practising leaders tend to meet groups that are similar in nature, so their thinking and discoveries about leading groups will have been constrained within the narrower confines of a particular context. A Scout or Guide leader will tend to conceptualise leadership in terms of the types of girls and boys s/he customarily leads and may see aims more in terms of working towards independency. The teacher of a remedial group handling youngsters usually less able to fend for themselves will have different ideas about leadership set in his/her mind and will be more inclined to operate with the group in a 'dependency' mode. Unless leaders are normally working with a wider range of different kinds of group, the point might not be realised that personalised ideas about the nature of leadership may be restricted if leaders have only ever worked with one kind of group. If the group is always all boys or always all girls or always mixed, or if they are usually juniors or adolescents or adults, the nature of the group with which the leader normally works will colour and, to some extent, limit the ideas a leader has about the nature of leadership.

Frequency of meeting can be another limiting factor. How well do you know them? Is it always a 'one-off' situation as in an outdoor centre or is it the first time or one of many meetings as in a youth club? Situation sometimes exercises a constraint on outlook too, and therefore practice, if the setting never changes. 'Where you always are means you always have to do what you always do'. Can individuals normally seen in the classroom, be expected to exhibit the same characteristics when in the outdoors or, as is quite likely, will the new and different situation throw up surprising traits and reveal unsuspected qualities calling for new and different responses from the leader?

Leaders thus need to be aware that thinking about how they lead, can be restricted by the uniformity of the group situation they normally experience. When their employment situation changes, as it sometimes does, and different kinds of groups present themselves, ideas about the nature of groups that were previously seen as immutable, are suddenly drastically challenged. Favoured ways of leading previously relied upon are no longer applicable or appropriate. Imagine the case of a university lecturer pitched into the middle of an inner city youth club (no disrespect to either intended). Methods and approaches which may have been ingrained by long usage, and with which one is comfortable, and to which one is unthinkingly accustomed, are more easily modifiable if the leader has been aware that other group situations exist that are different.

Conditional Theory of Leadership - Chase-Priest [8]

Chase and Priest's theory of Conditional Leadership identifies a number of factors which influence when a particular leadership style is used and integrates all these into one model. Leaders' general value-orientations may be **'people-centred'** by virtue of being focused on maintaining themselves, caring for individual members, building the group relations; or they may be **'things or task-centred'** because they are focused on achieving the task at hand, supporting the sponsoring authority, protecting the natural environment. These orientations and the range of leader styles available should flex and change depending on whether a high or low condition exists in five key areas: the favourability of conditions for a particular style is determined by the low/high ratings obtaining in the:

1. Degree of environmental danger.
2. Level of individual competence.
3. Degree of group unity.
4. Leader's level of proficiency.
5. Degree of seriousness consequent upon a decision.

The converse of these five factors would clearly imply a decreasing favourability for example if the group is divided, if leadership is deficient, if individuals are incompetent, if environmental dangers are many and if the consequences of a decision are major.

The degree to which there is a high or low condition in each of these five areas will create circumstances conducive to the adoption of either more directive or less directive styles identified by Chase and Priest as autocratic, democratic and abdicratic (delegatory).

The model is a sophisticated one and considerable effort is required to grasp its essentials sufficiently to be able to apply it in practice.

It is however a model more finely tuned to the needs of the outdoor situation where levels of concern for the care and well-being of the individual (services driven) are likely to be higher than in the cut and thrust realms of industry and commerce (market driven - aggressive competition for profit) from which most leadership models originated.

The key point to pick up here is that no one style can be right all the time. The most effective style is one that is flexible to changing situations.

Groups and Leaders - Interdependent

There is a natural tendency to concentrate on leaders, their needs and problems, when talking about leadership. But without a group a leader does not exist. The leader is only half of the equation. This is therefore a good moment to ask the question, "Who is the more important: the leader or the follower?" It might seem to be a silly question. But of what use is a leader if there is no group of people to lead? Conversely a bunch of people remains just that - a motley assortment - if there is no leader to bind it into a group or team. The leader is often presumed to be the one who influences the group more, but that influence which gives the leader status, recognition and esteem has to be paid for by the leader being obliged to provide direction, structure, resources and being available to the group. How far a leader imposes his/her will on a group or how far is it the case that s/he is controlled by the group can be a moot point. It can be said that a group only 'allows' a leader to lead it for so long as it suits them! Captain Bligh of the Bounty comes to mind. Crucial here too is whether the group thinks it can stop the leader leading when they wish it. Groups can become quite skilled in manipulating a leader for they know him/her better than s/he knows it usually. Groups at variance with leaders are not averse to side-tracking them from a proposed course of action. All manner of stratagems can be called upon. Orchestrated mayhem has to be experienced to be believed! In the outdoors the collapse of power and the resulting vacuum could entail catastrophic consequences. The point being made is that leader and group are inter-dependent; each is vital to the other; each is dependent on the other. A kind of symbiotic relationship can be said to exist between the two.

Group Development - B.W. Tuckman[10]

Although the notion of group has been mentioned frequently, it is now time to devote some space specifically to it because a leader needs to know something about groups or s/he will be very handicapped in carrying out leadership functions.

Reference was made earlier to the length of time a group has been, or will be together as a factor bearing on the leadership style to be adopted. There now follows a model, developed by B.W.Tuckman, which describes how the life cycle of a group generally evolves. It will be seen that time and timing is an important consideration for leaders.

When a group comes together for whatever reason, there are, allegedly, five identifiable stages it goes through as the group members become better acquainted either with the task or each others' strengths and weaknesses. As this knowledge develops so does their effectiveness and the need for leaders to adapt and modify their styles of leading. This scenario should be seen as more relevant to 'teenagers' and onwards than it would be for, say, junior children - but it is not necessarily so. Humans, happily, have a disconcerting habit of not conforming to order and expectation. And it needs to be remembered that the group is often not necessarily meeting each other for the first time when it gathers together with the leader. For many of the individuals in it, there may already be an attached 'past history' formed back at school, the club or some other voluntary organisation. Some of the impressions each already has about the other may be about to receive a drastic revision, as the outdoors works its impact on them in ways very different to that which they have experienced in the situation back home. One of the important reasons for that, inherent learning predispositions, already referred to earlier, will be discussed in chapter 8.

1. **Forming** - the forming phase occurs as group members make initial contact with each other and the leader - everyone is trying to 'suss out' everyone else - who is likely to be a 'buddy', who friendly, hostile or neutral, dominant or submissive. So it is characterised by a feeling of uncertainty about each other and whether there is some link to all present and whether there is, or will be, a common purpose. The life history of the group is coloured by the process of finding out the answers to these queries. There is a higher awareness of the leader as the group seeks information and direction and tries to come to terms with the task and each other. The leader has a fairly high profile at this time.

Often one of the priority jobs is to establish what are the limits on behaviour and to put a few rules in place, ideally with their agreement. So-called 'ice-breaking' activities are a means towards this end without a lot of 'aggro'. Many of the activities outlined in Karl Rohnke's *Cowstails and Cobras'* or *'Silver Bullets'* will be found helpful for moving through this stage positively and with fun.

2. **Storming** - as the group gains in confidence, and control of decision making begins to shift from the leader to the group, relationships begin to go through a more searching and sometimes an aggressive phase (see below '✪'). The transition can result in power conflicts and their resultant pecking orders, but the shift in control is essential if an effectively functioning group is to develop. This is also the shake-down phase which groups need to be helped through fairly quickly, and ideally with as little stress as possible.

✪ The storming phase can be much influenced by the leadership style adopted, with considerable subsequent repercussions on the 'norming' phase which follows it. The competitive aggression of insecure males (young or old) trying to dominate a mixed group is often allowed to prevail in the struggle for power and pecking orders because that is how the leader (male) operates naturally. Many able, perhaps less assertive, but probably more effective people, will become alienated and thus uninvolved in the group because they feel they can have no say or power unless they are prepared to descend to the jungle-like behaviour of the dominators. The leader has to make it quite clear that the 'survival of the fittest' ethic is not at all acceptable and that there are other more productive alternatives to the 'dog eat dog' way of being.

3. **Norming** - hopefully the result of the storming phase is that the group members manage to get on with each other sufficiently well to function effectively. Roles become apparent or are defined; strengths and weaknesses are recognised, compromises are negotiated. The group has arrived at an agreed shared goal and an acceptable culture to live by. A norm is a rule, either implicit or explicit, that says what behaviour is acceptable in that group, e.g. a speaker should not be interrupted. Do not 'put down' people for having spoken. Do as you would be done by.

4. **Performing** - all the group's energy is directed to achieving the goal. Everyone is playing a full part and problems are tackled openly. This phase is often described as *synergetic* , i.e. the sum of the whole is greater than the sum of the parts. Morale and achievement are high.

5. **Adjourning** - this is the winding down phase prior to the disbanding of the group. There may be sadness at the imminence of parting but the focus will be on tying up loose ends, reminiscing and evaluating. The leader can harness this climate for more formally directed reflection and reviewing aimed at drawing out the lessons to be learned from the experience that would otherwise never surface to conscious awareness. People like tidy endings to their experiences and a few concluding words from the leader is the sort of informal ceremony that fits the bill nicely.

Additional Notes on Group Life

Knowledge of how the life of a group develops is useful to leaders in giving them some idea of what to expect. They are able to view as relatively normal for example, the sometimes more alarming aspects of the storming phase. They are not prevented, by a defensive reaction, from monitoring the group's progress closely in order that their style of leadership is in accord with the current stage of progress.

It is as well to be aware, however, that this model, in outlining the various stages a group can go through, can convey the erroneous impression that movement in a group is always forward. Group development can regress and appear to deteriorate periodically, displaying what is best described as the 'peaks and troughs' phenomenon.

Things do not always occur in the theoretical order expected. And the extent to which any or all of these behaviour patterns are displayed is infinitely variable. A trainee leader might be agreeably surprised by an easy passage with his/her first group. Experienced leaders can be rocked back on their heels by apparently unsolvable chaos - and there are all stages in between.

This model, whilst very useful, only touches the tip of the iceberg. There is much more that leaders need to know about groups. For example, the different positive and negative roles that people can take on in groups which help or hinder the performance of a task or when engaged in building up the group itself. Some were listed earlier in the section on Adair's three circle model. (for more detail see Tables: 2-5 at the end of this chapter and 'people/task behaviours' in chapter 5). The role of peer group influences, past and present, is also significant knowledge for the understanding of the life of groups. The unseen emotional 'baggage' that group members bring in with them from home or school or club backgrounds, (e.g. rivalries, old scores, prejudices, even ways of behaving picked up from parents) that has nothing to do with the present group, can surface to sabotage progress. The film about a jury during a trial', *Twelve Angry Men'*, starring Henry Fonda, was a superb illustration of how the outside influences from the past, and future aspirations, brought into a group by its members, can affect the life of the group in the 'here and now'.

Leadership Style Stereotypes

Before leaving the subject, there are other important implications embedded in leadership styles that should be considered. They are best studied by looking at some polarised examples of leadership which will highlight the important differences for both the leader and members of the group.

The Coercive or Leader-Centred Style

The average person in the street asked for their idea of a leader will usually give the military model - leading from the front. The leader is conceived to be all-important and is very authoritarian. There is a very clear hierarchy of leader and follower. The required behaviour of the group is conformity and obedience to all orders. Independent thought is not normally encouraged or required. This style may be very good for the battle field, parade ground or emergency situations where both time and need require rapid and immediate action. But applied to other types of situations or tasks, it may be quite inappropriate. It can cramp initiative, dampen enjoyment, reduce the feeling of being involved and even hinder the development of those relationships essential for getting the job done. In the military situation it works because the 'team' realises in battle that survival may depend on unquestioning obedience, whilst off the battlefield there are the well known penalties that can be enforced for disobedience. Leaders here are perceived to be vested with a considerable power to punish or apply sanctions.

Leaders preferring this style tend to believe that there is a 'best way' to teach a particular body of knowledge, and by implication, only one way to learn it (see chapter 8 on learning styles). They spend a lot of time working out this best way and perfecting and updating it. Knowledge is presented comprehensively in as neat and logical an order as possible. Demonstrations have to be as near perfect as possible. Mistakes are perceived as time wasting and to be avoided. This style leads by presenting models of perfection to the group and the learning style is characterised by rote-learning, imitating or copying. Such leaders also tend to be very achievement-orientated and therefore set great store by efficiency, careful planning and preparation.

They will be very methodical, in order to avoid untidy loose ends and unnecessary time-wasting. Their treatment of their subject will be very detailed and comprehensive. The framework within which they work will tend to be rigid and not easily able to flex for the unexpected, or adapt to people of varying abilities and motivation. Such leaders often hold perfectionist values. The untidy nature of democratic methods is not to be contemplated by them!

*"Leaders are perceived to be vested
with a considerable power to punish"*

Out-of-doors, this style can be identified as the kind of leadership that leads by example - a force pulling the group along from the front. Unless care is taken, the tail-end may suffer. There is nothing more demoralising than being isolated at the back or being left behind when you want to be up with everyone. If leaders of this type are highly skilled and competent they may be so far removed from the level of skill in a party that they are unaware of, or unsympathetic to, any difficulties that individuals in the group may be experiencing.

Being at the front, they will tend to take all the decisions all the time. The group will not be involved in the experience as much as it might be and will tend to be tagging along blindly. It will have no real idea of what is happening or of the whys, wheres and hows of it all. No one will have any sense of ownership in the enterprise. Boredom and 'switching off' may be widespread. Some groups, perversely, do like this kind of leadership and prefer it - especially if the leader is a charismatic 'character' who can carry it off. But be aware that uncertainty as a pressure can cause leaders to drop into an authoritarian mode, ironically, at times when it is least appropriate.

The Permissive or Person-centred Style

Those with memories of the anarchic life-styles characteristic of the hippy 1960s-70s may remember that those decades earned, unfairly many would maintain, the label, 'permissive'. An unfortunate association of ideas gave to this leadership style negative connotations which made some leaders unnecessarily reluctant about its use. Their achievement-values inclined them to dismiss and discount the hippy, laid-back image in order to condemn it. But for those wishing to operate facilitatively in the social development dimension there is no other style that will suffice.

Here the leadership style has to be fairly low profile in order to encourage the people in the group to feel there is space and freedom to express themselves and take initiatives. So the leader adopts the role of a facilitator who helps the group make its own choices and decisions, identifies questions to be answered, decisions to be made, clears up communication foul-ups and helps to resolve any arguments, conflicts or personality clashes.The style may even seem to be, though it is not, *'laissez-faire'* in character, which is a complete absence of leadership when events are wont to take their course. Power is purposely devolved to the group in order to create the space for learning of a special kind, called experiential learning, which is concerned to involve people in real experiences. It is realised and accepted that some things in life cannot be taught. It is recognised that it is necessary, and only possible, for people to learn certain kinds of lesson by being left alone to get on with it and discover for themselves (heuristic learning) - sometimes the hard way. Being allowed to be responsible for one's own learning means experiencing one's own mistakes and successes in real situations.

There is a well-known definition of an expert as one who has made all the mistakes so knows the subject inside out - in direct contrast to the perfectionist who believes an expert is one who is so competent that they should never make any mistakes! The permissive method may be somewhat time-consuming, untidy and at times seemingly anarchic. But it can flex to the unexpected and be spontaneous. It is also individualistic or, to use the jargon, client-centred. If the level of self-motivation of members of the group is not carefully monitored by the leader, however, inter-personal competitiveness may arise to the extent that wholesome assertiveness may deteriorate into an undesirable aggressiveness which will block productive expression, creativity and initiative.

Understandably, leaders used to more authoritarian ways of working, may be unsure about how much freedom can be given to a group. There can be real worries about the apparent lack of the 'normal' controls on people's behaviour and things running away on them. It should be noted that controls exist in all styles but they will vary in kind. So the problem is a question of being able to identify them. One way of finding out is to explore thoroughly the labyrinth of the freedom/authority issue and what it means and implies with the group. If agreements/rules, democratically arrived at, are broken who makes them stick? Agreement can be reached by negotiation or by the leader setting limits. Such limits would normally include the four basic provisos that whatever is decided must not be illegal, unsafe, or harmful either emotionally or physically, to any member in the group. Neither can such decisions be binding upon anyone outside the group. This may seem to be obvious, but it can be forgotten in emotionally charged situations. Peer group pressure can often be a surprise force working for the leader since groups may often be more collectively conservative in outlook than the individuals in it. The leader does have one powerful sanction which is only effective if it is used sparingly. The warning that things are serious enough to warrant the withholding of his/her services or the resources available to the group is not abdication (yet) but notice that if things do not improve then that is it - finis.

This type of leadership would tend to be often found at the rear of the group - a force pushing the group from the back. This does not mean, as sometimes happens, that the leader goes to the back but continues to tell the group what to do from there. To be physically at the rear whilst continuing to project a directive lead is to display all the characteristics of the front-positioned leader.

Leading from the rear is a figurative attitude, but may, on occasion, be literally a physical position. The concern here may be to allow those at the front to feel they are involved and exercising some initiative in the shape of the day. There is also present a humane concern to encourage or support the others who tend to be at the back. Note that they are not necessarily the weaker ones for there can be all manner of reasons why someone might be towards the rear of a group. Can you think of some? The danger here is the leader's loss of control at the front unless some thought has been given to the problem. First-hand knowledge of the terrain, cave, river or coastline is needed so that a leader can anticipate when there may be a need to return to the front to cope with any tricky sections of the journey.

The leader needs to know the party well enough to be able to rely on them not moving beyond the contact range of eye, ear or voice, as necessary to the situation. Recognisable points can be set at which the front should halt to allow the rear to catch up. A more experienced group may be content to go at the pace of the slowest, but techniques need devising to cope with the impulsiveness of novice groups. This is particularly relevant to mixed groups at the start of the day when everyone is fresh and energetic, fit boys are prone to macho behaviour. The leader's skill is to maintain enthusiasm and enjoyment without losing control. To regard this role as one of maintaining control without killing enthusiasm is a negative way of approaching the situation.

*"Techniques need devising to cope with the impulsiveness
of novice groups"*

The Consultative/participative or Group-centred Style

This style tends to work either by consensus or in a formal democratic manner.

It requires a group to be confident and skilful enough to cooperate and participate, particularly in the process of communication and information exchanging so that opinions may be offered, worries are aired, problems solved, decisions made, and goals achieved. This style depends as much on the group for success as on the designated leader, for the group clearly has more responsibility for achieving success. In this it differs from the other two styles. When decisions about ends, aims or content are required, they are determined by the whole group. Where preferences about means are sought, (pace, speed, standard, pitch, degree etc.) they will be self regulated by the group. This style is underpinned by the belief that if the relationships in the group are right, anything is possible. The style also has the in-built flexibility to operate periodically under either of the other two styles if the group chooses to do so.

A morning meeting that was making decisions about the programme for the day was disrupted by the intrusion of events in the recent history of the group. Earlier on, a lot of resentment had arisen around the table-tennis table about whose turn it should be to play next. A lively exchange was now allowed to take place which became a matter of fierce argument about whether the winner of the previous game always earned the right to be one of the players in the next game or whether it should be a completely different pair. An important issue for them about fairness and justice was at stake. If left unresolved it would have had serious effects on the harmony and cohesion of the group and the achievement of their aims. The skilled players were using it selfishly as a ploy to keep the game to themselves. The priorities of an authoritarian regime concerned about getting on with activities (task) might have swept the whole thing under the carpet as an irrelevant side issue - with untold consequences. The democratic mode of operation required the leader to admit a different set of priorities which was prepared to put achievement in activities 'on hold'. It was felt important to give time to an exploration of the true nature of fairness, which was for the first time ever for some of them, and was instrumental in helping mistaken beliefs to be corrected. If this episode is read as putting table-tennis before more important matters, the whole point of it has been missed.

On the move in the field, a leader using this style tends to be found in the middle of the group - a position which epitomises the modern dynamic concept of leadership. Such a leadership style will be a combination of all of the styles mentioned above. The leader will only be authoritarian or military in style sparingly, at those times when occasion or situation demand it - perhaps only in emergencies or when physical safety is threatened by ignorance or fool-hardiness in the group. Using this consultative style, the leader can be at the front, centre or back according to the indications picked up from the physical environment and the group. The style tends to work democratically; helping, but not generally dictating to, the group to resolve their different impulses and inclinations, to decide for themselves, to adopt and carry through their plans. The leader is watchful to give support, encouragement, sympathy, guidance or advice to those individuals who need help. Leaders should be tuned in to signs of discomfort, stress or anxiety and be alive to possibilities that will arouse interest in, and enthusiasm for, the natural environment. The leader is at once consultant, counsellor, guide, mentor, chaperone and a source of information, knowledge, skill and experience. The leader is less a leader and more a person whose experience and resources are at the service of the group. The group is helped to lead itself as far as it is judged capable of doing so.

This style has one further advantage. When a group makes a decision about what to do, or go for, it has made an assessment of its own capability about what it thinks it can achieve - in a way it has measured itself against all the options and chosen this task because it believes it is equal to it. Whatever ensues - whether it is failure, success, under-achievement or over-achievement - self-learning will have taken place of a kind that could not occur if someone else (the leader?) had decided on the goal for the day.

A Comparative Note on Styles

The directive style tends to accentuate teaching behaviour. There is often an implicit belief that learning can only take place after teaching, i.e. teaching is essential to learning. There is a place for this and it is true in some respects, but not for everything (see chapter 8 on learning styles). Under this regime there tends to be a quicker and maybe a more systematic coverage of material - which can be mistaken for efficiency. But the criterion for efficiency is surely whether the thing that is taught is absorbed, learned and understood. However, much depends on what is meant by the term 'learning'. Directed learning tends to be at second-hand, somewhat mechanical and imitative, rote-learning for example, so understanding is not always as thorough as it should be. With experience-based methods, as found in permissive or democratic styles, the emphasis is on learning behaviour by discovery and actual, real experience of doing things. Self-motivated participation is required. Experience-based learning by definition is first-hand and real. Because it has been experienced in a real life situation, it is experienced by all of the capacities of a person working together simultaneously so it is integrated and holistic - unlike the 'didactic' approach (directive, dictating and autocratic) which tends to reduce material into its various separate parts in order to understand each in isolation (reductionist). But as with directed learning, experience may not be fully appreciated unless supported by a reflective, reviewing process afterwards to pull out the learning. Youngsters tend to remain at the shallower level of, "Great day - it's been fantastic" and do not delve into the deeper level of the experience under the tree bark, as it were, to get at the upper canopy layer of learning unless encouraged and helped.

Leaders should know that the same group of people will behave in markedly different ways under leaders who behave differently by using different styles; e.g. aggression and hostility is more frequent with autocratic and '*laissez-faire*' styles. There tends to be more scape-goating in an autocratic regime too. Most member satisfaction is associated with the democratic style and is highest in small interaction-oriented groups. As always, different styles are most effective under those different conditions best suited for them.

A Note on Starting the Democratic Process

It is sometimes difficult for leaders to know how actually to begin operating in the democratic mode. Is it done in a formal way by an announcement to that effect which may have a group of young people wondering what this new stunt is and begin testing out with outrageous suggestions to see what happens? One way that works is to outline the different operational approaches and to ask the group which method they would prefer. Implications in their choice of approach can be left to later or spelled out then as preferred or as dictated by the nature of the group.

If the change to using the democratic way is done informally and naturally in the course of events, it may be even more difficult for the group to discern when the offer of sharing power is being made. On the other hand, the transition from one style to another can be easily natural because the situation obviously requires it and the nature of prevailing relationships causes no problems.

How this style is introduced to a particular group may need some thinking about. It is sometimes necessary to spend some time on this in order to make clear what the implications for the group are in terms of their responses and behaviour. Especially if it is unfamiliar, they may need to understand in order that ground rules for operating this way can be established; even to the extent of reminding them how a proper discussion is carried out since good communication via the orderly exchange of ideas is crucial to the success of this style. Whether a lot is left to a process of discovery or not, at some time there will need to develop an understanding that the method depends on a number of things for success:

❂ Two-way communication must happen or the method will wither. It may prove necessary for the leader to establish some principles for speaking in groups - waiting your turn, timing your intervention, not shouting down things you disagree with, not dominating the debate, and so on.

❂ Nothing will happen unless the group exerts itself to make it happen. Even then it may not happen in the way that was expected or hoped since events sometimes have a disturbing habit of taking over or intervening. Unequal patterns of individual participation too can create a breakdown of relationships. If some appear to be doing or saying nothing, the inactivity or silence may be misinterpreted to arouse strong feelings about unfairness. Silence is perceived as a threat by some so some explanation of it helps allay worry. Asking the silent ones for an explanation, if they can manage it, can be a remarkably enlightening experience for the life of the group.

❂ Trust amongst the members is essential to make agreements about rules, or whatever, stick. Broken promises brought about by rule-breaking for instance, entails a lot of hard work by everyone before trust can be re-instated and restored. Groups used to 'quick fix' punishments as a way of resolving behaviour problems and trouble may be nonplused by the apparent absence of traditional threats or penalties. The effort required to restore trust between peers is in effect punishment and 'trouble' of a different kind as they suggest a range of solutions to solve the problem. It takes a while before they realise that the old leader/student relationship has been replaced by something rather different - a student to student to leader contract. The leader has one strong card to play *in extremis*. *"If we can't trust each other to keep this rule how can we trust each other when outside doing dangerous activities where trust is vital as in abseiling or whatever?"*

✿ Sincerity and consistency in the leader is vital. Cynical, worldly-wise attitudes of these times tend to see things like promises and agreements as so much naive optimism. Group discussions in reaching informal understandings or formal contracts about behaviour, can spell out the consequences of breaking promises or agreements and re-invest these social conventions with their need to be taken seriously.

There may be problems in introducing the democratic style with school groups such as:

✿ the testing out of staff by pupils to find out where the limits are in this new situation. Some of the deliberately outrageous proposals in this process can arouse immediate anxiety in the leader to such an extent that s/he reverts to the directive mode and brings the 'new way' into instant disrepute. A 'softly softly' approach engages the group in a short (or long if need be) discussion, riding the wave of testing behaviours with discreet interjections now and again to help the group arrive at reasonable decisions. There is usually a sane element in the group whose reasonableness can be harnessed to avoid catastrophe. Likely test questions are "What time do we need to go to bed?" or "Can we go to the pub?" Asking what they think and letting the discussion roll usually tends to reach a reasonable conclusion as groups are not as unconventional as they might like to think they are or as leaders fear they might be. Depending on the age of the group, is the appearance of cigarettes an immediate challenge or something to be ignored for the time being until the quality of relationships will permit a serious discussion of the issues with a more realistic hope of bringing about changes in that habit?

❂ the suspicions of staff in other departments about 'permissiveness' and apparent 'lack of control' need to be allayed by careful preparation of the ground with them beforehand. They need convincing that you have not gone 'over to the other side' - which is how they may tend to see it as it seems to them that you have lost control and are "letting them do what they like".

❂ old habits such as those acquired in school in response to the tight scheduling of normal time-tabling will be found to contravene the requirements of the democratic process, e.g. when expecting a response, the teachers often say, "come on, hurry up and answer, we haven't much time", the student feels, "no, wait, I need more time and space to think about or respond to questions that are quite different from those I usually get asked".

Democratic leaders need to be stable, secure people able to take the risky feeling of treading a knife edge. In our society, leaders will be held responsible for the actions of those in their charge even when the leader's power has been delegated. It is a different kind of risk-taking and must be backed by a strong belief in the rightness of the cause and by convictions that can be articulated to whomsoever sees fit to take you to task "for being irresponsible in letting them have their own way" - which is how Mr. or Mrs. Average Citizen regrettably tend to view it.

At times, leaders will be aware that they are close to flying in the face of normal conventions. If things go wrong the leader will be seen to be accountable.

I remember once being reprimanded by an irate member of the public who was justifiably outraged at the misdoings, in an unsupervised moment, of some of the young people for whom I was responsible. A philosophic discussion about the nature of man and self responsibility would not have been well received at the time and in a moment of inspiration all I could respond with was a promise that if the time came when the police would be held responsible for the wrong doings of the criminal fraternity, then I would be prepared to be responsible for the actions of my group. Whilst that floored him for the moment it did not exactly solve the problem. Mulling it over later, I reached the conclusion that if someone in a group decides to go off the rails, there is not a lot you can usually do about it at the time. The leader cannot really be held responsible for the anti-social decisions or actions of others who decide to go outside the rules of society.

But society is so over-protective of the young these days that it tends to overrule their need to become independent beings responsible for their own actions. The only way to guarantee wrong-doing did not happen would be to chain them to their beds! Ships are built for leaving harbour, we are told, and the same applies to people, otherwise what is the point of their existence? Later, what a leader can do, is be responsible for picking up the pieces, ensuring that damage of whatever kind is made good by the perpetrators and going over the episode with the miscreants in an attempt to get them to see the error of their ways or reach a tighter contract-type agreement with them. The age at which young people are deemed responsible for their own actions seems to be a swamp with shifting goal-posts.

" At times leaders will be aware that they are close to flying...."

A troubling question for leaders is, "if a child disobeys a rule or instruction and causes damage or injury to self or others, at what age can they be held responsible for their actions?" We used to think it might be fourteen years of age but now, seemingly, parents can be held responsible for older truanting sixteen-year-olds and even end up in jail. The whole business is much more complex depending on whether criminal law or civil law is involved. Any answer has to be governed by the phrase, "it all depends on the particular circumstances"; it is only possible to give an answer for a particular situation. Some of the key factors would be the previous known behaviour, skill and experience of the child as well as its age and maturity, whether an aberration or act of disobedience might have been foreseen.

Telling signs would be a history of unreliability, disobedience or unstable temperament, for example - whether the level of supervision and prior actions were reasonable and appropriate and so on.

Style Pitfalls

In adopting leadership styles, leaders need to be aware that after aims have been formulated, it is possible to choose a style which, if used as a general strategy rather than as an occasional, expedient tactic, may either help or hinder the aims.

It is sometimes not appreciated that:

it is possible to match up aims with a style of leadership which will ensure that the aims are never achieved!

For example, if the aim was to help the group become more self-determining and self-sufficient, as would be the case in preparing a group to undertake an unaccompanied expedition in the Duke of Edinburgh Award Scheme, the coercive style in requiring mindless dependence and initiative-stripping conformity, would be quite incongruent. It would be appropriate for an emergency situation where an authoritarian style is the best choice and may help to impart confidence in the group and get things done quickly.

Canoing novices, provided they were in a demarcated area, might be better allowed to learn, by discovery, the intricacies of paddling in a straight line, whilst reserving more directive coaching for the slower learner or the more complex strokes that may come later in the same session.

The autocratic style would be unsuitable to the teacher who wished the group to experience a more relaxed and informal environment in order to develop a better relationship with, and between, them. A group struggling with the complexities of navigation might be served better by a 'permissive' unaccompanied simple journey along the valley bottoms than by a coerced, complex, guided marathon over the hilltops.

Perhaps this is a convenient point to register the difference between informality and casualness and permissiveness.

Casualness is distinguished by sloppiness, and unthinking, unplanned behaviour which leaves people confused.

Informality permits a leader to be easy and relaxed but remain 'switched on' and aware so that nothing is missed or neglected.

Permissiveness is part of a strategy to make it possible for people to learn by finding out - discovery. So it is to do with the deliberate sharing of power with a group, and all that follows from that, such as deciding what to do, where to go etc.

A tent pitching session can be turned from a boringly directed ordeal into an hilarious, heuristic (finding out for yourself by discovery) problem solving exercise of the intellect by choosing to use the permissive style. "See if you can erect your tent without being told how to do it". On the other hand, it might be wise to give instructions to beginner canoeists about how to fit their life-jackets properly before going afloat to learn to paddle by finding out for themselves.

It is important to make clear if the point has not already been emphasised, that when a particular style is chosen, it does not have to be for the whole of a skills training session or for all of a more extended programme, but only for bits of it. To take the example about a Duke of Edinburgh Award expedition above, it may still be necessary to use a directive style on occasion to achieve a short term objective although the long term aim is independence and self-sufficiency. A particular style might only be used for five minutes, or it may be required for three hours, or three days because it is the appropriate tactic for the aim, the group, the individual or the occasion! The leader must weigh it all up and decide. Life is tough!

Limitations and Possibilities of Situations in Other Activities

Different outdoor activities have situations that are characterised by patterns of movement, visibility, speed and distances apart that impose their own particular limitations on the choice of leadership style. It is likely to be more difficult to give close support or coaching to individuals in their own vessels when canoeing or sailing, or in a restricted passage in caving, or on the open hillside when skiing, than it is, for example, to a group on a mountain walk, by the very nature of the way the activity is conducted. In some situations only one style is appropriate. What do you do in a cave where most of the group are out of sight for much of the time?

Whilst most of the novice-learner type situations require a fair degree of directive control, there are more opportunities for discovery methods than one might at first think. But where mistakes by a group member would have very serious consequences, supervision needs to be tighter. In light winds, an unaccompanied dinghy crew could be allowed to learn by experience in a way that would be unthinkable in very strong winds where a very authoritarian style from an instructor on board would be more appropriate. Also the sheer proximity of instructor and crew at close quarters in a dinghy makes it less easy to give the crew space to think independently. Even small detail is too easily directed, so the crew tend to stop thinking. Competitive racing is different obviously - but the habit of heavy command can overlap into recreative sailing.

The command structure in the less crowded situation of sea-going boats, is an interesting case especially when sailing in navigable waters. Boat skippers are like car drivers in that they have **legal** responsibilities to avoid collision.

This makes the activity of big-boat sailing an exception to some extent because it is circumscribed by legislation in a way that does not yet apply to the other activities in the U.K., though it applies to them now on the Continent. (But if EEC regulations relating to the suppliers of services became law in the U.K., anyone charged with negligence would be assumed guilty until proved innocent.) Skippers, who are training others on board, have a difficult task in trying to discern how far to be directive and how far to delegate. This is particularly so in an activity that has the nasty habit of disobeying the rules of learning by delivering the test before the lesson! If the crew becomes too used to democratic methods, will the habits encouraged by this style, such as expecting a say in the shaping of events, inadvertently arise during emergencies to endanger the ship or others in the vicinity? Skippers may tend to be directive on a boat because they are responsible and accountable in law for a wide range of liabilities. They may try to delegate but may understandably feel obliged to keep intervening in a way that will affect initiative and the means to foster self sufficiency.

"What do you do in a cave where most of the group are out of sight?"

There is also the pressure of being aware that there is a very expensive piece of kit beneath your feet! But being with a skipper prepared to be less directive is a very rewarding experience for the crew members. Skippers can't do everything, so it is better to plan what to delegate rather than let it happen casually.

Coaching Styles

Rock climbing can be an activity that is very flexible in providing situations that readily permit different leadership styles. This is illustrated by looking at the ways a person can be coached up a route. A directive style would point out every hold and instruct how every move should be made. No thought would be required of the learner, just acquiescence. With a permissive style no instruction would be given at all. But a safety structure would be provided by the rope and novices would be allowed to work everything out for themselves. A 'laissez-faire' style would provide more experienced students with a technical manual and guide book and, having delegated all responsibility to them absolutely, leave them to get on with it completely by themselves. A democratic style would allow everyone to be involved in, and responsible for, belaying and taking in the rope or securing and paying out the rope to another student - a situation obviously requiring closer monitoring by the instructor as the group have not yet progressed to the 'laissez-faire' level of operating.

Degrees of difference in between these styles are seen when the instructor is using a diagnostic and reflective approach (mirror-like) which, by summarising and identifying the situation, thereby helps to resolve the problem for the student. Thus: "You are not in balance, you need to find something for your right foot", or, "If you do not move soon, your arms will tire and you will fall off. Climb down to a comfortable stance and think again." On occasion none of these methods will work and it will become necessary to persuade and encourage the disheartened follower, "You're O.K. I've got you on the rope. You can do it. Have a rest first, then try again."

The skill of coaching is a whole other ball-game. It has similarities in principles with leadership styles as shown above. But when coaching a particular skill it is as well to remember that what worked for one person may not necessarily work for someone else. Even the words you use may be interpreted differently by different group members. An ability to observe, really observe, and analyse movement will be a great asset. Just think about all the factors involved in paddling a straight course for instance. Which one has the student got wrong? And there is always 'X', the possibility that it is some external factor at the root of the problem like a large repair patch on the hull causing an unequal flow of water inducing a turning moment on the canoe's motion. More on this subject later in chapter 8.

Tables - Highlighting Differences Between the Styles

An aspirant leader grappling with the novel intricacies of the different leading styles does not always immediately appreciate the important distinctions that must be drawn.

It takes time to understand; awareness of their finer points comes with experience: you can't tell the depth or temperature of a pool until you get in - the notices might be wrong!

- ❂ what differences characterise the variations in style
- ❂ what style variations mean in terms of the kinds of behaviour that both the leader and the members of a group must adopt
- ❂ what sorts of skills they both must have.

In an attempt to assist this process of appreciating differences in the styles, a number of tables[11] follow overleaf which try to tease out and show some of these differences. One tip is not to try and memorise them all!

TABLE 1

Table 1 on the following page can be read across the page so that a characteristic in one style column has its corresponding characteristic in the other two style columns.

THE DIFFERENT CHARACTERISTICS OF THREE TYPES OF LEADERSHIP STYLE

COERCIVE STYLE	PERMISSIVE STYLE	CONSULTATIVE STYLE
Leader directed.	**Individual** self directed.	**Group** acts collectively.
Authoritarian control.	Delegatory but not laissez-faire, which is non-control or abdication.	Consensus control by group.
Imposed aims/tasks.	Self selected aims/tasks.	Group determined aims/tasks.
Hierarchical structure necessary.	Anarchical structure can result.	Democratic /representative structure develops.
Conformity required.	Initiative & self-expression required. May become competitive.	Cooperation and trust required. Can include other styles if wished.
Rigid framework-rules etc. imposed.	Relaxed framework which depends on self discipline.	Flexible, adaptive framework. Rules agreed by vote or consensus.
✿ ✿ ✿	✿ ✿ ✿ ✿ ✿	✿ ✿ ✿
Activity highly organised well planned, methodical. May require much admin. to ensure it works.	Activity is self motivated or opportunist and spontaneous. It may be erratic and random.	Activity develops organically from needs expressed in the group.
Learn from 'models' of perfection and applying the theory.	Learn by discovery and from experience.	The necessary process of consulting and negotiating is an extra learning experience.
Perfectionist and tidy.	Mistake prone and untidy.	Mixture of other two styles.

Table 1. Continued on next page >

COERCIVE STYLE	PERMISSIVE STYLE	CONSULTATIVE STYLE
Success/achievement oriented. Getting there is all important. Activists love it.	Failure is possible and accepted. Diffident students feel more comfortable.	Mixture of other two styles and often self-correcting. The journey may be more important than getting there.
Mistakes frowned upon or punished.	Mistakes may be demoralising or fun and good learning experienced.	Mistakes are learned from.
Time saving if group can take it.	Time consuming, not time wasting.	Mixture of styles.
Uniform end product or effect on individual is visualised by leader.	End product is individually variable.	Construction about end product is built up by all.
Assumptions made by leader in selection of content/task etc.	Content/task self selected.	Content/task decided by the group.
Content, delivery, speed determined/ imposed by leader.	Self regulatory/ self imposed.	Self regulatory/ self imposed.
Concern is for standards of achievement and results.	Concern is for personal effectiveness.	Concern is for inter-personal relationships and social awareness.
The main focus is upon achieving the task/aim or learning about the subject matter in hand.	The main focus is upon personal interests.	The main focus is on the value derived from the group process in terms of social adequacy.
The style is thus task-oriented or outcome-oriented.	The style is thus interest oriented but elements are often interlaced with it.	The style is thus process-oriented and needs-oriented.

TABLE 2

LEADERS REQUIRE DIFFERENT ROLES/ BEHAVIOURS FOR DIFFERENT STYLES

COERCIVE STYLE	PERMISSIVE STYLE	CONSULTATIVE STYLE
Director	Observer	Observer
Supervisor	Recorder	Recorder
Instructor	Provider (resources)	Facilitator
Leader	Stimulator (ideas)	Commentator
Demonstrator	Opportunist	Helper
Pedagogue	Evaluator	Supporter
Organiser	Coordinator	Mediator
Planner		Consultant
Initiator		Advisor
Disciplinarian		Reflector
Motivator		Delegator
Selector		Evaluator
Judge		Reviewer
Assessor		
Challenger		
Analyser		
Criticiser		

TABLE 3

LEADERS REQUIRE DIFFERENT SKILLS
FOR DIFFERENT STYLES

COERCIVE STYLE	PERMISSIVE STYLE	CONSULTATIVE STYLE
Decision-making	Observing	Responding
Order-giving	Recording	Adapting
Controlling	Approving	Commenting
Dominating	Encouraging	Summarising
Asserting	Keeping low profile	Clarifying
Problem-solving	Suggesting	Identifying questions
Analysing	Supporting	Identifying problems
Confronting	Keeping silent	Identifying decisions
Setting limits	Providing resources	Compensating
Giving information	Providing back-up	Balancing
Giving answers	Organisation	Reinforcing
Summarising	Monitoring	Supporting
Pace-making		Persuading
Measuring		Giving information
Assessing		Providing resources
Imparting confidence		Catalysing
Taking responsibility		With-holding
Setting aims/tasks		Keeping silent
Criticising		Being patient
Censuring		Confronting
Scolding		Expressing
Disapproving		Interpreting
Approving		Observing
Praising		Recording
		Feeding back
		Evaluating
		Monitoring

TABLE 4

GROUP MEMBERS REQUIRE DIFFERENT
ROLES/BEHAVIOURS FOR
DIFFERENT STYLES

COERCIVE STYLE	PERMISSIVE STYLE	CONSULTATIVE STYLE
Conformer	Initiator	Collaborator
Obeyer	Forager	Participator
Follower	Discoverer	Sharer
Receiver	Explorer	Initiator
Absorber	Researcher	Recorder
Imitator	Pace maker	Organiser
Repeater	Selector	Planner
Performer	Decision-maker	Voter
Agreer	Experimenter	Communicator
Complier		

TABLE 5

GROUP MEMBERS REQUIRE DIFFERENT
SKILLS FOR DIFFERENT STYLES

COERCIVE STYLE	PERMISSIVE STYLE	CONSULTATIVE STYLE
Listening	Inducing	Solving problems
Memorising	Deducing	Making decisions
Reiterating	Relating facts	Carrying out plans
Concentrating	Drawing conclusions	Expressing
Watching	Organising self	Articulating
Copying	Assessing self	Communicating
Collating	Expressing self	Listening
Imitating	Defending self	Responding
	Asserting self	Suggesting
	Making decisions	Opining
	Making judgments	Feeding back
	Taking initiatives	Judging
	Taking responsibility	Relating
		Cooperating
		Evaluating Negotiating
		Taking responsibility

Personality and Natural Leading Style

One final point on leadership styles. The way you were brought up, the experiences you have had in your life and the nature of your personality will have tended to impart a set of values and attitudes which will cause a gravitation towards one of the three styles mentioned above. In other words, the way you are, and how you are, will determine the style you tend naturally to **prefer** to use. Without training or conscious effort, you are likely to adhere to that style and remain unaware of other styles, or when and how they are best used.

It is important to leading ability that leaders develop a conscious structure of concepts (a model) on which to base their own ideas about leadership. Without such a personal model, it is very difficult to form, develop, or manipulate ideas about a very intangible subject. But once it is acquired, do not forget to spring clean it occasionally! Learning is life-long for leaders as well as those in their charge.

To Summarise this Chapter:

The choice of leading style may be affected by:

- ✿ the aims or task

- ✿ the outdoor situation or circumstances - including weather and associated conditions.

- ✿ the nature of the group and its stage of development (maturity)

- ✿ nature of the terrain or water state

- ✿ certain types of activity situation.

It is important for the leader to keep in mind that the circumstances of a situation and the needs of group are continually changing. The ability to continuously monitor, perceive and evaluate these changes and the possession of a range of styles to be versatile in matching these changes appropriately, are key leadership skills.

Research indicates that leadership characteristics and situational demands seem to interact to determine the extent to which a leader will be successful in a group. Previously successful leaders may fail when placed in a situation that demands responses that are incompatible with the leader's personality, or his/her normal pattern of interaction or performance. Training helps to reduce this possibility.

❀ Chapter Five ❀

Leader Awareness

Difference Between Awareness and Understanding

One of the learning difficulties in leader training is the subtle semantic distinctions that have to be made in order to talk about it meaningfully e.g. what is the difference between awareness and understanding? Do we understand the distinction that is made between being told 'what to think' regarding certain topics (being given politically correct dogma perhaps) and being required to 'think freely about them' (making up your own mind)?

It is needful here to explain the difference between 'awareness' and 'understanding' because the two are often bandied about loosely and synonymously.

Awareness: is a state of mind which knows of the existence of something but without necessarily knowing the reason why it is there or what to do about it; e.g. entering a room and sensing a tense atmosphere.

Understanding: is having the necessary background of supporting knowledge which gives one the ability to diagnose the reasons 'why' which underlie that awareness and to form a plan of action if necessary. Thus entering the room and knowing that there is a recent history of peer conflict over who does the washing up, will enable the leader to avoid misinterpretations about the causes of the 'atmosphere' (e.g. not rivalry over girl friends) and be able to help the group to resolve the problem and move on.

There are lists in Appendix 2 detailing items of awareness and items of understanding which illustrate the distinctions being made here and which are part of a good leader's toolkit.

Comparison of Formal and Informal Party Situations

Leading a formal group in the outdoors is a very different 'game' from the informal situation of 'being with friends'. With friends of equal ability, responsibility and decision-making is shared in a casual almost carefree way. Each is tacitly understood to be self responsible (and for an informal group of adults this is the legal interpretation too) each having the skill and experience to know and observe personal limitations. If one of them has a problem it is assumed that it will be brought to the notice of the others. It would be less easy to do this in a group that often displayed 'one-upmanship' and aggressive competitiveness. Such groups are potential disasters looking for somewhere to happen!

Once the business of leading a formal party is embarked upon, a different world is entered with a new, extra, second dimension containing an additional set of factors to become aware of and to take into account. These factors are mostly to do with managing people and maintaining good working relationships. There is a large element of consideration for others involving self-discipline and self-denial in party leading which must have been thought through and accepted. It is well known that it is difficult for a leader to control others if self-control is lacking. The basis of self-control is self-awareness and self-knowledge.

Self Awareness

A raised level of awareness of self results in shifts in personal attitudes and predispositions, changes in preoccupations and priorities, changes in a general attitude to others. By way of illustration, take the case of a group with a leader not quite sure of his/her whereabouts in mist. It is important for this leader to **be aware** that there may be present an anxiety not to lose the way, and a need for immediate reassurance that the present position is correctly identified, and that a suitable line or track is being followed. The pressure to have immediate reassurance could cause the leader gradually to speed up the pace in the search for this reassurance and eventually cause distress to the group. In **an unaware state** it is built into the emotional condition that the leader is more likely to fall into this acceleration trap.

This kind of awareness could take years to acquire but a few well chosen words during training would achieve the desired effect in moments. The leader would then be aware that if acceleration is undesirable it can be avoided. Alternatively, if acceleration becomes necessary, the change of pace will be conscious and deliberate. There will be a *conscious awareness* that some of the group may be affected. Thus this small piece of awareness will have contributed to that quality of alertness and sensitivity one hopes to see in leaders. This is a typical example of how a piece of theoretical and apparently esoteric knowledge can have a practical use and application.

Another form of self awareness is being aware of one's own attitudes.

*"If acceleration becomes necessary, the
change of pace will be conscious and deliberate"*

One of the ways in which our values reveal and express themselves is through some of our attitudes which have a habit of popping out without conscious effort when something has triggered them - almost like bullets from a gun. Attitudes tend to fix people into particular ways of behaving or working (see chapter 6 for examples); the paths they follow is almost as predictable as the path of the bullet alluded to above. It is as if the attitude is a rear or fore sight that always causes a gun to aim at the same thing. There is no way of adjusting for lateral or vertical deflection - unless, of course, the aimer is aware of the limitations of what is being aimed with! So the more a person is aware of their own attitudes, the less they will be trapped inside them and more able to respond flexibly.

✪ Self-awareness has other applications which are slightly different, for example, as when trying to put meaning to some puzzling behaviour in a group (see also chapter 8 and the section on 'observation/ perception/ interpretation').

The conclusions a leader draws about human behaviour when it is observed are interpretations of perceptions. Not only is perception selective in tending to see what it wants to see, but the tendency is to judge others by the condition of oneself. This is particularly so when trying to identify motives in others. Sometimes there is no other helpful information to assist except what can be found from within the personal experience of the leader. The open, trusting sort of leader will find it easier to trust others. Positive motives will be ascribed to the actions of others or at least good and acceptable reasons will be assumed even if they are as yet unknown. An insecure defensive person will tend to suspect the worst in people because threats or insults to self are always being looked for. In looking, those negative motives will be found even when they are not there or not intended.

It is important for leaders to be self-aware so that personal prejudices can be prevented, as much as is humanly possible, from muddying the waters when interpreting the behaviour of others. Stereo-typing people is a form of prejudice for example. Leaders must try to be aware of it in themselves.

Lifestyle States

By 'lifestyle' we are not talking here about the way we live - as for example in having a 'consumerist' lifestyle or an 'urban' lifestyle. What will be discussed below is something more fundamental in the person which is concerned with certain inner basic stances in the way one looks at and deals with life, and certain basic aspects of living about which there are important choices to be made.

There are three main orientations with regard to states of self and life styles.[11] All of these are present to some degree in people, but one of them tends to be predominant. Leaders should be aware how it is for them personally.

❁ **'Doing'** kinds of people tend to act first and think later; they 'do' practical things. e.g. explorers, hunters, engineers, builders. In the outdoor context they are the 'autotelic activists'.

❁ **'Being'** people by contrast rarely act and are preoccupied with thinking about the state of how they are e.g. monks, mystics, hippies, (and maybe some therapists?).

❁ **'Becoming'** people tend to be a mixture of the other two states. Thinking is used to guide their actions (e.g. you and I - because I am writing this book about 'becoming' and you are reading it presumably with a view to becoming something different, better!). In this particular arena are found the social educationists, development trainers, the wilderness and adventure therapists - as opposed to the pure activist.

Leaders who are 'doing' people set greater store on more tangible, practical types of knowledge and will be less easily convinced about the value of information that falls into the 'awareness and understanding' categories. 'Becoming' people operating from a more balanced perspective will feel it to be relatively easy. Leaders identifying which orientation fits them personally, place themselves in a better position to see whether or not one of the other orientations is better suited to leadership and towards which personal movement is required.

Practical Points for Personal Awareness

It is important that the following points about the leading situation are realised:

❁ Although there will be a group present, it is virtually a 'solo' situation for the leader in the sense that there may be no other person with whom, in extremity, the responsibility of decision-making, navigating and monitoring can be shared - unless, of course, the leader is fortunate enough to have a second experienced person along as a designated assistant. Some 'accompanying adults' are not always equipped by experience to be able to help the leader in these things. The group may be encouraged to participate in these functions, but the onus will still be on the leader to check they are correct or acceptable. The leader is the one held responsible if things go wrongly.

✿ The whole group is dependent on the leader to the extent that, in the final analysis, s/he is responsible for their enjoyment, comfort and safety.

✿ You may have to do all the thinking for each and everyone of them - especially if they are novices to the extent even of telling them, for example, when to eat, drink, put on extra clothing/waterproofs or take them off, tie up loose boot laces, clip up a ski boot properly, adjust a loose spray deck or adjust rucksack straps.

✿ You may not assume that what you can do, they can also do. They may be able to do things that you cannot do - especially if it is an adult group.

✿ You may not even assume that what you want to do within the day will coincide with their desires and aspirations. This is one aspect served well by the democratic style of leadership which keeps channels of communication open and gives you vital feedback on how the group reads the situation.

Awareness of the Group's Condition - Signs and Signals

Leaders should not assume that because they personally feel comfortable, relaxed, confident, at any given moment, the members of the group feel the same.

"Leaders should not assume that because they feel comfortable, relaxed and confident....members of the group feel the same."

For all the leader knows, members of the group may quite likely be too hot, too cold, thirsty, hungry, out of breath, miserable, over-awed, anxious, tense, bored, fed-up or plain tired. Watch for 'signals' being displayed or broadcasted by the whole body or parts of it such as dragging feet, wallowing gait, head hung low, frequent tripping up, buttons or zips on anoraks not done up properly for the prevailing conditions. See chapter 8 on non verbal communication for more detail.

Awareness of Group Behaviour

Benefits accrue from an awareness of peoples' needs[5] and how they behave when they are in groups. As individuals in a one-to-one exchange with you, they can be quite pleasant people. In groups, the pressure of not losing face, keeping one's end up, establishing status in the group, being egged on to do things or "You won't be one of us" (and remember that they do want to belong to the peer group), being put down, being shown up, embarrassed, belittled and so forth are all very powerful pressures that can trigger people to behave quite out of character. Books[14] have been written which identify many of the so-called 'behaviour games' people play, often unconsciously, in their transactions with each other. It is well worth reading one or two to pick up a few tips.

A knowledge of some of the games is a useful aid to the understanding and interpretation of some of the behavioural aspects of group life. Knowing whether to tackle or ignore something seen, depends on how significant it is in relation to other things. This can be a minefield. To do something about 'games' is quite difficult because the behaviour pattern is likely to be quite deeply entrenched and often the product of home and neighbourhood experiences. Sometimes just being able to identify the game and cause a group to become aware of what is going on and that they have been 'rumbled', can be enough to stop it. Common games are: *'uproar'* (which is when a person uses some minor irritation to 'erupt' at authority in a way out of all proportion to the cause in order to attract status or avoid having to do something) or *'smoke screens'* (when a group seems to orchestrate a number of minor incidents in order to distract authority from dealing with the misdemeanour that started it all off) or 'how far can we push him/her before they lose their temper' or 'if we keep silent long enough "Sir/Miss" will give us the answer'.

People/task Behaviour in Groups

Groups or leaders when working towards some aim, tend to be in one of two modes. These are:

1. Getting on with the aim, goal or task

Such people tend to be 'achievers'. The job has priority and great store is set on 'getting there' even if people have to suffer a bit or a lot. Although this may be the case in the group generally, be aware that there may be one or more not of the same persuasion - the larger the group the more likely this is.

2. Maintaining or mending relationships

People preferring this mode tend to be gregarious and want to be liked. In the jargon they are 'affiliatives' or 'associatives'. Relationships have the priority and **how** you get to where you are going is more important than actually getting there. If the task is going to destroy the group then let the task go or find an acceptable compromise. Those who might be disappointed or frustrated can be taken out some other time in a group that would be specially selected because it is able to cope with the demands of a particular objective (miles covered, races won, summits reached, advanced study/exploration completed).

Roles of individuals in groups often reflect these two modes. Leaders may find them a useful tool to understand, or diagnose, who is doing what in the group. Some of these roles were itemised in the tables at the end of chapter four, but can be looked at in another useful way from the point of view of these two modes.

Any member of the group may show leadership behaviour by taking action that helps the group achieve the task or maintain effective relationships. If some individuals take on these roles more than other group members then relationship problems may arise such as jealousy, antipathy or resentment, which will require sorting out.

Thus we have:

Task actions which are leadership actions

Information and opinion giver
Information and opinion seeker
Direction and role definer
Summariser
Energiser
Comprehension checker

Maintenance of relationships actions which are leadership actions

Encourager of participation
Communication facilitator
Tension reliever
Process observer
Interpersonal problem solver
Supporter and praiser

Dominance/Sociability Behaviour in Groups

When two or more people interact, the nature of that interpersonal behaviour may be described in ways which seem to be the same as the actions described above since they are to do with authority/control or friendliness/intimacy. They are closely related in a way, but they are also distinct. For example, most people like either to control things (high dominance) or let others do the controlling (low dominance). We can be in one mode or the other at different times for various reasons. Also, most people tend to be either warm and personal (high sociability) or to be cool and impersonal (low sociability). Again, either is possible depending on circumstances. These four variables can be broken down into more significant classifications[15] as shown in diagram 5 below.

Being aware of these variables may help when it is necessary for a leader to know what is happening between and among individuals in the group and know whether to do anything about it in a way that will be positive and avoid unproductive outcomes. Interpreting human behaviour is a difficult skill. The ability to do it fairly reliably and consistently is a tremendous asset to a leader.

Diagram 5. Dominance/Sociability behavioural grid

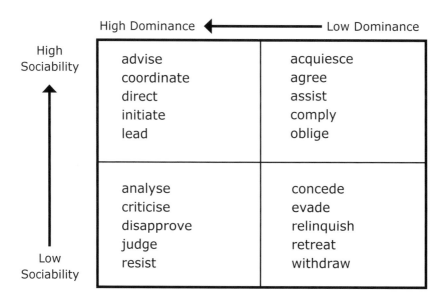

Most of us tend to rely for guidance on the teachings of our past experience in our dealings with others. Though useful, this particular kind of experience can be an imperfect information base at the best of times. Leaders wishing to improve their ability further in this field could consider studying some of the main elements of Transactional Analysis (T.A. for short). Despite its formidable title, T.A. provides a more understandable way for lay people to gain a better insight into human behaviour than an attempt to master psychology, which most of us have not the time to do. T.A. looks at behavioural attitudes as displayed by three states of self:

- the 'child' in each of us
- the 'parent' in each of us
- and the 'adult' in each of us.

Apart from the games we play with each other (the bad ones like 'uproar' are called 'rackets') it believes that there are five imperatives driving behaviour which are a simple way of understanding behaviour. The five 'drivers' are: 'Be Perfect', 'Be Strong', 'Hurry Up', 'Try Harder', 'Please Me' - all of which have clusters of particular kinds of behaviours attached to them. Regretfully, the nature of this chapter can only extend to the inclusion of one or two sources about T.A. for further reading at the end of the book.

Holistic Awareness of Situations

Training schemes do not set out to teach the aspirant leader/ instructor how to become infallible. They cannot even give a set of rules and procedures that will work to ensure the right answer in every situation. They can only offer a set of tools and show how these can be used in a general way. How they can be used in other certain specific circumstances can only be learned through experience.

Developing a comprehensive awareness encompassing the group situation, the immediate locale in which it is located and the total outdoor context surrounding it, provides a way towards finding answers to such problems. For better analysis, one may break down the situation into three areas of attention depending upon whether the leader's focus is 'micro', 'macro' or what may be called, 'super macro' at any one time.

Perhaps this point requires an example incorporating the three - micro, macro and super macro areas - on which the leader's attention may be focused at any one time. At the southern end of Crinkle Crags in Langdale, the descending path becomes a rocky section down the edge of a small gully. Where it leaves this edge a short wall has to be negotiated to reach the bed of the gully. A leader with a group coming across this 'bad step' obstacle, may feel a need to get out the rope to safeguard movement at this point and could become so engrossed with the technical aspects of the rocky situation (micro) to find a belay in order to protect the descent of the people into the gully, as to become oblivious of the wider super macro context. For, above this section is a slope of loose scree. Any other party descending it could send stones into the gully below where members of the leader's group will be standing after they have untied.

There is irony here in that the leader believes s/he is following safe practice in protecting the group by good rope management (micro) when, in fact, by not waiting until the party above is clear of the scree, or telling those of his/her party below to move to a safer place out of the line of fire (macro), s/he is in fact placing the group in some danger.

With experience it becomes easier for leaders to develop an all-round awareness which enables them to weigh up all the various factors of a problem situation and come up with:

- **the right response**
- **for a particular group**
- **with a particular job or task to do**
- **in a specific situation**

❂ Chapter Six ❂

Leader Attitudes and Approaches

If the contents of chapters four and five are absorbed successfully into leading technique, an attitude and approach will develop over time that is rather different from that of the person who pursues an activity purely for personal satisfaction and pleasure. Keep in mind chapter one about aims and values. Some pointers about key dispositions and outlooks now follow.

Selfish or Selfless Leaders

Leaders need to have examined their own personal reasons and motives for wanting to take groups into the outdoors and to have clarified for themselves why they are wanting to do it at all, and to what ends. There needs to be a clear realisation that the responsibilities of leadership impose a discipline that allows very little room for personal wishes, ambitions or aspirations. Leadership in this context is a state of mind that is largely selfless.

Ego-tripper

Leadership used for selfish ends is empty, non-creative and sterile. Leadership used to inflate or reinforce the leader's ego, such as needing to demonstrate personal expertise and 'superior' powers to the group, is a destructive exercise without value to the group. The group should be approached with humility rather than arrogance. Leaders should not assume they always know what is best for the group or think they understand group needs so well that there is no need ever to consult them or ask for opinions. Leaders can not hope to pitch things at the group's level of expectation, motivation, interest and capability without some degree of consultation.

✪ A leader's interest in an activity should not over-shadow interest in the group. If getting into the countryside or onto the water means more than leading a group, the leader should think twice before taking it on. If satisfactions are derived primarily from personal reasons such as so many miles covered, rivers descended, peaks ascended or species studied, a leader is going to be a disappointed, frustrated person who is unsympathetic to the group and a rotten leader. Very rarely will the motives, ambitions, interests and capabilities of the group coincide with that of the leader.

The Technician

The leader's concept of the role should not consist solely of imparting as much technical know-how to the group as possible. There is more to the natural environment than teaching the skills and techniques of a particular sport. These technical crafts are essential aids and tools, but a day so spent concentrating on techniques may be too clinical, too mechanical, and a bit lifeless - unless training for some competition is envisaged. The essential nature of a mountain experience, for example, may be missed. Under the mass of time calculations, distances, bearings, conventional signs, contour lines, do's and don'ts, the mountains may be so obscured that they never have the chance to reveal their inherent attractions to the group. If the garnering of the leader's own experience was a chore, it may never be possible to generate an atmosphere in which a love and feeling for the outdoors can be transmitted to the group. Time should be given for the aesthetic and, aye, maybe spiritual feelings, to impinge on the awareness of those in the group for whom such things will have meaning and great importance.

Rigid or Flexible

Some leaders find it necessary to impose a rigid structure on the group. Each person is given a place and number in a fixed order of march. This may be quite justifiable on a down-river canoe trip or a ski descent to discourage reckless competitive behaviour or overtaking in dangerous places. But where no deviation from the fixed order is permitted on a land based journey, the practice becomes questionable. Presumably such leaders either feel their responsibilities too acutely, or have an underlying anxious lack of self confidence in their ability to handle the fluidity of a group in the outdoors and feel a need to have a greater degree of containment about the situation. Hopefully this is an early stage that is passed through quickly. Such practice is sadly at variance with the freedom and informality of the outdoors. It is much more acceptable to see a group flowing freely and flexibly up a hillside path, interchanging according to the dictates of the social interaction going on within the group.

The leader only needs to intervene when weather (mist) or difficult terrain require it.

" *Time should be given for the aesthetic and, ...*
feelings to impinge on the awareness of the group."

Often these factors will exert their own pressures on the group without the leader needing to say anything. It is noticeable that the further away from the minibus drop-off point and the further up the hill a group gets, the less inclined it is to race off.

A feeling of being remote and far from civilisation works its own effect and a heightened awareness of their dependence on the leader. Safe leadership will become what it ought to be, more a matter of good practice used discreetly so as to detract minimally from enjoyment.

✿ Another kind of rigidity is to be found in leaders who are unaware of the values which inform their attitudes and beliefs about approaches, leading styles, methods and the criteria that constitute success. It is important for leaders to be able to distinguish between their personal values and the instrumental values which drive the aims of their courses or programmes. Instrumental values are of a different order or level and entail matters to do with, for example:

- ✿ dependency
- ✿ independency (i.e. self-sufficient or not)
- ✿ interdependency (cooperation and collaboration)
- ✿ specialisation in depth (competence)
- ✿ width of experiences (taster experiences and group processes).

✿ Unaware leaders tend to be single-minded and one-sided in their practice, for example, if a 'task' approach (which values getting on with the activity as 'efficiently' as possible), is held dear, then an authoritarian, staff-centred style will be favoured. Such a style is characterised by directive, perfection-seeking methods (using models) because it is believed they are conducive to specialisation and thence lead to the high standards of skill and achievement so greatly to be desired. The leader who embraces these values unconsciously, registers a sharp antagonism when meeting the values implicit in the 'people' approach which is often wrongly perceived as being in opposition. This is largely because their own values, being unconscious, are **felt** to be the only ones in existence. Anything which appears to contradict those values is seen as an attack, not only on those values, but on the self which holds those values. It is felt that these are the only values that it is possible to hold and if these values were to be defeated or dismissed, nothing would be left. The resulting state of non-existence is not to be contemplated. Salvation lies in resistance. The early days of 'outdoor pursuits', as they were called in the '50s-'60s, saw a lot of this type of leader because that is how it was then. The only people available with experience for the job of leading (no qualifications then) were those who were committed to an activity and had always done the activities as a leisure time pursuit. Hopefully such types are less common now in the 'leading game' which requires a more balanced outlook - no offence intended to the activist who has every right to be that way but who is only right for leading in certain prescribed circumstances where a single minded instruction in the skills is needed.

It will be seen that unawareness can lead to a defensive rigidity and a correspondingly extremely polarised attitude which will be exclusive in the values it holds. An aware state assists a flexibility of outlook because it brings a realisation that such values need not be seen as mutually antagonistic elements, but as complementary assets to be used as matters of degree - each for their appropriate purpose.

Diagram 6 below shows how it is not necessary to think in terms of polarised opposites (as depicted by the dotted lines in the diagram). There are advantages to be gained by treating all these extremes (instrumental values) as matters of degree. Embracing one of the approaches does not have to mean the outright rejection of the other. Thus, in this diagram, all the values most important to you are nearest to your chosen standpoint or orientation - towards either 'people' i.e. relationships or 'things', i.e. tasks.

It illustrates how the extremes of two different approaches can be used flexibly.

Other less important values are not dismissed or ignored, but are placed further away and so are still valid and available to act as a complement as necessary. The fear-enjoyment axis is common to both orientations but may tend to acquire a particular value depending on which approach, people or activity task, is acting upon it[16].

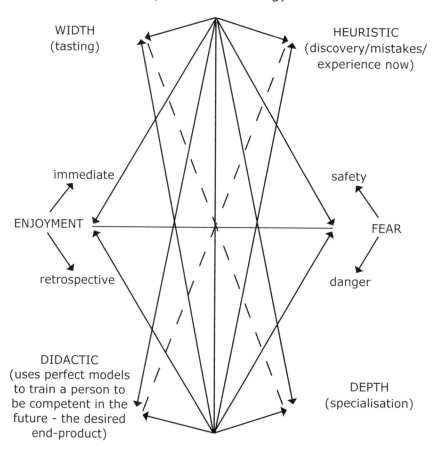

People Approach

Group Centred
Democratic - Consultative/Participative
(Self-Determining)

WIDTH
(tasting)

HEURISTIC
(discovery/mistakes/
experience now)

immediate

safety

ENJOYMENT

FEAR

retrospective

danger

DIDACTIC
(uses perfect models
to train a person to
be competent in the
future - the desired
end-product)

DEPTH
(specialisation)

(Conformist)
Authoritarian - Coercive
Staff Centred

Things Approach

Diagram 6. 'People' and 'Things' perspectives

Equipment Talismen

Beware of the tendency of placing too much reliance and trust in equipment. Carrying two of everything, for instance, does not double the safety factor either. Carrying equipment in duplicate results in a very heavy rucksack or canoe - a factor which, in itself, can affect safety margins. Part of the answer is to acquire the confidence that arises from good quality experience. One thing leaders can do in this respect is to carry a good repair kit as well as develop their improvisation skills. A different scenario and a difficult one for trainer/leaders is deciding whether the members of a D of E expedition group should each have a compass, map and whistle! The general oft-used dictum 'it all depends...' may apply, but in most cases it would be advisable for each to have his/her own bit of this special gear in case one somehow becomes detached from the group and has to continue to route find and operate on their own.

Outdoor Magic and 'Green Adrenalin'

Colour, light and shade, shape and form, textures, sounds and scents are all part of the outdoor scene. Sometimes they will work their own magic unassisted and individuals will experience what has recently become known as 'green adrenalin' - the exhilaration and excitement of experiencing high quality landscapes. Such feelings help create the reverential attitudes, referred to earlier, which are now needed to minimise environmental wear and tear.

At other times the leader may find it possible to heighten the group's awareness of their surroundings. The ability to interpret the natural landscape is of enormous value. Walking, for example, can be a monotonous business for many young people. They usually need to have been exposed to the hills a number of times before they come to appreciate that a good deal of the charm of mountains lies in their contrasts and infinite variety. Any snippet of information about flora, fauna, natural and man-made features, is grist to the leader's mill. Curiosity starved often dies quickly. Feed it and the results are often very surprising and fruitful. Beware of 'force-feeding' however.

*" 'Green adrenalin' - the exhilaration and excitement
of experiencing high quality landscapes!"*

Mention was made earlier that attitudes and their underlying values are expressed in practice in a number of ways. The following examples portray some of the more significant attitudes that it is crucial to keep in proportion.

The 'Buck Passer'.

"It's not me, it's the environment!"
Nature is hostile, impartial: there are life threats out there which are not always obvious. The harsh environment requires you must take steps to prepare yourself or you might get hurt. It creates its own imperatives.

"I am responsible for you. It's not me making you do all these things in a training programme like carry equipment, learn skills, suffer discomfort.

Don't blame me for the things I make you do. It's for your own good. We must be prepared. Please me by trying hard. Get a move on."

This is to do with imperatives which have their origin in the environment (see below).

Environmental Imperatives

The nature of the outdoor environment can sometimes be an over-dominating factor in the formation of a leader's attitude to group leading. The scenario is caricatured above: but the hazard-rich natural environment can be used more usefully to inculcate sound, safe practice in the outdoors. Just as man-made environments are not hazard-free and we all have to learn about the dangers of gas, bare electric wires, poisons, traffic, uneven surfaces, stairs, inflammable substances, glass (the list is endless) so the outdoors contains a different set of dangers that have to be learned.

There are serious hazards in the mountains or on the water which imply harm will come to humans unless they take these hazards into account and modify the 'survival-on-the-run' behaviour normal to man-made environments. In towns they can nip into a shop if it rains, get on a bus to travel, slip into another shop if hungry for a snack, use many signposts to find the way, ask a policeman if lost (!). The comparatively untouched outdoors present seven physical problems which have to be addressed in order to travel and live safely and comfortably in it. These problems constitute seven imperatives demanding attention:

Seven Survival Requirements in the Outdoors

- ❂ sustaining energy by ensuring a supply of food and liquid is available.
- ❂ keeping body temperature comfortable - by adjusting clothing, having warm under clothes and outer wind-proof clothing. Food intake also contributes to this.
- ❂ keeping dry - waterproof outer shell.

✿ finding the way - map/chart and compass **and** knowing how to use them. (GPS on its own is inadequate; e.g. it needs manual back-up skills if it malfunctions for some reason).

✿ avoiding injury - using eyes and other senses to select terrain and having correct footwear, equipment and skills.

✿ treating injury - first aid kit **and** knowing how to use it.

✿ calling for help - whistle, torch, mobile phone.

The gear carried in the canoe, rucksack or dinghy should be enough to solve these problems in the short term.

So behavioural adjustments to normal everyday living habits require us to have the right equipment, skills and knowledge to cope, making sound preparations, appropriate plans and taking proper precautions.

✿ These implications for survival - or the continuation of life - represent a set of imperatives which put serious responsibilities on leaders to ensure that all these requirements are met by their groups.

✿ So, the content of training programmes which leaders set up, will reflect these environmental imperatives.

✿ So, also, the course of training, which is limited by a finite amount of time, will reflect these pressures on the leader to fulfil his/her responsibilities.

✿ Together, the environment, the training content and the course of training may constitute such a set of imperatives that they are likely to be felt by a recipient group as an authoritarian approach. The training tasks, the pace, the level, the pitch and the overall aims will have been set by externals that have no reference to, or origin in, the group's needs and capacities. Ironically, if a group should voice protest, the leader feels justified in ducking the 'flak' and responsibility by placing the blame for all the hassle on the environment. If a group accepts all this as reasonable common sense there is no problem. Subtler approaches are called for when a group, ignorant of the natural environment and/or suspicious of authority is wary lest they are being 'taken for a ride' by all the 'hassle' of preparation. One way through this is the careful selection of a convenient locale which permits the abandoning of normal safety practices so that the group can find out by discovery! When/if they get wet, cold, develop blisters, get hungry it is not far to get back out of it. It is important to have forewarned them about unpleasant consequences otherwise they will be convinced the leader did it out of badness or spite. 'The *Brat Camp*' programme on Chanel 4 in March/April 2004 was an interesting example of this approach in a remote area of USA. Even though, well into the true wilds of Utah, there was a comprehensive back-up infra-structure to retrieve a situation if it got too serious.

The 'Ego-Head' and Expertise Imperatives

"Hey, hey, hey! I'm it - it's me, I'm the instructor folks. I have a lot of experience. I have all the qualifications. I can do all the activities. You are really lucky to get me. I know all the best places to go. I'm the expert."

Thinks: "I mustn't make mistakes. I must be perfect and strong".

"Do as I say - watch and copy me - follow me you guys."   "Off we go - way-hey!"

This is about the imperatives driving leader behaviour that can arise out of expertise inexpertly handled. Whereas in the environmental illustration in the previous paragraph, the leader wished to distance him/herself from some of consequences of leadership by disclaiming responsibility for the less pleasant aspects, the opposite extreme is when leaders over-mindful of their expertise, skills and status feel that they have a mandate to be authoritarian in all things. Because of all their expert training and extensive experience they think they know how to make the most of the possibilities of a situation and how best to use the time available. This conviction is even greater if they are faced with a group of volunteers, and even greater if the volunteers are unknowing novices. Such leaders may have made a number of erroneous assumptions about motives and expectations, like assuming his group are all willing volunteers prepared to take on anything, and may have neglected to take account of each individual's ability, fitness, needs, attitudes, security levels and background. In so doing, the ensuing low quality working relationships are likely to result in low achievement levels and low morale.

For your further delectation and entertainment, two more stereotypes are described below. They are extremes of course, but the flavour of them is to be found in some degree in many good outdoor leaders.

The 'Hippy Rebel'

"The outdoors is for the maverick, man! It's all about freedom, man! Doing your own thing you know? Rules? What are they? Blow your mind - go for it. Go with the flow. I really care about you guys having a good time. What you want is what you get. So let's go for it. Let it all hang out."

"Wow!"

The 'Groupie'

"I really care about you guys. I don't know much about you yet, so let's sit down, get to know each other before we decide what we want to do. And talk and talk and talk!!"

"When we've finally done what we said we'd do, let's sit down and see what we got out of it. And talk and talk and talk!!"

To Impel or Not to Impel

There is one attitude common among leaders and outdoor practitioners in general, which needs a detailed examination. It is to do with aspects of the management of risk[17] and the belief expounded by Kurt Hahn, the founder of Outward Bound, that "it is right to impel people into experiences". Whilst doubtless there are some occasions when this doctrine may be justifiable, there are many, many more times when it is not. In the wrong hands it can become a dangerous philosophy for sadists and all too easily be interpreted as a licence to dictate and to impose generally. It is needful to spend some time on the implications of this issue.

'Impelling' implies the use of compulsion
and coercion by the impeller

Between the extremes of silent apathy and open revolt, will be found all degrees of resentment, antagonism, hostility and resistance on the part of the impelled. The attitude receives some propping up from a school of ascetic thought which believes that "hair shirts and strength through pain" is a viable developmental approach. It is forgotten that the essence of this approach is that it should be voluntary. Whenever an element of unwillingness exists, positive consequences or outcomes become doubtful. Leaders are not sufficiently gifted with divine insight to enable them to predict whether they will be impelling their charges, both in the literal and metaphoric sense, in directions they do not want to go, at a speed they are unable to cope with, at a level they are not ready for, at an intensity that is too stressful to be beneficial. Just as importantly, leaders may run the risk of impelling people over their personal fear thresholds - which is the point beyond which fear ceases to have a useful survival function and becomes inhibitive, destructive, and even downright dangerous.

The business of pushing out personal limits and discovering them is an intensely personal and private matter. It is presumptuous and unethical for a leader even to contemplate doing it unilaterally for someone else. It may happen incidentally and often does, especially during unexpected "epics" and emergencies; but to set out with the deliberate intention of doing so is a very questionable practice. The balance between comfort and discomfort is closely allied to the danger - safety issue referred to earlier in chapter 1. See also the next chapter on the risk taking process.

Consequences - Effects of Being Impelled

A person who has an unpleasant experience, or who has failed in something into which s/he was impelled intentionally, can justifiably blame the 'impeller' for bad judgement and for the negative experience. Conversely, a person who has been allowed or encouraged to impel him/herself, and who fails or dislikes it, must undertake an internal evaluation to discover why. The responsibility for his/her own actions and development is still his/hers. It cannot be off loaded onto someone else. This self examination process in these circumstances leads to personal growth rather than diminishment.

✿ The success and enjoyment of a person who has had a self impelled experience is of greater worth than that where they were externally impelled. This is partly because of the need to go through the winding-up process required to generate the degree of motivation and commitment necessary to see the chosen task through. What you choose to do is a measure of what you think you can do. To do it and succeed confirms an estimate made of personal capacity - valuable self knowledge indeed. Success and achievement in self chosen activities imparts a greater degree of confidence and satisfaction than that derived from compulsory participation in activities. Even if an impelled experience is enjoyed, it merely confirms the impeller's fortuitous estimation of the other person and does not really contribute as much to the recipient gaining knowledge about the self.

When people are allowed a say or choice in decision making, their motivation and commitment tends to be higher and the nature of the activity is likely to be more closely related to their needs, abilities and capacities. Part of the leader's job is to help the group avoid the pitfalls of over or under-estimating their own abilities. Aspiration which exceeds capacity is doomed to disappointment and may be potentially dangerous. Under-achievement may be safer but sometimes can be worse than no achievement at all. Finding the right balance depends on the leader having sensitive communicating and negotiating skills so that challenges are pitched at the right level.

Compromising Ideals

An over zealous adherence to the ideals, principles and standards set by training courses for leaders can actually prevent youngsters from having any worthwhile outdoor experiences at all. By 'following the book' and requiring their groups to come equipped with all that they are supposed to have, leaders automatically debar those who have not got it, cannot borrow or afford it. Leaders need to be prepared to compromise on these things but in such a way as not to compromise safety aspects. The nature of the day out needs to be adjusted in order that it is possible for the group to go on a trip that is not over-ambitious for the equipment they have. Take the old hoary problem of wearing tight fitting thin trousers on the mountain. Many youngsters may have nothing else. Possible solutions are to stay lower down or walk shorter distances. If a decent waterproof shell is available it is probably reasonable to go anyway, provided the forecast is not talking about strong winds and low or sub zero temperatures at three thousand feet.

The hazards of the natural environment do require one to take certain minimum precautions or be prepared to suffer the consequences of ignoring them. The threat of these consequences is always present to a greater or lesser degree. The insistent pressure of these environmental imperatives to conform to all the sound advice received in training make it difficult to go against it. Yet that is what the leader must do sometimes. The group will rarely ever be perfectly equipped, trained or fitted to cope with the objective perils.

Being able to improvise can get the leader out of a scrape such as advising groups to use socks to replace lost or forgotten gloves on a D of E expedition or a towel or scarf for a hat.

Leaders must know enough about their craft to be able to handle those situations where the reality of a situation requires the setting aside of the book of rules. This can be as much an ethical problem as it is a technical one. For example, "This scree filled gully that I have to descend with this group is of such a nature that all the usual recommended procedures are unsuitable. I think I can work out a safe way to do it but have I the right to commit this group to what is virtually an experiment?"

Knots in Relationships

Relationships in groups can sometimes assume a pattern best described as a circular 'knot'[18] akin to the 'chicken and the egg' idea. There seems to be no way out of an unbroken circular situation. Until it is broken, movement forward for the group is impossible. Here are some examples commonly found in groups:

> ✿ "I would like to have a say in what goes on. But I dare not speak out and say what I think. I might make mistakes and be laughed at or punished in some way. I do not want to be punished, so I will not try. So I do not get a say in what goes on; but I would like to have a say."

"*The group will rarely ever be perfectly equipped,
trained or fitted to cope with the objective perils.*"

✿ "I feel somebody always seems to be trying to pull me down. Others will take advantage and hurt or harm me in some way if I show I am weak (making mistakes) or vulnerable (at fault). I cannot trust anybody. So I must always try to protect myself against others by trying to keep on top, never admitting guilt or mistakes and never giving in. I would like it to be different but I cannot trust anybody because I'm always being got at."

✿ Another is when the group is looking to the leader for a lead or a decision even though there are no critical reasons for the pressure. Before responding to this pressure, it is worth the leader trying to ascertain what these reasons are, especially if the leader wishes, or needs to have, a closer relationship with the group. There may be a genuine cause or it may be one of the typical games played by idle youngsters on conscientious leaders. It is all too easy to succumb and 'do it all' for the group, especially if the leader is one of those who enjoy the dependence of others.

In responding to this pressure the leader will most likely assume the conventional authoritarian stereotype of what a leader is in the group's eyes. This may not be how the leader wants to be perceived by the group. But anxiety to produce answers the leader can feel the group expecting, will set her/him further apart. For in yielding to the pressure the leader will become directive. This knot is resolved by resisting the pressure and pushing responsibility for the problem back to the group where it can be shared with them. This tactic will help move them out of the habit of dependent-mindedness and the abdication of responsibility towards a more resourceful and self-sufficient attitude. Leaders can help people to want to be more responsible by helping them to feel they have a real say in what is going on, that their say is valued and by explaining and showing them that if they do not say their piece, resultant outcomes may not be to their liking.

Need to be Coherent, Conscious, Systematic

Because of the serious nature of the leader's responsibilities, the approach to the leadership situation must be systematic. The 'woolliness' of the "being with friends" situation referred to earlier, will no longer suffice. All the detailed factors relating to good practice, comfort and safety must be identified. In this context of safety, there must be a reason for everything done or said and everything NOT said or done. The reason must be conscious. There will be many things learned in the early days by experience which are now done unconsciously without thought. For example, the way to walk uphill or downhill (not so simple if one is only used to the level, even surfaces of town) or pick the way up or down a hill, or how to hold and use a paddle or keep a canoe in a straight line, or whilst helming, being able to judge what the wind is doing without having to look at the tell-tales or burgee all the time. All these things now have to be brought, as it were, from the back of the head to the front and consciously stored ready for use.

In those areas which relate to safety and comfort, leaders must be able to justify in minute detail everything they do or choose not to do.

This implies a very articulate grasp of the outdoor situation which only a process of reflective, self-analysis and self-questioning about previous experience, outdoor and otherwise (both are relevant) will give. It is not enough to know the right thing to do. The leader must know why it is right and what the consequences will be if it is done incorrectly or differently.

✪ *Chapter Seven* ✪

The Management of Risk

This topic is sufficiently important, and has so many aspects, as to need a chapter all to itself. So this will not simply be a rehash of official advice or guidelines, though they will be touched on at some point because, it is argued, they tend to be skewed to particular kinds of situation and are thus unfortunately limited in their treatment of the subject. At one time there was a tendency to think one had slavishly to follow the 'Five steps' * method[28] of risk management but fortunately sanity reigned and it was accepted, even at the highest levels, that there are more ways than one to er....manage risk.

* see Appendix 3.

The first time I heard the phrase, 'risk assessment', and that there was a legal obligation to do it, I remember the feelings of anxiety that suddenly arose about what it actually meant and how on earth could it be carried out satisfactorily to meet the rigorous standards of a **legal** requirement. It seemed to bear the hallmarks of a mysterious new high-tech process imposed by some superior intellect which would make life very difficult. One assumed that it would somehow have to be very exact, since to be otherwise would render it useless, and penalties would be invoked to ensure conformity with the law. How could you ever hope to anticipate all the risks? To trip you up, Murphy's Law was there stating,

"If you think you have it all sorted out, there is always something waiting to spring out to prove you wrong".

Modern parlance might call it being 'statistically challenged' but I prefer to call it bad luck! Despite all the care in the world there will be incidents with good luck or bad luck to determine whether they end up as 'near misses' or accidents. But as I thought about it, and as literature on the subject began to issue from the Health and Safety Executive (HSE), it became less of a nightmare, although there still seemed to be areas that could prove troublesome. It soon dawned that we have been doing some form of risk assessment for years in a less formalised, intuitive way based on our experience. A lot of it was in the thinking that underlay many of our standing safety regulations relating to the use of the building we worked in, and from, and to the programmes of activities that we organised. Some of it occurred 'hot on the hoof' in the field with groups in response to a change in conditions. The knack was as much about learning how to think articulately about risk assessment as doing it.

After the Cairngorm tragedy in November 1971, when six children died of the cold in an unplanned bivouac on the plateau, the accent was understandably on 'safety' management. But many felt that this was an unhealthy way to look at it and preferred something that would send out more positive, less alarmist messages like 'good practice'. Where the talk used to be about safety and eliminating danger, a more realistic stance is now being taken with 'risk management'. This is fine providing it does not stray into the temptation to ask for 'risk elimination' or 'risk avoidance' which is unrealistic and impracticable - even undesirable. Developing real skills, however, does involve real risk such as the first time your dad let go of the bike you were learning to ride and you were suddenly on your own. Duke of Edinburgh groups are using real skills all the time on their unaccompanied expeditions. Leaders need to think through carefully their stance on this one. Abseiling skill only becomes 'real' when done without a top rope but most of us are not prepared to allow our groups to progress that far. Canoeing, sailing and orienteering lend themselves to real skill learning whilst hill walking in an accompanied group does not.

All the great leaps forward the world has seen by explorers, thinkers and inventors have been the result of taking risks - think Martin Luther, Christopher Columbus, Marconi, Pasteur, for example!

In the process of getting clear in one's head what is involved in the whole business of risk taking and risk management, one can become quite confused trying to distinguish between the hazard and the risk, which is the challenge, and which is the fear, because they are all so closely connected one with the other. One useful approach to clarifying ideas and concepts is to look at a few assorted examples of situations. By teasing out their constituent parts one can begin to get a better feel for what is involved. So a look at a few case studies first, before coming to definitions, may be found useful in sorting ideas out.

A Few Case Studies

Taking off in an aeroplane:

The hazard is height above the ground with gravity taking over in the event of mechanical failure or pilot error. There is the risk of a crash and fear. Because you are not the pilot you are not in control. So there is no challenge in the sense that there are no demands on your abilities other than to 'keep your cool'. This commitment at one remove involves your capacity to cope with fear and also your capacity to trust someone (the pilot). There are other implications to be touched on later about being a 'passenger' and whether it is an entirely 'passive' role with the air company seemingly carrying all the responsibility for your safety.

You submit yourself to all this stress because you hope to receive some benefit like a ski holiday at the end of the flight.

Canoeing down a rapid:

The hazard is the unstoppable commitment of running white water and obstacles. There is no cop-out half way down. The risk is capsizing and/or drowning. But this time the control is actively in your hands - literally. The challenge is to negotiate the obstacles which make technical demands on your skill. You have to judge if your skills are equal to it and whether you want to do it depending on whether you think you are likely to succeed or fail. A leader will find it difficult if not impossible (depending on the water state) to help anyone in difficulty.

You are on your own and success, the reward, depends entirely on your own skill and judgement.

Driving fast in fog on the motorway:

The hazards are poor visibility combined with speed and others around you similarly situated. Risk of a crash, hitting or being hit, is more likely than in the case of the aeroplane. But the semi illusion of being in control - you could control the speed but not the fog - makes it possible for the motive (whatever it is - 'late for a meeting' perhaps) to hold down fear and rise to the challenge such as it is in order to enjoy the pay-off of arriving at journey's end.

Rock climbing as second on the rope:

Although the hazard is very steep ground, there is no physical risk (of falling and hurting yourself) but there is the challenge of 'can you do it'. You are in control of the challenge but the leader above is the one controlling the risk. Any fear present may be a mixture of the fear caused by the illusion of danger, which is perceived not real, or of not being equal to the task and showing yourself up, or uncertainty about the leader's abilities which in certain circumstances might be perceived as part of the hazard. The reward is overcoming your own fears and discovering you are up to it. If you have been sent by your company to do this course then the possibility of promotion prospects might be at the back of your mind too.

Leading on rock:

The same type of hazard as being the second on a rope, but the risk is no longer perceived but real because the danger of a fall is possible, the seriousness of which depends on how bombproof is the protection you can put in place. The challenge is more acute because there is only oneself to rely on, although your second has to be able to control the degree and severity of a fall. But whether the perceived seriousness of the challenge will be greater or less, will depend on the leader's judgement about the difficulty of the rock route ahead and whether the degree of skill s/he feels they have is up to it. This will determine the level of fear present and therefore the degree of motivation necessary to offset it. Is it worth it? What will you get out of it?

Running down scree:

In principle this is the same as leading on rock. It is obviously less serious with perhaps less dire consequences of a fall but the situation is deceptive for the danger is real.

Some Useful Definitions

By now a few definitions will be becoming apparent, I trust.

⊙ **Hazard:** may be an objective environmental feature like a rock face or white water rapid representing a threat or challenge. But note that a hazard may not always be of an environmental nature. Behavioural aberrations in people can be equally as hazardous (See list itemising different types of hazards at the end of this chapter).

⊙ **Challenge:** is something arising out of the hazard that confronts you, which you might or might not choose to accept.
You may or may not be sure you can do it.

⊙ **Risk:** is the consequence of facing the challenge - especially if you should not be able to do it. The level of risk, which will be present in any degree from high to low, will depend upon how likely or unlikely it is that harm will ensue.

⊙ **Fear:** may be about any or all of the above items, hazard, challenge or risk.

⊙ **Pay-off:** of a positive sort is the dividend or benefit expected if the challenge is met successfully. A negative pay-off is the penalty if one is unsuccessful.

⊙ **Motivation:** is generated by the self internally when measuring the balance between the risk and the inducements of the pay-off. Pay-off is thus allied closely to personal motivation. The degree of motivation present, or absent, in a risk taking situation affects the nature and quality of the effect of the experience on the person. Absence of motivation tends to negate the experience - render it less meaningful. But note that motivation can also be provided by external events outside one's control, e.g. a prize or some other thing that may be attractive or even vital, like a train to be caught or a pursuing avalanche. It can be stimulated by someone else, but thereafter the motivation has to become yours or one enters the realm of external compulsion.

Note that values have now entered the arena here to provide a vital link between risk taking, motivation and pay-off.

"Motivation can also be provided by external events."

A value judgement will be made at some point in the risk taking process upon which everything will pivot - go, or back off (down?).

Deeper Level Definitions

At a deeper level we now need to look at other more basic definitions.

1. **Risk:**

"hazard, chance of, or of bad consequences, loss etc. expose to chance of injury."
Oxford Concise Dictionary.

The use of the word 'chance' implies that all is not predictable and therefore not controllable. Management implies an ability to control. So the 'management of risk' seems to represents a paradox - "the control of the uncontrollable" which is not very helpful but nevertheless basically true.

Since the implications of risk, as defined by the dictionary, all appear to be negative, a lay member of the public might feel compelled to question the validity of risk as a dubious tool for leaders to use. An ability to be able to articulate and justify what one is doing is therefore very important. One might more accurately restyle the title of this chapter, and more positively, by calling it, "The management of safety". But no doubt many of us feel there is too much of an accent on security in our society already. Perhaps a more acceptable title would be "The management of support" of which more will be said later.

To round off the definition of risk, it is emphasised that the word 'chance' is used in close association with the nature of risk. Chance implies uncertainty about the future. It is not predictable but we believe we can attempt to calculate probabilities. But the calculation is at best a dodgy gamble and at worst a jump in the dark. The ability to take risks is closely associated with the capacity to cope with uncertainty and the unknown. See also later in this chapter about the effect of MOA.

Some risks are more 'risky' than others and many of the risks associated with hazards in the outdoors are of the 'less likely' variety - otherwise our splendid safety record would be strewn with accidents - which it is not. Being able to assess the 'likelihood' of risk and its bad consequences is a key skill for leaders - which brings us to the subject of 'management'.

2. **Management:**
"Handle, control, wield, manipulate, take charge of, subject to one's control, gain one's ends, make proper use of, cope with, deceitfully contrive."
Oxford Concise Dictionary.

When a leader uses styles of leadership flexibly, any one of these meanings could be valid, whilst at another time they could, each of them, be quite out of place. When did you last 'deceitfully contrive'?

The interpretation of what is meant by 'the management of risk' appears to depend more on who you are, what you represent and what your aims are. Values again.

For Education Authorities and other responsible bodies, conscious of legal obligations and liabilities, 'management' means ideally the eradication of risk or its reduction to harmless levels - which seems to be too much of a contradiction of terms. Safe adventure?

For practitioners in the outdoors, it probably means the provision of risk mostly within the confines of 'perceived danger' as opposed to 'real danger'. But in this respect there is a tendency to visualise challenge and risk in purely physical terms. There has been critical concern voiced recently within the field that 'buzz activities' and instant thrills which rely on virtual risk (perceived risk) are replacing real experiences. In this category come bungee jumping, ropes courses and amusement park thrills where the instructor has taken over and disempowered the participator.

For the National Governing Bodies of the various outdoor activities it probably means the seeking out and active pursuit of real danger often to the degree of what is known as 'brinkmanship' - pushing things to the limit of one's ability and equipment.

If we are realists and accept that the management of risk implies the 'control of the uncontrollable' we have to find another definition that will be more helpful. Perhaps the nearest one can approach in management terms is a form of coping whereby one must be able to recognise when hazard and risk is present and when it is not; if it is present to recognise to what degree it is present, how perceived or real it is, and what sort of risk it represents i.e. is it physical, mental or emotional.

This leaves unanswered questions such as:
Can one guarantee that risk will be provided or eliminated *for others* at will?
Can one guarantee that risk will be reduced or increased *for others* at will?

This would be real management.

Societal Attitudes and Risk
Those who lead groups sometimes do so because they would like their charges to become better at managing risks and tackling challenges of various kinds. But what kinds of risks and challenges are we talking

about here? Any kind of risk? All kinds of risk? Only certain kinds of risk? Are there kinds of risk one could present to a group that society (parents or the law) would find unacceptable? If some kinds of risk are unacceptable we need to know which they are. Is the presently risk-averse society a reliable gauge for deciding what constitutes reasonable risk? Society has also been conditioned by unbalanced reporting in the media to the point where it is now characterised by a tendency to perceive risk and danger where, statistically, there is little likelihood of it. Yet society is taking risks all the time - speeding on motorways, gambling, over-eating, abusing drugs or alcohol, over-consuming, over-polluting, voting for MPs, investing in shares. Youth happily finds ways of making life adventurous - crime, base-jumping, parcours, skate-boarding, global travelling in the the gap year. But one does wonder how much harder it may be for younger children conditioned for years by overprotective parents to 'be careful' and not allowed to wander far from the home to develop an independence and confidence as once they were. Do they find it harder to cope with risky activities?

Self initiated risk-taking

We tend to prefer those sorts of risk where we have to trust our own judgement, which we feel are more or less under our immediate control and of which the result willl be fairly immediate or soon - witness the display on our motorways daily and see section above. We have also made a decision that the benefit of taking the risk is worth it for reasons personal to us. This is self initiated risk-taking.

Second-hand risk-taking:

But not all risk-taking is self-initiated. There is another kind, which I call 'second-hand risk- taking' of the kind which is experienced by those under the direct authority or power of others who have to decide whether or not to expose us to risks, e.g. parental concern to protect the young; the nanny state tries to make things safer; insurance companies attempt to limit their liabilities by putting up premiums; local councils try to avoid compensation cases by inflicting unnecessary bye-laws and regulations; party leaders never have to have accidents; teacher unions advise members to avoid taking school trips; HSE apparently determined, at the time of writing, to foist unnecessary and irrelevant Working at Height Regulations on an outdoor industry long recognised for its safety record. In these cases those directly feeling the effect of impositions from above have the choice of obeying or disobeying, conforming or rebelling and coping with the ensuing risks. If there is felt to be no choice - look out!

Third party risk-taking:

Another kind of risk-taking which is 'third party risk-taking' does not normally involve a party leader but is useful to know about. This is that kind which entails information, often unclear or contradictory, about various issues which carry risks, such as going into the EU, BSE, new variant CJD, FMD, GM food or genetic interference. It emanates from shadowy institutions and organisations who rely on the media and the politicians to present it to the public. Choices may be left open-ended without clearly stating all the pros and cons, all the benefits may be emphasised without revealing the downside which carries all the risks. This two-layered process engenders the perception of manipulators with undeclared self interests and hidden agendas who have not revealed all the information necessary for making proper decisions.

We dislike those risks which involve trusting others such as governments, politicians, scientists, multi-national companies because the results are usually far away on the time scale and often uncertain because even experts disagree about outcomes, e.g. the Iraqi war, climate change, going into the EU. Leaders do well to keep reminding themselves that they are the ones asking others - those in their groups - to trust them.

We think we can manage risk for ourselves, but can we really do it for others? Can we actually plan what sort of risk we want to be present? If so, what degree of risk is permissible? What degree of risk is it morally justifiable for us to provide for others? Can we manipulate risk as skilfully as the questions imply?

To answer these managerial questions leaders need to examine the nature of risk very closely:

- What makes a risk a risk?
- When is a risk not a risk?
- Is it the same for everyone?
- If not, for whom is it different, why, and in what way is it different?

De-bunking Some Assumptions About Risk

We also need to examine some of the assumptions that are held about risk in outdoor leading practice.

a) Outdoor leaders can be carried away by the assumption that 'risk' and 'challenge' are inter-changeable terms. They are not necessarily so - refer back to 'case studies' and see below.

b) There is the idea that challenge is always good for you, that it is the best (some think the only) and most worthwhile catalyst for developing people. So it is - sometimes! So it does - sometimes! But it is not always so. As ever, the phrase, "it all depends" has to come into the calculation/assessment.

c) If the outdoor leader is to do a proper job, it behoves him/her to provide challenge and that if this is not done, there is felt to be something lacking in the experiences offered.

d) Only challenge pitched at the right level will have any effect - this is "the grade III effect" described by Colin Mortlock in '*The Adventure Alternative*' [31] as "frontier adventure".

e) Only physical challenges are worth bothering about. This idea has already been challenged by the idea of holistic experiences. Whether there is such a thing as a purely physical challenge is debatable. Is there not an input of emotions and thought required to activate the whole risk taking process? What goes on between the ears when weighing up whether to 'go' or walk away?

All of these assumptions are half truths to be applied with great discrimination. A whole hearted, unthinking adoption of them would be unwise.

The Nature of Risk

There can be fear without challenge and even risk without challenge as when you think something dreadful is about to happen to you over which you have no control. There can be challenge without risk such as when trying to identify some flora or fauna from a book or taking part in a sponsored run. But there cannot be risk without fear.

Challenge can be risk-free; risk can be challenge-free.

Think about it.

Risk and challenge can be distinct, separate entities. Knowing the distinction is very useful. Risk is like a spinning two-sided coin. How it will fall is a gamble in the hands of chance. The result as it spins is unknowable. This 'not knowing' is what causes the fear supposedly characteristic of challenge. One side of the coin is fear of one or of a number of things - failure, pain, injury, losing, ridicule for example. The other side is the desired or hoped for 'pay off' or benefit - winning, succeeding, achieving or overcoming, self esteem, confidence, reputation for example.

Why one and not the other takes precedence in the mind is a very intricate process.

Diagram 7 which follows the explanation next, illustrates the risk-taking process.

The Process of Risk Taking

Many of the steps illustrated in the diagram and described below can occur so concurrently and instantaneously that it is difficult properly to separate them out. Some of the steps may not necessarily even occur in this order at all.

1. There has firstly to be some kind of hazard or problem presenting itself to be confronted. It may be of a physical, mental, emotional or even spiritual nature. It will require the possession of certain knowledge, skills and even qualities for overcoming or coping with it.

2. The person confronted by the hazard or problem, eyes it up and perceives the presence of a challenge representing a particular degree of difficulty and a possible uncertainty of outcome if it is accepted.

3. The presence of a degree of risk is also recognised as intrinsic to overcoming/solving the problem if it is taken on. The kind of risk involved is also recognised at this point.

4. The person then assesses whether the demands the challenge will pose will be within his/her capacity and abilities which also have to be weighed up. In the process of making this assessment, the person will become aware of the degree to which demands will be made on them and the task will be perceived in terms of degrees of difficulty, - easy, fairly hard, quite difficult, desperate or even impossible.

At some time there will be a realisation that the demands will be considerable to a point that the task becomes seen as challenging. There may be doubt about the outcome. Somewhere around this stage of the process another question, about personal values, is being asked. "Is this what I want?" "Is it important to me?" "If so, how important?" "Enough to take it on or leave it alone?" "Is there a choice in fact, because sometimes there is not?" Judgements about this are made prior to decisions.

5. By now the degree of motivation has been set. If the task is seen as undesirable for some reason or impossible then there is no challenge and no doubt and one opts out. But when uncertainty creeps in, the situation and the nature of the challenge changes. The quality of uncertainty itself may range from being quite weak to being very strong. The degree of uncertainty will be reflected in the feeling of taking a risk, i.e. the greater the uncertainty, the greater is the risk felt to be.

One is now on, or beyond the edge of, one's own known experience. When challenge takes a person into this alien landscape, feelings of uncertainty as to outcome ensue because competence and therefore success is in doubt. Risk is now present.

Only motivation can release any deadlock.

DYNAMICS OF THE RISK TAKING PROCESS

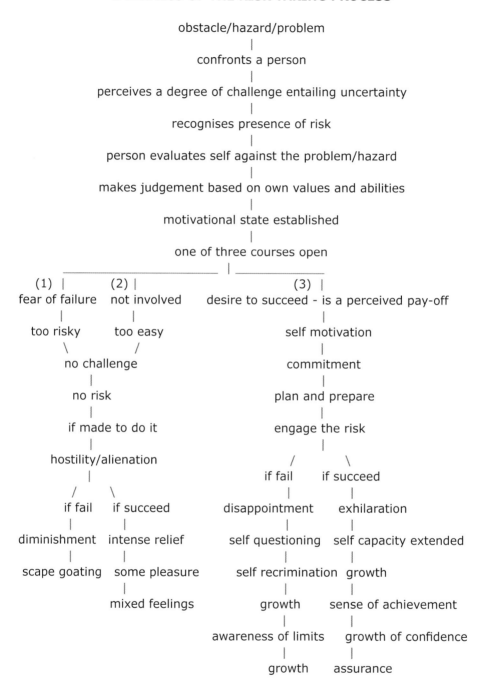

obstacle/hazard/problem
|
confronts a person
|
perceives a degree of challenge entailing uncertainty
|
recognises presence of risk
|
person evaluates self against the problem/hazard
|
makes judgement based on own values and abilities
|
motivational state established
|
one of three courses open

```
(1) |        (2) |                          (3) |
fear of failure   not involved    desire to succeed - is a perceived pay-off
    |                |                            |
 too risky        too easy                 self motivation
      \           /                              |
       no challenge                         commitment
          |                                      |
        no risk                           plan and prepare
          |                                      |
     if made to do it                      engage the risk
          |                                      |
   hostility/alienation                    /        \
          |                            if fail      if succeed
       /     \                            |            |
   if fail   if succeed             disappointment   exhilaration
     |          |                         |            |
diminishment  intense relief      self questioning  self capacity extended
     |          |                         |            |
scape goating  some pleasure      self recrimination  growth
              |                           |            |
          mixed feelings              growth    sense of achievement
                                          |            |
                                  awareness of limits  growth of confidence
                                          |            |
                                      growth       assurance
```

Diagram 7. The Risk Taking Process

[Note: there can be uncertainty in another way. Success perversely could bring risk because of uncertainty about its effect on others (e.g.jealousy/rivalry). To register the distinction being made, we could call that risk-running rather than risk-taking. It is based on an estimation of uncertainties outside the self, in others, not within oneself. It will be as well to lay this consideration on one side for the moment or things will begin to feel too complicated.]

Motivation determines if the pay off - the prize for succeeding - is sufficiently essential or attractive to make it worth accepting the challenge of the risk. In other words, the person's motivation now becomes the decisive factor. All the other factors are pre-set in the situation. Motivation is the one thing that is changeable and which can cause changes at this point.

**Perhaps we should be talking about
the 'management of motivation' in this process
for it lies at the heart of it?**

Motivation can be so strong that it can cause a person to overrule and ignore a realistic assessment of a situation and take on things that are not within their abilities. It can be so strong that it can enhance performance, as we all know, and make a person capable of feats they could not normally contemplate. The factors involved in the "to be or not to be" decision will include some of the following:

a) the extent to which various basic needs (see Maslow[5]) have, or have not, been fulfilled up to now in a person's life, and whether there is 'hunger' for the pay off.

b) the type of personality possessed by a person - the desire to achieve or win will have to overcome the fear of failure, or losing, or humiliation.

c) the personal level of security of the person.

d) other external stimuli e.g. competition, peers egging you on. "Don't be a wimp" etc.

e) to what extent the person feels some degree of control over the situation.

f) the level of vitality or energy possessed by the person at the time.

6. One of four decisions then follow:
   1. It is too risky - I am withdrawing.
   2. It is too easy - I do not feel involved - I am withdrawing.
   3. It is not relevant to my life - I am withdrawing.
   4. It is worth the risk - here we go!

7. In the first three cases, if the person who decided to withdraw is then overridden and made to tackle the risk, the likely scenario is hostility and/or alienation and a deteriorated relationship.

"Motivation can be so strong that it can cause a person to overrule and ignore a realistic assessment of a situation."

If failure ensues, there will be a sense of self-diminishment and the consequent resentment will seek an outlet for the blame to be placed, not on themselves, but on a scape goat - the person who impelled them.

In the event of success there will be intense relief, some pleasure perhaps - it will not be automatic, and a lot of mixed feelings that will block more positive outcomes. The result is the outcome of someone else's estimation of your potential. Their motivation may have no concern for your needs at all.

8. In the fourth case, there will be strong motivation and a high level of commitment. The self is on a self-chosen test. Confronting the task and taking the risk requires one to measure oneself against it. The result will therefore provide a measure of oneself. For this important reason, outcomes here will differ from those in the first two cases above. Failure here will be followed by disappointment, anger with oneself perhaps, self-recrimination and self-questioning. Sometimes an excuse escape is sought in externals. An article called '*The Art of Climbing Down Gracefully*' by Tom Patey in the compendium of '*Games Climbers Play*' by Ken Wilson (Diadem Books Ltd. London 1978) came up with all kinds of strategies for letting oneself down lightly - the weather, the wrong kind of equipment or poor gear, "bad night, last night" etc. Eventually there will be a gain in the new knowledge acquired about personal limitations which might set off a desire to be better trained, improved, developed or achieve even greater things. There will have been personal growth even in failure. Success will be followed by exhilaration and a new awareness about self potential. From the sense of achievement with its concomitant access of confidence and self assurance there will be growth in stature. As the song says, "you did it your way". Responsibility was yours not someone else's.

Kinds of Risk - Needs Related

A look at some of the types of risk found in adventure experiences will be useful since assumptions about what constitutes risk/adventure are often narrow[17]. Practitioners in the outdoors have tended to see risk purely in terms of the risk of physical injury. This selective perception tends unfortunately to be reinforced by official guidance on risk management[28] with its focus on natural hazards. But a list of most of the 'bad consequences' of risk shows that risk may entail danger to the '***thinking***' self and the '***feeling***' self as well as the '***physical***' self.

All risks represent a threat to basic human needs as listed by A.H.Maslow[5] (see chapter 4). Knowledge of these needs is a useful tool in helping to identify just what kind of risks are being run in a particular course of action. With reference to those needs, here are a few of the sort of risks that may be involved at any time. It will be seen that physical risks are only a part of a whole kaleidoscope of risk types.

i) On a **physical survival level**: loss of health, injury or death, could be caused by risk to food supply, shelter, rest and medicine - as well as accidents or mishaps.

ii) At the level of **physical security needs**, loss of property, money, valuables or equipment represent 'material' kinds of risks.

iii) On a higher level, the **need for self esteem** could be threatened by running the risk of being exposed to mockery, ridicule, disapproval and worst of all for a leader, loss of credibility. The possibility of being 'put down', 'discounted' or ignored is a fierce inhibitor/motivator. In asserting oneself to register or maintain one's position, or to avoid being left defenceless or vulnerable, one runs the risk of being given responsibility, of being held responsible and accountable, of being in the wrong, of being betrayed even.

It is a fine point whether it is worse to lose face in one's own eyes or to lose it in the eyes of others - one's peers in particular for example, which brings in the next set of needs.

In this context it will be appreciated that the issue of equal opportunity is very relevant. If people are not treated equally then many of the important needs outlined here will be thwarted.

iv) There are **needs of a social security kind** such as a sense of belonging, of being valued by others (prestige), of being part of a community without losing one's sense of being different. These could be threatened by the risk of rejection and possible eviction from the group, resulting in loss of status and companionship. Staying in the group might mean a risk of losing a sense of independence. On the other hand, standing up for what one believes in could attract the hostility that loses friends; could attract the attention or the responsibilities a present level of self confidence could not cope with; could attract the scorn or ridicule one's self esteem could not tolerate. The need to be understood and the risk of being misunderstood are uncomfortable bedfellows.

v) It would appear that all risk is ultimately related to whatever supports or constitutes a person's **sense of identity** and need for it. This includes the highest set of needs to do with a **sense of purpose** and the **values** associated with it.

It should be apparent by now that the perception of emotional risk in a situation can be just as powerful, or more, in its effect on individuals in a group, as is the possibility of physical hurt.

In this respect, as with planning highlights (see section on this in chapter 8), experiences can usually only be classed as positive or negative after the event, not before it. Their effect may be anticipated, feared or looked forward to, but cannot be predicted or guaranteed in advance or planned. The devices and tactics planned by leaders to increase enjoyment, excitement or interest and to decrease stress, discomfort and anxiety, may not always have their planned effect. Leaders have to try to do these things sometimes, succeeding more often than not, but they also need to monitor and test on-going group responses in case unintended negative effects indicate a need for a change of approach.

If things seem to be going awry, the most obvious change to be made is to reduce the assuming and presuming done by the leader in favour of more testing and consulting as outlined by Tannenbaum and Schmidt in chapter 4.

Blinkered Mindset in Leaders Ignores Holistic Nature of Outdoors

We have seen how leaders may be guilty of narrowly micro-viewing the nature of adventure (see types of risk above) which is caused by their looking through the selective facet of the outdoor prism as it were, and seeing only physical risk instead of viewing it through a lens that 'sees it all'. National guidelines have been guilty of this fault too in following traditional mindsets about safety management. They failed to register the existence of other sorts of risk. This was similar to another selective way in which leaders tended in the past to misinterpret the general nature of an outdoor experience. Leaders sometimes thought that because they were doing a particular activity, that was all that was happening. If they felt they were in an 'activity mode', this type of 'mindset' worked to exclude other considerations. For example, leaders sometimes thought that because they were doing environmental work or field studies, that was all that they were doing and that consequently because they were not involved in outdoor pursuits they did not need to take the safety precautions usual, say, to an activities group. They almost believed that they were immune from danger because their aim was scientific not hazardous activity. The fact that they might have been in a potentially hazardous environment eluded them. Risk is present in all outdoor experiences. Still on the holistic theme, a youngster belayed on a stance paying out rope to a leader and concentrating on the rope handling techniques of rock climbing, may also be enjoying the aesthetics of the vista as well as taking in the detail of land usage in the valley below. It is important for leaders to be aware that whatever they think they are concentrating on, all elements of the outdoor experience (recreational, environmental, spiritual and social) are present in varying degree and cannot be programmed out of the proceedings. This aspect is also touched on in the section on learning theory in chapter 8.

Having an open mind helps the the leader to be flexible, versatile and all-aware!

Leader's Character and Managing Risk

The risk-taking capacity of the person managing the risk elements of a situation has already been alluded to as an important consideration in the management of risk. It is sometimes the over-riding determinant in a situation. In this sense, the management of risk is not so much about techniques (of which more anon) or the leader's technical ability to weigh the numbers in the group and its ability/experience against difficulties of terrain or to manipulate equipment carried against some natural hazard or obstacle, as it is all about the leader's character. Risk-taking that is the result of too much courage, pride or rash bravado and too little judgement is reckless, foolhardy and likely to be accident prone. Too little courage and too much humility, thinking and consideration can result in over caution and not a lot of learning. Finding the right balance is all-important.

Ironically, in the dictionary definition as we saw earlier, all the consequences of risk are negative and bad. Educational practice in the outdoors overturns this dictionary view and regards the outdoors as a risk medium which can lead to **positive outcomes** such as increased confidence, self-esteem, self-knowledge and social awareness.

Using Risk-Taking as a Tool (i)

Years ago in the early 1970s, Colin Mortlock identified and categorised different intensity levels of adventure[30] as:

- ✿ 'recreational' - which makes only slight demands on a person's inner resources;
- ✿ 'skills learning' - is when it is felt to be reasonably within a person's capacity and control. Results are positive.
- ✿ 'frontier' adventure experience - is when you are being stretched on the edge (threshold) of what you think you can manage or want to do and outcomes are very uncertain;
- ✿ 'misadventure' - is when outcomes beyond that personal threshold will be negative.

This theory was a useful thinking tool. But people thought of it as a tool to be used and pro-actively applied in adventure education for the purpose of increasing the self knowledge or sense of identity of people in the group. It was held in some quarters that using risk taking as a means of pushing people towards so called 'frontier experiences' was quite justifiable for, it was believed, it was only at such a pitch that any personal development took place. So it did, but people seemed blind to the fact that there are other ways to encourage personal development than making them work fit to bust and in fear of their lives. The theory was limited by the narrow scope of the interpretation people tended to put upon it. Regarding our assumptions that underlie what constitutes a threshold/frontier experience - what are we to make of St Paul's experience on the road to Damascus? There, if any, was a superb frontier/peak experience and he was only walking along a road!!

I had a mind-blowing experience in the Plymouth Planetarium 30 years ago during a DES conference at Dartington. I was in a warm, absolutely dark room, in a very comfortable reclining seat listening to 'cosmos' type music and looking at points of light on the curved ceiling which simulated the sky at night and feeling I was literally in the very centre of the universe surrounded by all the stars. In absolute darkness there was no sense of near and far, distance was meaningless.

Sitting on the western slopes of Rum watching a golden sun set in the Sea of the Hebrides beyond the island of Canna with the Outer Isles beyond, was a similar type of 'never before' experience with a powerful impact - in both cases completely at rest! Finding a rare flower or butterfly could be another peak experience - being the culmination of a long search with similar feelings. I am not trying to belittle the potential of apparently physical adventure experiences - but I am trying to point out that it is mistake to think that peak experiences can only be experienced through them. OK, if that is your chosen medium then it is important to be aware of its limitations, strengths and weaknesses.

Using risk taking as a catalyst for development is not the simple straightforward process it might appear to be. An elementary trust exercise like standing behind someone you have asked to let themselves fall backwards to be caught by you before they hit the floor, illustrates that point well. How much of a dialogue is necessary before it happens? While on the subject of using risk taking as a tool there are other considerations relevant at this point.

Using Risk Taking as a Tool (ii)

Most advice and guidance in books is written from the standpoint of the leader taking decisions on behalf of the group with all kinds of legal liabilities in mind to be avoided by the leader who is seen to be the one carrying all the responsibility. Meantime the group stands by passively awaiting the outcome of his/her deliberations. The group is not involved in the process. But many practitioners do in fact involve groups in risk management processes in order to help them become practised at a skill denied them by a risk averse culture and which they are going to need throughout their lives. This is an extra dimension which entails a shift in the normal mindset of "the Five Steps" 28. The risk taking process diagram earlier in this chapter showed the need to involve the group in the risk assessment anyway. It was pleasing to see that the latest (2003) MLTUK official Hillwalking handbook taking this view also.

H.E. Brown[32 & 33] put forward some interesting and helpful ideas in *Horizons:* Autumn & Winter 2000). The process whereby leaders help individuals to progress from novices to independent operators (as in D of E expeditions) can be set within the Tannenbaum and Schmidt Continuum of Control and Power to show the way roles change from passive to active with improving skill - see diagram 8.

Novices can be likened to 'passengers', who progressively pass from that status to one of 'participant', then 'partner' and finally 'practitioner'. The role of the leader decreases as the novices gain in skill, experience and confidence. As the learners become more proficient in assessing risks, more decision making and responsibility for seeing the decision through is taken on by them until the point is reached where they are self sufficient, in control of the risk management and actively in charge of themselves and their goals - see diagram 8.

One of the benefits put forward by protagonists of outdoor experiences is that by being involved in how to assess risks and taking steps accordingly, youngsters can be taught how to become proficient themselves in the process of risk management itself. It can be seen as a means to their empowerment rather than being merely passive recipients of the leader's risk management ability. But even passengers, as on a boat, need to remain switched on to the realities of their situation and not misguidedly believe themselves to be completely safe because it is the expert operator's responsibility.

passenger →	participant →	partner →	practitioner
Leader controls situation	Leader is progressively less dominant		Leader not needed
Individual is passive		Individual progressively becoming competent	Individual is in charge of own destiny
Leader is directing and instructing	Leader is coaching	Leader is still supporting monitoring	Leader has delegated or abdicated*

Diagram 8: Tannenbaum and Schmidt's Continuum of Control and Power applied to the process of instructing, coaching and the acquisition of competence by individuals who progressively become able to assume responsibility of risk taking themselves.

"Even passengers, as on a boat,
need to remain switched on to the realities of their situation."

Human error or other external events like system failures or collisions have a nasty habit of impelling them out of situations where the operator was seemingly in charge of their well being and all they were required to do was abide by any instructions given, and into a situation which requires them to make rapid decisions and take independent actions to ensure their own survival. This was illustrated in a TV programme[34] which analysed the situation when the passenger jet caught fire on Manchester runway during take-off in the summer of 1985 (55 died) and the Estonia Ferry disaster September 1994 (900 died within thirty minutes of it losing its bow doors). Apparently, surviving is often much more than just luck. There appear to be links to the personality, emotion and training and even individual differences in brain chemistry. John Leach, a survival psychologist described a wide range of behaviour, linked to personality types, that was exhibited by people facing death and disaster. What he found was that:

- 10%-15% responded rationally - could reason things out, make a plan, were in focus.
- 70% were stunned - wanted orders instructions, were unable to plan or unable to help themselves.
- 10%-15% exhibited behaviour inappropriate to the situation- screaming, weeping, freezing, ignoring instructions.

One hopes no outdoor leader ever has to face such a death/disaster situation, but it gives some indication of what to be prepared for in group behaviour in that event. Whenever possible, prior training in emergency procedures was found to make a big difference in the way individuals might react - e.g. practice in self arrest in snow/ice conditions or canoe/dinghy capsize.

Pitfalls in Applying Risk-Taking Theory

There can be a lot of confused and woolly thinking when using risk taking as a developmental tool. The theory is all very fine in providing an insight into the nature of risk and adventure, but what those theories do not do, is point out the need for caution if a leader/instructor should apply them to someone else who will be, in effect, experiencing at second hand the leader's idea of what constitutes the adventure threshold. An indoor comparison exercise about low and high risk, later on in the section, 'what is adventure', reveals what a subjective business the perception of danger is. It is not just about the perception of danger either but whether the returns, the pay-off, for risk taking are felt to be worth it. What sort of return in personal development is presumptuously envisaged in the minds of the course designers? How do they know that what they have in mind is suitable or appropriate or wanted even? Is the risk-taking process so much in the control of the leader that all outcomes will be guaranteed and predictable? Is the intended result the same as the actual outcome? Whenever possible, vitally important dialogue (consultation) should have taken place beforehand with the participant about the choice of hazard to be confronted (e.g. in the 'I'm falling-catch me' trust exercise mentioned above you could ask, "how far behind you, do you want me to stand in order to catch your fall?" The 'faller' has a say in the degree of danger/risk to be encountered) and whether it is something they want to do. If there is no first-hand personal commitment, then the pay-offs resulting from risk taking are likely to be quite different from what was hoped for or intended.[17]

The theory of risk-taking as a catalyst to development may well be true. But how can you possibly plan to predict it as in a programme? How do you actually know when someone will be near or on their adventure threshold or crossing it? This is to anticipate the point, in the next section but one below, which looks at the question of what constitutes adventure. Clearly only the participant can feel when they stand on their own threshold. Whether it is an accurate assessment is another matter but is beside the point. It is vital that she/he feels able to voice disquiet if unhappy - and most importantly, without losing face with self or others. The 'impelling into experience' school of thought is very presumptive in believing it can plan in positive outcomes for every person in a group of ten!!! How do they know they are not 'compelling into unhappiness'. A lot is talked about the management of risk but the risks of management, or rather, of mismanagement, are just as important.[17]

The Nature of Danger/Risk

Mortlock also categorised danger into that which is 'real' and that which is 'apparent or perceived'[30] (and see chapter 1). Real danger tends to come from objective hazards like avalanches, rock fall or adders and mad bulls, and particularly for groups, situations where the leader would be powerless to reach a participant and prevent harm as, say, on negotiating a rapid, or something as simple as jumping off a wall or swinging unprotected on a rope over an abyss. Rightly, he said that adventure education (as he called it then) should have no deliberate, intentional truck with real danger.

But it is often mistakenly thought that if the leader is operating in the domain of 'perceived danger' (ropes courses, abseils, a heeling dinghy, seconding up a rock climb etc) then all manner of risks can safely be run - impelled even - because no negative outcomes are possible. Think again. Granted there might not be any physical harm likely but all manner of psychological harm is lying in wait for the unwary and the presumptive leader to have to deal with, or find they are powerless to cope with. It is important for leaders to be aware that some psychological risks have no physical element at all. An extreme example might be the trauma suffered by rescuers at an earthquake site. Can you think of other examples?

What is Adventure?

An important insight into the true nature of adventure can be gained by asking a group which is sitting indoors to write down 'five things' which they think are 'low risk' that they can actually do in the room. It is important they write it, rather than calling out, as an early revealing of replies would ruin what the result aims to show.

Then get the group to write down 'five things' (it is important not to say five 'different' or 'other' things) which they think are 'high risk' that they can do in the room.

Then ask them to call out their low risk items and list them on a flip chart. Do the same for the high risk items.

A number of points will become apparent:

1. It will be an unusual group if both 'low' and 'high' lists do not have some items in common - i.e. what some think of as a high risk, others think is low and vice versa. Here is the first big, big lesson - "one person's challenge is another person's nightmare or despair". That may come as a surprise to many if they have not thought about it before and blithely assumed that what they thought of as an adventure must be the same for everyone. That it might not be to someone else's 'taste' at all is a culture shock.

Do you try to find out beforehand every person's 'taste' in a group you are leading? Or do you ignore it and wait for it to show itself during the activity?

2. It is likely that a large number of the written items, or even all of them, will fall into the same category. Usually, all of the risky activities listed are up front 'physical' ones. Before trying to get them to think about possible psychological risks, one can introduce the topic in a roundabout way by saying you will need a volunteer in a short while!!! Any offers??? If you get a volunteer quickly, you have been lucky. Usually one has to work to overcome a reluctance. Why are there no takers? Why are they holding back? What are they frightened of? What is the risk they think they are running?

3. If you are really lucky, someone may point out that any physical risk is invariably combined with some element of the psychological and that it is artificial to separate them into different categories. It may be useful to reflect on what proportion of physical and psychological elements make up various kinds of risk.

Risk Management and Accident Control

Leaders can't be infallible. All the rules and regulations in the world won't neutralise the law of averages, or the randomness of 'chaos theory', despite careful planning and all reasonable care. After every accident there is a cry for more and better regulations in the belief that improved control systems will eradicate accidents. Not so. Motor racing, for example, is saddled with so much regulation it is now prohibitively expensive to run - but accidents still happen. The railways are equipped with more and better safety gear - but accidents still happen. Although the safety record of outdoor-group-leading over the last fifty years is remarkable and commendable - to which no less than the HSE attests, leaders need to accept that accidents will still happen despite more and better training. It is the nature of humans that they are frail and fallible. Parents too need to take this on board and accept that not all accidents are the result of negligence. There is 'bad luck' too as Sid Cross, one-time leader of Langdale Mountain Rescue Team, was often fond of saying. Those who say there is no such thing as 'bad luck' have got it all wrong. I wonder what the surviving passengers of the unsinkable *Titanic* thought about the 1500 who died?

Remember that by good management, you can have a high level of hazard with low risk. Conversely, you can have high risk with a low level of hazard if it is badly handled. Try and think of a few examples.

The Legal Jungle

The previous section began to touch on the legal aspects of leading groups so this might be an appropriate point to deal - but by no means exhaustively - with the legal framework within which leaders have to operate. Scottish law is very similar to English law but not exactly the same, particularly in relation to matters of access.

❂ Leaders in charge of minors (under eighteen-year-olds) by common law, in the UK (it could be different in another country), have a **'duty of care'** which is to take that **'reasonable'** sort of care, in any sort of situation where harm might be *'foreseen'* to occur to someone.

❂ The required **'standard of care'** is that which would be expected with the proper discharge of one's professional duties and it increases as one becomes better trained and qualifications improve one's ability to 'foresee' the possibility of harm.

❂ One is acting in the place of a parent (**'in loco parentis'**) and the leader can in no way be absolved from this duty until that duty is clearly ended. This responsibility does not end if it is delegated either. Neither does obtaining the necessary parental consent for a child to participate in an activity absolve the leader from this responsibility.

✪ In the context of a group, the leader's duty of care is higher than that which could be expected of a '**prudent**' parent at home because it has to be applied in the context of a school (or group) where there are greater numbers to deal with and for which one is responsible. Allegations of '**neglect**' kick in if these criteria are felt to be transgressed and legal proceedings are begun either to establish 'criminal liability' in the criminal courts (which deals with Statute Law created by Parliament for the protection of society) or in the civil courts to establish 'civil liability' (which deals with Common Law based on case precedents for areas not covered by statute). The court has to ascertain the truth of the allegation - whether responsibility was breached through carelessness or negligence and whether injury or death ensued as a result. Damages may be claimed for pain and suffering, the cost of medical treatment, loss of earnings, loss of potential earning capacity, loss of enjoyment of life - all of which are deemed foreseeable losses. Fault must be proved before compensation can be awarded. The opposite is the case in Europe where guilt is assumed and compensation is payable unless you can prove no fault on your part. In other words the onus is on you to prove you are innocent and were not negligent. You are guilty until proved innocent - a practice laid down in Napoleonic codes only two centuries old. It might be applied in Britain one day but not without a foreseeable titanic struggle.

Unfortunately these days litigation is booming. So-called 'Acts of God' once accepted with some philosophic stoicism by a generally religious population, now no longer carry any weight in a largely atheist and secular society. With the 'no win no fee' offer from aggressive commercial advertising driving it, people are easily tempted to try it on whatever the circumstances. This litigation landscape encourages people to hope for good luck since they have nothing to lose. An old idea from sport training about 'no pain, no gain' has been borrowed and turned on its head to become 'if there is pain there might be gain' by way of compensation! By 1995, claims against Local Authorities had increased eight fold in ten years - very few against outdoor leaders though!

Our risk-averse, overprotective, cotton wool society is also fertile ground for the impression conveyed that any accident must be someone's fault. Years of experts in various fields talking knowledgeably at us have convinced us that they have it all sorted and that everything is controllable, solvable or perfectible. Pilot error, driver error, human error, must be the fault when systems fail. So the 'blame and shame' process is set in motion with the media in attendance and, regrettably, all too eager for any dramatic or sensational details to feed to the gullible public in a trial by media. For leaders the message is clear: 'Get it right or look out'. Good intentions can be, but may not be, enough of a defence - it all depends on the circumstances - the devil is in the fine detail.

On the question of who is liable a distinction needs to be drawn between an employee and a contractor who might be one of many independent 'free- lancers' operating in this field these days. Employees are normally covered by their employers (e.g. an LEA) who are 'vicariously' liable for the negligent acts of their employees because they have a 'contract of service' unlike independent contractors working for an employer with whom they merely have a 'contract for services' and would require to carry their own liability insurance as protection against claims. However there is no one simple test to decide the status of a contractor. There are many aspects involved and any decision about this would depend on the particular circumstances pertaining at the time.

The emotionless legal phrases of the law are somewhat stark and bare and sometimes necessarily vague because it can only lay down principles to be applied in any particular situation, so case law precedents are needed to flesh out meaning and understanding. In the Glenridding Beck drowning incident in May 2002, for example, the leader was charged under section 7 of the Health and Safety at Work Act 1974. It was alleged that reasonable care was not exercised by the leader. The Judge said, the leader was "*unbelievably foolhardy*".... to allow any boy to plunge into that water was a very, very, high degree of gross negligence".

After the trial solicitors acting for Lancashire said that (and this is in the public domain) the leader acted with "*criminal recklessness*" and that "his actions amounted to gross negligence". The HSE Head of Operations, Janet Wilson, said:

"Outdoor adventure trips have great value in developing young people, and offer an excellent opportunity for risk education. The vast majority take place without serious incident."

"HSE would not want to see school trips stopped, or teachers refuse to lead them, as a result of this prosecution. But it is essential that they are planned properly and carried out safely."

The Lancashire solicitor had some reassuring words for these difficult times:

"All need the reassurance that, as long as they act in good faith, to the best of their ability, they will not be prosecuted, and they will not be sued. The law does not require people to be perfect - it does not expect that they are 100% right, 100% of the time. All it requires is that they do their best. If they do something, with the best of intentions, to the best of their ability, then they are 'bombproof' - even if it turns out that they got it wrong, or made the wrong choice.

As long as they **can show that what they did was not unreasonable,** *then that is all they need to do."*

But do not forget that Regulation 3 of the Management of Health & Safety at Work Regulations 1992 requires that risk assessments shall be made and appropriate action taken. Even before the Activity Centres (Young Person's Safety Act) of 1995, leaders were in fact legally required to carry out risk assessments. Note in passing that those 'Regulations', which are 'statutory instruments', set out the rules for how the law is to be administered and carried out - and as such they too carry the force of law.

It is estimated that there are 7 - 10 million pupil/days of out-of-school activities every year, The most dangerous thing you do is put all the group in a minibus in order to travel to some activity venue or start-point. Be warned that most 'activity accidents' occur on the activities which are considered to be the lowest risk. A common occurrence in accidents is that the actual risk is not foreseen or understood and so is unknowingly taken on. The Stainforth Beck double drowning in October 2000 was one such incident. In this case the finding was that the deaths were unforeseeable so the only possible verdict was accidental death. A lethal brew of minor omissions all came together in a particular sequence to result in tragedy - a characteristic common in many incidents.

"No outing or trip is risk free."

In law, ignorance is not deemed a valid excuse, so leaders would be well advised to keep an eye out for reports in the Press and to peruse the digests of the findings of a number of case histories in order to get the feel of how the law deals with certain kinds of incidents. Once an unforeseeable incident has occurred, it is no longer unforeseeable, for example. The '**unforeseeable**' becoming '**foreseeable**' is the juggernaut catalyst that can ratchet up regulations to try and ensure it does not happen again and the only brake on this runaway tendency is a judgement about whether it is ever '**likely**' to happen again or not.

Access

The other legal area in which the unwary leader can become entangled is the law of access. Most Governing Body and other training courses cover this subject so, thankfully, it need not be repeated here other than to underline the need for leaders to keep it in mind and to be familiar with the details of the recent Countryside Rights of Way (CRoW) Act 2000 which will give the public a statutory right to roam and will apply in England and Wales as from September 2004 together with a revised version of the long-standing Country Code based on the respect-protect-enjoy ethic. Scotland has its own version on access set out in the Land Reform (Scotland) Act 2003 with the rights and responsibilities contained in a new Scottish Outdoor Access Code developed by SNH and currently, as I write, being considered by the Edinburgh Parliament to be ready for Autumn 2004. In brief the Scottish Act gave the public a better deal than the English Act as it enshrined in law traditional rights of access on land and water whereas the England and Wales legislation was unfortunately less comprehensive. Indeed, it is quite ambiguous about whether or not certain groups/activites are outwith the CroW Act, such as wild camping, paragliding, hang gliding - mountaineering and rock climbing do not even get a mention! Crags in coastal areas are outwith the remit of the Act and any existing restrictions may still apply. Because the Act also only dealt with access on foot, access to water for canoing has remained problematic and a running sore which the British Canoe Union is attempting to get sorted in its River Access Campaign for a fairer deal. Be aware of the new revised maps as they come on stream from Autumn 2004. They will incorporate the changes initiated by the Acts opening up areas previously closed to the public,

Possible Defences Against Charges of Negligence

Charges of negligence will be easier to refute if...
- ❖ the accident/incident was unforeseeable.
- ❖ if the injured person had freely consented to participate in the risk causing the injury. It would also need to be proved that full knowledge of the risks involved had been given to the injured party.

- ❂ a partial defence is if the injured party had contributed to the injury in some way so that it was partly their fault. Although a child may be negligent, the age of the child is taken into account. This defence is rarely pleaded successfully.
- ❂ the leader was qualified to instruct the activity at that level. Appropriate and adequate supervision was provided.
- ❂ all reasonable steps had been taken to ensure the safety of the activity, environment and equipment.
- ❂ the group had been taught about the need for safety and had been warned against foolhardiness in a manner appropriate to their age, intelligence and experience.
- ❂ the group had been systematically prepared for the activities being undertaken, including attention to footwear, clothing and equipment.
- ❂ the activity and the manner in which it was carried out were compatible with regular and approved practice in other similar activity situations.
- ❂ parents of under-18 year olds had signed an appropriate consent form.
- ❂ a comprehensive risk assessment had been carried out and documented.
- ❂ leaders were aware of any special needs within the group.

The next section will be found useful in view of all that has just been said!

Some Important Management Priorities

So what can leaders realistically set out to achieve in the midst of all these unpredictables and imponderables?

1. Have the right kind of attitudes, experience, training and appropriate qualifications.
2. Have previous knowledge of the activity.
3. Have prior knowledge of the routes to be followed or locations to be visited so that hazards, problems and pitfalls are known. Be aware some of these change with the time of day, the seasons and the weather.
4. Ensure that correct and serviceable equipment is available.

5. Ensure that there is careful thinking and planning about how risk and challenge shall be presented. Why are you doing it?

6. Prepare pupils appropriately for what is to be, worn, carried, used and undertaken.

7. Know if there are any special needs in the group and what responsibilities can reasonably be given to young people of a particular age - i.e. know at what age they can reasonably be expected to cope with them and not suffer too serious consequences if they make mistakes. Do they understand what 'being foolhardy' means? But don't forget that some mistakes can be fun if the right attitudes prevail and the right context is chosen. Reprimanding mistakes stifles creativity, discourages experimentation and helps to promote a blame culture.

8. Have appropriate parental consent indicating adequate prior information has been given.

"Some mistakes can be fun if the right attitudes prevail."

Some Important Skills and Responsibilities for the Managers of Risk

1. To recognise when/if hazard is present and of what kind it is.
2. To understand the nature of risk taking.
3. To know when risk is present.
4. To know when risk should be present.
5. To know when risk is absent.
6. To know when risk should be absent.
7. To know what kinds of risk there are and be able to recognise them.
8. To know what levels of risk there are and be able to recognise them.
9. Be able to cope with uncertainty.

The management of risk implies an ability to control the provision of risk and the taking of risk within appropriate limits for the achievement of previously stated ends. It is using the medium of risk because acceptable specific outcomes are expected.

In an ideal world the management of risk implies an ability to ensure that risk is present or absent as required; that the level of risk is as great or small as is appropriate; that the risk is perceived or real by intention and not by chance.

In the real world it is sometimes not quite so simple for the world is not ideal. Waiting in the wings is the 'law of averages', 'chaos theory', 'Murphy's Law' or simple 'bad luck' - call it what you will. It is the 'X' factor able to introduce the unexpected, unwanted element into the situation that knocks all the plans and aspirations out of kilter.

Management Assumptions and Practical Difficulties

Leaders' expectations that planned outcomes will happen, is based on the belief that ability to lead or manage will be good enough to ensure this. For example:

1. It is assumed events planned to be highlights will turn out to be such (see section on planning highlights in chapter eight). A planned challenge will be the challenge it was meant to be. A 'stage III' risk will

happen as a 'stage III'. A planned physical risk will entail only physical risk. In other words, there is a belief that a leader can anticipate the way participants will perceive and experience what is given to them. Daily life shows that it does not work quite like that. Granted it may do for some, but very rarely will it happen for all of a particular group. What is risky or challenging for one may not be for another. It bears repeating that '*one person's challenge is another person's boredom or despair.*' Seeking a common denominator to ensure no-one is harmed may result in some being untouched by the experience - another risk of management.

2. There is the belief that challenge has to be at the 'right' level before it can have a beneficial effect. The 'politic-speak' type of euphemistic phrase for this is 'stretching'. This is achieved by injecting a requisite level of challenge and fear into the programme. Practitioners who believe that they can structure in the appropriate level of risk, challenge or fear to match a student's needs are either deluding themselves or possessed of unusual intuitive powers - a dodgy business at best! The business of extending the psychological boundaries of a person needs to be approached cautiously. It is a fine ethical point whether one has the right to do this or whether it is better left to individuals to do for themselves. Very few people actively seek risk as such. They do not want to be badly frightened. For most people, the risks that come to them unasked are enough. Many people have a defensive, reactive attitude to risk rather than an actively open welcoming one - see section on MOA below.

3. Although risk taking tends to have connotations of bad consequences, most outdoor risk taking tends to occur with hopes of positive outcomes. People who are motivated are more concerned about the rewards than the penalties. The remarks made by famous adventurers show that their mindsets are not concerned so much with risk as they are with achievement of some kind. They are success-orientated not failure or fear-orientated. But of course this is because they are self-motivated. The dynamics of exposure to risk change markedly when the risk is imposed by someone else. Commentators in the media give the fear/danger element in risk when adventuring, a disproportionate status through their desire to sensationalise. They could, arguably, concentrate more interestingly on the management of motivation or the management of achievement.

4. Depending on the person and on the way risk is presented to them, risk can diminish rather than enlarge them. The process by which managers of risk determine the level of risk and the kind of risk to be presented will be crucial. If the manager is authoritarian when s/he does not need to be and is too assumptive, s/he is likely to make many mistakes and cause harm. It is better if the leader shares these decisions with the student when there will be a better chance of positive outcomes.

5. The ability of people to cope with risk is unpredictable. It is important for leaders to know why so that they can respond appropriately to the unexpected reaction. For example, the amount of risk one is willing to take may be related to the degree to which one is aware of what the risks entail and whether the payoff is even relevant to oneself.

6. It is a well known phenomenon that providing a greater level of safety for some people merely gives them a higher baseline from which to take on greater risk, e.g. wearing safety belts allows some car drivers to go faster or climbers wearing helmets and using the latest protection devices to climb harder. But the degree of risk taking is only partly determined by one's personal sense of security. The TV Channel 4 programme 'Equinox', on 6th Oct 1996, 'Staying Alive'[34] and on 12th April 1999, 'Living Dangerously'[35], showed how the amount of the chemical, monoamine oxydase (MAO), which occurs naturally in the system, is now known to be a significant factor in the risk taking capacity of a person. High levels of MOA inhibit risk taking and low levels mean the individual is a stimulus seeker and able to enjoy the stresses of risk taking (e.g. a bull fighter). The amount of this chemical present in certain personality types reacted to affect the nature and determination of their ability to survive in emergencies. In sinking ships, some just 'froze' and gave in and died whilst others were hyperactive in seeking solutions and surviving. This was not just purely because there was motivation and something to stay alive for.

Anyone seeing those programmes would never perceive risk taking in the same light again.

Another allied contribution on brain chemistry pertaining to people's risk taking capacity popped up in the conference of the British

Psychological Society in April 2004. According to researchers at the Open University, babies born between October and March,

"demonstrated higher levels of sensation seeking, adventurous behaviour by the time they were in their 20s and 30s than people born between April and September and that type of behaviour continued until they were 45."

This was due to lesser amounts of sunshine in the winter months which adversely affect melatonin levels in the brain. Melatonin is a hormone that governs a person's response to daylight and the ability to sleep. More sunlight results in more melatonin, a substance which inhibits the production of Dopamine, a chemical that apparently allows people to feel sensations of reward, pleasure and motivation. So less sunshine in winter equals less melatonin and more dopamine in winter babies which enables them to enjoy riskier sports as they grow older. Leaders of older groups note that the effect begins to wane after the age of forty fivish so the desire to take risks becomes less.

A low sense of security is likely to be accompanied by a poor capacity to take risks. Increasing the level of support to someone may improve their capacity temporarily enough to cope with an immediate situation. For example, encouraging a group to be more actively sympathetic, more supportive and caring towards a person will re-assure that person that failure or even refusal will not result in scorn, mockery, censure or ridicule. This may well be all that is required to remove some inhibition. Again, it will bear repetition that the management of risk is as much about the management of support in groups as it is about the management of challenge or fear.

7. Personality type may also affect the degree to which a person may be motivated by risk. 'Achievers' and 'stimulus hungry' people (low MOA) are task orientated and tend to see self esteem and prestige as deriving from what they do. Deeds are rated highly by them. Conversely, people who set greater store by their associations with others, 'affiliatives', will expect to be valued for what they are rather than for what they do. So risk taking and achieving tasks will not be so important for them.

All Kinds of Hazards

Hazard can arise equally from the human condition and other factors, as well as from the state of the natural environment

This short section on the classification of hazards is included to emphasise the varied nature of hazard and to remind leaders that hazards are not all physical in nature. It also serves to provide leaders with a start-up check list, since thinking about hazards tends naturally to focus too exclusively and narrowly on objective environmental hazards. Can you think of others not listed here?

✿ Objective Hazards

1. **natural dangers** - rock-fall, cliffs, scree, mossy rocks, lichen on rocks, bogs, rivers, rapids, river banks, thin cover of snow on short grass, avalanche, cornice, steepness, height-exposure, distance, wetness, fast running water, flash floods, deep water, quick-sands, slipperiness, roughness, looseness, etc. Something as attractive sounding and seemingly harmless as 'remoteness' can be a trap for the unwary for a variety of insidious reasons which may cause a sudden emergency putting you out on a limb.

2. **artificial dangers** - radiation concentration in surf, crowded lakes, crowded ski slopes, river weirs, quarries (unstable quality of rock), mines (roof-fall, shafts, air quality, radon), tunnels, culverts, sunken wrecks, polluted ground, broken glass, barbed wire, polluted rivers, lakes, beaches or sea.

3. **weather effects** - hazards intensified by heat, cold, wind, squalls, rain, lightning, cloud, e.g: waves, tide times, snow, ice, mist, fog, hypothermia, cold injury, hyperthermia, heat stroke, sunburn, skin cancers.

4. **time of year/day/night:** - daylight duration, hours of darkness, time of sunrise and sunset, seasonal weather effects, set, speed and height of tides.

❂ Other Physical Hazards

1. **faulty equipment** - e.g. pressure stoves exploding or leaking gas, harnesses, life-jackets, buoyancy aids, ropes, ski-safety bindings, boats' buoyancy, safety boat propellers, kayaks, ice axes, crampons (to be serviceable all equipment requires checks, inspections, knowledge of limitations of usage, and ability to give instruction in procedures for usage).

2. **activity intrinsic/specific**
- e.g. various codes list dangers and how to avoid collision as on crowded ski slopes or water teeming with canoe-surfers, board-sailors and swimming public; swinging booms on boats or untidy ropes and heaving decks, scree-running; racing collisions, competition either formal or informal. Lifting loaded rucksacks or swinging a bulky sack onto shoulders can cause injury if a passer-by is hit - especially if it has an ice-axe and crampons strapped on it!

3. **animals** - e.g. pony trekking and some horses' erratic behaviour, habits and limitations. Certain farm animals - bulls, cows with calves, dogs. E. Coli-0157 bacteria contaminates farm ground where youngsters might go during farm visits.

Watching or disturbing certain forms of wildlife, e.g. adders, nesting birds like swans, great skuas, terns. Rat urine contaminated water causes Weil's disease, to be avoided by canoeists/swimmers.

Stinging insects - bees, wasps, hornets, horse flies or biting insects like ticks and ants - ticks can cause the quite nasty and enduring effects of Lyme's disease.

Some forms of marine life - jellyfish, lobsters, large crabs, stone-fish etc. How far global warming will affect this list in extending the range of marine life (great white sharks?) is impossible to predict, but the signs of that tendency are already there in the algae that certain sub tropical fish feed on, which were not previously around our coasts.
Beaches infected by sewage E.coli bacteria.

4. **vegetation:** poisonous fruits, berries like yew or deadly nightshade and some varieties of stinging plants. Some umbelliferous plants in the carrot family are quite poisonous whilst the Giant Hogweed has long been one to be wary of, being similar to our native cow parsnip. When its watery sap touches the skin followed by exposure to sunlight it causes painful, burning blisters that may develop into purplish or blackened scars.

Some people are allergic to normally harmless substances which cause troublesome reactions. Recent estimates showed the percentage of people in Britain with allergies has risen to around 15% to 20%. Even daffodil sap and the hairs on primrose stems or leaves can cause nasty rashes on some people.

❂ 'Human' Hazards

1. **leader related**
- inappropriate level of leader qualification or training or experience; poor perceptiveness; inability to distinguish between 'real' and 'perceived' danger; poor judgmental ability; weak group management skills or inflexible leadership style.
- absence of staff accompanying group. i.e. group unaccompanied and independent.

2. **group related**
- age of group mismatched with the challenge.
- number in group mismatched with the terrain or water state.
- type of participator - intelligence, able-bodied, disabled or impaired, special needs, medical conditions, psychologically disturbed or abnormal.
  NB: Some factors interact to create other problems. e.g. rock-climbing novices who are orally and/or aurally impaired, require extra people to assist with communication.
- nature of group - strangers or friends, sociable, friendly, argumentative, violent, conflict-prone, cooperative, competitive, anti-social, uncommunicative, authority 'hang-ups'.
- level of group competence/experience - relates to hazard-awareness and likelihood of panic or ability to cope with difficulties.

- standard of involvement - level at which activity participation is envisaged. e.g. novice, intermediate, advanced or expert.
- differences in individual's perception of danger, when in the actual outdoor environment. Unawareness because of unfamiliarity with natural environment - the result of generations of living wholly in towns and cities. This makes it difficult for leaders to know how much one should leave to an individual to discover for themselves before accusations of neglect creep in. As an aside, but an example of the level of innocent ignorance that can be found, I once had a fifteen year old who did not know how to light a match! Non-smoking parents living in high-rise, all-electric flats don't use them.

3. **Subjective Hazards** - Potentially Danger Causing:
   ⚙ **psychological**
   - **of the variety generated by internal causes**: there is: vertigo, agoraphobia, claustrophobia, dizziness, panic, fear, recklessness, other behavioural abnormalities etc.
   - **of the variety generated by external causes:** there is: abuse, bullying, violence, prejudices, sexism, racism, compulsion, poor leader judgement in matching ability to risk etc.

Hierarchy of Hazards

Now that formally recorded risk assessments have been going for a number of years, ways have been sought to make the process simpler and less onerously paper heavy. Some hazards are constantly there in an activity and others tend to come-and-go for a number of reasons. Starting a risk assessment with the 'constants' first, tends to make the process a bit easier - a kind of hard core on which to hang the other variables. So there is a growing tendency to think in terms of a hierarchy of hazards in which some hazards are always present in a particular activity (permanent and known or generic); some are site specific and some are seasonal (more or less predictable and known); some relate to the size of the group and the nature of individuals in it which have to be taken into account because it is always changing (current and known) and then there is the continuous on-the-hoof monitoring of changing circumstances to watch out for (the unknown, unexpected variety) when a group is on the move.

Some classification systems do not work for some people. Again, it is a thinking tool only. Make your own if this does not feel right for you. An interesting exercise would be to try and re-arrange the list of hazards above into this kind of hierarchic order.

Mac's Ten tips when facing the media

One harrowing ordeal leaders hope they will never have to go through is being interviewed by the media following some incident to a member of their party. The worse the incident the more cause for anxiety and worry. "Will I get it right?" "Will I put my foot in it?" "Will I be able to spot and correct the tricks some reporters (fortunately few) slide into the interview to create more 'newsworthy' copy?" "Will I come across OK?" "How will I react to being confronted by a TV camera and a microphone thrust under my nose?" It may be some comfort to know that most reporters are in the business of information, not investigation or annihilation.

The important thing is to have thought an interview through beforehand and to have your own agenda to follow rather than meekly react to theirs. Having a list of points clearly in your mind that you want, or need, to say helps you to stay in charge of the grilling you might get. If you do get caught in an unprepared state it is OK to say you are not yet in a position to say anything but that you, or a more senior person in your organisation, will make a statement for them at an agreed time and place.

Alistair Macdonald, an able and energetic broadcaster/journalist, who has been in the game for over thirty years (he was the one who 'discovered' Fred Dibnah, the charismatic Lancashire steeplejack) has kindly allowed me to include his own list of the following tips.

Never:

1. Speculate or apportion blame - your insurers won't like it and the true cause of an accident may be unexpected. A widely-reported 'gangland killing' in Liverpool some years ago turned out to be a straightforward suicide by a bank employee who had been sacked a few hours earlier for embezzlement.

2. Name victims - unless you have absolutely rock-solid confirmation that police have informed next of kin. Even if next-of-kin know it can be a dreadful shock for other family members to learn of a close relative's serious injury or death via a radio or TV bulletin.

3. Embroider - Keep Interviews Short & Simple (KISS). You need to provide a few basic facts to prevent the more disreputable hacks from making up the story but you should not be in the business of writing a reporter's story for him. A reporter's requirements may conflict with your responsibilities to the clients or children in your care. Any extravagant or colourful language or overstating the case will almost certainly come back to haunt you in court later.

4. Say 'No comment' - you'll sound guilty even if you're innocent. This may seem to conflict with No 3 (above). Generally, you will be able to give a few basic facts which will help a reporter tell their story.

5. Add fuel - rather try to take the heat out of hot moments. You may be under great stress - and reporters may put you under even more pressure - but it's not a good idea to make things worse by antagonising journalists. Don't raise your voice or appear rattled as this could suggest that you are 'guilty'.

Always:

6. Keep promises to the media - i.e. timing of news releases and interviews. Journalists - particularly broadcasters - work to very tight deadlines. Nothing is more guaranteed to attract negative coverage than failing to deliver information to them at, say, 10.45am. 11.05am is no good - they've missed the bulletin and will be facing untold grief from their news editor. This will rapidly be transferred to you.

7. Be human and sympathetic - a crisis involving employees/clients requires tact and understanding. Using appropriate language sounds so obvious, yet many interviews on sensitive subjects sound as impersonal and lacking in feeling as an instruction manual for assembling flat-pack furniture.

8. Offer appropriate sympathy - in the case of death or serious injury. This is not an admission of guilt and should be second nature to anyone doing an interview involving a tragedy - yet it's so often forgotten. Imagine how you would feel if you were a close relative of the person killed or injured.

9. Stay calm - panic can very easily turn a crisis into a disaster.

10. Tell the truth - a few white lies early on never proves to be a Get-Out- of-Jail-Free card in the long term. It took years to bring Jeffrey Archer to justice but relentless investigation eventually revealed the truth and he went to prison. When you know the truth, a 'quick bleed' is usually better than allowing the facts to emerge. If you've made a mistake, admit it. But, don't say too much too soon. You need to know the full facts first. Journalists and the general public can accept mistakes - we're all human - but we all want to know that lessons have been learned and that this is less likely to happen again. Of course, no two accidents are ever quite the same and accidents, by their very nature, will continue to happen.

Follow these guidelines and you may prevent a Crisis turning into a Disaster.

Be aware that inquest and court case verdicts can sometimes hinge on public perception rather than legal argument.

❂ Chapter Eight ❂

Leadership and Management Skills

"Leadership is doing the right thing and management is about doing things right."

Implicit in all that has been said so far about leadership, are a number of general functions specifically pertinent to the exercise of leadership. These are some of the more important ones:

Functions of the Leader [3]

1. To set the aims and goals:

Ideally by helping the group to identify or define them. A touch of charisma helps here to reassure a group that does not really know yet what it wants to do. It is not unusual to find a group like this. Sometimes it is just shyness about speaking out which needs to be overcome (time for ice-breaking activities?). Sometimes they genuinely do not know or lack the information to be able to make choices (time for a quick Powerpoint presentation or a less formal chat about the possibilities?).

2. To take responsibility:

There are subtle distinctions to be drawn here. It is not enough to be responsible, i.e. to be the place where the 'buck' stops. One can be the person responsible and do nothing; in which case, one is acting irresponsibly. To **be** properly responsible, one must also **act** responsibly.

An aside here on the use of the words 'responsible' and 'accountable' may be in order as they are sometimes mistakenly used synonymously. A leader is responsible 'for' something but 'accountable 'to' somebody.

3.   To control:
Allocating jobs appropriately and managing time; keeping things on track; by being aware, observant, perceptive; by anticipating, planning; by praising and disciplining.

4.   To care for:
Everyone - not the same as 'caring about' which is also important.

5.   To support:
Those who need it; those struggling, those falling behind; those over-reaching themselves; those hurt or fearful; those over confident and prone to making mistakes; those having a go at taking on responsibility which can set them apart from the others and induce feelings of insecurity.

6.   To set and maintain standards and limits:
About behaviour, commitment, output, equipment, safety.

7.   To make decisions:
This is the function that traditionally identifies the leader from the followers and sets him/her apart, although the extent to which this happens can depend very much on how the decisions are arrived at and delivered - imperiously, curtly, impartially, civilly, assertively, courteously, sympathetically, empathetically, apologetically, hesitantly, diffidently etc. Each of these stimulates its own distinctive set of reactions in a group

8.   To make decisions about how decisions are made:
The leader cannot, indeed should not, always do all decision making personally. Some tasks are best delegated, and some require a consensus, for example. In some cases the state of maturity or make-up of the group will affect how the decisions are made.

9.   To sustain the group's energy:
Individuals have differing work rates and they also have different requirements for rest. The caring leader will ensure that whatever task the group is engaged upon, the rate of energy output is paced and controlled so that 'burn out' does not occur in one or all. The pressures of responsibilities on the leader tend themselves to be a generator of

energy which must be tapped at those times when the group is flagging or morale is low, and used to jolly them along, encourage, re-energise and re-motivate. This function is closely related to the next one.

10. To engage and commit personal energy to the group's achievement of its task:

Without something to hold it together, a group of people tends to take on a fragmented character bordering on chaos or anarchy in that it will tend to lack purpose or direction.

"Individuals have differing work rates and they also have different requirements for rest."

The leader needs to be like a magnetic field holding the various atoms together in order that they may be something greater than the parts. If the energy required to maintain that 'field' drops, so then does the cohesiveness of the group. Even if the task has been chosen by the group rather than the leader, the group may not always be as motivated as the leader to see a task through. Its commitment as a whole, and that of individuals in it, will tend to wax and wane periodically, putting the achievement of the task in doubt. It is the leader who has to do the chasing up, checking that each is doing their part and that each has the necessary equipment to do it.

11. To be aware of and be able to respond appropriately to the reality of:
- the task.
- the group in your charge.
- the individual differences in the group.

This is a question of reading the signs correctly and proposing or adopting courses of action that will not deter the fainthearted or disappoint the gifted. It is a simple matter for a leader to be blind to the reality of the task or group or individual. Is the task too much or too difficult for the group or is it so easy that under achievement will result? It is no use trying to treat a group as if it were experienced if it is at the novice stage. Leaders can want too much for their groups with their eyes set on some idealised vision in the future. Similarly they can want too little. With their eyes looking backward to past experiences of disappointments and let downs, they may be too unambitious or cautious, so afraid of making the same mistakes that the group does not receive what it deserves or is capable of. Which takes us nicely into the last function.

12. To be aware of and responsive to:
- your own feelings, wants and needs.
- the feelings, wants and needs of the group as a whole.
- individual members of the group.

It is impossible for leaders to judge how far to keep their own ambitions out of the equation if they are not aware of them. It is only from a state of self awareness that a withholding of self can occur. Complete denial of personal needs, wants and feelings is also undesirable as it can lead to a bottling up of frustrations that may be taken out on the group. The group also needs help to see the leader as a person as well as the taken-for-granted figurehead leader in order to have the accurate perception of him/her that makes for good relations. The leader also needs to be aware when the feelings, wants and needs of the majority are causing excessive discomfort for the few and take steps accordingly. But the needs of the 'one' can, on rare occasions, outweigh the needs of the 'many'.

To carry out these functions properly and effectively, a leader needs to be able to call on a range of both technical (task orientated) skills and relationship (people orientated) skills. The technical skills are to be found elsewhere in other books or manuals. Chapter 8 focuses on some of the more important 'people' skills which are trainable skills and which can be acquired to assist the leader in the function of leading. Indeed, the attempt should be made so to develop these skills that they become ingrained habits rather than skills.

Attitudes/Prejudices Causing Learning Difficulties

Much of the information that follows throughout this section is abstract in nature and is of the kind that is intangible and therefore difficult to pin down. It is so much a part of everyday life that it is taken-for-granted. The obvious often goes unseen. If, before reading about them, you were asked to make a list of these leader skills, describe them or the processes of which they are a part, say how they are used and what their significance is, you might find it quite difficult to do. But as you read about them they will seem to be so familiar that you will think you already know them. In a way you do. You use them every day. But your use of them may have been largely **reactive** or subconscious. As a leader your use of them will need to be more **proactive** and consciously deliberate. An effort of memorisation and practice is required before some of them will be effectively absorbed into your usual way of doing things.

In the U.K., especially in sport or adventure type activities, because the accent tends to be on 'doers' and achievers, there has built up some prejudice about getting involved in the intricacies of leadership skills (see remarks in the introductory section). There used to be a fairly widespread deficit in the possession of, or belief in the value of, inter-personal skills. Since this book was written there seems to have been some improvement, not all because of this book I hasten to add. "Psychology and all that" was one way, and a mistaken one, of how the field of inter-personal skills tended to be perceived and was thus seen as rather intellectual or esoteric and remote from the job of leading - it still is by those who see themselves purely as activity types. It is argued here that leadership should be informed by a good knowledge and understanding of people. When a leader is not so informed, an unaware state will tend to render leadership formless or rudimentary, insensitive or unskilled, and prone to ill considered acts likely to arouse conflict.

There are, perhaps, lessons to be learned from this country's long history of discord and strikes in the relationships between the labour force and management which has too frequently accentuated getting on with the task and neglected the good relationships required to get the job done.

Interestingly, management training, development training and adventure therapy are all growth areas these days.

Another source of resistance possibly arises from the image of thinking, sensitive leadership being perceived as not quite 'masculine' enough or 'practical' enough for the majority of British leaders who are male. For reasons to do with the cultural mores of our society which imposes assumptions on, and prescribes behaviour for women and girls, female participation in outdoor activities generally and in mountain activities in particular, has been much less in extent and not as varied as that of male involvement. The last twenty years or so have seen some tremendous achievements by women in the outdoors to shake the complacency of male attitudes of superiority - marathon runs, ascents of Everest, Ellen MacArthur solo sailing around the world, Catherine Destivelle performing superhuman unroped feats on awesome rock faces, five women led by Caroline Hamilton in 1999 on an expedition to the South Pole. It is pleasing to see that the degree to which male leaders outnumber female leaders is changing. But the majority of participants being male in this field has tended to mean a preponderance of male values with the accent on technical excellence (i.e. competence) and achievement (all about the task). It does seem however that the input of leadership theory into leaders' practices is effecting some value shifts here.

Probably, because it too is a result of our socialising culture, women tend to be better at the 'people' skills and men better at the 'technical' skills. Is it possible that men subconsciously, and wrongly, deduce from this that the relationship skills are feminine and therefore to be kept at a distance in order to avoid being branded by their peers as 'womanish'? The terminology currently in use to describe technical skills as 'hard' and the inter-personal, relationship skills as 'soft' is misleading, crude and idiomatic. It does not seem to help a proper discernment, recognition and acceptance by the male community - despite the fact that other professionals who work with people regard the 'people skills' also as the technical skills of their work.

A more positive and productive line of approach would be to use the term 'technical skills' for so-called 'hard skills' and apply as appropriate, the terms 'inter-personal skills' or 'leadership skills' for so-called 'soft skills'.

Gender Issues: Male:Female Differences

Discussion about 'gender images' above, leads to a consideration of the part played by gender differences in outdoor activities. What do leaders need to know about gender to do their job more effectively? The next few sections on this topic can only lightly touch a large subject and try to highlight a few of the more important issues. I am also conscious that anyone attempting to write on this topic enters a minefield. But the subject has to be addressed in an attempt to establish some guidelines for dealing satisfactorily with mixed groups. Difficulty is no excuse for avoidance.

Whether with a mixed group, an all-female or all-male group, it is essential for leaders to take account of certain fundamental differences between the sexes. To ignore them, will be to allow all manner of injustice, resentment, alienation and opting out to take place. The biological differences are obvious, but until the onset of puberty, the other physiological differences are less marked and the sexes are almost equal in physical ability. Thereafter, boys in the main are heavier built and stronger than girls.

Beyond this point the way in which these differences are overlain with other misapplied meanings, creates a whole mish-mash of misinterpretations and misconceptions. 'Stronger' suddenly becomes 'better' or 'superior'. 'More powerful' becomes 'domineering' and 'over-powering'. Power values for weight-strength ratios are discounted as are the benefits of being 'light' or having a low centre of gravity. There are curious contradictions too! The 'weaker' sex is expected to be able to carry a three year old and a full shopping bag or lift a bedridden parent. Such feats or tasks are conveniently dismissed by male outlooks as "women's work". Asking boys to help with the washing up is sometimes a great lead-in to discussing their acquired gender prejudices.

Boys

From birth, boys are bombarded by a set of attitudes which hark back to the values of those times when food had to be hunted and territory or possessions defended. There was a need to be hard, aggressive and brave in order to succeed. Rearing methods still teach boys to strive to be strong mentally as well as physically. "Be a man!" "Don't cry". "If he hits you, hit him back". "Do not show weakness". If he cannot do these things, adult disdain reveals to him that he is not a real boy. So to prove to his peers that he is a boy he has to try to do these things.In all boys' groups, in times of stress, disagreement or conflict, these pressures are at work, elevating or degrading (depending on your point of view) their collective behaviour into one resembling the law of the jungle. To survive you have to prove yourself by showing that you cannot be taken advantage of. It is important not to appear vulnerable, so mistakes, or feelings of being incompetent or inadequate, cannot be voiced or admitted. To be put down or discounted is not to be countenanced. To "get somewhere" in such a climate, you have to prove yourself worthy of a place in the pecking order. To do that you have to enter a competition, either at least to stay off the bottom, or at most to reach the top of the pile. Desire to belong in the peer group creates a strong compulsion to conform to this way of behaving. It is an unusual or strong personality that can resist the pressure of this ethos and go his own way. Needless to say, ways of operating in this maelstrom, vary from the raw, naive, blatant use of crude physical aggression to subtle, obscure, cunning, psychological manipulation.

A subsidiary, but no less important, theme of this book is the need for male leaders to devote more time to getting across to boys that "being a man" does not mean acting out all those aggressive adolescent behaviours that our culture has indoctrinated males into believing are the socially approved ways to behave.

"To survive you have to prove yourself by showing that you cannot be taken advantage of."

'Maleness' is too often perceived to be all about proving oneself by being competent, doing things and showing off to females, coming out on top by being aggressive and competitive, never admitting to vulnerability (being perfect, never making mistakes) nor admitting to being, or feeling, inadequate or incompetent in case it is taken advantage of and exploited to the detriment of oneself.

'Manliness', on the other hand, is all about leaving most of this immature, adversarial stuff behind and replacing it with helping rather than fighting; cooperating with others; taking more account of the less strong, or those in a minority; coming down off the power driven pedestal of fear and refraining from indulging in all those non-productive behaviours such as the down-putting, point-scoring antics and the combative wasteful, adversarial tactics that males of all ages engage in too frequently. To convert boys' groups from these culturally determined inclinations is no easy matter.

They live in a competitive world and it would be a mistake to try to eliminate competitiveness completely from their personalities. What has to be attempted is their acceptance of the idea that a total dependence on this adversarial style as a way of life is undesirable. In the long run it is inefficient and wasteful - witness the combative exhibition we see daily in Parliament! They have to be convinced that it is unworthy and immature. They need to be shown that there are alternative viable ways of behaving and relating to others that can be equally effective in achieving aims.

A simple exercise can give an invaluable insight into the thoughtless way males tend to operate. Place a group of boys in a circle facing inward with their arms linked tightly together. Then ask the one boy you have kept out of it to try to get into the circle by any means he can devise. The resulting spectacle is illuminating. It usually becomes a violent attack/defend test of brute force. Bribery might be tried sometimes but rarely does the outsider resort to subtler methods. Positive, straight tactics such as a civil request or an appeal to friends are never given a thought.

Whilst not all male leaders exhibit the macho characteristics of maleness as it has been culturally determined in most societies, a sufficiently high proportion of them, and the boys in their groups, do. Age-old attitudes which support this male stance, may hinder the acceptance of ideas which challenge the customs and practice characterised by male behaviour. Bullying, for instance, is one form of macho behaviour which should be discouraged at every opportunity. Reluctance to show or admit interest in wild flowers or wildlife is another example where it can be felt to be 'not quite masculine'! How quaint!

Leaders' resistance to the acquisition of relationships skills can be overcome. They may have the belief that being outdoors is 'good' for young people but may not have thought through how that 'goodness' comes about. Such leaders can be compared to the vague mystic who relies on faith or random chance to produce desired results. This is not very professional. Most of the 'good' outcomes that are looked for in young people, arise out of the inter-active, inter-personal processes that go on in groups. These need time and space to emerge, develop and flourish. The only way to make this potential 'good' more probable is to avoid using leadership styles that inhibit group interaction and to use styles that actively promote it. The traditional directive style of leadership at best damps down, at worst paralyses, such interaction because it is over concerned with the activity and the skills needed to do it. Certain styles which can guarantee that issues will arise, are those which rely on interaction between people for success, i.e. the democratic, participatory, delegatory styles of leadership. They do not attempt to predict specific outcomes but they do ensure that there will be the supportive contexts or favourable climates necessary for their existence. This is what will ensure that desired outcomes receive their due in time and attention.

**By using these styles,
the opportunity for personal development and effectiveness
is structured into group life.
It is no longer a matter of optimism or chance.**

Girls

Girls have developed alternative strategies for achieving their objectives. I enter this arena with some trepidation and a wish not to be seen as patronising. I hope I succeed. As a male I cannot really speak about an all-girls' group when no males are present, but since their physical abilities would be equal as peers, relatively speaking, I could imagine that sometimes conflicts might not be too dissimilar to an all boys' group. The struggle for a place in the pecking order may, or may not be, as physical and though the quality of the psychological warfare might be quite refined it could be just as vicious!

In general, girls could quite probably be a lot stronger physically than they actually are. But they are like boys, in that the manner of their upbringing is culturally determined too, but along different lines. Girls are exhorted to take care of themselves in case "they hurt themselves", the underlying (never mentioned but implied) concern being to ensure that their reproductive capacity is unimpaired. So girls learn early not to get wet or muddy or do dangerous things. One noticeable offshoot of this is an observed unwillingness for girls to make big, massive movements, as, for example, when scrambling over rock. It seems to stem not so much from a sense of physical inadequacy as from a wariness not to be over exposed to a commitment to danger. It may also be the early consequence of wearing a dress which tends to inhibit big movements. The command "be careful" is probably more used now by parents during the last two decades that ever it was previously for both boys and girls.

From an early age, girls observe and experience what it is like to lack either power or physical strength. Later in life, as mothers, the job of looking after children places them in a vulnerable position. Without the benefits of power, alternative ways need to be found to achieve what they want and these strategies are passed on to the next generation. So negotiation and cooperation, the only method available to them when you think about it, has developed as the favoured method. Along with cooperative negotiation come all the other skills and qualities concerned with persuasion, tolerance, consideration, sympathy and compassion. Is it little wonder that women appear to outshine men in the sphere of interpersonal skills? For this reason it is quite common for many male leaders to prefer to have all female groups. Not because they may be more biddable, indeed often they may not be, but because there is less hassle in the group amongst its members which makes it pleasanter to be with and easier to relate to.

Mixed Groups

Problems of a particular kind tend to arise in mixed groups when the time is spent battling on unequal terms. If the brash, aggressive, adversarial behaviour of insecure boys is allowed to obtain, if their compulsion to prove themselves is allowed to prevail, choices about activities will tend to reflect their male preoccupations with physical strength, stamina, and courage. Competitiveness about skill competence is also likely to be present and it may even be compounded by the presence of girls in one or two ways. The boys may perceive it as an opportunity to show off their paces to the opposite sex in an attempt to impress them and appear more attractive. If these influences are allowed to run unchecked, most girls will find themselves constrained to operate at a disadvantage. Naturally they will not like it and will lose interest, or as a response to this enforced powerlessness, 'egg' the boys on in order to gain some sense of effectiveness from the situation. Girls tend to have a different approach to life. Taught by nurture and experience to be less assertive or aggressive, they are just as likely to decide not to join the dismal fray and stand back to remain uninvolved, letting the boys get on with it, possibly resentful but certainly not impressed. In such circumstances they are likely to feel let down, cheated of justice, even betrayed by the authority figure in which they have had to place their trust. Their seeming passivity (I nearly wrote 'seething passivity', which I have no doubt it often is) may go unnoticed by a male leader, who may be either insensitive to their reactions, or too personally involved himself in the power struggles to rise above them. Attention, regretfully, often stays focussed on the disrupters, the noisy ones with a lot to say, the extroverts and those who seem to know what they want.

With mixed groups it would be standard practice to have at least one adult from each of the sexes with the group and especially if overnight camping is planned.

Gender Implications and Consequences

The style of debate adopted by males, is usually characterised by posturing, boasting and position–taking. Because it closes off the possibility of flexibility or open-mindedness as well as the ability to change your mind, express doubt, or admit you were wrong, it is unsuited to the female disposition. It often deliberately creates an intimidating environment that discourages dialogue of the kind with which girls feel most comfortable. Girls are good at listening because they tend to be interested in what is happening, and boys are good at interrupting because they see it as a battle for "air time". Whoever gets to talk longest, wins.

Female silence is greatly misinterpreted by males. If it is taken to mean ignorance, intelligent girls are likely to find themselves being told what to think by boys whom they may perceive as their intellectual inferiors - a situation fraught with suppressed resentment at least and heatedly expressed outrage at worst.

If it is construed to mean uncertainty or indecision, things will be decided for them. More silence will be conveniently seen as consent.[18] Should the silence be broken by protesting or accusatory girls, the boys will be unable to treat it seriously because they cannot handle it and will take cover behind appeals to logic and attempts to deride emotional outbursts. "You are being childish." "You are too emotional-you must try to be more rational." "You are not being at all reasonable." This sort of denial of feelings can be very corrosive in its effect on relationships in a mixed group. Perhaps because they feel they do not have as much face to lose as do the boys and because they operate mostly in the cooperative mode, it is easier for girls to confess when they feel unable to do something or express doubts about their ability or competence. Sometimes girls, who are only too aware that this kind of behaviour is perceived by boys as "being feminine", make use of it as a tactic. This seeming lack of confidence is often construed by males as inadequacy or incompetence when in fact girls are just as capable as the boys. The difference is that boys, who are likely to be just as uncertain about themselves, will rarely, if ever, admit to feelings of inadequacy for fear of a loss of status in the group.

"Female silence is too often misinterpreted by males."

There are rare times when leader intervention enables a mixed group to see beyond the customary masks. When each sex sees in the other a mirror image of its own fears and anxieties, meaningful dialogue ensues.

It will be apparent that in the context of teamwork and groups, boys and girls labour under a plethora of disabilities in the realm of personal skills. It is a wonder anything ever gets done. Achievements are likely to be at no little cost to some in the group in terms of self respect and a sense of personal identity. Girls are more likely to be used to, and skilled, at compromise and negotiation. Cooperation depends upon it.[20] But some girls taught by their own life experiences that these do not work are likely, out of sheer frustration or a sense of injustice, to be as bad as boys, or worse, in their use of raised shrill voices, screaming, shrieking and yelling to get their way.

Need for Leader Intervention

Parity of opportunity, either in discussion time, or in choosing activities, or in decision-making will not occur unless the leader takes positive action to ensure that conditions are conducive for parity to take place and prevail.

It is worth emphasising this truth for the simple reason that it lies at the heart of the issues surrounding the futures of young people themselves and the nature of their development. It is as much about whether they themselves will derive maximum benefit, as whether the potential of the outdoor experience itself will be fully utilised - this is what is at stake.

Leaders, male and female, can do much in providing, by their own example, good positive role-models from which both sexes can learn.

Women Leading All-male Groups

A note about women who have to lead all-male groups might be useful at this point. The remarks that follow are arguably more observable with, and applicable to, all-male groups coming from inner city contexts. As with all generalisations, not every all-male group will exhibit the type of reaction now described below.

The normal macho expectation of boys involved in some kind of outdoor activity is that a male will lead them in their sessions. When this does not happen and a woman appears before them, their ideas about leader role-models in the outdoors receives a jolt. The severity of reaction may range from mild surprise to outrage. Some may feel that they are being sold short; some will feel that they are doomed to soft options - there is a sense of some kind of betrayal at work. At bottom is the feeling that "women don't do these things as well as men so we won't have as good a time as we should." These feelings of disappointment and/or resentment will show themselves in a variety of ways all designed to test out and discover the mettle of the leader, whether this woman leader is worthy of respect and of course, who will be the boss. Leaders of such groups can expect: cheek, overt disobedience, attempts to knock the leader off-track by hustling her through induction processes at a hurried pace, arguing with the leader's proposals or decisions, brisk questioning of her actions. The strategies required to cope with or counter this sort of situation will be as varied as the leaders themselves.

The reaction of an all-male group to a woman leader will be dependent partly on how the group perceives that individual. The first impressions and initial conclusions they draw about her will determine what form their action takes. Is she attractive or not, young or not, athletic or academic looking, and so on? It cannot be the purpose of this section to give answers on this one but simply to flag up its existence and the need to have thought out ways of dealing with it. A leader faced with this situation in an unprepared condition could be in for a bad time, not to mention the possible dangerous spin-offs that could accrue whilst pursuing potentially dangerous activities. Suffice to say that the leader has to find means to impose her personality on the group to the point that gains their respect without antagonism - not easy to do and sometimes unavoidable. It is likely that a stand will have to be taken sooner or later about something. Very few women leaders win through on charm alone. So if a stand has to be taken, it would seem prudent for the leader to be aware what sort of ground she is strong on and herself choose the terms of any confrontation.

The advice about mixed groups having adults from each of the sexes also applies in this instance. Women leading all male groups should have a male assistant accompanying the group.

Leading Adult Groups

Whilst on the subject of different types of group, it has been assumed that most group leading will be with younger groups. But a few short notes on leading adults will not be amiss as this situation will be met by any leader required, for instance, to help train a group for a governing body award qualification or be involved in the intricacies of developing a senior management team from corporate industry. Many commercial groups specialise in holiday or recreational treks for adult customers too. One would expect that leaders given these responsibilities would be quite experienced in the ordinary way, but leading adults is in a different league and leaders may find themselves on unfamiliar ground, metaphorically speaking, at times. The first and obvious difference is that leaders have lost that edge that age gave them with minors. Leaders may be dealing with peers so will need to be more skilful (subtle?) in their relationships or may have a group of retirees far beyond them in years, maturity, wisdom and experience - and up to all the dodges too!

Leading adult groups may be both easier than when handling younger persons in some respects, and more difficult in other ways. Adults may tend to be more prepared to be conformist, patient and attentive generally about routine stuff, but they may be more pernickety and choosy about what they want to commit themselves to when plans are being discussed. They may also be less willing to make mistakes outdoors for fear of showing themselves up. By adulthood we have learned to suss out most of the stuff we need to 'get around' and get on with the routine business of living. And we have grown used to being comfortable with jogging along with what we've got/learned. To suddenly find oneself once again on the edge of one's experience having to learn new things can be a sharp reminder of the less comfortable more anxious days of our youth when learning was on a steeper curve. By adulthood there suddenly seems to be more to lose in stepping into the unknown. Losing face seems to have more serious ramifications, irrespective of whether you are among a group of work colleagues or relative strangers. Self respect has developed harder edges over the years. It has become more defined.

"By adulthood there suddenly seems to be more to lose in stepping into the unknown"

It may be less easy to flex. Conversely, some adults are more inclined to see themselves as free agents and liable to shoot off unexpectedly at a tangent. Whilst a 'light rein' may show that you respect them as people and might ensure a greater likelihood of their cooperation, there are hidden dangers. Some may still be into 'showing off' behaviour and end up putting themselves or the group in real risk situations. It could just be genuine curiosity about something seen of course that results in their shooting off away from the group.

The taxing question about how far adult group members are responsible for themselves and to what extent the leader should intervene when someone is 'pushing their own boat out' too far, is a possibility forever present. One of the questions the leader has to attempt to resolve is whether what the maverick individual is attempting is the result of a careful personal judgement based on that person's experience which might enable him/her to make an accurate, informed judgement about the course of action they are taking. Or is it the result of some rash, impulsive emotion like the desire to show off and impress. The leader in effect has to judge the person as much as the overt action which is an extremely difficult task as this depends greatly on how well that person is known.

In such situations it may be unclear who is responsible for what when one goes off to do their own thing whilst nominally in your charge. So it may be necessary to point out that as adults they are responsible for their own actions if they seem unwilling to take your advice (the leader having been careful to ensure they have been given any relevant information about particular hazards and risks involved in what they propose to do).

Legally, provided the leader has made the adult fully aware of the consequences of their intending independent action, then the leader is in the clear as provided by the law of 'volenti non fit injuria', - no harm is done to those who consent. The leader has fulfilled her/his responsibility and with a consenting adult no question of leader negligence arises. This applies to adults and not minors of course.

However, is this really the right time for such an individualist to be amassing experience and learning by discovery? Uneasy and difficult questions arise about whether the leader has the correct balance of control and responsibility and whether the client has the right to act independently. Where will liability be seen to lie in the event of an accident? Ideally these matters would have been resolved in a prior contract of understanding and agreement.

Generally, however, it will be possible for the leader to manage an adult group by suggestion and proposals to arrive at a consensus about aims and objectives with it understood that on-going feedback is desirable.

What this particular point underlines is the need for the detail of the 'contract of understanding' between the leader and the adult group member to have been spelled out beforehand as to the level and nature of the danger and risk to be confronted and the challenge to be tackled, i.e. where the responsibility of the leader begins and ends.

I was once walking with a group of trainee mountain leaders on a line just under Cust's Gully on Great End in Lakeland when one of the group suddenly decided to 'have a look' at the moderate scramble up the gully and set off up it without announcing his intention. By the time I became aware of his move a short while later, he was already some way up the rocky route. What was I to do? He seemed to be moving confidently but the harder part was higher up with the potential for disaster if he became unstuck. If he fell off, was I responsible for having allowed him to go on or could one reasonably maintain that he was responsible for his own actions? He was an adult so I was not 'in loco parentis' but there was an implicit contract. I was in charge of his training programme that he expected to be designed to fit him for walking the hills with a group. He was a fairly experienced hill walker in his late twenties, fit and strong and reasonably level-headed, not given to immature behaviour. I came to the conclusion that he was genuinely attracted by the appeal of the route and had judged that he could manage it. However, as leader of the group in a training capacity I felt, in crude terms, that if he wished to chance his arm in the hills it had to be on some other occasion.

"We're off to the pub"

"Uneasy and difficult questions arise about whether the leader has the correct balance of control and responsibility"

This was neither the time nor the place as there were other pressing training needs to be addressed. I invented some spurious reason that persuaded him to descend without losing face. It might be thought that here in a training situation was an ideal time, if any were ever to exist, for someone to try themselves out. I have a feeling however that a lawyer would say that if a person is taking part in a training session, then by definition that person is not yet ready to exercise judgements of the nature under discussion, particularly when the type of activity in question is not part of the session. This incident also illustrates the risk-taking capacity of the leader as a factor in the situation.

Categorising Skills

The need to categorise skills and the skill to be able to categorise, should not be regarded merely as an academic luxury but as a crucial aid to assist leaders in the task of internalising a mass of information so that it can be more easily handled, managed and used.

Various ways of categorising and classifying the 'relationship' skills are possible[3]. Some suggestions are included below but in time leaders should find their own ways to do this because their own devised system will work better for them.

The relationship skills required by a leader for operating effectively could be listed under three general headings:

Communication Skills	Group Management Skills	Assertion Skills
Listening	Planning	Influencing
Expressing	Organising	Controlling
Informing	Decision making	Positive assertion
Questioning	Supervising	Confronting
Clarifying	Monitoring	Responding to criticism
Facilitating	Mediating	Directing

Skills could also be classified according to the object on which they are used:

⚙ **the self:** which is intra-personal e.g. self analysis or self awareness.

⚙ **others:** which is interpersonal as in one-to-one relationships. e.g. feeding back.

⚙ **others as a whole:** which is the group - with one relating to many e.g. briefing, summarising, managing.

As well as the activity-specific physical skills of the 'how-to-do-it' sort and the mental skills of the 'need-to-know' variety - both of which are dealt with on training courses, there are other kinds of leader skills which can be categorised by their type or nature:

- **awareness skills:** such as looking, listening, sensing and intuiting which is:
    - to do with **knowing** what is going on.

- **understanding skills:** such as analysing, diagnosing, inducting, deducing and prognosticating which implies having the necessary models, pertinent concepts and sensitive perception which is:
    - to do with **understanding** what is going on - in order to know what to do next.

- **adaptive skills:** such as having a range of real behavioural choices. Being aware of and able to control personal feelings will help to avoid being locked into one style of leading for example.
    - to do with being able to **respond flexibly** to situations.

Simon Priest's 'PEOPL' model[21] looks at the whole picture and classifies skills in another way under eight separate headings which I have re-grouped under 'things' and 'relationships' sub headings with a few illustrating examples for each. These are :

Things or Task Oriented

- Technical activity skills - navigation, packing a rucksack, camping, paddling, helming, rope handling etc.

- Safety skills - e.g. first aid, casualty evacuation, pace of slowest, appointing tail end, keeping group together, predicting, anticipating, awareness of difficulty, controlling and managing risk etc.

- Environmental skills - e.g. actively observing country code, reducing impact of group, recognising and avoiding sensitive areas.

❁ Organisational skills - e.g. planning, preparation, setting goals, setting tasks, managing time etc.

❁ Instructional skills - e.g. teaching, coaching, supporting, encouraging, demonstrating etc.

Relationships or People Oriented

❁ Problem solving skills - e.g. analysing, diagnosing, judging, decision making.

❁ Flexible leadership skills - the ability to use all styles appropriately e.g. directive, permissive, collaborative.

❁ Group management skills - e.g. listening, communicating, informing, mediating, compromising, delegating, praising, disciplining, motivating, resolving conflict etc.

All these classification methods are but tools to assist leaders with the identification and integration of them into personal practice. Only when they are known about, can they be built up into a usable framework, to be then fleshed out, improved and amended by experience. There is not space fully to do that here. In any case it is preferable that leaders evolve their own ways of meshing them into an interrelated, integrated structure. It will be the one that they understood best. Filling out of some of the more significant skills follows below, but for the most part the intention is mainly to raise levels of awareness about them and give some indication of their range, scope, depth and importance.

Planning and Forethought - Anticipation

Accidents are often the result of simple omissions arising out of poor planning and/or weak preparation. Prevention is better than having to find a cure. Good planning eradicates at a stroke, many potential causes of trouble. Perusal of the annual reports of rescue units quickly provides affirmation of this point. Many incidents occur through the neglect of some very basic precaution such as ensuring that suitable footwear is worn or equipment checked before use. Even something as basic as not ensuring or ascertaining everyone has had a decent breakfast could result in an incident. Urban lifestyles make breakfast less important because consequences can be quickly remedied there. Novice groups do not immediately realise that a heavy physical day will make unaccustomed demands on the body which needs to have been 'stoked up' more than usual.

Planning is as much a habit as it is a skill which will enable leaders to meet difficulties in a greater state of preparedness. It will often provide them with a ready made course of action when emergencies arise and will mean that the necessary resources to meet them are to hand too. It is of course, undesirable to go about continually expecting crisis after crisis. But it is wise to be ready for them when they happen and have a rough plan of action already prepared to meet them.

Typical examples would be, "What equipment am I likely to need on this expedition I am planning", or, "If someone had an accident here, what would I do?" and, "If something happened to me could the group cope?" Alternatively, "If I had to take this group down there, how long would it take and who would be the ones to watch?" or, "Where is the point of no return on this trip?" What is my alternative plan B?" if events conjoin to make it advisable not to pursue it further - like a shallow ankle deep river crossing likely to be a raging torrent after a rainy night. Anything over knee height of the smallest group member would be 'off limits' anyway.

"where is the point of no return on this trip?"

A law of hydrodynamics states that water running at twice normal speed can shift obstacles many times greater than double the size it could shift before it rose. Those two eminent naturalists, F. Fraser Darling and J.Morton Boyd in '*Highlands and Islands*', 1964, (pg 311) reckon that a current able to shift a one ounce pebble will be able to move a four pound boulder when the water velocity doubles!

Then there is the possibility of unseasonal snow such as fell in Lakeland on 2nd June 1975 or August 20th 2000 to sabotage plans or something as commonplace as transport having to pick you up earlier because it is needed elsewhere.

✿ But beware of over-planning and over-preparation. There is a point beyond which it chokes spontaneity both in the leader and the quality of the experience for the group. Be willing and able to flex and change when it is advantageous to do so. Once upon a time leaders were wary of digressing from the detailed planned route left behind in the hostel, camp or centre, whilst nowadays, notices pinned to minibuses merely invite their theft. With mobile phones it may be felt that, despite 'blind spots' and the inevitable discharged battery, there is, maybe, less need to feel bound by the planned route provided an updated risk assessment is made mentally about walking time required, sunset and darkness times, food supply and the group's fitness and so on. But it would be inadvisable to rely on a mobile phone to get you out of a jam. Digressions because of changing weather or minor injuries can be taken as read. It is the deviation caused by some attraction pulling the group off course that used to invite criticism and may still do so unless it is justifiable. A confident and capable leader should be able to do that.

❂ Unlike caving, river canoeing or piste skiing which operate in clearly defined or constrained places, where it is less easy for a group member to become separated and lost, for a walking group one easily overlooked piece of forethought is keeping the group informed about where it is, where it is headed and what are some of the names of the places, peaks and passes. Groups are very soon disorientated if they have not been very involved in the planning of a journey or tracking its progress on the map. Not really knowing where you are can be very disturbing. Knowing a few names gives the comforting illusion of making strange ground seem familiar. If one of the group should become detached or lost, both leader and the lost will have red faces when it becomes apparent that the strayer did not know whether s/he was in Langdale or Llanberis. It can be as basic as that.

Good Luck and Bad Luck

Even with the most perfect planning and preparation system for good practice and safety in place, there can still be incidents where good luck and bad luck have a say in the way events turn out - in determining whether an unexpected interlude remains an incident or whether an incident becomes an accident or deteriorates to the point of a fatality. Leaders should not allow this to induce a fatalistic attitude, "Whatever I do is pre-ordained so there is not much point in trying to prevent accidents" or "his/her number was up" or "the gods frowned on us" is populist mumbo-jumbo. Some say that bad luck is the culmination of a series of minor misjudgements and there are many recorded accidents illustrating this. But this is not invariably the case.

I was once traversing around the north side of Ill Bell above Troutbeck in South Lakeland with an adult group. The traverse line was going straightforwardly along a narrow path when we were confronted by an unexpected obstacle - a long gutter-like depression from the top of the slope to the bottom, normally scree filled, which we had to cross. It was choked with hard packed frozen snow. This steep snow-covered slope was about twenty yards wide. Two hundred feet lower down it ran out onto bare frozen scree, with a nasty rasp-like surface if slid over. Further progress required the chopping out of steps with an ice-axe to ensure none lost their footing on the snow and slid down onto the scree rasp. One of the group exasperated with the slowing of progress caused by the chopping of steps, or unable to appreciate what all the fuss was about, decided to by-pass above us all and charged onto the steep hard snow where he only then suddenly realised what the danger was. He was told to freeze until he could be reached and a platform was chopped out for him to stand on. If I had been unlucky he could have panicked or moved his feet a fraction and he would have been away. It had never crossed my mind to explain to the group what the difficulty was and what my reasons were for taking pains to improve the footing - they could all see the problem, I thought. If I had, the incident might not have occurred. Was I neglectful or reasonable in assuming that everyone appreciated the nature of the hazard and was it luck that the situation did not become serious. Winter is the time when the weather is more likely to pull sneaky tricks. A "Call 999" series on TV in the early 1990s recounting various accidents on land, air and water was full of degrees of luck.

Planning in Highlights

All leaders want their groups to have enjoyable experiences. This causes some leaders to try to plan into the programme what they call 'positive' experiences. They also plan to avoid negative ones. It should be noted that though this is laudable and understandable, it is to a certain extent unattainable for everyone in the group. The old dictum that "One man's meat is another man's poison" has an application in the outdoors. An individual's perception about what constitutes adventure or enjoyment is quite subjective and personal to the extent that one person's idea of challenge can be quite different from someone else's. Some will revel in the challenge and exhilaration of wild, wet days, rocky scrambles or long treks into remote places. Others will be turned off by them. Dark, wet, cold caves or the look of very turbulent waters when afloat can have a similar effect. This point was touched on earlier in the management of risk in chapter 7.

Checking

Cultivate this skill until it becomes a habit.

✿ Check that both the leader and the group have the necessary food, clothing and equipment before setting off. In a concern for others, leaders should beware of forgetting to check that their own gear is complete. It happens sometimes.

✿ Check that any instructions given are heard, understood and obeyed. This is obvious and should be basic but it is often neglected, particularly in the informal, fluid circumstances that are characteristic of parties outdoors. Noise from strong winds, rain on anorak hoods, rushing rivers or streams, inattention simply caused by the distraction of people moving about are features common to many types of outdoor situation; they all affect the hearing quite considerably.

✿ Check how things are going with the party. With practice this becomes a 'sense' that is always 'switched on'. If the leader is at the front, there should be frequent looking back. It is so easy to forge on unaware of the mounting chaos behind. Taking a head count now and again is a good idea - the bigger the group the more frequent it should be.

Observation, Perception and Interpretation

These skills are supplementary to the habit of checking. Together they constitute the foundation of the leader's system of control. The leader needs to know what is going on around - in the environment and in the group. Seeing and checking what is going on gives that knowledge. The ability to perceive things varies greatly in people. Work to improve it. This is one of those skills where, if it is desired hard enough, it will happen.

"It is so easy to forge on unaware of the mounting chaos behind."

❂ Be aware that observation and its co-partner, perception, is often selective too. Like a self-fulfilling prophesy, one often only sees what one expects or wants to see.

Try to avoid tuning to particular wave-lengths, as it were, and keep the 'receiver' wide open. In practice this means not jumping too quickly to conclusions about what you see or being too judgemental about what will happen. This is not as easy as it sounds. Being 'tuned' to everything is rather like being tuned to nothing and akin to the feeling of being switched off. Learn to distinguish between the two states. Listen for the 'static'!

❂ Perception is followed by an almost compulsive process of interpretation, a desire to assign meaning to what is observed. It is too easy to make a prediction and jump to conclusions. This is a fine ethical problem where it is difficult to know whether to judge an action by the intention that caused it or by the effect it produced. When observing behaviour, people tend to interpret and judge it on the grounds of what they see or feel - the effect it has on them or the consequences it has for other people. What they do not see often are the causes of that behaviour or the motives that drove it. These can often put things in a very different light. Sometimes hostility between people in a group bursts out in violence. The leader sees furniture broken, tents torn, or others kept awake by the din. In the heat of the moment, incorrect motives may be read in to the events observed. It may seem on the face of it to be one of many varieties of delinquent behaviour - wanton damage, mindless violence, vandalism, bullying, inconsiderate anti-social behaviour. It is important to find out the real reason. It may not have been the pecking order type of aggression on the offensive, but prove to have been a defensive, inner act of survival, or a reaction to severe provocation. The link between cause and effect is often quite different from what one imagines it to be. The trick is to avoid being too judgmental too early and, providing circumstances permit, allow more time for things to reveal their true nature.

The practical point for leaders here is that, just as their judgement skills in more concrete, physical situations in the outdoors can be improved, so can their skills in relationship situations be honed by keeping simple records for a time about their impressions and expectations of events occurring in their groups and the decisions and actions to which those events gave rise.

✪ It is mainly by observation that a leader will get to know the characteristics, strengths and weaknesses of each member of the party. Although a lot of chat may be exchanged with the group, it is the non-verbal sounds, facial expressions and body signals that will provide the needed knowledge about conditions in the group. Mainly by observation will the leader become aware of signs of tiredness, boredom, low morale, tension, anxiety stresses, personality conflicts, acute discomforts, feelings of insecurity, lack of a sense of balance, lack of powers of coordination, sloppy, uneconomic, energy-consuming footwork and so on.

" It may seem....to be one of the many varieties
of delinquent behaviour."

It is important to be tuned in to the positive signals too which tend to be overlooked because they do not represent trouble like the negatives. All these signs and many others, leaders will usually have to discern for themselves, for the members of the group will tend not to want to say anything about them. The pressure of a group on the move, for example, is a palpable thing and may cause people within the group to feel reluctant to slow it down, or stop it. The leader may have to find out by asking direct questions. It is a simple matter to give them an opening by making it clear that their comfort or enjoyment is as equally important as pushing on.

⚙ The need to keep observing the environment is basic and should be obvious. Continuously assess its implications for the party in terms of enjoyment and pleasure, danger and effort. On land, assess the terrain and which routes offer most interest, protection from head winds, reasonable footing - not always footpaths which may be badly eroded or dotted with greasy rocks or interrupted by unbridged streams requiring to be crossed. Watch out for changes in the weather such as mist on land or fog at sea; and particularly for water borne activities, be aware of changes in the strength or direction of the wind, rising water levels and accelerating currents, tidal or otherwise. Many of these have implications for requiring greater energy outputs from a group.

Instructing and Coaching....

Since the two terms are often and mistakenly used interchangeably, it is useful to know that 'Instructing' is about establishing a skill and 'Coaching' is about improving and fine tuning it. Unless leaders come from a physical education background which gave them training in the teaching of 'physical' skills, they tend to be conditioned by the way the training scheme in their chosen activity treats the skills of instructing and coaching and how a person acquires a skill. Such leaders tend, understandably, to teach in the way they were taught. There probably aren't many leaders left who still do the land-drill that purported to help novice canoeists learn how to handle a double-ended paddle! But that was the recommended method for introducing beginners at one time.

In the matter of learning physical skills, it is prudent to give some learners time to assimilate the skill. Some seem to manage it effortlessly and instantly; some need to think themselves through whatever movement is required whilst others 'visualise' themselves doing it - much in the manner of modern athletes in competition; some need to understand the theory before trying to put it into practice. When learning to roll a canoe, some learners doing this 'thinking through' seem to tie themselves in knots, get completely screwed up and inhibit any improvement in performance. Others try alternative ways like hanging by their bent legs from a beam or bar, even the edge of a table or chair (held by someone), anything which helps them get the 'feel' of what has happened to the world when they turn upside down. Sometimes when all else fails, the answer is to "relax, think of nothing and do it" - it does work. I came late to swimming and by the time I was twenty three I had never dived into a swimming pool - even off the side! Struggling to overcome all sorts of mind blocks one day on the side of the pool a friend said, "Think of nothing and fall in headfirst." It worked! I know of a few eminent personages in the outdoor world who tried this method when attempting to roll a canoe and came up so fast they nearly capsized on the other side again!

Leaders of walking groups can gain considerable insight into the level of skill in terms of the balance and coordination of the group by observing them as they cross over a stile. Some move over easily with hands in pockets, others fumble for the hand rail or catch a toe on a step. Of particular interest should be how they descend the other side as descent is a skill most likely to be lacking in the range of skills they need to have. Who has to sit down on each step and lower themselves cautiously down, who skips down unconcerned - and all conditions in between the extremes? A convenient sloping slab of rock at the right angle, at ground level, without the troubling factor of height, can be a good coaching place to practise the correct distribution of body weight on the feet and build up confidence in descending skills.

Historically, the received body of wisdom regarding the theory and practice of the acquisition of physical skill exists within the public sector of education, in Physical Education. But amateur governing bodies of outdoor sports were not a part of this at one time. Without access to, or disregarding developments in currently accepted theory, these bodies tended to become outdated and insular in their approach to skill-coaching. Operating from the simple belief that the quickest way to achieve proficiency and competence in a skill is the method that appears to be the most direct and straightforward way, they put their belief in traditional, didactic, directive methods. Most coaching methods geared to improving physical performance in most activities conformed to this model. I remember BCU coaches horrified at the sight of 'play' discovery approaches to skill sessions and failing instructors, under test for an award, for using them. The ski-school was the typical stereotype of the approach with its stylised regimentation, involving lots of time standing watching others, and pursuit of the perfect 'end form' movement. The RYA had its official 'method' for teaching sailing.

Things eventually changed for the better, however, and there is, for example, a book of games designed specifically to improve canoeing skills. But the residual net effect of the past on many leaders is that the process of coaching a skill is assumed to be purely physical in nature. Sometimes it is, but sometimes it is not. Olympic Coaches, for example, now place considerable emphasis on their athletes developing powers of concentration and 'visualising' themselves performing a skill. Zen is alive and kicking! Skiing adopted some of these internalised techniques with the idea of 'inner skiing' like skiing blindfolded over short stretches of easy-angled snow to develop awareness of where the body weight is, or should be, when turning.

....and Supporting

In situations where people are experiencing difficulty or distress, the reason or cause of that is often not obvious. It is therefore hard for a leader to decide what the right kind of assistance should be. Because of this, the skills of coaching and supporting are often poorly executed. Analytical observation or remembering past experience and feelings can often help a decision about what kind of help to give. How often is advice given about walking skills when ascending and especially descending? If it is given, is it given to everybody or only to those in need who are making heavy weather of it?

How much use is the advice to "try and keep a rhythm", or "try to conserve energy"? In these cases the need is to give the person a tip about "how to do it". Advice must mean something quite specific in terms of what sort of movement to make which will result in an action that will affect the appropriate group of muscles.

For the canoeist learning a support stroke, advice to press upwards with the knee opposite to the paddle in the water will bring a greater feeling of stability.

A model of a difficult movement to master is turning on skis because it is an unnatural movement. For the learner skier, the tip to, "Press down with the outside big toe", will help the ski to turn more effectively than the usual, "bend zee knees" which usually resulted in the skier's body piking at the waist with legs remaining obdurately straight and stiff.

For the hill walker, "Put your feet down flat" or "get off your toes" or "push up with the heel instead of the ball of the foot" or "look for flat spots to place your feet" will bring relief. If there are no flat spots, "put your heel on small bumps or stones to lift it up and make the foot more horizontal".

Negotiating an awkward move as when crossing a stream on stones, stepping across a gap or when moving up or down a rocky scramble, are similar situations where decisions have to be made about whether advice is enough. "Trust your feet" or "use that hold there" might suffice for some. But bellowing correct instructions to others may be quite inappropriate since a deeper level of emotional support may be needed such as, "take my hand" or "hold onto my rucksack strap" or "I'm right behind you". Will getting out the rope intensify anxiety or relieve it? It may decrease the leader's but will it add to theirs?

Unfortunately these days the question of 'touching', which no leader once needed to think about, needs approaching with sensitivity lest accusations of abuse ensue. Where touching is likely it is advisable for the leader to outline to the person the reasons for it even though it may seem obvious, to avoid possible shock or surprise and misinterpretation of the supportive actions.

Some leader training schemes did not pay a great deal of attention to the skills of teaching or coaching in the past. This was the case because it was known that the majority of people electing to do leader training then were themselves either teachers or youth leaders. The policies and contexts which created those earlier conditions began to change radically in the 1980s and '90s to create a different future. The arrival of national vocational qualifications (NVQs) for people wanting to work with groups out-of-doors made career paths more accessible to individuals who were outside the two traditional public sector sources for recruitment to leader training. The newly established Learning Skills Council now also assists in this process. It has therefore become more necessary to lay a greater emphasis on teaching and coaching skills in schemes of training in order to maintain quality in leading and managing groups. This will be no bad thing in any case. It is often forgotten that, whilst teachers and youth leaders may have been trained to teach, they are not likely to have been trained in the arts of coaching and teaching physical skills. Whilst there are some resemblances, is not quite the same thing. Quite different capacities and skills in the other hemisphere of the brain are entailed. Writing this revision in March 2004 it would seem that coaching is moving up the agenda of various National Governing Bodies with talk of identifying 'generic skills in coaching'. It will be interesting to see what transpires.

Insight

One of a leader's most invaluable aids in coaching and supporting will be the **ability to recall past experience**, particularly feelings when a beginner. It will enable a leader to appreciate and to be more acutely aware that, if there are occasions now which are felt to be personally extending in the slightest bit, there will be some in the group in whom these feelings will be greatly magnified. This kind of recall whereby one is able to put oneself in another person's shoes, facilitates 'insight'. Probable examples are fearfulness when negotiating sections of rocky scrambling or narrow paths across steep slopes or steep descents, feelings of cold, hunger, thirst and fatigue to which a leader is more likely to be acclimatised than the group. Insight is partly rooted in some degree of self awareness and sensitivity to others, but it can be developed by the frequent reflection and evaluation of personal experiences.

In recalling past experience to aid a coaching problem, it would be a mistake always to equate it with personal technical skill. The, "I found it easy, why can't you?" type of response is narrow and lacking in understanding and empathy.

It is the personal recollection of <u>feelings</u> at moments of great personal challenge or during times of stress, such as when very fatigued or frightened, that are of greater importance for leaders since they are the very foundation for empathy with others in stressful situations.

If such feelings of struggling and inadequacy have never been experienced by, say, a very able and athletic leader, such a person will have to work very hard indeed to imagine what it feels like.

It will be remembered that in the chapter on risk, the perception of risk and its attendant feelings was seen to be an intensely personal thing which varies greatly in people. Leaders seeing youngsters faltering over a physical movement or skill should not hastily view it as a purely technical problem but recognise it as perhaps an emotional one requiring a very different set of responses from them. (see examples in the preceding section on 'supporting')

Problem Solving - Needs/Wants - Rules

One of the things the leader of a group is often called upon to deal with is helping the group to come to terms with the conflict between its needs and its wants. What you **want** is not always what you need. A minibus group travelling from home to a distant campsite may want to stop at every motorway cafe they meet for a drink or snack. But they may **need** to arrive at the campsite early enough to avoid the difficulties of setting up camp in the dark in a strange place. A leader's task will be to help a group to understand and accept this. It will be just as important that the outcome is achieved without seriously impairing the leader - group relationships. It is very easy for a leader feeling the pressure of responsibility and able, from experience perhaps, to foresee the consequences of bad decisions, to override objections and protests and heavy handedly decide needs come before wants. Leaders have to be able to judge whether such autocratic decisions will result in serious reactions from the group or just minor grumbles because they do in fact see the sense of it.

There are times when wants may have to come before needs, especially in the early history of a group, when to deny wants may so seriously affect relationships that it would be unwise to do so. Wants tend to be short-term and needs tend to be long-term in nature. But the denial of a short term want could be long term in its effect on relationships in a group!

Sometimes it is the needs of others quite outside the group that have to be considered. A common example is after the end of camp with people neglecting or unwilling to do all the equipment maintenance jobs such as drying tents, cleaning utensils and crockery, repairing damage and replacing missing items. The next group to use the gear will need it to be serviceable. The current group may want to dash off now, because there is a special T.V. programme or an important local soccer match it wants to see now and leave everything for 'somebody' else to do. It is quite prepared to ignore the needs of some unknown group in the future. How a leader resolves these difficult choices will exercise a key influence on the future life of the group. It may even bring about its demise. To release the group unconditionally is a 'group win, leader lose' situation. To insist they stay is a 'leader win, group loses' situation. The ideal situation is where everybody wins. One possible solution would be for the leader and group to agree to disperse now, but promise to re–assemble at an agreed time in the future to complete the job. The old amusing tale comes to mind that leaders may be able to use in a 'situation' one day about four people named Everybody, Somebody, Anybody and Nobody:

"There was an important job to be done and Everybody was sure that Somebody would do it. Anybody could have done it, but Nobody did it. Somebody got angry about that because it was Everybody's job. Everybody thought Anybody could do it, but Nobody realised that Everybody wouldn't do it. It ended up that Everybody blamed Somebody when actually Nobody accused Anybody."

The conflict between needs and wants is often to be seen in the process of making rules to demarcate the limits of acceptable group behaviour. The older the group, the more important is it to involve the group in the formulation of them. Detailed discussion about the need for a particular rule will ensure that at least everyone understands the reasons for it. Negotiation about the particular form a rule assumes is more likely to ensure that it is observed. If it is not, then the group has to look at why and may become involved in a whole range of moral discoveries to do with trust, group loyalty, how to deal with disobedience, the nature of punishment and justice and so on - which is just as important for young people to know about as how to read a map or cope with moving water on a river. 'Doing' types may find this difficult to accept. But it is important to remember that, **above all, one is teaching people not a subject.**

Judgement

Judgement involves the application of intelligence to a problem in order to:

a) assemble all the facts and factors which bear on a situation.
b) identify and consider the options this information reveals. This will be the specific, relevant information necessary to enable a correct decision to be made about selecting from many possibilities.
c) decide on which is the right course of action needed to solve the problem.

The skill of accurate judgement is greatly dependent upon the quality and quantity of past experience. But this experience-base is of limited value unless it has been processed in an internal reviewing procedure[23] which sifts, measures, analyses, synthesises, evaluates and draws conclusions from the facts of the experiences. It can be further enhanced by the creative use of the imagination to visualise situations where similar circumstances might exist in different permutations of degree or even sequence. Drawing up a critical path analysis of causes and effects for a developing situation is a roughly comparable example. The diagram of the risk taking process in chapter 7 can be viewed as a critical path analysis exercise. These acts of processing provide a more conscious store of information in the memory from which to develop criteria and standards which are used to help estimate the value, nature and significance of conditions confronted at some time in the future. Information is required in this form to enable predictions about possible outcomes to be made.

Judgement is often a matter of comparing questions of degree. How closely does this compare with the last time? A simple example is when the map shows there are five kilometres still to walk which one can normally expect to take about an hour. But there are other factors present to be taken into account. There is a strong head wind, it is towards the end of the day, and the group is tiring. The memory is scanned for previous similar circumstances and similar groups to enable you to estimate how long it is likely to take this group to cover the distance. You judge it is going to be longer than you would like, and a short cut would help matters greatly. So, "If I took this short cut down here I could probably save half an hour. The angle of the slope is fairly steep and the group could probably manage it. But because of the angle of slope, the ground surface needs to give a good grip for the feet. From experience I know that bracken, tallish grass or a soft surface would help. But this is hard with very short turf and wet from that last shower. Nasty! I predict the consequences of trying to descend it could be greater than the problem I'm trying to solve. Better leave it." Or on another day, "There is no wind down here but I see those clouds up there are moving very fast. I remember noticing that once and finding it pretty wild on the tops. These clouds are moving even faster than that time. Maybe I should not take this group of beginners that high on their first trip out today." Or, "The last time we went sailing/canoeing with the waves that high, we were lucky to get back. And they were a good group - this is not. Better postpone it."

Judgement relies heavily on a person's ability to analyse situations. Present in any situation are hundreds of factors to be scanned and identified. The problem and the skill is to discern those factors whose effects will be the most significant in a chosen course of action. Skill in being able to correlate all such vital factors is also needed. No situation is ever exactly the same. Previous successful solutions will not necessarily prove workable again. The ability to see why quickly, is a great asset. It cannot be emphasised too strongly or often enough that the path to success in this area lies in frequent, conscientious reflection and evaluation of one's experiences. Becoming wiser after the event can be used to develop a future sound, judgmental skill.

❂ The really difficult times are those when the leader is on the fringe of known experience, when previous experience is not much help.

"The really difficult times are when the leader is on the fringe of known experience."

Being able to control feelings of insecurity and anxiety caused by the unknown or doubts is a definite requirement in leaders. It is very similar to recognising when all of a whole group must be on the edge of its experience.

I discovered this one winter's day in the early 1970s coming off Hartsop Dodd south of Ullswater with a hazard that could not be avoided and questions in my mind as to whether the group would be able to cope. The route down normally crosses a steepish grassy slope downwards and leftwards to the ridge which leads down from the top of the Dodd to a descending wall lower down which is followed to the valley floor. Normally uncomplicated. This day the slope to be traversed was hard packed snow with a long smooth run-out below to the wall - an unavoidable and unwelcome backstop to a long slide if one slipped! Higher up there had been no sign of frozen snow all day. This north facing ridge without sun combined with it being a windy place to produce conditions specific to its location and quite unexpected. Getting off the top would involve an awkward descending traverse of about thirty to forty yards (no metres then) with an awareness of considerable exposure below.

It was near the end of a winter's day with darkness not all that far off so reversing tracks to an alternative and rather distant descent point was out of the question, particularly as the group of eight fifteen year old schoolgirls, who had had a full and enjoyable day in the snow up high, were tiring and would be in no condition to back-track.

They all had ice axes but had not yet practised self arrest. Any solution had to be better and safer than reversing the route for an hour or two (at least) in darkness. Cut steps would be necessary for the traverse bit. But how to protect each individual across the exposed slope which would require a good sense of balance, cool nerve and an ability to drive in the axe on the uphill side as a potential anchor to prevent a slip? Could they do it? The only protection available was 120 ft of number two hawser nylon rope, the standard practice 'emergency' rope for a hill-walking group then. A handrail was out of the question as it would be too long and too inclined to sag to be effective. There was also the chance that anyone slipping might not be able to hang on long enough to get back up. If they tied into a rope held by me it would have to be singly - more than one ran the risk of one bringing down others on the rope. Even if just the one came off there could be a long pendulum. This method would mean my having to take the rope back to those still waiting their turn each time it became vacant. All this would be very time consuming and time in abundance we did not have.

Eventually options boiled down to cutting generous steps for each to use as they were individually shepherded across by me standing below them. They all did very well and we were soon off the bad bit and thankfully on our way. I suppose you could say I had good luck as well that day. Meeting an unavoidable hazard on the edge of the group's experience is one of the occasions when the risk taking capacity of the leader is called upon because solutions are not 100% bombproof - we've all had to do it at sometime - so be ready for it one day!

Faced by something quite new or unknown, a leader may first have to screw down anxiety before the mind can begin to observe properly and apply the processes of induction, deduction and maybe intuition, to unzip possible causes, consequences and implications. A good imagination may even be of assistance here - or it might not!

❂ Sometimes it is difficult beforehand to decide what kind of moral value to put on a course of action because it is in the sphere of conflicting bipolar values. By this I mean when an action can be judged to be either foolhardy and reckless, or courageous and strong depending on the point of view. Another act can be either cautious and wise, or cowardly and weak. How does one decide which it is? The fear of being judged wrongly by others, or the desire to be judged fairly, is not to be lightly dismissed. Sometimes all there is to help is the integrity of personal inner resources and convictions - aims and goals again! Leaders have to be able to justify their actions articulately to themselves as well as others.

Decision-Making Methods

Decisions stem from judgement and are meant to promote action to resolve problems or achieve aims. Since leaders have to make decisions about how decisions are made, it will be useful to describe the various ways in which decisions can be made. In no order of priority they are:

❂ **By authority without discussion:** as when 'authority' makes a decree. It is quick and efficient for emergencies when time is short and speed important. But it may not be very effective if the group who has to implement the decision does not fully understand it or feel involved in it. Motivation is likely to be low or even non existent if they do not agree with it.

✪ **By an expert member:** who 'pronounces' a verdict or opinion. This may be fine for some situations but how do you tell, or ever know, who is the expert? In most outdoor situations where a technical problem is posed, it is likely to be the adult leading the young people who has the technical expertise. But in a peer group as found with Award expedition groups it is not so obvious. Popularity may be substituted for expertise. Individuals with power tend to overestimate their expertise. With a group of adults the leader may be obvious, providing it is a technical problem, but if non technical matters are the issue, confusion may arise as to where decision making power lies. But overall, this method is better than the next one.

✪ **By an average of members' opinions:** this is rather like majority voting. A straw poll is taken to find the popular view. The most common opinion is unlikely to be in the majority. Also, the best opinion may be cancelled out by an ignorant or uninformed view. Because opinions are not allowed to interact and modify each other, decision making is likely to be of a low order. Motivation and commitment, despite apparent consultation will be poor too.

✪ **By authority after discussion:** since the leader initiates the process in calling a meeting to present a problem requiring solution, the group is aware that a rough decision has already been made and that the function of their contribution is merely to approve or modify it slightly. The final decision will still be made by the leader so the sense of involvement is weak. Leaders using this method need to be good listeners in order that the eventual decision benefits fully from what the group says. Members may also try to impress the leader or tell him what they think s/he wants to hear.

✪ **By majority control:** this is such a common, taken-for-granted feature in our society that it is used thoughtlessly without a real understanding of the implications of the 'numbers game' that is being played when the winner is the 51% 'first past the post' or the sub group with most votes. The 'most' win but many more can lose. It is sometimes even a minority which makes the decision. The famous example being the Referendum voting which propelled the UK into the European Community in the early 1970s when the total of 'don't knows' and 'against' was greater than the 'yeas' and which, wondrous to relate, was hardly mentioned or commented on by the media. Unlike the electoral system however, in this method minority opinions are not always respected and may be brow beaten by the winners. 'Yes/No' thinking is raised to such a sacred level that it creates blindness, irrational, polarised argument and discourages the consideration of viable alternatives. As a method for deciding rules where it is important that everyone agrees, it is patently unsuitable. Effective majority decision making requires that everyone feels they had a fair hearing.

✪ **By minority control:** known as an 'oligarchy' in which a sub group such as a committee is given authority to decide. This is useful when there is not enough time to shift a lot of business or when the consequences are not too serious if poor decisions are made. But there are risks that only the decision makers are committed to the course of action and resistance from the rest may be passive or positively reactionary. This type of decision making also occurs when a powerful sub group attempts to 'railroad' through a proposition. The manner of the railroading not only denies people enough time to think, but may make some afraid to speak out against it. The danger then is that silence is read as consent whereas in reality, silence develops into a form of underground resistance.

✪ **By consensus:** a thorough ventilation of the problem and all points of view about it, permits the group to reach a point that is agreeable to all. i.e. all win. This is the most effective method for decision making which involves the resolution of conflicts and controversies, but it is time consuming and requires a high degree of member skill and energy. High quality decisions ensue from this method.

Since all are fully involved, the degree of motivation and commitment to carry out the decision is high. Duke of Edinburgh Award groups, for example, consisting of peers, would find the consensus method of decision making perhaps best suited to their situation when on expedition.

Group Decision-Making

Group decision making confers benefits which, by contrast, are absent when only a single person is making a decision. There is an exchange and use of a greater diversity of information and hence a stimulation of new thoughts.

There is likely to be increased motivation since the weaker members will tend to imitate and compare themselves with peers felt to be of higher ability.

There is a feeling of more support and encouragement than when on one's own. Members will feel a greater accountability to the others, therefore group loyalty will increase.

There is more motivation to rethink if one meets disagreement with one's own view. The processing of information whereby it is rehearsed and elaborated increases its meaning, facilitates comprehension, imparts a deeper level of understanding and aids its retention.

Insight is gained into a variety of ways in which to view the decision. Security of numbers creates a willingness to adopt more extreme or dynamic positions than would an individual alone. But good decisions also depend on how effective the group is. The quality of their relationships, which largely depends on how much respect they have for each other and how much tolerance and trust there is amongst them, will affect their ability to communicate well, resolve conflicts and disagreements, define goals and agree on a course of realistic action to achieve them.

A group is effective when it is able to set high but achievable goals. Then it is motivated to achieve, and is willing and able to take responsibility for itself. But this desirable state of affairs might only apply to one specific situation and not necessarily to other tasks. It is possible for a group to be highly mature in the pursuit of one task and low for another task - 'peaks and troughs' again.

"Security of numbers creates a willingness to
adopt more extreme or dynamic positions."

An effective decision is one where:
- time and the resources of the whole group are fully used;
- the decision is implemented fully by all the group or those designated;
- the future problem solving ability of the group is not inhibited by further sets of grievances or problems created by the present decision.

Factors Hindering Group Decision-Making

Whilst there are many advantages to be derived from group decision making it is as well to be aware of certain negative aspects.

These relate to group decision making which will minimise those benefits. Here is a brief review of them.

❂ If the group has only had a short time to get to know each other, this will reduce the degree of group maturity. It is after the passing of the 'storming' phase that groups tend to mature and work more effectively. When the personal goals of members conflict with those of the group, this will slow down, impoverish the decision or even prevent it. When such goals are undeclared they are known as 'hidden agendas' and may or may not thus sabotage the group's efforts, cause conflict or disruption. Hidden agendas are always present and should be accepted as legitimate - not to be complained about or scolded for having them. Consensus agreement about group goals would help avoid this sort of negative situation.

❂ The failure of individuals, because of shyness, laziness or reluctance, to participate equally, or their inability to communicate well, listen and use information will cause resentment, disharmony or suspicion.

❁ Self centred outlooks of members unable to step outside the limits of their own prejudices and attitudes will cause side issues to arise which will conflict with, and detract attention from, more serious matters.

❁ Pressure sometimes comes from individuals to reach agreement too quickly or prematurely. This may take the form of compromises pushed too early before there has been time for a realistic appraisal of a problem; or seeking solutions before the problem is understood; or the quick suppression of disagreement or the stifling of discussion which might give rise to possible conflict.

❁ An insufficient diversity of types of people might not provide the desirable and necessary variety of skills and outlooks for a richer, wider interaction. Leaders need to monitor the quality of dialogue in case a poor discussion otherwise doomed to flop, would benefit from their helping input.

❁ Those unskilled in the art of discussion will experience interference with, or blocking of, their contributions to discussion because they are unable to find a slot for it at the right time. Ground rules for holding and taking part in a discussion may be needed.

❁ Groups larger than eight or nine will tend to be held in thrall by the dominant ones. Inappropriate group size will gravitate against the involvement of everyone.

❁ Many groups have in-built power structures that have appeared early in the group's life. These cause power differences or inequalities between members. When this occurs, fear, defensiveness and distrust inhibit frank and open exchange.

Time Requirements for Decisions

Diagram 9 below illustrates the fact that group processes also take quite a lot of time so there needs to be as much time as a particular task of decision making requires to be properly carried through. The size of the group affects the process too; the bigger the group, the more time is needed. But size is not everything and sometimes it is the depth or seriousness of a controversy that is the determining factor in the time needed.

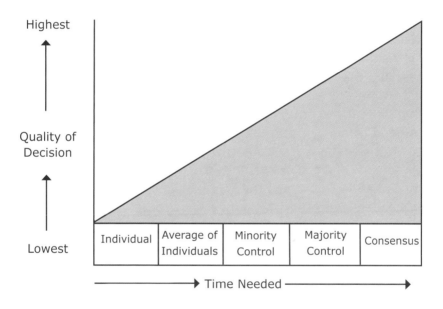

Diagram 9. Time requirement related to
the number making the decision

Skill and Practice for Group Decision-Making

Good decision-making by groups is only feasible when members possess the necessary skills and motivation to work collaboratively, which means they must be able to communicate effectively and manage conflicts constructively and not sabotage group efforts. Leaders of groups of young people should be aware that these skills do not arrive overnight and that, like every other skill, they require practice. Young groups learning these skills will make plenty of mistakes as they fumble towards competence in this arena. So leaders will need lots of patience and understanding as they witness much frustration in the group and must be quite convinced about the value of time spent learning decision making. Leaders may be tempted to wait until the group is more mature before permitting group participation in these important functions. It is so easy to say that the time is not yet right. But when will the time ever be right for acquiring this important skill? The answer has to be that the time must nearly always be right.

A good leader will normally try to get the group participating in as many decisions as is consistent with safety, and as is compatible with their age and ability. For example, the group could be given the chance to say what sort of things they would like to see or do on a particular day. Leaders too often think they know best and maybe sometimes they do. But people of any age like to feel that they have discovered or decided some things for themselves.

A group of remedial youngsters were quite determined in their desire to be in dinghies on Lake Windermere on a day so wild and windy that the staff had already written off sailing in the programme for the day. But these youngsters would not be shifted from their aim. 'Swallows and Amazons Forever' had nothing on this lot. Continuing good relationships required some kind of 'all win' compromise to be found. The eventual answer was to allow the group to row the dinghies in the lee of a convenient headland. Whenever the dinghies began to drift into wilder water, the safety boat towed them back into calmer waters to carry on. Staff on their own would never have dreamed up such a day believing it to be too low a level of involvement. The youngsters had a great day and got a lot from it.

Feedback from group planning sessions are invaluable to the leader in providing insight into the level of student aspiration and ambition and of what they think they are capable. This may not be as feasible with some novice groups. But much can be done by skilful prompting to help them identify their expectations and feel involved. Often when people are asked what they want to do, they just do not know. It is necessary to spell out in some detail the choices that are available. It is rather like dressing a shop window. One of the outdoor leader skills is to be able to identify for a novice group, a choice of objectives in such a way that degrees of challenge and/or attractiveness are readily apparent: "Would you like to visit a small lake surrounded by trees and bushes halfway up a hill today, or scramble up a rocky ravine with a stream running down it, or walk uphill for three hours to reach a high rocky summit with great views?"

"The youngsters had a great day and got a lot out of it."

When alternatives are involved, it is a shrewd move to itemise the implications of a particular choice or course of action because it is probable that coming to them 'cold', the group will not have had time to realise the consequences such as the amount of preparation needed, or the time required to do it or the effort it will entail.

More experienced groups are quite likely to have ideas about what they want to do which will be useful, not only for gearing up their sense of commitment, but for providing the leader, often incidentally, with feedback on their assessment of themselves.

The 'dressing the shop window' idea has useful applications in other situations. For example, when faced by setbacks or minor disasters many youngsters do not really know how to respond, so they react. All they have to rely on are their gut reactions which are more than likely to be unproductive. A leader can help everyone at a crucial time in providing the needed information.

This would be by pointing out the various ways that are open to them to respond to a situation and asking which one it is going to be. Positive choices are usually made when the information base is comprehensive. When some of the tents blow down, group members have the choice of blaming each other or the leader for not checking properly, blaming the wind which won't listen and anyway the wind that did it is miles away now, blaming the pegs for bending or pulling out, or if they ever hope to spend a comfortable night, making the best of a bad job by pitching in (no pun intended) to re-erect the tents as quickly as possible. If they finish their own tent soon, is it better to scramble into it out of the wind and wet, or instead, help others less fortunate to complete theirs as well?

This was a real life situation and the decision making that resulted from laying out the choice of alternatives before them was very surprising and pleasing. Often for young people, the choices are not obvious until pointed out. The way through a morass of emotions to reasoned productive behaviour is not always easy to see.

General Note on Quality of Decision-Making

What makes a high or low quality decision is fine in theory, but in the real world we are not often in possession of all the facts; we are not usually aware of all the good or bad consequences of our decisions; we are not as rational as we would like to think either, because our decisions are often based on rationalisations of emotional stances which decided the way we would go before we even realised it. We are rarely sure of the rightness of a decision and are usually worried or doubtful about it. We often look for the line of least resistance, the answer that will cause least trouble/upset, or have minimal impact or the solution that requires least effort and resources so is the most easily carried out. We sometimes prefer to do nothing because change creates a fearful uncertainty about the future and so we carry on regardless as before. Sometimes, by contrast, we hope a change might work a miracle and opt for it without really comprehending the consequences. If we are faced with a number of unattractive alternatives we are likely to feel that we are damned if we do and damned if we don't, so we waste time, put it off, delay, pass the buck, anything to avoid the stress of the controversial decision. The 'down' side of consensus decision making is that in trying to design a horse one might end up with a camel! Trip to the Sahara anyone?

Achievement Versus Group

One of the difficult major planning decisions to resolve always is whether the make-up of a group should be determined by the nature of the objective such as a designated hill ("it's a long day so only the fitter ones qualify to go"). Or should the nature of that hill to be climbed, its distance, height, roughness, remoteness, be determined by the structure of the group, the number of members in it, their age, experience, skill and ability. Do you only recruit/select the few elite performers to accompany you on a difficult journey? If the number of members in the group are too many, do you reduce them for a testing objective? If the characteristics of the group are very variable, do you take them all but select an objective within the capacity of the lowest denominator? Since the variety and range of objectives or challenges available for choice is almost infinite and since the members who present themselves in front of you to form a group is often already predetermined, there should not be much doubt about which alternative to adopt.

Other outdoor activities have their own particular type of 'hill' to deal with. A river to be canoed will be assessed for its remoteness, access points, length, general water speed, roughness and frequency of rapids, clear or obstructed banks. A ski slope will be scrutinised for its steepness, the depth, texture and condition of the snow, open or restrictive spaces for manoeuvring, density of other skiers and so on.

It is usually much easier to match the challenge to the group than it is to match the group to the challenge. Group discussion about the objective for the day should facilitate the resolution of this problem in the early stages of planning. During any journey over land or water, there are many decisions in which the group should be encouraged to participate such as, when to stop for lunch, where to go next, identifying landmarks, who navigates next or takes the helm, and even whether to go on or not.

Crisis Management

It is the emergency/crisis decisions that are the particular province and concern of the leader. If the skills and habits already outlined have been developed strongly enough, the business of personal decision making by the leader should be half accomplished already. For the big important decisions relating to the group's safety, the relevant factors will have been already observed or anticipated. It is then a question of using past experience to assess all the factors, for and against, and picking out the best course of action from a number of possible alternatives.

Emergencies are a special case however:

Coping with an emergency situation, 'crisis management' as it is sometimes called, is a good example of a 'frontier' experience referred to earlier. If it occurs suddenly and unexpectedly in the form of an accident, it will be an unusual leader who does not experience some shock caused by the realisation of the need to shift from a relatively relaxed state of mind into the 'red alert, all systems go' mode. The mind is numbed temporarily and this paralysis can induce a form of panic caused by the fear of not living up to the expectation of being the leader who always knows what to do. This is followed by a mass of unrelated, half-baked plans, courses of action, ideas, facts and figures flooding the brain that can compound the feeling of helplessness. Leaders should be comforted by the knowledge that this is a normal reaction to the situation. By keeping calm and waiting for the surge to pass, as pass it will, rather than going off at half cock too early, a lot of distress will be avoided all round. There is an admirable piece of advice from the States for this situation, "Don't just do something, sit there". Obviously if a patient's blood is pumping all over the place or breathing has stopped, urgent, immediate action is required. The difficult part is arriving at a workable plan to evacuate the patient. By the time ten, even thirty, seconds have elapsed, which may feel like ten minutes, you should be in a sufficiently calm state to be able to think more clearly and get on with sorting the myriad of detail into an organised plan of action.

Even if the emergency has developed slowly, the realisation that you have one on your hands is likely to be sudden and the effect on you similar to a surprise accident. A depth of previous experience will be of tremendous help in the formulation of answers to the problems posed by the situation.

Thus we return again to the quality of this all important previous personal experience. Learn about your personal limitations in your chosen activity before ever leading parties. Get to know not only the inner self, but how the self is in various technical emergency-type situations, for example, beware against anxiety causing undue haste whilst navigating in mist on land or fog at sea. Learn beforehand what it feels like to be lost temporarily; what it is like to be out in foul conditions; how to handle different types of terrain both in ascent and descent in the different seasons or varying conditions of wind and water; what it is like to be out at night. Try a planned bivouac.

There is no doubt that mobile phones have removed quite a bit of the load on a leader in an emergency. Some bemoan the passing of times when being remote meant being remote! Beam me up Scotty!

People Have Different Learning Styles

The subject of how people learn is hugely important for anyone handling a group of people for whatever reason - information to be passed on or physical skills to be acquired, insights to be teased out of them or time given for creative, self-directed learning. If the group aren't taking it in or learning, it's a waste of their time and yours. The theory about how people learn was once thought to be a simple matter. The brain of a young child was thought to be rather like an empty page that has to be written on or a pot that has to be filled. So teaching methods concentrated on ramming in by rote-learning (memorising or copying), as much book-based knowledge (often referred to as the '3Rs'- reading, writing and arithmetic) as was deemed would be necessary for a young adult to lead a useful life. Some pots conformed and meekly accepted what was ordained whilst other pots seemed always to be leaking, unable to retain much, whilst others were 'smart' pots able to reject what was inserted and managed to learn in their own way! So learning was likely to be a bit haphazard and unpredictable. Some research in the 1920s-30s had concluded that a person's 'cleverness' was measured by their 'intelligence quotient' (IQ), that is their ability to handle academic, intellectual (cognitive) kinds of knowledge. Hence the value placed on the dreaded 11+ exam as a way of differentiating between the 'clever' ones and the 'slow' ones. Intelligence, as then defined, was thought to be inherited with a system of rewards (some) and punishments (many), known as the 'behaviourist' method, used to encourage learning. In the mid 1950s things moved on a little and most leaders have probably heard the old saying then current that,

"To hear is to forget, to see is to remember,
to do is to understand".

These auditory, visual, and performance styles of communication were held to have differing degrees of impact on memory and learning - i.e. on how much was retained by the learner. Research claimed to be able to establish, in terms of percentages, the effectiveness of each of these different learning styles. By the mid 1970s these generalisations had been modified to the extent that it was recognised that this hierarchy of learning was not rigid; it could be flexible or idiosyncratic i.e. it was inherited in people that they tended to have their own preferred 'learning medium' which was specific to themselves.

Some learned better through the auditory rather than visual and vice versa. But it was believed that more enduring learning took place when people were living and participating in an experience - doing it. All the capacities of the 'thinking', 'doing', 'feeling' self were more engaged because they were more comprehensively involved and in an integrated way - which was not the case when merely being talked at. This gave outdoor education (as it was commonly called then) some foundation for its claim that experience-based learning was the more effective and levelled the learning playing field previously favouring the intellectually gifted. A popular quotation of the time was that "All learning is experiential, but some learning is more experiential than others."[23] Despite this, secondary schooling remained entrenched in the old ways, but primary schools, always keen, even from the 1920s, to try new ideas, had latched on to it. So those trying to promote outdoor education/learning in the secondary sector and upwards, always had an uphill struggle against those persisting in seeing it as a "Whoopee trip for the Hooray Henry's.

The mid 1970s was also the time when it was discovered that the left and right side of the brain had different capabilities or functions. The left side was for logical, analytical, mathematical scientific types of methodical thinking whilst the right side was more imaginative, intuitive, artistic and creative and adapted to handling physical movements in space. As a result we became more aware that conventional education, as characterised by the drive to pass exams based on intellectual knowledge (cognitive) had been neglecting and ignoring the whole other half of a person's capacity to learn. By so doing, a large percentage of the population has been condemned to have a poor image of themselves when they failed these exams which were designed to test only one form of learning. One might have expected to see a huge revolution in the way information and other material was presented to pupils. Politicians, however, were more inclined to respond to the conventional and enduring perceptions of parents that 'education' and good exam results got you the best jobs and guaranteed your children employment. Incredibly, politicians were more intent on turning the clock back a century and changing education once again into a sausage-machine type system with its prescribed core curriculum and league tables of exam passes to ensure teachers did it 'properly'. Formal education was as much in a strait jacket as outdoor learning came to be in the 1990s.

In the 1990s, learning theory benefited from a surge in brain research facilitated through the use of sophisticated scanning techniques with intimidating names like Positron Emission Tomography, Computerised Axial Tomography and functional Magnetic Resonance Imaging which enabled researchers to see how the brain actually worked.

"All learning is experiential, but some learning is more experiential than others."

This research developed into new learning ideas and theories which seemed to reinforce some of the progressive ideas which had in fact been around in a less scientifically articulated form for a very long time. But because earlier notions had seemed to be just unsubstantiated convictions they had been conveniently ignored by the State system. The vested interest of teachers, tutors and lecturers unwilling to change were part of the log jam too. Those in the outdoor learning world were to find this research supported much of what they had been saying and doing for years. The specialised left and right brain idea was extended. An academic consensus began to emerge that the nature of learning was biological rather than mechanical. Evolutionary psychology was discovering that the way the brain had developed over millennia of hunting and gathering, subsistence living in small groups, problem solving and needing to collaborate, had resulted in modern humans inheriting a set of learning predispositions (preferred ways of learning) which vary in each of us and which amounted to different types of 'intelligence' possessed by us all. What this was saying was that people reinterpret what we say in terms of their own experience, interests and patterns of inherited predispositions. These are the ways we learn best. The brain is now seen as a product of its biological evolution. It is not the machine that the teacher dominated educational methods want it to be with just an ability to soak up, memorise and regurgitate facts which are kept in their own distinct compartments unrelated to other subjects. This uses a mere fraction of our potential and muffles our creativity, imagination and energy.

In '*Frames of Mind*', Howard Gardner described seven different sorts of intelligence or inherited predispositions:

"over the course of evolution, human beings have come to possess a number of special-purpose information processing devices".

1. Linguistic - able to put thoughts into words.
2. Logical / Mathematical.
3. Spatial Intelligence - the way we relate ourselves in space.
4. Musical.
5. Bodily - Kinetics - able to do things using our bodies.
6. Interpersonal Intelligence - able to work with and understand others.
7. Intrapersonal Intelligence - able to assess one's own thinking.

Of these types of intelligence, 1 and 2 are the major part of what happens in school. Items 3, 4, and 5 tend to occur outside curricular time which is in short supply these days as schools struggle to maintain a good place in the league tables based on exams in intellectual knowledge.

The significance of all this for outdoor leaders is that now more than ever there is scientific evidence to support what they are doing which has cut the ground from under the feet of their objectors, demeaners and belittlers. But do not expect changes to be quickly on the scene.

Successful teaching and leading has to take account of these 'multiple intelligences' as much as possible in order to maximise the talents of young people. At the moment there is a mismatch between theory and practice in schools and higher education. For outdoor leaders there is less need to worry about it because the way they work, and have worked for the past fifty years, incorporates all the theory - small groups; using various ways of learning by experience; using achievement and a sense of success, problem solving and collaborative team approaches to develop all the social qualities deemed desirable - self esteem, confidence, being tolerant, considerate, cooperative, initiative-taking, self-sufficient, active life-style, environmentally informed etc. Methods which use learning-by-doing mean that all the faculties of the person are engaged in the process of learning because many different kinds of knowledge or experience have to be assimilated and integrated, rather like the cross curricula work that used to be common in schools. When this is happening the leader becomes a manager of open ended learning rather than a teacher operating within the closed confines of a specialised subject.

One other newly emerging item on learning has significance for a nation noted for its 'stiff upper lip' and 'bad form to show your feelings' culture. The last two items in Gardner's list, 6 and 7, combine to form what is being called 'emotional intelligence' increasingly being recognised as an important part of our potential. Dr. Daniel Goleman in his book, 'Emotional Intelligence', suggests that performance in emotional maturity tests may become more important than traditional intelligence tests. Social competence may be a better predictor of success at work than academic or technical ability. The traditional idea we have about emotion fouling up clear, rational thought is quite wrong. Decision making needs the input of an emotional dimension to give it the right emphasis in the same way that the presence of motivation is a vital factor in risk assessment. The situation may be analysed using logic, but emotion provides an overall check on the wisdom of the decision to be made. We like to think we make rational choices everyday of our lives but the 'hidden persuaders' of advertising know differently!

The term 'emotional intelligence' embraces five elements or qualities such as understanding your own feelings (self awareness), having empathy with others, like being aware of other peoples' emotional states, motivation (self direction), being able to control your impulses (self regulation), and adeptness. Your ability in these areas could be called an 'emotional quotient' (EQ), though the idea of giving something emotional a number is rather quaint. If you badly misjudge others' intentions by misinterpreting the emotional cues people give off, it could result in your making some poor social decisions. A large part of our evolution has been spent living in groups, we are social beings, and survival and success has been dependent in large part on our ability to be socially sensitive and competent. This is, as it were, wired into us. Research has established that one of our inherited predispositions is towards social, collaborative and team building skills. If we do not provide young children with the nurturing and supportive environment needed to develop these skills, the young brain reacts with amazing speed and efficiency to the violent world it experiences around it to develop habits of an aggressive nature needed for self protection if support is absent . This is the 'use it or lose it' evolutionary imperative at work. Quality time with youngsters is time well spent. The style a leader adopts can do much to assist or hinder this positive development in the young.

*"Misinterpreting the emotional cues people give off
could result in your making some poor social decisions."*

Robert Rosenthal, a Harvard research psychologist, found that people who are good at reading emotional cues tend to be successful at work and in their relationships. The ability to understand our feelings means we have a better chance of handling them in a more creative and productive way. A decision based on a shock/surprise reaction will be quite different to one made if the shock/surprise effect can be controlled enough to make a calmer judgement. This is one of the big differences between ordinary and emotional intelligence. With IQ you are stuck with what you've got whilst with EQ there is the possibility of change.

Finally, to round off this section, research has also discovered that their surroundings also make a big difference to how well people can learn because they have definite preferences about the conditions of the learning environment. There is no one environment that suits everyone (which is what schools have imposed on pupils for years) and there appear to be three types of learner who respond well to some environments but not to others.

'**Global learners**' learn better with something soft to sit on, or the floor, low lighting and background music with a number of tasks on the go so that they can flit from one to another as they get tired of concentrating on one, whilst some like to be doing something physical as they learn.

'**Analytic learners**' prefer hard upright seats, no distractions, silence and bright light (typical classroom conditions), to help concentration and like being able to stay focused on one project until it is completed.

'**Integrated learners**' have no particular preferences and are happy with a variety of situations. So in terms of practice whilst one student might be happy to sit through a talk another might prefer to tape it and play it back whilst out on a training run, whilst another would be happier listening whilst lying on a cushion on the floor. So the old 'sing and clap' style used by primary schools and some voluntary organisations was on the right track - even the mass recitation of tables, so often criticised today, would suit some learners better.

Reviewing and its Benefits

"We had the experience but missed the meaning." T.S.Eliot.

Whilst there are leaders who take groups on an outdoor activity with the single-minded aim of doing it purely for its own sake - which can be an OK thing to do, most leaders have some broader aim in view to facilitate the personal development of each group member in some way. This sub-section is relevant to such aspirations.

Reference has been made already to the benefits that a leader can enjoy from looking back over an experience in order to extract important lessons from it. It cannot be repeated too often that the adoption and exercising of this practice regularly is one of the best aids to self improvement that the leader can have. It helps develop insight and judgmental skills. Very often there are other lessons to be learned which do not become obvious until an experience has been reflected upon. If it can not be retained in the memory to be easily recalled when necessary, it is lost learning. Reflection guided by a structured process (see below) facilitates the degree of retention and improves the quality of what is retained.

Reviewing Experiences for Groups

Whilst some of our learning has to be received second hand through normal directive and didactic, teaching methods, much has to be learned for ourselves heuristically - by experiencing and discovering it.

The experiential learning process is distinguished by having four main components:-

- ✿ planning;
- ✿ execution and action;
- ✿ reflection;
- ✿ application.

A shortened simple version of this is the 'plan, do, review' cycle which has the in built benefit of enabling one to make progress as a result of learning by reflection and modifying future behaviour because of the lessons learned thereby.

Experiences are only special if we think about them in order to make them personal to ourselves. We do that to discover what was important or significant about them and what may be of future usefulness.

Members of the leader's group will benefit, no less than the leader, from this kind of reviewing process. But beware of over-doing it lest the group become bored or alienated by too frequent exposure to it. Remember, too that because people have different learning styles this means that some people express themselves better in ways other than talking or writing. It is a good idea to allow them to use different ways of reviewing as for instance using poetry, play-acting, painting, modelling, video, cartoons, drawing to name a few possibilities, to illustrate what they believe they have learned. To get the best out of it however, it should be preplanned to ensure that there is adequate time for it and, most importantly, to give the group fair and advance notice. To spring a review session unexpectedly on a group is to invite all manner of brickbats!

A Suggested Basic Model for Reviewing

Reviewing should be properly structured by having a conceptual model on which to base one's ideas about how to organise and proceed in such a session. One useful model follows a sequence of levels of thinking which progress from the simplest to the more complex. These levels are:

1. Knowledge - which is the **memory level**: remembering facts by recognition or recall.

2. Comprehension - which is the **understanding level**: explaining or interpreting knowledge in a descriptive way - knowing why and how.

3. Application - which is the **usage level**: using knowledge correctly.

4. Analysis - which is the **relationship level**: breaking down knowledge and perceiving relationships between the parts.

5. Synthesis - which is the **creative level**: putting bits together to make a whole.

6. Evaluation - which is the **opinion level**: forming opinions, making judgements about the value of ideas, solutions, events.

The point about this structure is that information on a particular level is not accessible to a person until the previous level has been adequately dealt with. To ask for an opinion (level 6) before syntheses (level 5) have been made is futile. You can't build a ceiling if you have no walls. So experiences have to be 'processed' in an orderly manner to gain maximum advantage from them.

A commonly used shorthand device to aid the memorisation of this process is:

- What?
- So what?
- Now what?

The 'action' orientated leader, or indeed the group, who may feel this exercise of the brain is pointless, needs to ask the question, "Is it more important to experience much or is it more important to make meaning out of that which is experienced?" It is possible to have had a lot of experience but have learned very little from it. It would be possible for example to keep making the same mistakes and be quite unaware of it, locked as it were in a cycle of innocent incompetence.

Reviewing bestows a number of benefits. In the process of looking at the sequence of events ("what did you do?"), and the various processes ("how and why did you do it?") such as consulting, negotiating or decision making and the part played by individuals, much valuable feedback can be generated which, provided it is of the right, positive kind, will result in improvements in motivation, self awareness, relationships, group unity and performance ("how do you feel about it?"). Reflection is conducive to insight.

The leader's ability to generate a caring climate of trust and cooperation is very necessary to successful reviewing. The aggressive, competitive, point-scoring atmosphere characteristic of some male behaviour needs to be discouraged since this would severely disrupt the chances of positive results. (See suggestions for further reading at end of book for more on reviewing)

Recording

Allied to the reviewing process is the practice and skill of writing down and recording events, experiences and thoughts as another aid to the leader's self improvement.

It is very easy to jumble up sequences of events when trying to recall them. Changing the order in which they occur can impart quite a different meaning or interpretation to them - in the context of group conflicts or misunderstandings this can be crucial.

"A cycle of innocent incompetence"

It is very easy to be deceived later after the event into thinking that predictions and expectations turned out exactly as it was anticipated and judged they would, or that the results or consequences of decisions were what it was intended they would be. If they had been written down beforehand the difference might be very surprising. Recording keeps leaders firmly grounded in reality!

Some events can't always be explained immediately. Recording means there is an opportunity to keep working on them. The act of writing, besides requiring the sorting out of the material into an orderly manner, also reinforces the process whereby events are imprinted on memory. But to be successful, recording requires an act of personal commitment and much self discipline for it is not the most attractive of tasks.

Communication Skills

Communication is a four stage process in which everyone sends-receives-interprets-and infers. There is no set order in which these functions occur; indeed they usually happen simultaneously. Effective communication takes place between a 'sender' and a 'receiver' when the receiver interprets a message in the way that the sender intended it to be understood.

Communication can be affected by 'interference' either at the sender's end (sender's attitude, frame of reference, appropriateness of speech such as very long words or swearing or coarseness) or at the receiver's end (receiver's attitudes, prejudices, background, experiences that affect the decoding process) or certain kinds of 'noise' in between the two people communicating (environmental sounds, speech problems such as a mumble, stammer, or distracting mannerisms).

Communication is the basis for all human interaction and group working. Every group must take in and use information. The very existence of the group depends on communication. Set in this context, the leader's ability to communicate effectively is crucial since it is the all-pervading means by which leadership is delivered or exercised. So clearly the quality of leadership can be greatly affected by the quality of the communication skills possessed by a leader.

Whilst actions do speak louder than words, and leading by conscious example is important in many ways, it is as well to remember that leaders can lead by unconscious example, in that non verbal communication, which has already been mentioned as a means of detecting signals from the group, also works in reverse - groups pick up the leader's non verbals and very quickly!

But for most of the time it is the spoken word which permeates everything, whether it is giving information, issuing instructions, selling an idea, recommending a course of action, helping to resolve a conflict or knowing when to be silent (of which more anon). It is necessary to be aware that it is not just the 'content' of what is said that is important but the emotional tone with which it is delivered. A telling off is more likely to be received if it is delivered in a neutral tone than one in which the voice is perceived to be scolding, nagging, whining, angry, censorious or indignant (but paradoxically with some people, a reasonable tone does not work and it is sometimes only an emotional message that gets through to register). It is quite possible for a statement to be made in which the tone of voice absolutely contradicts the intent of what is being said. This is called a 'crossed message'. Sarcasm is a good example of this. "Please *do* take your time" can be said with an inflection that means quite the opposite. It is important to ensure that the 'emotional message' matches the message content.

It is vital to express oneself positively. It is helpful to avoid the use of 'always' in the manner "you always do that" (no one 'always' does anything). Refrain from an over-use of negatives (don't do that; you can't do this; that's no good at all!) which so often cause feelings of frustration and resentment.

It is vital to express oneself clearly. Try to avoid loose or careless expression in the spoken delivery. Even when you are trying hard to be positive and clear, be aware that there are many opportunities for being wrongly interpreted. What means one thing to person A, will mean something quite different to person B. Heedless, thoughtless ways of expressing yourself can mislead the listener. Leaders can check if a wrong image or impression has been presented by resorting to a system of feedback. To check out what has been received ask one of the group to play back by re-stating to you what they think you have said. This also gives an opportunity, that would otherwise not have arisen, to clarify misunderstandings or correct any misinterpretation. With this point we have moved on to the skill of listening.

Listening

Since communicating with others is a two-way process, the ability to express oneself by 'sending', is only a half of the story. It is equally important to be able to 'receive' or listen properly. Good listening is an art, a skill and a discipline and not the simple process it is usually conceived to be. It is possible to listen, but not hear what is said. It is possible to hear, but not understand, or even misunderstand, what is said. Hearing only becomes listening when close attention is paid to what is being said. This requires a sense of humility or respect for others that keeps one's own ego quiet. Good listening also needs practice and patience.

Most of us have bad listening habits - here are a few of them which tend to foul up 'reception' and prevent you understanding the speaker.

✿ How often in the middle of listening to someone, when you hear something you do not agree with, do you apparently keep listening, but in fact shut off whilst you begin to marshal the elements of your counter argument? (On-off listening). This is because the act of speaking is four times slower than we can think, so we have time to think other thoughts whilst listening to others speaking and sometimes tune them out.

✿ How often listening to some boring account, does your head continue to nod and make all the minor signals of receiving, when in fact you are far away and could not afterwards repeat or 'play back' any of it or even summarise it? (Glassy-eyed listening).

❂ How often when you hear something that seems to oppose the very essence of your being or some important value held dear, do you get so angry you tune out and stop listening? (Red flag listening). Examples of red flags might be 'hunting with dogs', 'GM crops', the growth of wind turbines, 'E' additives in food, experiments on animals discrimination, bullying, drugs.

❂ How often do you conclude too quickly that you know what is coming, or feel the subject is boring or too incomprehensible and decide there is no further reason to continue listening? (Open ears-closed mind listening).

Good listening requires an emotional, intellectual and behavioural control that comes only with effort and practice. Good and careful listening can be astonishingly energy-draining. In a group it is important that people talk freely about matters and problems that are important to them. The more information a leader has about these matters, the better the leader will be able to know how to go about dealing with them effectively. This is where knowing when to be silent is a leader's priceless asset. Then there will be a minimum of leader-initiated argument, interruption, unwanted advice, premature judgments and hasty conclusions, all of which are barriers to good listening.

Silence can be taken too far, however, to the point where it inhibits interaction. So silence used to minimise negative communication must be complemented by 'noise(s)' to show interest, understanding and empathy with the speaker(s) e.g. "that's interesting, I see, uh-huh, geez, wow, crikey", and so on as appropriate. Your facial expressions also help or hinder the speaker! Trying to be neutral and keeping a straight face may mean you are seen as a stony faced, emotionless person, hard to read, who gives nothing away and keeps everything close to their chest.

Some Do's and Don'ts of Listening

Good listening is helped if we try to:

- ❂ show interest
- ❂ be understanding of the other person
- ❂ express empathy

- single out the problem if there is one
- listen for causes to the problem
- help the speaker associate the problem with the cause
- encourage the speaker to develop competence and motivation to solve his own problems
- cultivate the ability to be silent when silence is needed. Successful leaders usually know how to keep their counsel.

To listen properly, don't:

- Argue
- Interrupt
- Pass judgement too quickly or in advance
- Give advice unless it's requested
- Jump to conclusions
- Let the speaker's opinions or attitudes react too sharply on your own.

Silence

There are times when silence can be used deliberately as a means of extracting a response when one is needed. But it should be used with caution. Most people react uneasily to silence and will try to fill it, not necessarily with what you are looking for. If the silence rebounds on the leader by becoming protracted and very 'heavy', this may be because the group do not yet understand what is being asked of them. The exact nature of the problem they are being asked to solve, or a decision they are expected to make, may not have occurred to them yet. Quite often the group too will use silence to exact an answer from the leader who must then attempt to discern whether they are too lazy, tired or bored to exert themselves because each of those conditions requires a different kind of response.

Communication as an art and skill is a very big subject and all that can be attempted here is a little to whet the appetite for more. It is inadvisable to think that what skill you have is quite adequate. In this particular area of human activity there is always room for improvement, especially for those who would lead others successfully.

Non Verbal Communication

An in-depth knowledge about the nature of verbal and non verbal communication is very useful. For all manner of reasons, people do not always mean what they say. A boy's response to a concerned query which draws a, "Whose afraid? Not me!" may be blustered out in such a way as to mean the opposite. But signals may not always be verbal. There are vocal clues in the pitch, speed, volume, inflection, tone and emphasis of the voice - grunts, groans, sighs, various noises and worst of all to interpret, silence. It is the non verbal modes of communication which give a more subtle but reliable feedback. Very revealing indications come from facial expressions, gestures, attitudes of body posture, restlessness, gait and other mannerisms.

Harder to detect are some of the involuntary signals the body gives out - rapid breathing or pulse rate, dryness in the mouth, pupil of the eye dilation, fear induced sweating. Does that yawn mean fear, tiredness or boredom? Is that redness caused by sheer physical exertion, blushing or flushing? Is that white pallor a symptom of imminent sickness, caused by pain or fear or is it a low body temperature? Anxiety, physical distress, feelings of inadequacy, dangerous levels of exhilaration or exuberance (as when high quality environments are experienced) which could lead to life endangering foolishness or recklessness, all need to be watched out for and monitored in case your intervention is required. Be aware of the group. Awareness is one of the foundation stones of control. Desmond Morris gives further insights into this fascinating topic in his book '*Manwatching*'[13]. It is amazing how we give ourselves away without realising it - leaders included!

Meta Skills

We saw earlier that skills may be classified in many ways. Some skills seem to be fairly simple and are quickly acquired; others are more complex, not as easily learned, not as easily mastered, if ever. Once you learn how to tie a bowline knot for example, that is it. Or is it? There is more to learn about it for there are two or three other ways of tying it which are useful to know. Thereafter, there is nothing more to learn about the actual business of how to tie the knot, but you could go on to learn many different applications for the knot and the circumstances in which it can be used. This so-called 'climber's knot' is much used by sailors, for example. The ability to use a skill in a number of different ways is one form of the skill of versatility and the example of the knot was a very elementary way of illustrating the point.

A similar sort of higher level process applies to the use of relationship skills. As knowledge, awareness and understanding grows about various aspects of group behaviour, it becomes possible to operate on more than one level at a time. The process can be likened to 'multi-tasking', which is the way a computer is able to do a number of jobs simultaneously. Females are also apparently better at multi-tasking than males, able to keep a number of things on the go at the same time. You can be paying attention to the content of what individuals in the group are saying (one level) whilst monitoring the non–verbal effect on the whole group (second level) and at the same time, be using this in-coming information to monitor the quality and content of discussion in order to decide whether an intervention from you is necessary or not (third and fourth level).

Above all this (fifth level), you could also be trying to make an overall evaluation of what is going on, i.e. how worthwhile is it to spend time on this, are lessons being learned, does it help the group to move on to achieve its objective or is it leading to disruption?

This kind of multi–activity is of a higher order of skill which may be called a 'meta skill'. It is a fairly sophisticated skill which takes time to acquire and can only be used in short bursts as it uses a lot of energy.

One other skill might be mentioned in this category. It is allied to observation and is the ability to see what is **not** there. If this sounds like nonsense think again. Most people find seeing what **is** there to be less easy than they believed. Ask a few witnesses to an accident to describe what they saw and the number of different versions is astounding. But to recognise when there is something missing that ought to be there requires the level of skill required of a scanner working with a perfect model in mind for comparison.

As an example, I was talking to a visitor on the island of Tiree once and in the course of conversation mentioned the lack of trees. He was astonished. He had had a feeling that something was different but had been unable to put his finger on it until I spoke of it.

The big embarassing example of 'not there' is when a member of the group has absented themselves for some reason (e.g. loose bootlace; attention caught by something interesting; get something out of rucksack; call of nature, stops paddling to blow nose) and no-one notices. Developing the practice of frequent head counting as a habit is a good idea. The group should also understand that if any of them do stop for some reason they should let someone know - preferably the leader.

'.....but you could go on to learn many different applications for the knot '

The Skill of Using Skills

There is another skill which can be included in the 'meta' category. It is based on discretion and discrimination, to match up the use of particular leadership techniques to the right person or group, at the right time, in the right place for the right reason or job to be done. If a wood chisel, for example, is used as a screw driver, the end result will be imperfect. There is a risk of damage both to the tool and the material being worked on. In a similar way it is possible for a person to be technically highly proficient but still be quite inadequate as a leader because of an inability to relate to people and a tendency to mismatch 'people' skills. This may be either because s/he does not want to, or because s/he does not know how, or because personal qualities, such as shyness, are such as to make it unlikely that s/he ever will. The sensitivity with which all these skills are used greatly affects the way they are used and therefore the effect that they will have in a group. Technical skill in a leader without the seasoning of human understanding has little value. Without this sophistication to inform his/her actions it is possible for the most technically, highly qualified leader to give the group a negative experience.

Getting leadership right is a never-ending task. It is an alive, ever-changing and open-ended process, whereas the purely technical is inanimate and relatively static and predictable. With leadership there are rarely neat answers or solutions. Situations will elicit from leaders, responses they never knew they had. Therein lies some of the fascination.

Do not be afraid of making mistakes - we all manage to do that every day. But have a positive attitude about them. Mistakes are about learning not about feeling guilty or being punished. That applies to the group as well as to the leader. Let them know this too and a lot of suppressed initiative will be released. The thing is to have good intentions, more especially, conscious intentions, allied to sound convictions. It helps to make intentions known in order to reduce the probability of being judged by the effects of your actions - especially when they go wrong. If mistakes in relationships are made they can be rectified, but it is necessary to know, or to have worked out, how to do that and repair any emotional damage. If such mistake-mending is neglected, hurts and resentments stack up to erode the leader's standing and credibility.

Some leaders feel it is unprofessional ever to admit to making mistakes. "Professionals do not make mistakes, only amateurs do that". To admit to such vulnerability would be to breach the infallible aura that they think should surround them.

On the subject of mistakes, it is amazing what a simple thing like a sincere apology will do to mend relationships. It does not cost much, but it buys a lot.

Outdoor leaders often being the only adult in the group, may tend to feel awkward or downright resistant about apologising to young people out of a belief that it might undermine their authority or that it will place the leader at their mercy. Nothing could be further from the truth. Leaders tend to be seen by their groups as people who know what they are doing, where they are going and who know many of the answers. Groups become very troubled when the evidence seems to contradict this belief. Feeling troubled causes trouble. Leaders need sometimes to burst the bubble of infallibility perceived by groups to be around leaders. An apology sincerely made and sincerely meant will often be the way to show young people that adults have their limitations too and are not as different, inhuman, unapproachable or unreachable as was thought. Humility is an asset.

One could almost be excused for thinking that apologising is a meta skill too because it is felt to be so difficult. Subjective obstacles are the most difficult of all challenges to overcome. To reach an apology, it is sometimes necessary to be able to overcome a deep-rooted attitude or a strong emotion in order to acquire the humility that makes it possible.

Concluding Remarks

Many of the skills touched on in this book should have been explored in greater detail, but space does not permit a full and comprehensive coverage here. For now, it is sufficient that the attention of aspirant leaders has been drawn to them. They are mostly the skills which contribute to the quality of working relationships in the leader-group situation: the art of dealing with and relating to people; the skills and intricacies of communication and listening; dealing with conflict; the relieving of tension, using humour; roles in groups; understanding the dynamics of group life and encouraging the full development of the individuals in your group; fostering self-sufficiency, confidence and self-determination in people.

For most of the group, the aim for the day may well be in getting to the top of the hill or the end of the journey and enjoying the experience. Whilst a leader's more basic responsibilities, in order of priority, will be the safety, comfort and enjoyment of the members of the group, they should feel it happening in exactly the reverse order for most of the time. It is often said that, "It is better to journey than to arrive". In this respect, hopefully, leaders will be aware that there are many times when the processes of group interaction are just as important as the achievement of the aim.

Leaders, with an informed and more liberal interpretation of their role and a broader awareness of the potential of the outdoors as a marvellous medium for helping people to develop their capacities to the full, will be able to provide the atmosphere, the context and the setting for this to take place, whilst taking care to remember, in this day and age where sustainability is becoming an ever more vital issue, to minimise environmental damage, and promote awareness, respect and care for it.

HOW TO KEEP GOING WITH THE SPIRAL OF LEARNING

We shall not cease from exploration
And the end of all our exploring
Will be to arrive where we started
And know the place for the first time.

T.S.Eliot, "Four Quartets"

APPENDIX 1

Beginner's Guide to Aims and Values for Leading Outdoors

Brits are by culture and tradition a practical people who tend to avoid having to think too deeply or abstractly about things. Psychological stuff is perceived as anathema by many. So people as a rule do not find it easy to talk or think about values as a stand-alone subject. Any such discussion tends to become abstract and philosophical and people soon begin to feel a bit out of their depth. Debate may become confused and rambling in nature. Understanding is not helped by the fact that some words are overly long and their meaning hard to grasp. One way to help prevent confusion when talking about values, is firstly to identify the context - the situation under discussion, after which the sense follows more easily. But as we shall see, we all have values - most of them effortlessly acquired.

I felt that some kind of beginner's guide might be useful here. The kinds of questions to be answered are:

- ✪ what are values?
- ✪ where do they come from?
- ✪ how do we acquire them?
- ✪ does it matter whether we have any?
- ✪ what use are they? Do we really need them?
- ✪ do we need to know what they are?
- ✪ what are the values applicable to using the outdoors for learning?

What are values?

Values are often associated exclusively with spiritual matters - but this is a mistaken view. Values exist at many levels of importance. By value we do not mean the value of the economist who 'values' things in terms of how much money they cost or are worth. It is necessary to distinguish the difference between value as 'worth' and value as 'price' or 'cost'. Something can cost a lot of money and be valuable, but be valueless; and something can be worth no money and have much value and be priceless. And in all of this, the idea of value may be determined by the situation. To be in Amsterdam with a bucket of water and a bucket of diamonds will give each container a particular value which will be changed radically if one is suddenly placed in the middle of the Sahara. A bull in a china shop may be a liability, but on a farm a great asset. Using different scales of measurement, drugs have a high commercial value but from a social point of view they have low or even negative value.

All aspects of our lives have values associated with them. This is because everything we do, make decisions about, plan to do is based on beliefs, attitudes and values we hold either consciously or unconsciously. Values are therefore closely intertwined with our behaviour our choices and preferences. But often we are not very clear what they are, partly because there is not one set of values in which everyone believes anymore - parents, school, work, peer groups and politics all seem to have different sets of values saying different things. Alternative value systems can be a bewildering maze. But hang on to the idea that values in any outdoor context are closely associated with behaviour.

Values are ideas, or concepts that you believe in, which you feel are important to you - "this is where I am at", "this is me". Conversely there are other values that may not appeal to you, "I'm against that", "Don't want it"

So, in a sense, values determine the very nature of your being, 'how you are' and 'what you do' and 'what you intend or hope to do' and 'what you are not'.

The dictionary defines a 'value' as a "*quality, calibre, grade, rating, priority, importance, significance, excellence, goodness, merit, stature, worth - that which is appreciated, cherished, admired, adored, considered, coveted, esteemed, honoured, idolised, loved, prized, regarded, respected, treasured*".

What all that means is that values are all those concepts which help you to decide what are your preferences and priorities - as such they figure in what motivates you. These concepts are thus all the criteria or tests you use for making judgments; for making choices; for deciding tactics, strategies and policies; for resolving conflicts about what is important and what is not; for deciding on courses of action. In this sense these values are the means to reach the goal or target - things for aiming **WITH**. They are called 'instrumental values'.

Goals and targets also have values for they are things worth working to achieve, worth aiming **FOR**. These things are worth aiming for, because the values we have, incline us to see them as valuable, beneficial, worthy, desirable things that will help us to become what we want to be, or achieve something we think is worthwhile.

In brief, values are used to judge actions, evaluate behaviour, measure goals and achievements. They permeate all aspects of life and are unavoidable. For example, are you a conforming, challenging or antagonistic sort of person; are you passive or active; reactive or proactive; are you extravagant or frugal; competitive or cooperative; materialistic or mystic; practical or academic?

Values can be classified by their level of importance

There are many ways of classifying values. All of the classification ideas are largely useful, but not vital, tools to help you think about, manage and deploy values. Here are a few ways of classifying values:

✿ Absolute values include:

✿ Cardinal values -
which tend to be general, unchanging, fixed, universal and applicable in many fields. There is only one state of it like honesty, conformity, spontaneity, selflessness, efficiency. These absolutes are the ethical and moral imperatives recognised by all societies such as incest or fratricide.

✿ Institutional values -
because they are distilled out of experience and wisdom over a long period, tend to be permanent. They describe how things are in a society. They give meaning to life - 'this is how it is'. They tend to be old but do not go out of fashion. e.g. kindness. For the individual they represent a larger whole, greater than the individual, against which the person can measure themselves and discern their own significance.

❂ Less permanent values include:

❂ Relative values -

are flexible, a question of degree such as being rich (or poor) or not very rich, or very rich, or immensely rich, i.e there are many different states of being rich, unlike being honest where you either are or you are not.

❂ Instrumental values -

describe how things get done. They are the means towards achieving ends and the ones used for aiming 'with'. They are the values, such as competence or efficiency, used in designing plans and programmes and the methods, approaches to be used for achieving specific goals, targets and outcomes. e.g. by copying, discovering, practising, being careful or hasty or careless, perfect or messy, neat or untidy, broad non-specialist or narrow specialist treatment, accuracy in navigation, spelling or woodwork and 'consideration' in driving. They offer no help about ends.

Instrumental values in Physical Education would be 'strength, stamina and flexibility' as a means to promoting health, skill and efficiency - which still leaves unanswered the question, "for what, or to what end?" Social instrumental values in Physical Education would be 'cooperativeness, friendliness and tolerance' as strategies to help you achieve your aims. It should be apparent that a concentration on instrumental values will not help to discover or decide about the more permanent values indicated above. The methods, procedures and techniques that are central to science do not tell us whether science is a good or bad thing. Human actions need to be assessed/evaluated from many different angles at the same time.

❂ Higher values -

are used for the more important categories attaching to the aesthetic; spiritual; moral; social; intellectual; physical. Outdoor Learning, for instance, embraces all these domains.

❂ Values can have a number of sub aspects:

❂ **Unipolar values** - are those about which there is no choice other than to accept or reject them, e.g. honesty, loyalty, truth, goodness. The principle is clear.

❂ **Bipolar values** - require a sense of proportion where values are twinned as extremes of the 'either/or' variety; two alternatives, one or the other, which are sometimes opposites such as young or old; self-control or spontaneity; competition or cooperation; sometimes they are aspects of a central concept such as the attitude to danger which can be reckless or cowardly depending upon your value-laden point of view. The value you put on an action can even depend on the emotional state of your mind - so what is perceived as cowardly could be cautious or prudent and what seen as reckless could be brave or courageous.

❂ **Multi polar** - values can exist in a cluster or as a set of options in connection with a central theme. e.g achieving 'control', or getting things done might be by 'autocratic' or 'democratic' methods with 'heuristic' (self discovery) as a third alternative method. You might regard the natural environment exploitively as a resource to be plundered and bent to your will, or a precious asset to be conserved and lived with as harmoniously as possible, or a dominating system of powerful forces over which one has no control and to which one is helplessly subject.

Function of values

So what purpose do values serve overall? What is their function? It would be easy to overlook this point in the long scramble looking for one's own values. Fundamentally, values are about providing a sense of certainty in one's life. They are about what you are doing, where you are going and for what purpose. Like leading and managing, people need to know if they are doing the right thing and doing it right. One way of looking at this is to see life as comprising five basic value orientations each of which carries a number of options (multi-polar) in the search for a coherent sense of self.

What will your attitude be in relation to:

❂ inner self - see yourself as good; bad; or a mixture of both.
❂ active self - 'doing' - all planning and action; or 'being' - all inertia and meditation; or combine both in 'becoming'.
❂ others - live in a hierarchical (conformist) society; anarchy (competitive); or democratic (cooperative) society.
❂ the environment - be subordinate to it; exploitive of it; or in harmony with it.
❂ time - backward-looking and hide bound by precedents and tradition, living in the past ignoring the present; or forward looking and concentrated on your goal living for the future ignoring past and present; or living in the present using past experience to make a better future.

Outdoor Values Diversity:

Depending on whether one is educating or learning in the environment, **about** the environment (scientific and natural history type data), **for** the environment (conservation and sustainability agendas) or **through** the environment (means to other ends like personal development not directly connected to environment), will cause the hierarchy of values to change - in other words, each has its own specific hierarchy of values, for example, when the environment is used as a **medium** for learning about oneself and becomes the **subject** of study rather than the vehicle, aims and outcomes must change.

Lookout - Values are About!

How to recognise when values are in fashion or conflict? People with a strong interest in values often have a finely tuned sense that "things aren't what they used to be", or that "things aren't right and that something needs changing". The object of concern may be oneself, other people or some aspect of the world in general. Usually they mean other people because it is their behaviour that they feel has made the mess. There is a strongly felt need to change the way "things or people are now". So people talking about values may have an underlying agenda to change 'things --- you', as when politicians talk about citizenship and emphasise its responsibilities rather than its rights and freedoms.

Acquiring Values

Values are concepts or ideas picked up during the course of one's life from parents during one's upbringing, from role models whose deeds must match their words, by finding out for yourself from experiences received and lessons learned. They tend to define:
- how you are - what you aim with, your thinking state of 'being';
- what actions you choose to do or not do - your active state of 'doing';
- what you are aiming for - your aspiring state of 'becoming'.

Opinion making, decision making and action are all determined by values. Everyone of those values chosen entails a decision about whether it is attractive to you or not.

Values can refer to some context posing choices which imply that there are some values in conflict.

Note on Environmental Values

The environment possesses innate qualities which are impartial and objective - slippery, steep, cold, hot, muddy, rocky, rough, smooth. We humans are affected by these objective qualities in a number of ways via our senses, so we assign to them other values to do with the feelings they arouse in us. The environment thus acquires subjective qualities, or values, such as hard, thirsty, energy-sapping, brilliant, fantastic, soothing, horrid, mind-blowing, treacherous, hostile, difficult, dangerous etc. We also rely a lot on the potential of Nature to pass on to us values for life through the vehicle of the metaphor - brave as a lion is a common one. A stream symbolises the flow of life - canoeists learn to harness the flow rather than to fight against it - 'go with the flow'. Note the power of parables for modifying behaviour - at the outset an expedition appears as a formidable undertaking with so much to be done. But one learns to take it steadily a bit at a time, a day at a time, and it gets done. When faced by two alternative routes at a fork in the track, you learn to consider carefully in order to avoid mistakes in the execution, the action bit. If you do not observe an environmental imperative and the need for preparation or precautions, you suffer the consequences of getting wet, cold, or hungry - and it's no-one else's fault but your own.

Outdoor Learning
- List of Values

The following Tables illustrate, not exhaustively, the values to be found in the states of 'doing', 'being', and 'becoming' in the person when outdoor learning is looked at from the point of view of its potential as a subject in Table 6 and in terms of its potential outcomes when used as a means for *personal development* in Table 7.

Table 6. Potential as a *subject*

"DOING" AS A SUBJECT	"BEING" AS A SUBJECT	"BECOMING" AS A SUBJECT
new skills potential	informal	remedial
process friendly	personal	new values
new responses	small groups	socialisation
experiential	contrast experience	citizenship
direct, real, first-hand	novel experiences	more positive self view
commitment	unfamiliar experiences	
purposeful activity	attractive experiences	
new learning styles	captive situation	
different teaching styles	protracted	
recreational activities	intense	
field study-environment	sustained	
social relationships	egalitarian start for all	
inter-personal skills	holistic	
group skills	subject integration	
affective skills	cross curricular	
cognitive skills		
learning to learn		
physical skills		
holistic		

Table 7. Potential outcomes for people

"DOING" FOR THE INDIVIDUAL	"BEING" FOR THE INDIVIDUAL	"BECOMING" FOR THE INDIVIDUAL
success	anti social behaviour addressed	new awarenesses
new skills-competences	self discipline	personal effectiveness
maintaining relationships	self responsible	social awareness
initiating relationships	sense of identity	tolerant
communication skills	sense of belonging	cooperative
listening	not isolated	diverted from crime
contributing	better motivation	sense of purpose
cooperating	positive self view	sense of achievement
challenging		confidence
inter-relating		self measurement
collaborating		self esteem
discussing		self assessment on-going
team work		expanding self-view

APPENDIX 2

Diagram 10.
Model Showing Elements in Leader Training/
Development and their Inter-dependent Relationship

*Explanation of Diagram 10.

- Leader development embraces COMPETENCE and SENSITIVITY, both of which greatly depend upon a solid core of PERSONAL EXPERIENCE in the particular activity to be taken up, and in the particular type of environment in which operating and of people.

The PERSONALITY should not be seen as a minor part of this concept because of its apparent small size. Rather it should be regarded like the core of a nuclear reactor which may be smaller in size than the buildings housing it, but it infuses all around it with its power and is the reason for their existence and purpose.

- Training builds on this core by giving KNOWLEDGE and by developing SKILLS in the "OBJECTIVE area" (which is mostly concerned with dealing with problems to do with activities, environmental data and environmental hazards; and in the "SUBJECTIVE" area which is concerned with 'people' tasks of a managerial (relationships) nature; and by facilitating greater UNDERSTANDING and AWARENESS (which is mostly concerned with the degree and style with which skills and knowledge will be used).

Thus:
- skill and knowledge increase competence.
- Understanding and awareness increase sensitivity.
- All four elements, Knowledge, Skill, Understanding and Awareness depend on further personal experience after training if they are to develop.
- Properly integrated, all four elements inter-act with the PERSONALITY to produce EFFECTIVE LEADERSHIP

Appendix 2 concludes by listing all those items which may properly be included under the headings of each of the four main areas of training shown in the diagram.
   1. Knowledge.   2. Skill.   3. Understanding.   4. Awareness.

Some of the items listed, which are are already well known, will be summarised in a very condensed manner. Other less well known items receive more detailed treatment. It will be noticed under the 'knowledge and Skill headings particularly, that a number of items are included which relate not to 'activity' problems, but to 'people' problems. At this point of the book I hope it does not come as a surprise that some 'hard' material is not necessarily 'activity' related. Concepts about what may properly be called 'technical' need to move on to a stance more in keeping with modern party leadership theory and the comprehensive nature of party management.

The Leader - 'needs to know'

This list is concerned with data, foundation facts and theories necessary to the carrying out of practical tasks.

1. Contextual data such as environmental knowledge about the anatomy of mountains, mountain hazards, caves, rivers, coastlines and sea, flora and fauna, meteorological theory, man's effect on the environment. Details mentioned under item 12 are also valid here.
2. Scientific and technical data about tools and instruments (e.g. suitable clothing footwear, ropes, maps, compasses, canoes, buoyancy, paddles, life jackets, and other equipment. Medical data.
3. Principles governing design, care, choice and use of equipment.
4. Procedures for planning and arranging day trips or extended expeditions.
5. The administration and organisation of mounting any type of excursion. e.g. keeping accounts, records, check lists etc.
6. Legal matters and the level of the leader's responsibilities: liability insurance, access law.
7. The structure and purpose of the organisation within which the leader works, e.g. City Council, Social Services, School, Youth Club etc.
8. The strategies of leadership - co-leadership, team work, project leadership.
9. The physical and emotional development of young people.

10. The resources and opportunities available to young people e.g. sources for equipment, transport, other operating agencies, other more distant locales.
11. Current social and economic issues affecting young people, e.g. racism, sexism, unemployment, violence, obesity, active life style, over protectedness etc.
12. The allied work and interests of other organisations, e.g. National Governing Bodies of Sport (NGBs), National Park Planning Boards, Conservation bodies, John Muir Trust, Landowners etc.

The Leader - 'needs to be able to'

This list is concerned with all the 'hard' practical skills and also with the many 'people' skills required for effective relationships with others.
1. Plan and assess the effectiveness of your work.
2. Anticipate the requirements and actions of young people.
3. Employ the range of skills required by the relevant activity.
4. Use a range of creative skills e.g. improvisation, photography, role -play, motivate.
5 Use and extend your range of leadership skills (directive, persuasive, assertive, consultative etc.)
6. Be alert, observant and perceptive.
7. Analyse situations accurately.
8. Make accurate judgements.
9. Assess people's abilities, attitudes and capabilities.
10. Interpret observed behaviour in the group.
11. Recognise fear, fatigue, anxiety, boredom, apathy, low morale, instability, enjoyment, exuberance etc.
12. Provide guidance and support.
13. Develop confidence and self-responsibility in young people, delegate, challenge etc.
14. Communicate effectively with young people.
15. Relate effectively with, and closely to, young people.
16. Work with young people in groups rather than with individuals.
17. Seek out new situations in which work with young people may be developed.

The Leader - 'needs to be aware of':

Note: This list is largely concerned with things internal to the self and with the 'here and now'

1. Own aims, objectives, personal philosophy and its implications.
2. Own motivation, attitudes, prejudices, preferences and predilections.
3. Own aptitudes, capacities, strengths and weaknesses.
4. Own training needs and opportunities for personal development.
5. What is happening immediately around the leader to people and the environment - i.e. to be observed, perceived and interpreted.
6. The influence the leader has on others.
7. The influence others have on the leader.
8. The influence young people have on each other.
9. The unspoken needs of young people.
10. When, and when not, to intervene, speak, be silent.
11. The importance of feelings in human affairs.
12. The special needs of minorities e.g slow learners, various physical impairments, ethnic minorities etc
13. The opportunities for extending young peoples' responsibilities.

The Leader - 'needs to understand'

To underline the distinction made earlier in chapter 5 between understanding and awareness a further list is included here for interest. This list is concerned with causes and effects, with why things are the way they are, or how they work, and with these influences and pressures, external to oneself, which affect the condition in which, and under which, a leader has to apply his/her skill and knowledge with a nicety of judgement.

1. What is expected of the leader by young people, parents, the organisation, society.
2. Where the leader's responsibilities end and the other support available to the group begins, e.g. delegating upwards.
3. Leader's own personal theories of leadership and how they relate to established practices.
4. Different types of authority and leadership and young people's responses to them - teaching styles are included here.
5. How people learn - the process of understanding which is too often confused with the process of teaching, i.e. what is taught is not necessarily learned.
6. The effects of discomfort , failure and success on young people.
7. The effects of weather upon the environment and upon the body.
8. The implications of doing things badly, wrongly, differently or carelessly.
9. The needs and interests of young people and ways of providing for them.
10 Young people's relationships with each other, with leaders, parents and other significant adults.
11. The behaviour of young people in groups.
12. The influences on young people - media, social, political, educational etc.
13. The communities in which young people live and how they function.
14. What other leaders are doing.
15. The inter-relatedness of all the elements of training and how they interact with each other, and depend upon each other, i.e. 'getting it all together'.

APPENDIX 3

The '5 Steps' Process of Risk Assessment

This is a shortened version of the 'Five Steps' with the main points is included here so that quick reference can be made to what HSE actually says. The first big point to get hold of is that it is designed with **industrial** practices of the workplace in mind which means it is not always relevant or appropriate to what leaders do in the outdoors. As a basic procedure for tackling risk assessment it is sound as far as it goes. The main intent of the advice is good in identifying a simple and usable process, but a number of important refinements need adding for the leading outdoors situation. The underlying premise that the leader should be doing all the risk assessment is unethical if not unsustainable. It also ignores the existence of non physical hazards/risks because it is "aimed at firms in the commercial, services and light industrial sectors" and therefore concerned with eliminating or minimising physical risks present in a normal industrial workplace as opposed to the outdoors. My comments are in square brackets, e.g. [---]

1. "LOOK FOR THE HAZARD" - what could '**reasonably**' be expected to cause harm'. Ignore the '**trivial**' and concentrate on the '**significant**' hazards - [these terms are capable of wide interpretation outdoors, particularly as the 'trivial' can become 'significant' on occasion. Fortunately a consistent industry-wide agreed definition for some activities exists in the shape of NGB approved practices - but this only goes so far as certain activities do not come under any governing body].

2. "DECIDE WHO MIGHT BE HARMED AND HOW" - i.e. employees, young workers, trainees, cleaners, students, other visitors, public at large.

3. "EVALUATE THE RISKS & DECIDE WHETHER EXISTING PRECAUTIONS ARE ADEQUATE OR MORE SHOULD BE DONE" .

❁ "after all precautions are taken, some risk usually remains. Consider how **likely** it is that each hazard could cause harm. You have to decide [whether the remaining risk] for each significant hazard is '**high, medium or low**' ." [This scale of degree may appear a bit crude but it is a practical rule-of-thumb method adequate to our needs. A more sensitive scale would raise more problems than it would solve]. The "aim is to make all risks 'small' ideally by 'getting rid' of the hazard or controlling it so that harm is unlikely".

❁ Are "generally accepted industry standards in place?" HSE regards observance of legal requirements as a first priority, followed by things like National Governing Body recommendations where they apply, the ACAC Code of Practice, Local Authority guidelines, sponsoring body regulations, manufacturers' instructions for use of equipment or materials etc. Beyond this you must also look at your situation to see whether there is anything special or unique that can be reasonably foreseen which requires further action to minimise risk.

❁ The "aim is to make all risks small" [The scale used earlier related to the 'likelihood of risk'. But what is also needed is a scale of the 'level of harm' such as:- 'no harm; very slight harm; slight harm; some harm; considerable harm; serious harm', to indicate what reduction of risk has been achieved, e.g. in a cave the risk of head injury from a low roof hazard is very likely and potentially serious, but the precautionary use of a helmet will reduce this risk of harm to an almost non existent level. Whilst the degree of confronted hazard may remain constant, the degree of harm may be reduced by safety precautions or the acquisition of greater skill. But sometimes the degree of confronted risk arising from an outdoor hazard may remain constant in spite of all precautions taken, e.g skiers off piste in avalanche conditions or sailors on a lee shore in strong winds or hill walkers surrounded by thunder and lightning.]

4. "RECORD YOUR FINDINGS" - (if you have fewer than 5 employees there is no need to write anything) Employees must be informed of your findings.

There is no need to show how you did the assessment, provided that:
- you can show that a proper check was made.
- you asked **who** might be affected.
- you dealt with all the obvious significant hazards, taking into account the number of people who could be involved.
    [For leaders this is important at the staff-student ratio level. What is O.K. for a group of three or four may not be appropriate for ten - a good example being the Crib Goch route up Snowdon in N.Wales.]
- the precautions are reasonable and the remaining risk is low.

✪ Assessments are expected to be 'suitable and sufficient"', not perfect.

5. "REVIEW YOUR ASSESSMENT AND REVISE IT IF NECESSARY"
    - any significant changes giving rise to significant new hazards should be added to the assessment.

Note that because these regulations are framed primarily with industry work-places in mind a difference exists between the approaches of the Outdoor Learning world and the rationale of the HSE.

✪ The former sees safety as means, a tool to be used and *aimed with*; and may actively seek or use challenge (hazard/risk) in order to:
  - teach/learn how to recognise, cope with, control, overcome hazard and risk.
  - progress towards independent client participation in risk pursuits.
  - promote personal and social development.

✪ HSE sees safety as an end, the thing to *aim for*; and seeks to minimise or avoid risk in the workplace wherever and whenever possible.

Happily however, the HSE is known to regard the 'outdoor industry' as one with a very good record. They are not too worried about us. Many other industries give them greater cause for concern. The differences in outlook can produce nasty hiccups on occasion however as evidenced by the tortuous negotiations needed to get them to see sense over the 'Working at Height' EU Directive during 2004.

References

1. *Outdoor Education - Safety and Good Practice. Guidelines for guidelines* (p12-15) (1988) Duke of Edinburgh Award.
2 . R.A.Hogan (1992) *The Natural Environment in Wilderness Programmes. Playing Field or Sacred Place?* Journal of Adventure Education and Outdoor Leadership (JAEOL) Vol.9:No.1.
3. Mary Cox (1983) Leadership MLTB Conference, Ripon.
4. John Adair (1983) *Effective leadership; a self development manual.* Gower Press.
5. A.H.Maslow (1954) *Motivation and personality.* Harper & Row
6. R.Tannenbaum and W.Schmidt (1968). *How to choose a leadership pattern.* Harvard Business Review.
7. P.Hersey & K.H.Blanchard (1969) *Management of Organisational Behaviour.* Utilising Human Resources. 3rd edit. Prentice-Hall. 1977 McGraw-Hill (1970).
8. R.Chase & S.Priest (1989) *The conditional theory of outdoor leadership style.* 1989. JAEOL Vol.6:No.2.
9. T. Dixon & S.Priest (1991) *Confirmation of the Conditional Outdoor Leadership Theory.* JAEOL Vol.8:No.1.
10. B.W.Tuckman (1965) *Development sequence in small groups:* Psychological Bulletin.
11. K.C.Ogilvie (1974) *Dare to Live - a philosophy for outdoor education.* Unpublished.
12. G.Rattray Taylor (1972) *Re-think.* Pelican Books.
13. D.Morris (1978) *Manwatching.* Triad Books.
14. E.Berne. MD (1964) *Games people play.* Penguin.
15. D.W.Johnson & F.P.Johnson (1987) *Joining together: Group theory and Group Skills.* Prentice-Hall.
16. K.C.Ogilvie (1985) *Adventure Activities - a perspective view.* In Report by Sports Council for Northern Ireland of Adventure Activities Conference at Runkerry Outdoor Centre.
17. K.C.Ogilvie (1989) *The management of risk.* JAEOL. Vol.6:No.4.
18. R.D.Laing (1970) *Knots.* Penguin.
19. Article in "The Independent" 17/10/91 about the trial of Clarence Thomas in the U.S.A.

20. Dr.John Nicholson. *Men and women: How different are they?*
21. S.Priest (1988)*Preparing Effective Outdoor Pursuit Leaders* (PEOPL) JAEOL Vol.5: No.1.
22. S.Priest (1990) *Everything you always wanted to know about judgement, but were afraid to ask*. JAEOL. Vol.7:No.3.
23. L.K.Quinsland & A. Van Ginkel–Summer (1988) *How to process experience.* JAEOL. Vol.5:No.3.
24. K.C.Ogilvie (1998) *Re Values.* JAEOL No:1
25. G.Cooper (1998) *Outdoors with Young People*. Russell House.
26. J.Graham (1997) *Outdoor Leadership*. Cordee
27. P.Barnes (2002) *Leadership with Young People*. Russell House.
28. HSE Books (1994/2003) *Five Steps to Risk Assessment.*
29. G.Cooper (Spring 2004) *Changing Roles for Outdoor Education Centres*. Environmental Education.
30. C. Mortlock (1973) *Adventure Education and Outdoor Pursuits.*
31. C.Mortlock (1984) *The Adventure Alternative*. Cicerone Press.
32. H.E.Brown. *Working with Risk in the Outdoors*. Horizons 11. Autumn 2000.
33. H.E.Brown (2000) *Passengers, Participants, Partners and Practitioners-Working with Risk*. Horizons 12.
34. ITV Channel 4: Equinox. (6th Oct 1996), 'Staying Alive'
35. ITV Channel 4: Equinox. (12th April 1999), 'Living Dangerously'
36. HSE Books (*1996)* Health & Safety Commission. *Guidance to the Licensing Authority on The Adventure Activities Licensing Regulations.*

Suggestions for further reading:

❂ Various (1988) S.Priest - *Outdoor Leadership around the World*. S.Priest - Bibliography for outdoor leadership. Journal of Adventure Education and Outdoor Leadership. (JAEOL) Vol.5:No.1
  J.Hunt - Ethics in Leader Training Models.

❂ K.C.Ogilvie (1985 *Planning an Adventure Experience in the Outdoors*. JAEOL. Vol:2.No.4/5.

❂ S.Priest (1988) *Avalanche-Decision analysis*. JAEOL. Vol:5.No.3.

❂ D.Hammerman & S.Priest (1989) *The enquiry/discovery approach to learning in Outdoor Education*. JAEOL. Vol.6:No.2.

❂ S. Priest (1989) *Teaching outdoor adventure skills*. JAEOL. Vol.6: No.4.

❂ R.Chase & S.Priest (1990) *Effective communication*. JAEOL. Vol.7: No.1.

❂ Groundwork (1989) *Creative Reviewing*.

❂ R. Greenaway (1991) *Reviewing by Doing*. JAEOL. Vol.9:No.2.

❂ M. Cox (1984) *Facilitative Intervention in Adventure Activities*. NAOE Conference Report.

❂ D. Johnson (1990) *Women in the outdoors*. JAEOL. Vol:7.No.3.

❂ B.Humberstone & P.Lynch (1991) *Girls concepts of themselves and their experiences in outdoor education programmes*. JAEOL. Vol.8.No.3.

❂ Abi Paterson (1989) *Gender Issues: Case study of a Women's Leadership Course*. NAOE Occasional Publications:No 4.

❂ S.Priest (1987) *Preparing Effective Outdoor Pursuit Leaders*. University of Oregon Press.

❂ S.Priest (1991) *The Ten Commandments of Adventure Education*. JAEOL Vol:8.No.3.

❂ T.A.Harris (1973) *I'm O.K - You're O.K*. Pan Books Ltd.

❂ C.M. Steiner (1975) *Scripts people live (transactional analysis of life scripts)* Bantam Books.

❂ M. James & D.Jongeward (1971) *Born to win* (transactional analysis). Addison-Wesley Pub. Co.

❂ Dr.J.LeGuen (1999) *Reducing Risks, Protecting people*. HSE Books.

❂ Adventure Activities Industry Advisory Committee (1999) *Adventure Activity Centres: Five Steps to Risk Assessment*. HSE Books.

❂ R. Ornstein (1977) *The Psychology of Consciousness*. Penguin.

❂ D.Kolb (1984) *Experiential Learning*. Prentice Hall.

- J.Abbott (1999) *The Child is Father to the Man.* 21st Century Learning Initiative.
- S.van Matre (1972) *Acclimatization.* American Camping Association.
- S.van Matre (1998) *Earthkeepers.* Institute for Earth Education.
- Karl Rohnke *Cowstails and Cobras.* Project Adventure Inc.
- Karl Rohnke (1986) *Silver Bullets.* Project Adventure Inc.
- H.Gardner (1983) *Frames of Mind.* Palladin.
- H.Gardner (1991) *The Unschooled Mind: How children think and how schools should teach.*
- H.Gardner (1993) *Multiple intelligences: the theory in practice.*
- D.Goleman (1995) *Emotional Intelligence. Why it can matter more than IQ.*
- D.Goleman. *Working with Emotional Intelligence.* Bloomsbury.
- Judi James (1999) *Body Talk.* Industrial Society.
- Allan Pease. (1999) *Body Language.* Sheldon Press.

A few quotes to leave with you to inspire or keep you thinking

✿ Leadership is of the spirit; management is of the mind, a science.

✿ Leadership is the ability to open up possibilities for others.

✿ If you are not confused you don't know what is going on.

✿ Leadership is the intelligent and sensitive use of power or using persuasion to work towards a common goal.

✿ People want direction, hope, trust.

✿ Transactional leadership is now transformational leadership.

✿ Leadership is mobilising people to do adaptive work.

✿ A leader is best when people barely know he exists; not so good when people obey and acclaim him; worst when they despise him. Fail to honour people, they fail to honour you. But of a good leader, who talks little, when his work is done, his aim fulfilled, they will say, "we did this ourselves"..... Lao-Tse.

✿ From Confucius to Plato to Machiavelli, many of the world's most famous scholars have theorised about how humans lead one another. Despite all the attention, leadership truly remains an enigma.... M.Z.Hackman & C.E.Johnson 1991.

✿ Present at the MLTB conference of 1983, I heard Mary Cox say that "Leadership permeates the minds and practice of Outdoor Experiential Training practitioners on the assumption that it is a critical component in the way groups function". Wow!

✿ Leadership is one of the most observed and least understood phenomena on earth.... J.M.Burns 1978

- Leadership can produce useful change...management can create orderly results which keep something working efficiently.... J.P.Kotter 1990
- Leaders are people who do the right thing; managers are people who do things right. Both roles are crucial, but they differ profoundly... W.G.Bennis 1991

- Leadership is like the wind; we can't see it, but we know when it fills our sails...anon

- Leadership is more of a performing art than a science.. M.W.McCall & M.M. Lombardo 1978.

- I am not a leader; I am a servant... Nelson Mandela.

- The task of leadership is not to put greatness into people but to draw it out... John Buchan.

- Never think you are superior to others just because you are the leader teaching and promoting learning in others... Anon.

- All leadership takes place through the communication of ideas to the minds of others... H. Gardner. Leading Minds. Harper Collins 1996.

- Leadership is something you gain by invitation from those you work with... Shaun Hopwood.

Are YOU...
an Outdoor Leader,
Teacher or Youth Worker?

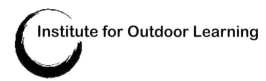 **Institute for Outdoor Learning**

Do you help others use the outdoors for learning?

Membership of the Institute for Outdoor Learning offers a wealth of services to help YOU

As a charitable organisation 'IOL' is run by its members with the aim of supporting safe, high quality outdoor and adventure-based education, development training and recreation through professional development, networking and the supply of a variety of specialist services.

Benefits of membership include:
- Recognition as an Institute Member
- Professional Accreditation
- Discounted professional insurance
- Safety Officer
- Free advertising of jobs, courses and events
- Big discounts on clothing, gear, minibus rental, travel, etc.
- Discounts on purchases from IOL's own Bookshop
- Access to Networking, Courses and Conferences
- Membership of active Regional & Special Interest Groups
- Members' Quarterly Newsletter
- Access to Newsgroups & Contacts
- Discounts on these and other outdoor related publications
  - Horizons magazine
  - Journal of Adventure Education & Outdoor Learning

(Visit the IOL Bookshop online for a full list!)

These important services are only available to Institute members. The cost of membership reflects the balance achieved by a professional charitable organisation run by its members for its members.

Choose either individual or organisational membership

If you believe in the value of high quality outdoor experiences for all, join us.

Visit: www.outdoor-learning.org or ring 01228 564580
or email institute@outdoor-learning.org

Professional Development and Accreditation with the Institute for Outdoor Learning

Institute for Outdoor Learning

IOL has developed a range of Professional Accreditations for practitioners at different stages of work in the outdoors.

R P I O L

Registered Practitioner (RPIOL) - IOL's entry level accreditation; for people who have consolidated experience of facilitating outdoor learning sessions but who are not yet working in "challenging environments". RPIOL is IOL's entry level accreditation; it's for you if you have:
- consolidated experience of facilitating outdoor learning sessions
- are not necessarily working in "challenging environments"
- are working in any branch of outdoor learning (including traditional "outdoor pursuits" but also environmental studies etc)

RPIOL does not "retest" specialist skills. It records and recognises the way you have used these skills in your work with groups and individuals.

There are 5 key areas in RPIOL:
- the core skills of **Facilitating Learning** and **Managing Risk**
- backed up by **Personal Philosophy** of outdoor learning, **Values and Ethics**, and **Reflection and Career Development**.

A P I O L

Accredited Practitioner (APIOL) – IOL's accreditation for practitioners who have consolidated experience of leading outdoor learning in challenging environments. If you have experience of the following:

- being responsible for groups in challenging outdoor situations
- designing and managing tailored outdoor learning programmes
- reflecting on and developing your practice in the outdoors
- putting something back into the outdoor field?

APIOL is about Accrediting independence of decision-making and reflective practice.

L P I O L

Leading Practitioner (LPIOL) – the accreditation to aspire to after your APIOL; this is for people who are making a significant contribution to outdoor learning at regional level. Leading Practitioners demonstrate in-depth, professional development in outdoor learning, and have made a significant regional contribution to the outdoor sector. Leading Practitioners are the next generation of movers, shakers and leaders in the outdoor field; they are ambassadors for outdoor learning and guides for younger practitioners.

Find out more here:
www.outdoor-learning.org/professional_accreditation/index.htm

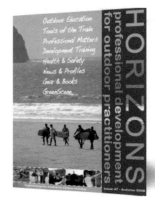